*Come my friends,*
*'tis not too late to seek a newer*
*world ... That which we are, we are—*
*one equal temper of heroic hearts,*
*made weak by time and fate, but*
*strong in will to strive,*
*to seek, to find and not to yield.*

– Tennyson, **Ulysses**

JOSEPH ROBERTS

# SMALLWOOD

## JOURNALIST, PREMIER, NEWFOUNDLAND PATRIOT

### WILLIAM R. CALLAHAN

PROLOGUE: HONOURABLE BRIAN TOBIN, PC

FOREWORD: DALE RUSSELL FITZPATRICK

BLACK TOWER
Productions

*with*

Flanker Press Ltd.

**National Library of Canada Cataloguing in Publication**

Callahan, William R., 1931-
    Joseph Roberts Smallwood : journalist, premier Newfoundland patriot / William R. Callahan.

Includes bibliographical references and index.
ISBN 1-894463-33-1

    1. Smallwood, Joseph R., 1900-  2. Newfoundland--Politics and government--20th century.  3. Prime ministers--Newfoundland--Biography.  I. Title.

FC2175.1.S63C35          971.8'04'092          C2003-902690-6
F1123.S565C35 2003

This book was conceived and researched by the author who acknowledges with thanks the kind permission of the Smallwood family to quote extensively from the writings of Hon. Joseph R. Smallwood, in particular his autobiography *I Chose Canada* (Macmillan, 1973).

The author is especially grateful for their support and encouragement to Jeff Blackwood, Aidan J. Maloney, John A. Nolan, the late F. Burnham Gill, the late James R. Thoms, Hon. Brian Tobin, Dale Russell Fitzpatrick, Hon. Kevin Aylward, M.H.A., Dr. W.L. Goodwin, Councillor Frank Galgay, James G. Callahan, Dr. M. Joan Whelan, Dr. Melvin Baker, and Staff of the Centre for Newfoundland Studies Archives, Memorial University of Newfoundland.

ISBN 1-894463-33-1

PRINTED AND BOUND BY FRIESENS,
ALTONA, MANITOBA, CANADA

Design by Black Tower Productions
with Arlene Wells of Wanda Cuff Young Inc.

— FLANKER PRESS LTD. —
*P O Box 2522, Stn C, St. John's, Newfoundland, Canada, A1C 6K1*
Toll Free: 1-866-739-4420   Telephone: (709) 739-4477   Facsimile: (709) 739-4420   E-mail: info@flankerpress.com
www.flankerpress.com

*The publishers acknowledge the support of the Department of Education, Government of Newfoundland and Labrador, which helped make this publication possible.*

ENDPAPER
Freshwater Bay, Gambo; Inset, Luben Boykov's rendering in bronze of Joseph R. Smallwood in Gambo's village square. (TA)

FRONTISPIECE
*Architects of Confederation*
Rt. Hon. Louis S. St. Laurent, Prime Minister at the time Newfoundland joined Canada, officially opened Confederation Building on July 5, 1960. He was photographed with Premier J.R. Smallwood in the new House of Assembly chamber. (JN)

# TABLE OF CONTENTS

*For my parents,*
*William and Alice Marie,*
*who gave me life;*
*and for my wife, Daphne,*
*and for Sean, Maureen, Sheilagh,*
*Ann Marie, Mark*
*and Brian,*
*in gratitude for*
*their unfailing love and support.*

# PROLOGUE

*The sixth Premier of Newfoundland and Labrador, Brian Tobin, frequently expressed his admiration for the first man to hold that office, and on August 30,1996 unveiled a bronze sculpture of Honourable Joseph R. Smallwood by artist Luben Boykov in Gambo, Bonavista Bay, Mr. Smallwood's birthplace. Mr. Tobin returned on June 1, 1999 for the opening of the Smallwood Interpretation Centre. We are pleased now to offer the below tribute, specially written for this occasion.*

*He exhausted himself (for) those who without privilege, education, or means sought a better life for their families.*

"Take a good look, my son, for once he is gone, you'll not soon see his like again."

These words crossed my mind when I last visited the Honourable Joseph R. Smallwood, affectionally known as Joey, as Newfoundlanders and Labradorians and indeed all Canadians called him during and after his time in public life.

Joey was at home on Roaches Line. He was small, frail. A stroke had left him bereft of speech, and he sought the steadying assistance of walls, doors, and helpful arms as he navigated around his retreat at the entrance to Conception Bay. He had met Fred Mifflin, Eric Dawe, Jack McCarthy and me as we drove up the long driveway to his home. It was a warm, sunny day and a strong breeze danced through the long grass in Joey's fields. Joey stood alone, hair blowing in the wind, waving a warm welcome as we approached.

As we rolled to a stop my heart went out to this man who had so dominated for more than two decades the political life of Newfoundland and Labrador. The heartache didn't last long.

Joseph Smallwood's body was failing him, his love of oratory frustrated by his inability to speak, but his eyes blazed with life and determination. He shook each of our hands like the energetic campaigner he once was. His arm swept over the horizon as he invited us to admire the beauty of the day and his special place under the sun. Then Joey led us inside his home.

Ever the master communicator, he slashed a hand at newspaper headlines indicating by his expression either agreement, or disagreement, with what was being said.

His eyes and expression sought from each of us our views on the subject at hand.

Then, like a well-practiced tour guide, he invited us to join him on a tour of his office and library. The memories of a fascinating life were everywhere. Pictures with dignitaries, plaques of appreciation and recognition, samples of offshore oil, silver shovels that unearthed the potential of countless development projects, and letters from presidents, prime ministers and royalty were among the countless collectibles Joey had amassed. The centre of his attention and pride remained, however, one of the best collections of Newfoundland and Labrador literature in existence. Joey selected with reverence and affection special first editions to be admired and acknowledged.

Joey Smallwood, old, ill and not long for this world, quite literally exhausted himself as he delighted in entertaining and informing his visitors. That was always Joey's way. To the end of his life he quite literally exhausted himself in pursuit of the task at hand.

Newfoundland and Labrador and Canada were always, beyond family, Joey's absolute preoccupations. He personified the ambitions and dreams of the many who without privilege, education, or means sought a better life for their families.

Joey understood that Confederation with Canada was not a cause for the benefit of the comfortable few, but quite literally liberation for the many in pre-Confederation Newfoundland whose existence for generations was feudal in nature. He knew that Confederation could never be negotiated with those who had all the power, but must be won at the ballot box by securing the support of those who were powerless and afraid.

Joey Smallwood, the Barrelman, spoke aloud that which could only be whispered by the toiling masses.

No other single individual, in the 500-year history of Newfoundland and Labrador, has striven so mightily and had such a positive impact upon the life of the people who live here.

Joey Smallwood, in my judgment, is too often remembered as a master politician. It is true that he was clearly without equal in that game; but he was much more than an incredibly gifted rainmaker. He was a visionary who understood the importance of education, health care and a diversified economy to those who had never known more than the basic necessities of life.

The first act of the new Smallwood administration post-Confederation was the establishment of Memorial University. This decision to move quickly towards the attainment of educational excellence reflected Joey Smallwood's huge ambition for Canada's newest province.

He and his government set a frantic pace in building the infrastructure of a sadly underdeveloped Newfoundland and Labrador. "Develop or perish" became the cry, and mistakes were made, as Joey Smallwood himself would acknowledge. However, his were mistakes of the heart. He died a relatively poor man. He poured his last energies and resources into the making of the *Encyclopedia of Newfoundland and Labrador*.

To the end he was this province's greatest ambassador and greatest advocate. I am proud to salute his signal achievements, and the work Bill Callahan has done to celebrate his life.

*– Brian Tobin*

# FOREWORD

*Dale Russell Fitzpatrick remembers her grandfather, Honourable Joseph R. Smallwood, and family moments at Roaches Line, Conception Bay. As Secretary and later Business Manager of his publishing company, Newfoundland Book Publishers (1967) Limited, she was closer to the former Premier than anyone outside the immediate Smallwood family.*

*Everybody has
a strong opinion
of Joey Smallwood
... his name is never
spoken with
indifference.*

I have known both the author and the subject of this book since birth—or should I say more correctly—both gentlemen have known me since my birth! The paths of these men have crossed many times and they have in many remarkable ways paralleled each other over the years. The former has covered many news stories and written about the subject of the book in his role as a journalist; the latter created much of the news! They have served, side by side, as elected legislators in our House of Assembly, both holding Cabinet posts, but always in the latter's administration. Patriots to Newfoundland, they each have chosen to preserve our Province's rich history by the age-old tradition of writing and publishing.

In that role and stage of his life, I am personally grateful that I was able to be a part of my grandfather's life. It has shaped my career path and deepened my love for my home province. What a teacher!

When that fateful election of October 1971 was called, I had just finished high school and, like many young people, didn't know precisely what I wanted to do with my life, but did know some of the professions I didn't want to be. I didn't attend university that September and, boy, am I glad now! All the years my grandfather had been involved in elected politics, my idea of an election was hearing a date on the TV, driving with my mom and dad to the polling booth on that announced day, and knowing as each of them came back to the car that each had voted Liberal. We knew many of our Members personally and they often would drop by to visit, but as with most busy politicians, primarily at election time.

In 1971, I travelled with Grandfather as he made his way around his district doing what he did best—talk! I saw a new area of the Province and even was asked to make a short speech to a group of ladies who were holding a baby shower party at the same motel I was staying at (I was so nervous and they were so kind to that young lady!).

I sometimes rode in the lead car that blared over a rooftop speaker that he was coming and holding a meeting at the such-and-such hall—

sometimes I was in the back seat of the car he was being driven in and thus, could hear all the commentary and "backseat politics." I got to view the commercials that were being developed for airplay and I got my first ever helicopter ride. Exciting days for a 17-year-old! I worked throughout the campaign and on election day he won—again! And I went on to find a job while I decided what I wanted to become when I grew up, while Grandfather went back to his job of being an elected politician.

Less than two years later, my world turned upside down when my father was killed in an accident on his farm. I was working and living in Montreal at the time and moved back home one year later to take over running our family farm—Russwood Ranch. Dad was the "Russ" and Mom was the "wood." They are Ed Russell and Clara Smallwood and my grandfather is Joseph Roberts Smallwood—in case you hadn't guessed.

Well, about a year after moving back to Roaches Line, Grandfather came to my rescue when I needed a paying job and he needed a secretary for his small elected band of Liberal Reformers—I became that person in 1975. I evolved into the Business Manager of his publishing company, Newfoundland Book Publishers (1967) Ltd., when he yielded to his first love and turned his attention primarily to publishing.

We did six books together before the staff of the *Encyclopedia* came to the small apartment/office in a lane off Portugal Cove Road, chosen by him for its proximity to Confederation Building. St. John's City Council has honoured his years there by giving the lane his surname. I thanked the Council through a letter to Mayor John Murphy at the time, but I do secretly wish they had called it instead Encyclopedia Lane, my inbred sense of history overriding my personal pride. At number 119, we did two of the five volumes of the *Encyclopedia* together before his stroke curtailed his work.

It was at that office, after returning from lunch with a dear friend at the Battery Motel on September 24, that it became apparent to me that something was terribly wrong with Grandfather. I was pregnant at the time, and called my personal doctor (he still, at 83, didn't have a regular family doctor!) to see if he could see Poppy. Dr. Vaughan-Jackson saw him immediately and, after he collapsed getting back in the car, arranged for him to be met at the Health Sciences' emergency department. His daughter-in-law, Marcella (Walsh) Smallwood and I spent a tense afternoon there while what had happened to him began to unfold and sink in on us. I'll never forget that day.

While many things changed in our family life because of Poppy's stroke, many good things came from it also and he would be the first to point (even count!) them out. The *Encyclopedia* was indeed finished (and my career in writing, publishing and heritage work was sealed) and he was able to see, and hold, and read Volume Three before he died (just before midnight on December 17, 1991).

He learned to write a little with his left hand, but particularly to do his signature, thus enabling him to continue to autograph his books. He learned to speak again, albeit with one-word questions or responses, not at all the Joey everyone knew on that front. His being at home gave us greater access to him, but was a big transition for Grandmother having him at home all the time. And he accepted the Governor General's appointment to the Order of Canada, something he would never have done before (I was with my grandparents in London, England when he had declined the telephoned invitation in 1972 because, in his opinion, they hadn't offered it for the right reason concerning Confederation, and that they should offer it to many more than he, if it were for bringing about Confederation).

What a pleasure for me to meet Esmond Butler, who made that 1972 telephone call, at Government House in St. John's on December 11, 1986 when he was invested as Companion in the Order by the Honourable James A. McGrath, Lieutenant-Governor, and to hear his side of the reaction in Ottawa to someone declining the honour.

All growing up, today and for years into the future, being related to J.R.S. has come with its downside: people tended to judge me and the other 12 grandchildren by their own political stripe, but I was luckiest when they were not Liberal. I could become an obscure Russell from the Bay Roberts area and not be immediately identified as being related; the others all bore the Smallwood name, so once they spoke their name, that was it! There was also an upside: the opportunities to be part of so many wonderful occasions in his and the Province's life, and if they were Liberal, you were immediately welcomed. Everybody has a strong opinion of Joey Smallwood—his name is never spoken with indifference. I always will say he was either loved or hated, never in between!

Bill Callahan's book will no doubt give you all sides of Poppy. While a strong Liberal and an obvious admirer, he is foremost a journalist who aims to give a complete story. If Joey were to read this I'm certain we would hear him say, "It's all there—warts and all!" As it should be.

*DALE RUSSELL FITZPATRICK*

Dale Russell Fitzpatrick and her famous grandfather at Roaches Line, 1975

# INTRODUCTION

## "JOEY," COLLEAGUE AND FRIEND

*My purpose is to pay personal tribute to a Newfoundland patriot for whom I had during his life, and still today, unbounded admiration.*

Joseph Roberts Smallwood, born in Gambo, Bonavista Bay, on Christmas Eve 1900, became the first Premier of Newfoundland when he was not quite 50 years old. The oath of office was administered by Lieutenant-Governor Sir Albert Joseph Walsh at Government House, St. John's, a few minutes after 11:00 A.M. on Friday, April 1, 1949.

Then for 8,327 days—a few weeks short of twenty-three full years—he presided over the governance of Canada's tenth province. His was an administration faced by challenges far outstripping in sheer magnitude anything then, or perhaps ever, to demand the attention of legislators, provincial or federal, in the nation's history.

Anyone who had travelled "upalong" to the Maritimes, and especially beyond to the cities and larger towns of Quebec and Ontario—which Mr. Smallwood, of course, had done; as had I myself (as a university-level student based in Toronto for four years) in the late Forties; as had my father before me—had seen with their own eyes the incomparably higher levels of economic and social progress enjoyed by Canadians. It was difficult, if not impossible, not to come quickly to the conclusion that Newfoundland's worst tragedy lay in popular rejection of the idea of Confederation as long as 80 years earlier, and to realize that the time had long since come to revisit it.

The decision to become part of Canada, when finally taken, was decades too late for Newfoundland to participate fully in the benefits of the prospering union to which earlier joining provinces fell heir. But to Mr. Smallwood, it was abundantly clear that late or not, Confederation alone held the prospect and the promise of real progress for his long-suffering fellow countrymen and women.

A few days before becoming Newfoundland's first Premier in 1949, he wrote in the *Toronto Daily Star*:

"When I launched the fight for Confederation two years ago, I did so with the belief that union with Canada was Newfoundland's only hope of escaping poverty and oppression. Today, on the very eve of Confederation, I am more certain of this than ever. I am convinced we have broken with an unhappy past, arrived at the dawn of a glorious new era.

"As a small, isolated nation, striving to get along by our own unaided efforts, we were doomed to endless want and an endless but futile struggle to keep our chins above water. No people in the Western world have finer qualities of industriousness, ingenuity, frugality and sobriety than our Newfoundland people. But these qualities, by themselves, are not enough."

Newfoundland became a province impoverished by the handicap of massive underdevelopment that left her far behind even the least-favoured of the other nine in the availability and quality of public services of every kind. Gertrude E. Gunn in *The Political History of Newfoundland, 1832-1864* (Toronto University Press, 1966) rendered this judgment:

"Policies, geography and economy have kept Newfoundland eccentric and peripheral in the British North American scene. The Island never really belonged to the old colonial system, in that it was not a colony until 1824. It did not really resemble the colonies of the Second Empire, with their American components, in that its roots were in the Old World, though its aspirations were in the New."

She continued: "It was not ready to federate with its neighbours in 1867, for it was held back by the bonds of its own origin, history and way of life—by insular patriotism and pride, prejudice and fear. It could not retain its Dominion status, for it had lost its viability by 1933. When Confederation was finally accepted, almost half the population was still against the change."

The task and responsibility assumed by Mr. Smallwood involved much more than persuading a majority of Newfoundland voters to his confederate view—difficult as that obviously would be. He also undertook to obtain, in negotiating the Terms of Union, provisions that would result in the raising of backward or not-yet-existing public services to an "acceptable" level—that is, acceptable by comparison with those provided generally in Canada and more particularly in the Maritime Provinces. And this in a fraction of the time it had taken to develop them there … without resort to more onerous taxation than existed in those nearby provinces, if not Canada as a whole.

In his biography of the first Premier, *Joey* (Stoddart, 1989), Harold Horwood—one of Mr. Smallwood's closest collaborators in the Confederation enterprise, later perhaps his severest critic—has written that in negotiations with powerful ministers and bureaucrats of the Canadian government, between June and September 1947, "Joey carried the ball about 90 per cent of the time" for the Newfoundlanders. He was "the only delegate who was completely familiar with the Canadian federal system, knowledgeable about federal-provincial relations, and determined to secure from Canada a realistic offer that would give (his countrymen) something worth voting for."

From the perspective of a key participant in the campaign for union, and notwithstanding their subsequent estrangement, in his "Political Notebook" column in *The Evening Telegram* Horwood recalled that Mr. Smallwood "negotiated hard and long, arguing cogently with minister and mandarin" so that the meetings, instead of being concluded in two or three weeks as expected, stretched out for months through the entirety of a long, hot Ottawa summer.

His judgment is extraordinarily generous: "This was one of Joey's finest hours. He showed he was no mere propagandist, no simple populist politician, but that he was also a statesman, capable of compromise, of considered negotiations, of putting the case for his country appropriately, and of manipulating the art of the possible."

When Newfoundland became a province in 1949, memories were still fresh of the so-called "dirty thirties," of the virtual bankruptcy that led to the abdication by Newfoundland's political leaders of elective Responsible Government and the quasi-independence of a dominion of the British Empire. Images of the despotic rule of the Commission of Government which, however benevolent, had robbed the people of any effective say in their own affairs, obviously were too recent to have gone away. My maternal grandfather, Edward John Rogers, a molder at the United Nail and Foundry, was given to lament, "Our poor little country, the bottom is gone out of her."

Although there are some, even today, who continue blindly to insist that conditions were otherwise—that there was no poverty, or none worse than other places endured—the Amulree Royal Commission, which gave birth to that British-appointed administration, rendered a stark finding that is not seriously challenged.

In the midst of the Great Depression, it reported, Newfoundland was a place with "no (financial) reserves, its primary industry neglected and its credit exhausted … disillusioned and bewildered people, deprived in many parts of the country of all hope of earning a livelihood, are haunted by the grim spectres of pauperism and starvation."

Circumstances would alter dramatically thanks to the Second World War which spawned a period of unprecedented prosperity in the construction, equipping and operating of U.S. and Canadian military bases, an unbelievable temporary reprieve from reality. But the war over, the struggle to keep body and soul together quickly resumed.

Deliberating behind closed doors and ruling by edict, the Commission of Government dedicated itself to accumulating fiscal surpluses ahead of improving public services. By the second winter of the war, cash balances were such that on its winding-up in 1949, it left the new provincial government a nest egg of about $45 million, including a wartime loan of $12 million advanced to the U.K. For Mr. Smallwood, this was perhaps the best news after the Confederation decision itself—a source of funds to kick-start his administration and its New Industries Program, of which more later …

◆　◆　◆

The opportunity to establish more than a passing acquaintance with Newfoundland's first and greatest Premier—which, I am proud to say, would grow into a lasting friendship—arose as a direct outcome of my tremendous good fortune in landing a news editor position at the fledgling Newfoundland Broadcasting Co. Ltd., also known as Radio Station CJON, "First With the News in Newfoundland."

I was recruited in the first instance by the station's senior news editor, Brendan "Minty" Walsh. He interviewed and hired me on the spot, in his room in the stately Glynmill Inn in Corner Brook, to be CJON's first Western Newfoundland "stringer," as part-time correspondents were called.

Having recently parted company, albeit reluctantly, with *The Western Star* after a couple of summers and a year-and-a-half full-time as a general assignment reporter-photographer, I was holding down a non-news day job writing up General Motors Acceptance Corp. financing contracts for one of my high-school teachers-turned-sales manager, A.D. "Al" Pittman (father of the poet and playwright of the same name) at the appliance division of Corner Brook Garage Ltd. Several nights a week were taken up playing piano in a dance combo (the Riverside Quartette, which often carried five and occasionally six players) at Ray Wellon's popular roadhouse on the Deer Lake Highway. Walsh's offer represented the chance to get back at what I really wanted to be doing, working in news.

Shortly, because my piece-work reports to CJON (filed in "long" telegrams, the high-tech business communications tool of the time!) due to frequency and detail were proving as costly, or nearly so, as having me full-time in St. John's, the legendary Don Jamieson made me an offer that I did not hesitate to accept.

Journalistically, and in all-round technical and programming innovation, the team of president Geoff Stirling and Jamieson, his vice-president, had been building, in a rambling, converted wartime Royal Canadian Navy structure at the top of Prince of Wales Street, an enterprise that in 1953, only a couple of years after first going on the air, was numbered among Canada's broadcasting leaders.

There I found myself in the company of such top-of-the-line journalists, in addition to Stirling, Jamieson and Walsh, as Jack A. White, Jim Thoms, Jim Quigley and Jack Howlett, Arch Sullivan and Russ Roberts, to be joined in time by Burn Gill, George Perlin and Ed Roberts, Ed Bonnell, Wally Millman, Gerry Ottenheimer and Newfoundland's first TV cameraman—"video-journalist" today—Nels Squires.

Newfoundlanders awoke in those times to the voices of such on-air luminaries as Bob Lewis, John Nolan and Muriel McKay, Greg Bonner, Bob Lockhart, Gerry Wiggins and Jim Turner, Sally West, Ethel May Whitham and Jim Regan, Merv Russell, originator in Newfoundland, if not all Canada, of the "open line" radio format, Howie Meeker (who succeeded me in 1959 as Sports Editor), and by no means least, the talented Clark Todd. He would become a foreign correspondent for the CTV Network and die a lonely death from wounds inflicted on the sands of Lebanon while covering conflict in the Middle East. To complete the station's roster of future politicians and activists, the Advertising Sales and Programming staffs included future MP and Lieutenant-Governor Jim McGrath, millionaire businessman Harold Duffett and international hockey impressario Art Harnett, and not to forget literally dozens of essential non-air staff including Charlie Lang, Albert Ryan, "Dubie" Jamieson, Florence Dawe, Emily Davis, Colin Jamieson, Shirley Crocker, Cathy Yuill Brodie, Len Walsh, Ches Chafe, Bob Holloway and Oscar Hierlihy, to name a few. Getting on staff at CJON was rather like going to broadcasting heaven, and to this moment I marvel that I could have been so lucky!

The station's reputation for news integrity and its remarkable popularity across the province meant top newsmakers, both local and visitors to the city and province, made a point of coming to our radio (and later, television) studios for interviews and "voice clips"—today called sound bites. Or, armed with the latest equipment and transported in a fleet of classy news wagons, we covered them in mobile "remotes," either live or recorded. Mr. Smallwood, himself a broadcasting pioneer as the radio "Barrelman"—on Station VONF from

1937-1943, a program to "make Newfoundland better known to Newfoundlanders"—as Premier was chief among them, no stranger to CJON and its people.

Despite the fact Stirling and Jamieson had been at the forefront of Chesley A. Crosbie's Party for Economic Union with the United States, and thus on the opposing side to his campaign for Confederation, the Premier backed their application for a broadcasting licence. Yet, Jamieson recalls in his memoirs *No Place for Fools* (Breakwater, 1989), he never looked for favoured treatment:

"… He knew how much the station's credibility depended on objectivity and the thoroughness of the coverage provided. He also knew the folly of attempting to manipulate the news-gathering team we had assembled."

The truth was he hardly needed to. It was barely five years after Confederation, and Mr. Smallwood easily was the most newsworthy, yet most accessible, public figure of the era. Most reporters had his "private" telephone number, and he could be reached day and night and weekends, no trouble.

◆　◆　◆

This book is not, nor intended to be, a biography of Joseph R. Smallwood, the greatest Newfoundlander of all time. His own autobiography, *I Chose Canada*; Richard Gwyn's *Smallwood, The Unlikely Revolutionary*, later revised and expanded; Harold Horwood's *Joey*, Ron Pumphrey's *The Last Days of the Last Father*; together with such works as Reg Smallwood's *My Brother, Joe*; James R. Thoms's *Call Me Joey*, in two editions; William Connors's *Best of the Barrelman*; Robert Moon's *Peril and Glory*; and the writings of Dr. Melvin Baker and others—each fills the role in its own way, and I have no wish to enter on that field.

Regarding my friend Pumphrey's book, at pages 255-6 Mr. Smallwood expresses beyond question his preference for Newfoundland's flag—"the pink, white and green … in conformity to heritage and tradition … with the Coat of Arms of Newfoundland and the Union Jack emblazoned on it," hence its display on this book's cover. A decade earlier he requested and obtained a prototype copy from the Provincial Flag Society, of which I was Secretary, for inclusion in the endpapers of Volume 2 of the *Encyclopedia of Newfoundland and Labrador*.

My purpose is to pay personal tribute to a statesman and friend, a Newfoundland patriot for whom I had during his lifetime, and still today, unbounded admiration as the man who "dragged Newfoundland kicking and screaming" into Confederation with Canada, and an era of incomparable progress and relative prosperity—"relative" only because, as he himself was the first to recognize, the union was not and is not in all respects perfect, a work in progress still. We remain a so-called "have-not" province and we do have to continue to work at it as he did in literally spending himself in an unrelenting effort to make this a better place for all future generations of Newfoundlanders.

Descriptions such as "the Cinderella of empire" and "the sport of historic misfortune" are not much heard anymore; as concepts they almost literally have dropped off the screen of our consciousness, and with pretty good reason. Newfoundland and her people are forever changed in outlook and in prospects, and the credit must go to one man. Few Newfoundlanders alive today realize just how great was the task to which Mr. Smallwood set his hand *after* the initial battle for Confederation had been won. That, in a real sense, was the easier part. Though painful, perhaps, to admit, Newfoundland became a province in 1949 with the lowest standard of living by far to be found in North America: an economy frightfully thin, and but for the few industrial towns and those still enjoying a military presence, cash wages were virtually non-existent or pitifully low. My parents William B. and Alice Rogers Callahan, certainly experienced this, as I did, I am sure, my wife's father and mother, John J. and Amy Bailey Ryan, did too.

I remember a fellow theology student from a Conception Bay fishing village telling me in Toronto, that during a lifetime of unbelievable toil, his elderly parents had never had cash in their hands until Confederation came. This was not strange or unusual, not a new phenomenon for thousands and thousands of Newfoundland families. It was much as it had been for most of our proud but poor history—what some of us took ruefully to describing as *ragged* individualism, as we nevertheless carried on, determined to make our own way against the whole world and perpetual adversity.

Every time it appeared Newfoundland might get solidly on her feet, some great, unforeseen calamity occurred to knock her down again. It was, therefore, always an uphill fight, always a losing battle, always an history of deep and tragic suffering for our people, hounded by isolation, unemployment, malnutrition, ill health, and catch and market failure in the fisheries.

It must have seemed to many Newfoundlanders that we could never, no matter how long they lived or how long this Old Colony endured, come to enjoy the full and fruitful life that is in keeping with the dignity of human beings as children of God and subjects of the Queen. It would have been terribly easy to despair, to throw in the towel, to abandon our birthplace, all of us—as many, indeed, have felt they had to do—and leave it to the wind and the waves and the seagulls.

A few years before we became a province of Canada, a great British newspaper sent out a senior reporter to investigate first-hand what was going on, to see how the Commission of Government was performing the job it took over from our own elected government and legislature. What Morley Richards of the London *Daily Express* reported, hoping perhaps to stir the U.K. to do more, makes for difficult reading:

- Half of the 300,000 people were near starvation, a quarter getting only six cents worth of food a day; malnutrition was widespread and increasing
- Children as young as 10 were still sent to jail; education was neither free nor compulsory; nearly 10,000 children did not go to school
- Many women and children could not go out all through the winter because they had no clothes to wear
- There were at least 20,000 active cases of tuberculosis, one in every 15 people; the one TB sanatorium was overcrowded, with thousands on a waiting list
- Ten thousand fishermen had no equipment; theirs was still a salt cod industry with fresh and fresh-frozen production still unknown
- Manufacturing industries (the pulp and paper mills of Grand Falls and Corner Brook predominated) employed fewer than 4,000 men
- There was no highway across the Island and few other roads had been built, none longer than 40 miles
- The trans-Island railway ran three times a week in summer, twice in winter, and had closed several branch lines
- There was one airport, without a name and near to nowhere (we know it today as Gander International)

Never in his extensive travels as a journalist, Richards reported to *The Western Star* of Corner Brook and to his own paper, had he witnessed such extremes of wealth and poverty. He was appalled by the wide separation between "the poor and the comparatively rich" as well as the "lack of means of transportation and communications, a serious detriment to economic development."

"It is wrong," he wrote, "that a community of nearly 300,000 free-born Britons should not govern themselves. It is a humiliation which, I imagine, every proud Newfoundlander finds difficult to bear."

Was it all exaggeration as some claimed, and still do? In fact, it is strikingly similar to what Frederick Griffin, then Superintendent of Missions for the United Church of Canada, wrote in the *Toronto Daily Star* a bit earlier, that "many in Newfoundland (are) wearing clothes made of flour bags." Of a population of 280,000, he wrote, "70,000 are on dole of $2.20 a month." (Griffin blamed it all on ignorance, bred by a system of "small, scratchy, poor … sectarian schools" whose church owners, he charged—except for his own—refused to give up control.)

There is also the haunting description of Rev. Lester Burry, Labrador delegate to the National Convention on Newfoundland's future governance: "… Going into homes of these people and seeing their bare cupboards and hearing the cries of the children, cries of hunger, cries that never leave you once you have heard them … I fear the return of Responsible Government (which) might bring back these conditions again."

Why recall now what Newfoundlanders old enough to remember might just as soon forget? Simply because not to know is to fail to appreciate the tremendous change that has taken place in Newfoundland in a very short time, in a generation or two—change that is little short of a miracle, concerning which we have become complacent and tend to take largely for granted, about which we are perhaps a bit too satisfied.

And how did it come about … by accident, perhaps? Did it just happen? I think the vast majority, indeed all Newfoundlanders who think seriously about it, know better: It was the result of the vision and unrelenting drive of one man.

On the eve of the 21$^{st}$ Century Newfoundland's oldest and most important newspaper, *The Telegram*, offered its readers the opportunity to nominate the Newfoundlander of the Millennium. Who, in the estimation of these citizens, was the greatest Newfoundlander in the 1,000 years of our history?

As they had done in the historic Confederation referendum, and in six straight provincial general elections and very nearly a seventh, his fellow countrymen and women chose Joseph Roberts Smallwood in that pre-Millennium vote, and by what can only be described as an overwhelming majority.

And because the man and his accomplishment are inseparable, as Harold Horwood suggested in another context, by placing their confidence in Mr. Smallwood, there could be no question the people demonstrated support for what he had wrought. Another of his biographers, Richard Gwyn, suggested at one point that rather than the development of Churchill Falls, the creation of Memorial University, or building roads, hospitals and schools, Mr. Smallwood would best be remembered for bringing Newfoundlanders out of their centuries-old inferiority complex—and of course, for leading them into Confederation.

The province's first Premier could talk with people like the Rothschilds, federal politicians and Quebec Premier Jean Lesage "as an equal, something no Newfoundlander had ever done before … They gained such self-confidence during his years in power that they could reject him in the election of 1971 because they didn't need him anymore."

The period following Mr. Smallwood's debilitating stroke in 1987 was very difficult—for him, for his wife Clara and his family, for his friends. He had been robbed of what was his most important facility, the power of speech. The inability any longer to communicate normally was the source of frustration, even embarrassment. Every public appearance was marked by a deep aura of sadness and regret.

By the time the 1980s were winding down, fate had surpassed my wildest expectations—I had succeeded to the managing editorship of *The Evening* (as it then was) *Telegram* where my old friend Steve Herder was still publisher. (This gave me the unbeatable record of occupying the chief editor's chair in all three Newfoundland dailies published in this century, including *The Western Star* and the since defunct *Daily News*.)

I understand from family sources that when word of my appointment came on the TV news, Mr. Smallwood clapped his hands and though unable to speak, he smiled animatedly. *The Telegram*, after all, was where his own career as a journalist (which, to a large extent, underpinned everything else) began in earnest. I like to think that he saw my going there as one more common interest that we shared as well as one more sign of approbation for one of those whom he had chosen to share with him the burden and responsibility of government. I know he was happy for me; I like to think that he felt a little proud.

My copy of *I Chose Canada*, to which I refer often in this book, is inscribed as follows:

> *"William R. Callahan …*
> *With greetings and affectionate*
> *regards to my colleague and friend!*
> *Joseph R. Smallwood"*

The remains of Joseph and Clara Oates Smallwood are interred in Mount Pleasant Cemetery in St. John's. Standing at their grave on this, the 100$^{th}$ anniversary of his birth, I reciprocate those greetings and regards with the warmest personal gratitude for his life and work, and the opportunity to share in them.

*St. John's, Newfoundland*
*December 24, 2001*

# CHAPTER 1
## COVERING THE PREMIER

ST. JOHN'S, NEWFOUNDLAND

## The Daily News

THE EVENING TELEGRAM, ST. JOHN'S, NFLD., FEB. 23, 1959 PAGE

# New Violence In Loggers Dispute

## Pop Bottles Or Injuries

**Charges of Police Interference; Claims, Denials Lead Strike New**

# 17 Appear In Court, Food Theft, Assault

## 150-200 Men Raid Camps

GRAND FALLS, Nfld. (CP) — RCMP reported new violence in the strike of Newfoundland pulpwood loggers Tuesday. Both police and union sources said women relatives of striking loggers attacked a motorcade trying to pass through a picket line of the International Woodworkers of America, CLC, near Millertown in central...

ST. JOHN'S, NEWFOUNDLAND

GRAND FALLS, Nfld. (CP)—The RCMP's role in the strike of 1,200 Newfoundland loggers...

CORNER BROOK (Staff)—SEVENTEEN MEN APPEARED IN MAGISTRATE'S COURT HERE AGAIN THIS MORNING AND WERE REMANDED FOR TRIAL ON CHARGES OF THEFT OF FOOD AND ASSAULT IN CONNECTION WITH A RAID ON A LOGGING CAMP IN THE SANDY LAKE AREA

# LOGGERS REMANDED IN CUS

## Charges Laid In Court

CLC Director Due...

# Police Constable Dead

**IWA PICKETS DUMP PULPWOOD ON ROAD**

# Loggers Tried 2nd Time, Three Men Get $200 Fine

**MASS ARRESTS FOLLOW**

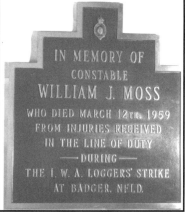

IN MEMORY OF CONSTABLE WILLIAM J. MOSS WHO DIED MARCH 12th 1959 FROM INJURIES RECEIVED IN THE LINE OF DUTY — DURING — THE I.W.A. LOGGERS' STRIKE AT BADGER, NFLD.

*He was blessed with
a photographic memory
(and) a journalist's
ability to quickly
absorb ... the most
complex information.*

My first contacts with Premier "Joey" Smallwood—the appellation had stuck, according to my friend Jim Thoms, after being applied by a small boy on the edge of a campaign crowd—came during the early 1950s as a broadcast journalist covering, among other things, politics and especially the House of Assembly.

Its sessions then were held in the historic, century-old, creaky and dusty Colonial Building, brought back to life after 15 years of Commission of Government rule as the seat of the restored elected legislature.

In time the politicians would move to the modern Confederation Building skyscraper that would rise on the St. John's northeast landscape. It was built under a lease-back financing arrangement, a turnkey contract for 25 years at $665,000 a year, by Whitney-Hansen Limited of Hackensack, NJ. (The same firm undertook in 1959 to construct, on a similar contract, the initial buildings of the new Memorial University campus.) Newfoundland Engineering & Construction Co. Ltd., a Crosbie & Co. subsidiary, was principal subcontractor. The city pretty well ended at Empire Avenue, and many said, "Joey must be crazy to put the government so far out in the country!"

With the formal offices of the Premier and his Cabinet located elsewhere than the Colonial Building (Mr. Smallwood's in his Canada House residence on Circular Road, those of ministers with their departments scattered over a dozen or more locations around the city of St. John's, while private members almost literally had nowhere to go) opportunities to avoid the media and the public during House breaks and recesses, if the politicians wished to do so, were sorely limited. Thus they and their staffs, news reporters, photographers, and little knots of spectators lounged around, some drinking tea—some, no doubt, something stronger—and it was hard to tell us apart. The limited space afforded minimal privacy to the Premier and his Ministers, the tiny Opposition, and the Speaker. (In the basement, a place had been found for the Director General of Economic Development, Alfred A. Valdmanis.)

After Confederation Building became available (officially opened by former Prime Minister Louis S. St. Laurent on July 5, 1960) with a new legislative chamber and related offices occupying the ninth floor, and virtually the entire government bureaucracy under the same roof, any politician who so wished could remain in or escape to his office (no gender lapse here; the first post-Confederation female MHA, Liberal Hazel McIssac, was not elected until 1975) or Members' Common Rooms without need to encounter reporters or the public. Mr. Smallwood, however, had had more and more varied media experience—

in Halifax, Boston, New York and London, as well as in Newfoundland—than any reporter on the scene at that time, and his attitude clearly was the more media the better. He really did hold with the adage that "There's no such thing as bad publicity ... so long as they spell your name right!"

He was blessed with a photographic memory, to match a journalist's ability to quickly absorb and synthesize the most complex information, and would regurgitate it at length and repetitiously, to the chagrin of news people, particularly those of lesser ability, making sure they "got it right." Some came to hate him for it. Tough, probing questions and criticisms by those few who dared take him on were regarded as challenges to be summarily disposed of—and not always without an element of rancor and even personal attack, as senior journalists such as Burn Gill and Harold Horwood could attest!

(Interestingly, in time the Premier would appoint my friend Gill as Provincial Archivist—I admit to having a hand in that. Horwood, who had served as one of his right-hand men in the Confederation campaign and then as Liberal MHA for Labrador, only to become his sharpest media critic, would author a biography that is nothing if not kind to his former leader.)

I not only covered Mr. Smallwood for CJON Radio and TV and Geoff Stirling's *Sunday Herald*, but also for *Time* as that magazine's Newfoundland correspondent, and found him unfailingly cooperative.

For example, I had scheduled for *Time* a photograph of the Premier against the background of Confederation Building under construction, to accompany a forthcoming story. The date was Saturday, March 14, 1959—which happened to be the day Newfoundland Constabulary Constable William J. Moss (the prefix "Royal" would be added years later) who was murdered in a savage encounter on a loggers' picket line at Badger a couple of days earlier, would be going home for the last time.

It occurred to me that the Premier might be much too engaged to worry about my photo shoot. After all it was he who, in effect, had sent Moss to his death as a member of a contingent of St. John's officers ordered to Central Newfoundland to help the Royal Canadian Mounted Police, on contract as a provincial force, to keep the peace.

(This became a more difficult duty after Prime Minister John G. Diefenbaker countermanded RCMP Commissioner Leonard Nicholson's order, in response to the province's legal request under the contract, to send reinforcements from the mainland. A planeload of Mounties, already in the air, was grounded in New Brunswick and then sent back. In consequence the force's national commanding officer resigned, and the Premier saw to it he was immortalized in Harold B. Goodridge's historical mural in the lobby of Confederation Building. Attorney General Davie Fulton, who had approved Nicholson's order, was badly embarrassed; that he didn't resign over Diefenbaker's show of non-confidence probably cost him his own chance to succeed as prime minister.)

But I was not disappointed. Promptly at 9:00 A.M., the appointed time, the Premier crossed an empty, snow-covered field to give me my picture. Then he left to join Moss's funeral procession which, after a brief service conducted by Canon R.R. Babb of the Church of St. Mary the Virgin at the home of the officer's mother on University Avenue, wound up at the railway station. There the coffin of the dead Constabularyman was put on the train for his native Port Blandford where, the following day, Babb presided at the final obsequies at the Anglican Church and Cemetery of St. Aidan with an honour guard of Constabulary, RCMP, firefighters and Orangemen in attendance.

■   ■   ■

After I returned to the West Coast in 1959 to be managing editor of *The Western Star* the Premier rarely failed to let me know when he would be coming to town.

Breakfast table interviews at the Glynmill Inn became fairly regular practice, and ideas proposed editorially by the paper not infrequently found their way into public policy. These included suspension of the new city of Corner Brook's municipal government until public finances were got under control, development of a badly needed public housing program for the Second City, establishment of the Harmon Corporation to take over and manage the assets of the U.S. Air Force Base of the same name at Stephenville, creation of a junior college for the West Coast (the idea would develop into the Sir Wilfred Grenfell College of Memorial University) and a stone's throw away, the Corner Brook Arts and Culture Centre.

In the meantime, I covered Mr. Smallwood in dozens of situations. They ranged from his speeches in the House of Assembly, to the Term 29 brouhaha, to numerous sod turnings and plant and mine openings in various parts of the province, to election campaigns, to the November 1958 trans-Island safari by four-wheel-drive Land Rover. This was the only civilian passenger vehicle then capable of traversing the muddy track that in less than a decade would become the Trans Canada Highway.

The first person ever to walk clear across the Island, which Mr. Smallwood had done in the 1920s to organize railway section-men into a union and stop a pay cut, now became the first to drive a motor vehicle from St. John's to Port aux Basques. As he led a motorcade into the Southwest Coast town, I rode in the second Land Rover.

In mid-1966, after some seven years as managing editor of *The Western Star*, I was appointed, with the Premier's concurrence, to the position of Regional Officer for Newfoundland and Labrador of the federal Centennial Commission. Headed by "Mr. Canada" John Fisher, it was the organization responsible for arranging the celebration of the nation's 100th birthday—and never mind the irony of Newfoundlanders being encouraged to take a full part after quite less than two decades in the union!

To offset any negative reaction—of which, as it turned out, there was precious little—I developed a rationale for service club speeches, talks to youth groups, and for use in motivating municipal officers and local committees to take an active part.

In the first place, I liked to point out, Newfoundland was not alone; there were in fact only four "charter members" in the Confederation of 1867—Ontario, Quebec, New Brunswick and Nova Scotia. Manitoba (which joined in 1870) wasn't there, nor was British Columbia (1871), nor Alberta (1905), nor Saskatchewan (1905). Even Prince Edward Island, the "cradle of Confederation" whose capital Charlottetown was the site of the September 1864 meeting at which amalgamation of the British North American colonies was first discussed, did not join until 1873. And Newfoundland did send delegates—House of Assembly Speaker and future Prime Minister Frederick B.T. Carter, and Opposition Leader Ambrose Shea, if only as observers—to the further discussions that took place later that fall at Quebec City.

This was not greeted with general favour on the part of Newfoundlanders and is commemorated in a piece of rather pejorative doggerel:

> "Remember the day that Carter* and Shea
> went over the bay to barter away
> the rights of Terra Nova?"

*As Premier, Carter's pro-Confederation government was roundly defeated in the election of 1869.

Nonetheless, it was clear that if the 1967 celebration was only for provinces that had been "in" for a hundred years, a large part of the country would have to be left out! At the same time, I pointed to the unassailable fact that tens of thousands of young Newfoundlanders had been born Canadian citizens since 1949 and many were obviously proud to display the Maple Leaf emblem, especially as they travelled the world, on headgear, shoulder patches and backpacks. (Most people, I judge, unfortunately were and are unaware that the flag of Canada that we honour today was recommended by a parliamentary committee headed by none other than a Newfoundland Member of Parliament, Herman M. Batten, native of Bareneed, Conception Bay, and formerly the highly respected principal of the Corner Brook Public School, while Deputy Speaker of the House of Commons.)

And a further, notable consideration—that in excess of half the Newfoundlanders who cast votes in the Confederation referendum had freely chosen to become Canadians. All taken together it made a logical, even compelling case.

With Mr. Smallwood leading the way, the vast majority of Newfoundlanders entered enthusiastically into the spirit of the celebration and special events and lasting community projects blossomed on every hand. Most impressive was Newfoundland's official project, the St. John's Arts and Culture Centre, an $8 million facility towards which the province's contribution far exceeded Ottawa's $2.5 million.

Newfoundland's "special tribute to Canada in the 100th year of Confederation"—the Premier's description—served as the venue for the Centennial Year edition of the Dominion Drama Festival. The national extravaganza for the first time featured all Canadian plays, headlined by Tom Cahill's adaptation of Harold

Horwood's novel *Tomorrow Will Be Sunday*. Attending with the entire Cabinet and in company with federal Transport Minister J.W. Pickersgill, on May 22, 1967, Mr. Smallwood declared his "indescribable pleasure of declaring this centre open … in the hope that it will become a powerhouse, an inspiration for everything cultural in this province." He saw its role as being "the cultural heart of the province … a people's place, and not merely for the arty-arty people, as important as they are, but for the toiling masses too."

■ ■ ■

My Centennial Commission appointment became the entry-pass into the often confusing, always deadly serious game of politics and government. It also took me and my family back to St. John's where, by late summer, it was a foregone conclusion in the media, at least, that a General Election was in the offing.

Niagara Falls MP Judith Verlyn "Judy" LaMarsh, a law graduate of the University of Toronto and Osgoode Hall, as Secretary of State ran the Centennial. She also brought in the Broadcasting Act, and appointed the Royal Commission on the Status of Women. As Minister of National Health and Welfare, she mothered both Medicare and the Canada Pension Plan. But she had her hands full with the Centennial Commission, established by Diefenbaker, that was in a state of deep turmoil. Beginning with Fisher, close personal friend and aide to the former Prime Minister, it was seen as heavily laced with Tory loyalists, and a struggle ensued to wrest control from friends of the late administration.

The solution, at least at the top, was that Georges-Etienne Gauthier, said to be an equally close friend of Liberal Prime Minister Lester B. Pearson, became associate commissioner, raising immediately the question of who really was in charge and had final authority. (It made sense, at least to the extent the leadership was now bilingual, thus correcting an oversight seen as critical to French Canada's participation. Reviewing LaMarsh's memoirs, *The Evening Telegram* reported that she considered Fisher, although brilliant, potentially a disaster, and doubted he and Gauthier could operate as a team. It seems she saw Pearson as "gutless … (preferring) to talk rather than fight," and other Cabinet colleagues as "hopeless, apathetic, drinking too much and working too little." In 1968 she quit politics, disgusted over Pierre Trudeau's election as Liberal leader.)

Instructed to proceed to Ottawa for departmental orientation, I settled in with counterparts from across the country at the Beacon Arms on Albert Street, the hotel made infamous by the Munsinger scandal that had helped grease the skids under Diefenbaker's biggest parliamentary majority in Canadian history. That's when I found out, to my astonishment, that the minister—allegedly because I was "Joey Smallwood's man"—did not want me on her staff, and had refused to confirm my appointment.

Each morning we would leave the hotel and proceed to top-level briefing and strategy sessions in a government office building several blocks away at which top secret information concerning plans for the Centennial celebrations was systematically revealed to those charged with carrying them out. The ticklish situation in which I found myself—and I was not alone; commission members and staff also were uncertain, perturbed—was that not having been confirmed in my position, and not having taken the civil service oath, I really had no right to be present at these confidential sessions. At the same time, as a virtual intruder, having become privy to what was being discussed, there was nothing to prevent me, a journalist, from writing about the disagreements and the divisions seen as interfering with good and efficient operation of the commission.

In fact, as the week wore on and my status remained unclear, some of my would-be colleagues began to suggest it would constitute a real public service were I to walk out and go public with the whole sad story—a temptation to be sure!

It was an open secret that Pickersgill, as Newfoundland's representative in the Pearson Cabinet and in behalf of Mr. Smallwood, was bringing heavy pressure to bear on LaMarsh to relent. Finally, just before noon Friday, the last day of the conference, and literally minutes before our scheduled departure for the airport and home, New Brunswicker Jack Golding, chief of regional offices, entered the room and whispered in the ear of the chairman. Fisher, in turn, announced to the meeting, to scattered cheers and applause, that my appointment (by now a virtual *cause célèbre*) had been confirmed.

I had not personally met the minister to this time, but that would soon change. In an effort to finally mend the splits and divisions plaguing the commission, LaMarsh arranged an Air Canada charter and flew the whole kit and kaboodle to Victoria, B.C., for a full-scale staff retreat in the posh Empress Hotel. Late one night Ross Lawrence, my opposite number for Ontario, came knocking at my door to inquire as to my technical skills, being a veteran of radio broadcasting.

"Do you know anything about sound-recording equipment?" he asked. "There's a tape the minister needs to listen to."

"Depends on the equipment," I replied, "but I'm willing to give it a try."

Off we went to LaMarsh's suite. I got the equipment going, playing and replaying a children's chorus that the composer, musician Bobby Gimby, was promoting as the Centennial song. Eventually, she gave an enthusiastic thumbs-up: "CA-NA-DA" would be the 100th birthday anthem.

The minister thanked me profusely—actually smiled!—and I somehow got the impression she might get used to my being there, after all.

## NIGHT OF THE BADGER RIOT

The night of March 10, 1959 I headed for the St. John's Memorial Stadium to do the play-by-play of game three of the St. Bon's-Guards senior hockey finals for CJON Radio, while hoping for eleventh-hour permission to carry it "live" on TV. (In the end this was denied by the Stadium Commission, reflecting the St. John's Hockey League's fear of lost revenue if fans chose to watch the game at home. St. Bon's won 4-0 to break a series tie and wrapped up their 26th Boyle Trophy with a decisive 5-1 win in game four.)

The colour commentator was my cousin, Dennis "Dee" Murphy. Also in the booth was prominent Guards supporter and CJON vice-president Don Jamieson who had handled play-by-play hockey for the station before he tabbed me for the job.

Halfway through the game the studio phone rang. It was for Jamieson who listened briefly, then called me aside to say there had been a loggers' riot in Badger and it looked like a policeman was fatally injured. I was to follow him to the station after the game; we had to plan our handling of this latest, tragic development in a continuing, tragic story that I had covered from the earliest days of the IWA's certification hearings.

The British Columbia-based International Woodworkers of America (IWA) had made its appearance in Newfoundland three years earlier under the leadership of tough, articulate Harvey Landon Ladd. He won Mr. Smallwood's grudging admiration as "one of the most capable and apparently one of the straightest trade union leaders ever to set foot on Newfoundland soil." However, the Premier was not so kind to Ladd's associates, or the union's tactics in pursuing improved wages and camp conditions for loggers cutting pulpwood for the newsprint mills in Grand Falls and Corner Brook.

The IWA struck woods contractors supplying the Grand Falls mill on New Year's Eve 1958 and in the Premier's words, from that moment "did nothing right ... for what the union started on December 31 was not a strike, but a war; and not an ordinary war, but a blitzkrieg." Contrary to accounts that the government ignored the strike until it reached crisis proportions, within days after it began Attorney General L.R. Curtis, on radio and TV and by means of leaflets distributed on the picket lines, provided sage advice to the strikers, the plain-spoken message couched in classic Smallwood style:

"Don't break the law. Don't let anyone persuade you to break the law. Don't block any roads. Don't attempt to attack men in the camps or the camps themselves ... Obey the law. Keep out of jail."

But it had little effect. Mass picketing, barricading company roads and public highways, stopping privately owned trucks and dumping their pulpwood loads, night raids driving men from contractors' camps into the winter woods and across frozen rivers in their underwear, damage to vehicles and equipment—the temperature of the dispute soared leading up to the confrontation in Badger.

Curtis lost no time ordering the police to "prosecute those responsible ... No union, whether on strike or not, is entitled to forcible possession of the property of others, to set up road blocks, to prevent the free movement of property, or to molest any person." The Royal Canadian Mounted Police, he announced, had been instructed "to prosecute those who commit such breaches of the law, including those who incite others" to do so. *The Evening Telegram* said "the Attorney General … (was) to be commended" on his firm application of the law.

Meanwhile, a split occurred between sister mill unions in Grand Falls and Corner Brook, the latter coming out for the IWA, the former strongly against it. A split occurred as well in the executive of the Newfoundland Federation of Labour. As tensions increased the police presence in Central Newfoundland multiplied, as did the numbers of strikers charged and jailed. Officially the strike was against contractors supplying the Anglo-Newfoundland Development Company's Grand Falls mill, but by late January the union predicted Bowater's in Corner Brook would be out of wood in a matter of days.

"Sickened" by reports of Newfoundland workers assaulting each other, and concerned over the threat to a struggling economy, on February 12 the Premier took to the airwaves. The IWA strike had failed, he declared in a highly charged statement. The IWA itself was a failure in Newfoundland. It was a menace. The loggers should get rid of it and form a new union, and he would help. Thus was born the Newfoundland Brotherhood of Woods Workers (NBWW), to be replaced later by the Carpenters International Union.

As for the IWA, which had vowed never to abandon Newfoundland's loggers, the murder of Const. William Moss sounded its death knell. Appalled by the viciousness of the strike, the vast majority of Newfoundlanders supported the Premier's action, notably the Opposition PCs, the churches, most unions, and the media.

*The Telegram* praised the Premier's "Brave, Wise Stand." He had made "a difficult choice (that) should have the admiration of his fellow Newfoundlanders …" but the province's leading newspaper asked, "How much more bloodshed and violence must we see? How many lives may be lost before this terrible business comes to an end? Are we to see the ultimate … the spectacle of troops being brought in to uphold law and order? Before that comes we should act upon the Premier's suggestion … 'Send them (the IWA) packing!'"

*The Daily News* praised the Premier as "the first political leader in North America to take legislative steps to outlaw unions which are considered to be inimical to the well-being of the province … The necessity out of which this course was born may be deplored, but it was created by the actions of the IWA whose conduct has provoked the censure of people of all classes and the condemnation of all but three of the eleven international locals of the Trades and Labour Council of Central Newfoundland …" In a further comment, *The News* referred to "The Terror at Badger" and suggested that "If necessary, the militia should be called out to control the situation," and a public inquiry into the causes of the violence and "to place the blame where it properly belongs"—the newspaper clearly had decided this already—"should be started without delay."

Decertified by unanimous vote of the legislature, its name and image anathema to most people, its treasury depleted to the tune of $500,000 compared to the $35,000-$40,000 cost estimated for its organizing campaign in Newfoundland, the IWA soon disappeared from the province, its officials actually advising loggers to join the NBWW.

(Moss's death was not the only one to result directly from the IWA strike. Few people remember, perhaps, that three men from the St. Barbe coast—37-year-old Leslie Hiscock, 39-year-old Guy Pittman and 22-year-old Arthur Maynard, returning home from IWA picket line duty in the Deer Lake area—died when a 3-ton truck in which about 20 loggers were travelling plunged off Laing's Bonne Bay ferry, throwing many of them into the icy water. *The Western Star* reported the tragedy January 27, 1959 under the headline "Truck Breaks Loose, Three Loggers Dead." They deserve to be remembered too.)

The evening the Premier went on the air with his decisive speech condemning the IWA, I was at Trade Printers on Duckworth Street where we were holding the press on the latest edition of the *Sunday Herald*. Although provided with an advance copy of the speech, we well knew the danger of committing a story to print *before an event has actually happened*—no matter how certain and nailed down it appeared to be. Finally, about 8:45 P.M., the CJON newsroom called to advise it was okay to let the press run.

# CHAPTER 2
## CONFEDERATION'S SAVING CLAUSE

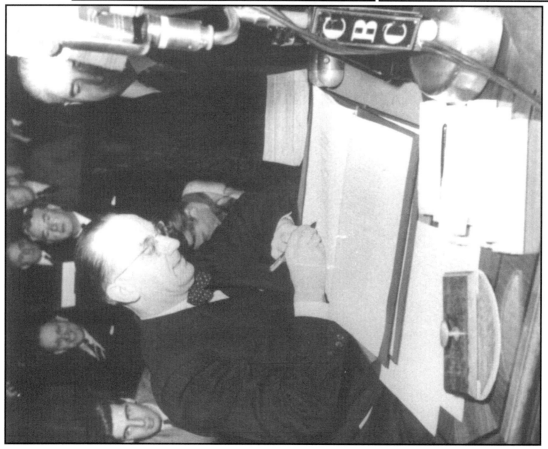

*"If (he) is acting*

*towards us the way he*

*is because of a*

*grudge against me…*

*if he will*

*treat us fairly,*

*and give us a fair deal,*

*I'll resign Tuesday."*

PHOTOS CLOCKWISE:
■ As a member of the Newfoundland delegation, Joseph R. Smallwood signs the Terms of Union with Canada (MA); ■ As Premier he hosted Eleanor Roosevelt, widow of the late U.S. President, and Prime Minister John G. Diefenbaker at the official opening of the new Memorial University campus (TA); ■ Albert B. Perlin, editor of *The Daily News*, accused Diefenbaker of "unexampled arrogance" in the Term 29 affair; his brother-in-law, businessman Chesley A. Crosbie, had refused to sign the Terms claiming they were inadequate (TA).

A vastly more complex, and consequentially more hazardous field of operation than local or provincial politics, is this province's relationship with Canada. It involves a broad range of issues, most of them clearly articulated in and by the Terms of Union by which Confederation was consummated, but some unfortunately not.

The key provision that was believed, with great confidence, to have been fully covered off in the Memorandum of Agreement of December 11, 1948 would collapse, a decade later, into the contradiction of an empty promise. This was the Term 29 commitment to fiscal adequacy, as determined in hindsight by a Royal Commission, but now revealed as being seriously flawed and subject to partisan political whim.

The complex financial arrangements, on their face, appeared to be satisfactory and even generous. Haunted by the size of the public debt, in the range of $100 million, Newfoundlanders were relieved to have most of this financial obligation taken over by Canada, and other costly burdens (for example, the money-losing operation of the Newfoundland Railway and its coastal steamers) as well. The real challenge for their negotiators was to ensure that the new province had the fiscal resources to develop and maintain a broad range of public services on a par with the rest of Canada—or at least its neighbours, the Maritimes. The question had bedevilled them; at the top of their list of concerns was replacement of critically important revenues, e.g., customs tariffs and excise duties (over $22 million in 1949) that would vanish when the two countries joined.

Far from happy with proffered solutions, including substantial improvement in Canada's original offer under the head of transitional payments, one Newfoundland team member, Chesley A. Crosbie, chose to boycott the ceremony to finalize the agreement.

On the 10th anniversary of Confederation, CJON vice-president Don Jamieson sent me down to 18 Rennie's Mill Road to interview his former leader from the days of the Party for Economic Union with the United States. Mainly we sought to determine, in light of his December 1948 refusal to sign the Terms of Union, how Crosbie felt about the Diefenbaker government's announced intention to terminate Term 29.

Seated in the gloom of a back parlour, a smoky coal fire on the hearth to banish the late March chills, he gave no sign of regretting the decision.

"My refusal," he explained in his gruff voice for CJON listeners, and for readers of the *Sunday Herald*, "was based on my knowledge of Newfoundland over a period of many years, some of which were prosperous but unfortunately, many of them left our people with very little … The members (of the Newfoundland delegation) felt that a Transitional Grant of

$40 million"—precisely, $42.7 million paid in diminishing amounts over 12 years—"would not be adequate, and with that I agreed."

However, their financial advisors "were not able to forecast with any degree of accuracy" what the actual needs would be. And this precisely was the problem that gave rise to Term 29, literally the saving clause of the Confederation contract:

> 29. ***Review of Financial Position:*** *In view of the difficulty of predicting with sufficient accuracy the financial consequences to Newfoundland of becoming a province of Canada, the government of Canada will appoint a Royal Commission within eight years from the date of Union to review the financial position of the Province of Newfoundland and to recommend the form and scale of additional financial assistance, if any, that may be required ... to enable it to continue public services at the levels and standards reached subsequent to the date of Union, without resorting to taxation more burdensome, having regard to capacity to pay, than that obtaining generally in the region comprising the Maritime Provinces of Nova Scotia, New Brunswick, and Prince Edward Island.*

The irony, Mr. Smallwood would point out in *I Chose Canada*, was that the Newfoundland *people* would do very well; it was their *provincial government*, which would have the obligation to provide them with public services—formally, "to carry out its responsibilities under the British North America Act"—that would be struggling!

"... It was clear," the Premier recalled, "that the union, if it could be brought about, would be good—better than good, excellent—for the great majority of Newfoundlanders. Canada's famed family allowances, old-age pensions, Veterans' Charter, and all the rest of its social security system would go far indeed toward blunting the sharp edge of social poverty in Newfoundland ...

"Everyone would benefit from Confederation—everyone, that is, but the government of the new province. As we negotiated in Ottawa, we couldn't see much more than poverty, or even bankruptcy, for the Newfoundland government under Confederation. A people who would be much better off headed by a government that would be near bankruptcy; such was the contrast that seemed to make Confederation unworkable ... The solution of this problem was the *sine qua non* of making the deal."

In other words, there could be no Confederation agreement without it!

The solution the negotiators came up with was open-ended. It gave no guarantees, except this—that in the event the various fiscal provisions contained in Terms 23-28 (including the Transitional Grant, annual subsidies, and the assumption by Canada of most of Newfoundland's public debt) as well as savings resulting from Canada's takeover of the Newfoundland Railway, steamships, posts and telegraphs, and a range of public services, were not enough to provide the province with sufficient equity in the union, there was one more that would require a reassessment based on the experience of the early years. That financial review, conducted by a federal Royal Commission, would determine whether additional assistance was required, and if so, how much.

"Quite frankly," Mr. Smallwood wrote, "it was a confession by the two teams of negotiators representing Canada and Newfoundland, that they couldn't, at that stage, make final terms of Confederation for the two countries. We could do most of it; we could cover an enormous part of the field, duly sign the terms, and get them put through the constitutional processes that would make them binding.

"One part we couldn't do ourselves, but we did make provision for that very thing to be done that would complete the Terms of Union. That is what Term 29 was ... Without that clause, there would have been no Confederation. Even with it, Chesley Crosbie refused to sign ... without it (Newfoundland Terms negotiator F. Gordon), Bradley and I and all the others in the Newfoundland delegation would have refused to sign."

Term 29 imposed a developmental straitjacket in advance of the federal Royal Commission. The new province, in those first years, would have to strive to raise public services to the highest levels and standards possible—for these were what would be assisted to "continue." But it would have to be done without visiting on the people a heavier tax load, keeping in mind ability to pay, than existed then in the Maritime Provinces—and without resorting to massive borrowing that would endanger the young province's still fragile credit. It would prove a near-impossible task.

In Mr. Smallwood's words, the Royal Commission "would be everything. Our fate would be in their hands, and we had to prepare our case more thoroughly than we had ever done anything before."

But he also recognized a fundamental weakness in Term 29, namely that so much depended on Canada's "full honest intention of living up to the literal and moral obligation implied in the term." Would it feel "bound in honour faithfully to carry out the findings" of the Royal Commission it had undertaken to appoint?

There was, he was sure, "no human possibility" of doubting Prime Minister Louis S. St. Laurent's honour in the matter. But the courtly Quebecer was long gone from office by the time the report came down, his Liberals were out of power, the Conservatives were in, and "John Diefenbaker was the Prime Minister on that fatal day."

St. Laurent was careful to consult the Premier in the selection of John B. McNair, Chief Justice and former Premier of New Brunswick, to be chairman of the federal Royal Commission, and his co-commissioners—distinguished Canadian economist John Deutsch and Newfoundland Chief Justice Sir Albert Walsh. The province, to prepare its case for presentation to McNair, established its own Royal Commission chaired by Philip J. Lewis, Q.C., with *Daily News* Editor Albert B. Perlin and businessmen Gerald S. Doyle (who died before the work was completed) and Philip S. Gruchy as members.

After nearly four years and the most exhaustive examination ever made into Newfoundland's public services, the Lewis commission decided that the province would require $15 million a year to maintain them at current levels. But the McNair commission surprisingly reduced Lewis's finding by nearly half. In a report dated July 25, 1958 it recommended that the Transitional Grant, in planned decline, be raised back up to $8 million a year until 1962, and at that level paid annually "thereafter."

It was a "bitter disappointment" for Mr. Smallwood, the inadequacy of $8 million being "appallingly obvious." However, much worse was to come.

With the province in deteriorating financial shape and needing every penny it could lay its hands on, he got the House of Assembly to pass unanimously a resolution urgently requesting an interim payment from Ottawa "while we argued the larger question … (but) Diefenbaker did nothing."

Next, as journalist Richard Gywn recorded in *Smallwood: The Unlikely Revolutionary* (McClelland and Stewart, 1968) the Premier "put on the mantle of supplicant" and travelled to Ottawa to plead with the Prime Minister to adopt Lewis's recommended $15 million payment. Diefenbaker wouldn't say yes and wouldn't say no.

Then Newfoundland MP J.W. Pickersgill approached the Prime Minister with a message from Opposition Leader Lester B. Pearson—Gwyn says it was at the Premier's behest: If Diefenbaker would accept McNair's recommended settlement of $8 million in perpetuity, Pearson would stand in Parliament and lavish praise on the Prime Minister as a great Canadian statesman. But still there was no clear response.

Finally, the best part of a year after McNair had reported and virtually on the eve of the 10th anniversary of Confederation, on March 25, 1959, Diefenbaker gave his answer … and it was a political bombshell: The award would be the $8 million McNair recommended—but only until 1962. It would be "quite inappropriate," the Prime Minister told the House of Commons, to settle on a fixed annual amount payable "over a period of unlimited duration."

And then this: The payments would be in "final and irrevocable settlement" of Canada's special obligations to Newfoundland under the Terms of Union. From 1962 on she would receive consideration in accordance with the "general methods of providing financial assistance to provinces."

Taken by surprise, Pearson at first rejected the decision as "quite unwarranted" and said it did not seem "compatible with the obligation which the Government of Canada accepted in the Terms of Union." Subsequently the Leader of the Opposition condemned Diefenbaker's statement in stronger and more direct terms:

"This is a complete misrepresentation of (the McNair) report," he declared, pointing out that the commission had recommended additional assistance of varying amounts for the four years ending March 31, 1961, "'and thereafter $8 million per annum.'

"Nothing could be clearer … (T)he Prime Minister's interpretation now given of the commission's recommendation is both false and misleading."

Pickersgill, who charged "unequalled bad faith," wondered if the Prime Minister realized that "every person in Newfoundland will regard this as a breach of a solemn contract?" But he was also interested in pinning down Diefenbaker and the Conservative government beyond any possibility of future misunderstanding. Rising in his place in the House of Commons he said quietly:

"I should like to ask whether I understood him (Diefenbaker) correctly to say that the legislation which he announced the government had the intention of bringing down, to implement the recommendations of the McNair commission, contemplated the complete discharge of the obligation under Section 29 of the Terms of Union, by that legislation, which will expire on March 31, 1962?"

Diefenbaker's reply was brief and unequivocal: "That is so."

Coming on top of his intervention to prevent RCMP reinforcements in the IWA loggers' strike—Newfoundland would sue in Exchequer Court for breach of contract—and the failure for many months to name a new Chief Justice to succeed Sir Albert Walsh who had died in December, Diefenbaker's action in unilaterally writing *finis* to a key provision of Canada's constitution affecting the new province took many Canadians aback and raised a political firestorm in Newfoundland.

Mr. Smallwood condemned the Prime Minister's announcement that payments to 1962 would "discharge in full Canada's liabilities" under the Confederation contract as meaning Term 29, considered to be the province's sheet anchor in the deal, "will no longer exist." It was, he said, "a betrayal of Newfoundland and of Canada's honour" that "plunged (the province) into mourning"—the latest instance of harsh treatment at the hands of the federal Tories. He had Public Works Minister James R. Chalker order flags flown at half-staff and government buildings hung in black crepe to emphasize the "betrayal of Newfoundland." (The signs of mourning were removed after three days as not being "in keeping with the spirit of Easter Sunday.")

The Premier pointed out: "For nearly ten months Prime Minister Diefenbaker had the McNair commission's report and recommendations, and all Newfoundlanders were convinced by this otherwise incomprehensible delay that he intended to agree with our contention that the amount recommended was far short of the amount needed. Now, ten months later, he announces that we are to get only the amount recommended and not a dollar more …" And that for only a brief period.

The message was not lost on students at Memorial University's increasingly inadequate Parade Street campus. Carrying signs deriding Diefenbaker and condemning the Term 29 decision, they staged a funeral march, complete with motor hearse, with members of the public joining in. The crowd of more than a thousand wound its way to the Colonial Building to be met at the legislature steps by Mr. Smallwood who left a Cabinet meeting to join them.

"I hope no Newfoundlander among the half-million of us will blame Canada or the people of Canada for what one man has done," he told them. "The whole responsibility lies with Prime Minister Diefenbaker."

Would a constriction in anticipated federal funding cause cancellation of plans for a new university campus? "No! It will make no difference," the Premier told them to loud cheers. "You'll get your university, and it will start this year."

Meanwhile, he took aim at an old foe, Diefenbaker Minister without Portfolio William J. Browne: "If (he) has a shred of Newfoundland patriotism left, he will stop trying to hide the infamy of this betrayal and resign from this government without an hour's delay. Otherwise, he will go down in history as a Newfoundlander who helped his leader betray Newfoundland."

Browne insisted that there was no justification for the conclusion that payments to Newfoundland would cease four years hence: "The whole situation can be reviewed in 1962," he explained lamely, "and Newfoundland's case will be considered at that time in the same way as all other cases put before the government are considered …"—thus conceding, perhaps unwittingly, that this province would no longer be entitled to special constitutional consideration.

As for leaving the Cabinet over the issue, he said: "I see no useful purpose in resigning. Payments will continue until 1962. The whole matter has to be discussed in Parliament and bills in relation to Term 29 have to be debated … There are representations to be made on Newfoundland's behalf and I shall be there to represent this province."

(Privately Browne was given to complaining that as only one member of the government he was powerless to influence the decision. In fact, it appears he and fellow Tory MP James McGrath were caught unawares, neither consulted nor informed in advance of Diefenbaker's decision, and suffered for it at the polls. In the 1962 General Election, Browne's previous 6,000-vote majority evaporated as he was narrowly defeated in St. John's West by Liberal Richard Cashin, 12,650 to 12,626. McGrath was re-elected in St. John's East but his margin of nearly 9,000 was reduced to less than 2,000.)

The four-member Conservative representation in the House of Assembly disintegrated over the issue. Opposition Leader Malcolm Hollett (St. John's West) and G. Rex Renouf (Browne's law partner, who succeeded him in a by-election in St. John's South when Browne moved to federal politics) stood fast in support of Diefenbaker. But James D. Higgins (St. John's East) switched to the Liberals and A.M. Duffy (St. John's Centre) left the PCs to form the United Newfoundland Party (UNP) supporting the Smallwood government.

When Hollett and Renouf refused unanimous support of his stand on Term 29, the Premier called a General Election for August 29, 1959 in which they paid with their seats. Mr. Smallwood left Bonavista North to take on Hollett in strongly Tory St. John's West, beating him by more than 2,000 votes, while John R. O'Dea of the UNP narrowly defeated Renouf in St. John's South. The PCs returned three members, all new faces—James J. Greene, who defeated Higgins by 147 votes in St. John's East and would become Opposition Leader, Richard J. Greene, Bell Island, and Albert E. Furey, Harbour Main.

Final standings reflected the public's anger: Liberals 31, PCs 3, UNP 2. The fledgling Newfoundland Democratic Party, formed out of labour reaction against the government's handling of the IWA strike with former *Western Star* managing editor Ed Finn as Leader, fielded 18 candidates but elected none.

*The Daily News*, whose editor, Perlin, had been a member of the Lewis Royal Commission, declared the Prime Minister had "arbitrarily torn up the terms of the Confederation agreement (and) arrogated to himself with unexampled arrogance the right to alter the Constitution of Canada." Brains-thrust of the anti-Confederate forces in the 1940s, Perlin wrote that it was "an infamous betrayal … which has horrified Newfoundlanders and shocked millions of mainland Canadians."

*The Evening Telegram* declared Diefenbaker's announcement on the eve of Confederation's tenth anniversary "sounded the death knell of Newfoundland as a happy and prosperous province … with timing that seems almost malicious."

It went on: "What a feeling of disappointment and disillusionment he has created! What a shocking betrayal of a sacred trust he has presented to us! And this performance has been further demeaned by sanctimonious mouthings that seek to explain away an utter failure to honour a solemn obligation (refusing to implement even the recommendations of the McNair commission) which almost everybody … considered to be ungenerous and unwelcome to Newfoundland."

But however "narrow and niggardly" the Royal Commission proposal, the Prime Minister, the newspaper said, had taken "a completely unexpected, unprecedented and unjustifiable step of arbitrarily ruling out the most crucial portion of the McNair recommendation." The result was that a "solemn contract and sacred obligation," binding on whoever was in power in Ottawa, had been abrogated.

As the lone holdout when the Terms of Union were signed, Crosbie said it was the "distinct understanding" of the Newfoundland negotiators that whatever amount was arrived at by the federal Royal Commission would be paid indefinitely—"not limited to a certain number of years … But although I am disappointed, I cannot say that I was surprised. I had no faith in that contract at the time, and time has borne me out."

It was neither "satisfactory or sufficient," he added. "I felt we were not getting enough financial aid, and also, there was nothing in Term 29 which said that the government would implement the recommendations of a Royal Commission."

Almost identical reaction came from prominent lawyer J.B. McEvoy, K.C., third chairman of the National Convention (after Cyril J. Fox and F. Gordon Bradley) and like Crosbie, a member of the Newfoundland delegation that finally negotiated the Terms of Union; unlike Crosbie, however, McEvoy had chosen to sign the binding document. He charged that Diefenbaker had "overruled the constitutional guarantees (and) nullified acts of the Parliament of Canada and the Imperial Parliament (that are) as binding on the Prime Minister as they are on me."

There would be no Confederation anniversary banquet that year. The organizing committee announced the Term 29 decision "left nothing to celebrate," and the 600 who had bought tickets would get refunds on request. Instead a dinner would be held to honour the Premier, thus giving Mr. Smallwood yet another opportunity to upstage Diefenbaker: This time it was to offer to resign if the Prime Minister would give Newfoundland a "fair deal":

"If Mr. Diefenbaker is acting towards us the way he is because of a grudge against me, I now make this offer through The Canadian Press, that if he'll treat us fairly and give us a fair deal, I'll resign Tuesday" on the resumption of the legislature. (Of course, Canada's national news agency immediately flashed the story across the country, but the Prime Minister declined comment.)

The "grudge," the Premier speculated, might have to do with the fact that Newfoundland stood out strongly against the Diefenbaker election sweep of 208 seats in 1958, or even the embarrassing fallout over RCMP reinforcements not sent to Newfoundland in the IWA strike, in violation of a binding federal-provincial contract.

*The Evening Telegram* took very seriously what it headlined as the "Premier's Challenge":

"… Mr. Smallwood is usually as good as his word, though he has, from time to time, made some elaborate promises which he could not hope to fulfill. But, in our estimation, he was not making an idle boast when he offered his resignation if this would change the Prime Minister's view. Mr. Smallwood is not short on courage. He has been a fighter for a long time, unafraid to climb in the ring with anyone. He is also a master political strategist, one in which the visionary Mr. Diefenbaker might well have found his match.

"Mr. Smallwood's challenge is something like that loaded question, 'Have you stopped beating your wife?' Any answer is wrong. Mr. Diefenbaker probably knows that he has no choice but to keep silent on the Premier's offer. Either way he will place himself in an extremely bad light, politically and personally."

Other skirmishes marked the Smallwood-Diefenbaker relationship—a long-drawn-out dispute over ownership of the former Pepperrell U.S. Air Force Base property, settled after the province agreed to withdraw its court case for breach of the RCMP contract; a tiff over appointments to the St. John's Housing Corporation which, while heavily supported by federal funds, was nonetheless a provincial Crown corporation; and the mean-spirited eviction of the Premier and his family from Canada House, the pre-Confederation residence of the Canadian High Commissioner. (To end a protracted vacancy on the three-man Supreme Court, prominent Conservative lawyer Robert Stafford Furlong, Q.C., was named by Diefenbaker as Chief Justice of Newfoundland.)

Despite it all, Mr. Smallwood was anxious that the Prime Minister of Canada attend the spectacular official opening of the new Memorial University campus. In light of all that had occurred, many were surprised he did so.

The Premier told the story in *I Chose Canada*:

"I had quite a time of it getting Mr. Diefenbaker to come down to St. John's for the opening by Mrs. Eleanor Roosevelt of our magnificent new Memorial University campus in October 1961. I phoned him several times, and he kept evading, saying neither yes or no. I tried to enlist the help of some of his staff by telephone.

"At last one day, Diefenbaker said quite frankly on the telephone, 'You want to get me down there to make a victim of me.' I was sincerely shocked and told him so. 'You're our country's Prime Minister, and we are good Canadians down here. You come, Mr. Diefenbaker, and I guarantee you right now that you'll get as good a reception as you ever had anywhere in Canada.' 'Do you mean that?' he asked. I assured him vigorously that I did. He said that all right, he'd come. He was as good as his word, and I was as good as mine. I had an immense crowd to greet him at the airport. At Government House, where we met immediately after the public reception, I grinned at him and asked him, 'What did you think of our reception?' He liked it …"

If he did not know it in the beginning, the Prime Minister quickly learned that to tangle with Newfoundland's peppery Premier could be extremely hazardous to one's political health. There seems little doubt the fallout from their encounters contributed in a major way to Diefenbaker's rapid decline in popularity across the country—from Canada's biggest parliamentary majority in 1958, to minority government in 1962, to the status of Official Opposition in 1963. He resigned as leader of the Progressive Conservative Party of Canada on September 25, 1967.

By that time the Liberals, back in power, had corrected Diefenbaker's blunder and restored the Term 29 award according to the recommendation of the McNair commission—$8 million a year in perpetuity.

The Premier, meanwhile, added this:

"I had, frankly, hoped that on the tenth anniversary of Confederation I would see our financial agreement with the federal government brought to a successful conclusion and the province secure, so that I might make this a good time to drop out of politics."

Of course, it was not to be—not for another decade and more, and an additional four provincial and four federal election campaigns, by which time the entire Diefenbaker saga was a distant memory.

Mr. Smallwood's ambition was to return to writing, most especially compiling what would become the *Encyclopedia of Newfoundland and Labrador*, unique as the only such compendium of history, biography and general information about any province of Canada. But that would have to wait …

# CHAPTER 3
## TO THE BALLOT BOX WE GO

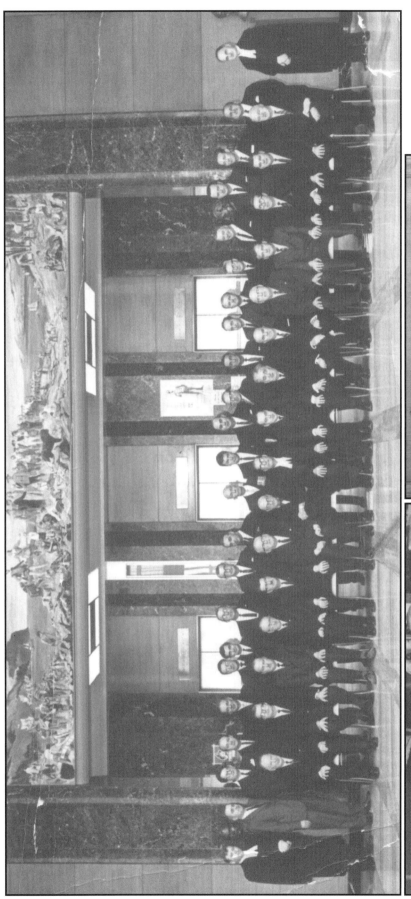

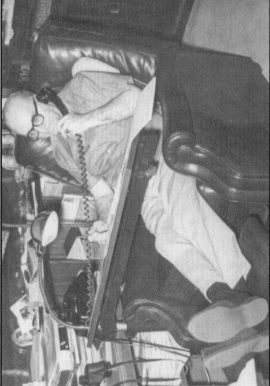

*PHOTOS CLOCKWISE:*
■ MHAs elected to House of
Assembly, 1966, and officials: Front
row - C.R. Granger, J.C. Crosbie, E.S.
Jones, G.A. Frecker, J.R. Chalker, L.R.
Curtis, J.R. Smallwood, G.W. Clark,
G.R. Ottenheimer, W.J. Keough, F.W.
Rowe, B.J. Abbott, T.A. Hickman, A.J.
Maloney, C.K. Wells, H.R.V. Earle;
Back row: F.J. Aylward (Ass't. Clerk),
S.A. Neary, E.M. Roberts, J.A. Nolan,
N.S. Noel, A.D. Moores, W.N. Rowe,
H.E. Starkes, U.F. Strickland, E.W.
Winsor, A.E. Hemmens (Sergeant-at-
Arms), T.W. Burgess, G.H. Myrden,
E.N. Dawe, W.P. Saunders, W.R.
Callahan, G.I. Hill, W.H. Hodder, A.B.
Wornell, J.A. Mahoney, T.V. Hickey,
A.J. Murphy, Henry Cummings (Clerk
of the House.) Absent from photo:
MHAs Ross Barbour,W.R. Smallwood,
P.J. Lewis, P.J. Canning, J.M.
McGrath, C.M. Lane (TA); ■ Liberal
Party Leader introduces candidate
for District of Port au Port (TA); ■
Premier Smallwood working on
election strategy at home (MA)

Media speculations about an impending election were confirmed for me early one Saturday morning in late summer 1966 when the telephone rang in our temporary residence on Roche's Farm, Torbay Road. An anonymous female caller (as I learned later, the Premier's long-time personal assistant, Muriel Templeman) asked to verify our telephone number. Moments later it rang again, but this time it was the Premier himself.

Could I come to see him at his home (at Roaches Line, Conception Bay, about 50 km west of St. John's) and could I come at once?

From the perspective of my position with the Centennial Commission, it was natural to assume he wished to discuss Centennial business. I was surprised and somewhat shocked to learn that instead, he wanted to advance the possibility I might become a candidate in the forthcoming trip to the polls ... whenever that might take place.

When the election was held in early September, my name was on the ballot for the Liberal Party in Port au Port. But this was not what Mr. Smallwood originally had in mind. In fact, his intention was to run in Port au Port himself, the better to take command of an economic rescue operation designed to offset the imminent, devastating closure of Ernest Harmon Air Force Base, the economic heart of Stephenville and its surrounding area. (Years later I would discover that extensive and expensive pre-election propaganda had already been printed in support of this plan.)

In the scenario outlined for me that Saturday morning, a prominent Corner Brook lawyer with strong ties to the Young Liberals organization, Clyde Kirby Wells, would stand in Humber West. I would be the Liberal candidate in Humber East.

But I was unhappy to run there against my friend Noel Murphy, recently become leader of the Official Opposition. Together with Rev. Andrew Montgomerie of the Presbyterian congregation, and others, we had laboured to establish a successful adult literacy program in Corner Brook, we had joined in efforts to improve the area's tourism potential, and we were much involved in pursuing the idea of a junior college, a new public library, and theatre facilities for the city. The thought of now turning against Murphy did not go down well. I argued that in any case, I would fare better in the overwhelmingly Roman Catholic constituency that included Stephenville and the Port au Port Peninsula.

(Mr. Smallwood cautioned that friendship might find it hard to survive the slings and arrows of political warfare. I soon saw that he was right, and was taken aback, quite frankly, by a hard-hitting Murphy polemic condemning the so-called "Stephenville Letter"—no letter in fact, but a modest "Householder" flyer supporting my candidacy. In it the Premier reviewed what had been accomplished to date to support the economy in the face of the planned military shutdown, advised residents that he would keep on working in their interest, and asked that they elect me to be his "eyes and ears in Port au Port District."

This was characterized by the Opposition as political blackmail, a threat to residents that nothing would be done for them if they dared elect a Tory.)

Boldly I went on to suggest that Wells, Anglican and a lawyer, would be better matched against Murphy, prominent family physician and a Roman Catholic, in what I perceived to be a predominantly Anglican district.

The Premier could run virtually anywhere and anticipate victory, but to me his previous connections with the West Side (or Humber West) as campaign manager for Sir Richard Squires, as labour organizer for mill workers, and especially as founding editor of the short-lived, populist weekly *Humber Herald*, would be to his advantage. (That was when, in a light moment, he named the muddy—or dusty, in season—boardwalked main street Broadway in ironic reminiscence of his reporting days in New York.) Subsequently absorbed by *The Western Star*, the smaller weekly is remembered in the naming of Herald Avenue, a rocky laneway off Broadway that for years provided a convenient shortcut for mill employees walking to and from work, and now elevated to the status of an important city street.

I reasoned that under my suggested alternative arrangement, we would have a good chance of winning all three districts, instead of one or perhaps two. Mr. Smallwood did not respond right away. But a couple of days later there was a further summons, this time to the eighth floor of Confederation Building. I was invited to drive with him to the former Pepperrell U.S. Air Force Base hospital for its official reopening, having been converted by his government at a cost of $8 million, and against the objections of most of the medical establishment, into the magnificent Janeway Child Health Centre. It would become the centrepiece of the government's all-out attack on Newfoundland's tragic record of children's diseases and infant mortality.

Along the way I received the news that would seal my fate, as it were, and shape the future for our family for all the years to come:

"You were quite right, Bill…You'll be going in Port au Port—but don't say anything now; wait until I announce it." I was instructed to go at once to the offices of the Fishermen's Protective Union, off east-end Water Street, and make myself known to William J. Petten, the Liberal Party treasurer and a future Senator. Unbelievably, this man whom I had never before met (but would come to know and like) handed over an envelope containing $4,000 cash, no questions asked, to get my campaign started!

(The era of candidates being chosen in a nominating process by party supporters in the constituency, rather than being named by party leaders, was about to arrive in Newfoundland and Labrador—but not quite. The General Election of 1966 was the last in which candidates of all parties were not chosen by popular selection as a general rule. It also marked the end of a 100-year-old tradition which took seriously into account the faith of a prospective candidate *vis-à-vis* the dominant religion in the district.)

There was not long to wait. That very afternoon my brother James G. Callahan, a reporter at *The Western Star*, telephoned excitedly to tell me that they had received word of the Liberal lineup in Humber East and West and especially, from the point of view of himself and my former colleagues at the newspaper, Port au Port. It would be as I had suggested—and as it turned out, we did win all three seats.

The election took place on September 8, and as the results rolled in from around the province, it became obvious Mr. Smallwood had fashioned yet another tremendous electoral victory, his sixth in a row, and in terms of the number of seats his biggest electoral success ever. The final count: Liberals 39, Progressive Conservatives 3.

Nothing succeeds like success and thereafter, it seemed Mr. Smallwood and those around him who previously knew me only as a journalist—newsmen always being under a degree of suspicion—came to regard me with new respect. This was underscored when the Premier picked me for the high-profile assignment of seconding the Address in Reply to the Speech from the Throne at the opening of the new legislative session.

Unfortunately, I could not always claim political judgment so astute.

◆   ◆   ◆

If there is one notable trait that I inherit from both sides of my family, the Rogers (my mother's) side as well as the Callahans—and can take little credit for it, of course—it is a tendency to worka-holism. They definitely were not lazy people.

I came to admire a similar quality in Mr. Smallwood, and not only his capacity for work, but also for his inventiveness and imagination. He was both an idea man, and an eternal optimist. He was not one to beat his head uselessly against an immovable, impenetrable wall, but neither would he throw up his hands in defeat and give in easily. Rather, his approach was to insist there must be a way around barriers, to press for a constructive solution to a problem even if it (frustratingly!) would take even more time and effort. And patience was certainly not his most evident virtue!

This attitude, I was certain, would make all the difference in dealing with the difficulties that beset the people of Port au Port, then one of the worst-off and neglected areas in an historically poor and neg-lected province. It would require the dedication of workaholics blessed with the patience of Job to make noticeable progress in solving its immense economic, social and infrastructural problems.

Closure of the U.S. Air Force Base at Stephenville in 1966 left the town and the surrounding area destitute—employment limited to the few jobs provided by a poor and seasonal fishery; a scattering of shops and garages, mainly in Stephenville; a handful of government welfare, public health and high-ways department positions; limited numbers of lay positions in schools largely staffed by religious Sisters. Many saw Stephenville Airport, with its airline and aircraft servicing jobs, as the area's main asset. But with the economy at its lowest ebb since the Americans had arrived in the 1940s, the need for a civilian airport now appeared to be very much in doubt.

Once I got my MHA's bearings, and was able to document the problems, I sent off a lengthy, detailed request to Zenon W. Sametz, then Deputy Minister of Social and Economic Development and the provincial government bureaucrat directly responsible for implementation of the federal-provincial development programs. I urged that my District receive generous treatment under the latest agreement (the Fund for Rural Economic Development or FRED) and wrote:

"... The area of most concern is the Port au Port Peninsula, although the communities of Port au Port East, Port au Port, Point au Mal, Aguathuna and Boswarlos ... and the communities of Kippens, Noel's Pond and Cold Brook should also fall within the scope of any rural development plan. The Peninsula itself is well off the beaten track of industry, commerce and communications. And what geo-graphical location has not decreed ethnic background, isolation, poor education and difficult circum-stances have ordered to the point that this can be considered ... one of the most impoverished and backward areas of Newfoundland. I do not pronounce judgment. I merely state the fact.

"Recently, following much insistence and what was in effect an order from the Board of Commissioners of Public Utilities, the Avalon Telephone Company declared that the Cape St. George area with a population in excess of 2,000 people could not support a compensatory service, and I judge from their figures will not for a period of perhaps 20 years."

In the end it would take a Cabinet order to bring the first telephones to more than a dozen com-munities—assisted to no small degree by the fact Mr. Smallwood knew the area having agreed to go with me to the ends of the primitive, unpaved roads snaking dangerously along the sides of the natural triangle of the Peninsula, sticking like a sore thumb into the Gulf of St. Lawrence. (In time they would be joined to close the gap between the Cape and Mainland, in the first language of most residents, La Grand Terre.)

I can still see the faces of the children of Mainland and nearby Three Rock Cove, staring in wide-eyed anticipation as it seemed the Premier's heavy Chrysler must crash through a tiny bridge into the brook dividing the communities. But it and we emerged unscathed, and the fact of his visit enormously helped the Peninsula get the support it required.

He never slackened, aided and abetted by myself and Bill Keough, the MHA for neighbouring St. George's District and then Labour minister, in working to build an alternative economy for the area. We turned Stephenville, in particular, from a potential ghost town into a bustling industrial community with our all-out support of John C. Doyle's Javelin (Melville) Paper Company, together with a dozen lesser industrial and business ventures; establishment of provincial adult education and training facilities and programs; highway upgradings; telecommunications and airport facilities; and opening the Sir Thomas Roddick Hospital in former U.S.A.F. medical facilities. The District was now on its way to becoming arguably the most prosperous part of rural Newfoundland.

But all this activity contributed, as well, to a housing shortage, to higher rents, to school overcrowding, as people flocked into Stephenville from all over the province looking for jobs.With industry came labour disputes and work stoppages. It all built up into an atmosphere of public dissatisfaction that would translate into political backlash.

(It was a rather different story on the Peninsula where paved roads, telephones, improved schools and libraries, plus development of municipal government and community services, along with the new opportunities for work at Stephenville, were factors to improve the government's standing.)

One major irritant, in particular, boiled the blood of taxpaying property-owners in the town of Stephenville. Upscale housing on the former military base, once occupied by officers of the United States Air Force and their families, now was being made available for rent by the Harmon Corporation, the agency we had set up to take control of the imposing military property. According to rumour, some tenants paid what were said to be scandalously low rents (which perhaps some did, as an incentive to new industries to establish in the area.) By the same token, living outside town boundaries, they also escaped municipal taxes. Inevitably, we were accused of favouring "outsiders" compared to local people.

As the General Election of 1971 approached, there was increasing, worrying evidence of deepening tensions among Liberals in Port au Port District, or to be more precise, Stephenville, its capital. This grew largely out of the bitter 1969 Liberal Party leadership contest in which Mr. Smallwood ran to succeed himself—the last thing he wanted, I continue to believe, but he was left little choice: fight, or be forced out.

In the course of the fractious leadership exercise I crossed swords frequently with John C. Crosbie, several of whose influential supporters happened to be members of my district executive or key constituency workers. They included, particularly, the president of the Port au Port Liberal Association, Robert Isaacs, the manager of my constituency office, Theresa Ryan, and a young lawyer and native son of the district, Fred Stagg. In fact Stagg, whom I judged correctly to have political ambitions of his own, pledged as a Liberal to support my re-election. I was publicly nominated by acclamation in 1971 in a new, democratic candidate-selection process, upon which I had insisted.

But after Crosbie finally decided his place was with the Tories, Isaacs (who had absented himself from my nomination meeting and the motorcade that preceded it), Ryan, Stagg, and a couple of thousand voters who had marked an "X" for me in my first election, followed him. Stagg was elected as the MHA for Port au Port which thus went Tory for the first time.

◆　◆　◆

Consummate practitioner of "the art of the possible," it is fair to say that Mr. Smallwood ate, drank and slept politics. It wouldn't be far wrong to say he was at it 20 hours a day, seven days a week. Hardly ever did a day pass but he was on the phone, calling around the province from a list carried in an inside suit pocket, often on the back of an envelope, to keep in regular touch with trusted observers and politically sensitive situations. Consequently it was rare for him to be taken by surprise by any happening with political implications, and rarer still to be caught unprepared.

His constant, repeated advice to the Cabinet and the caucus consisted of this central reminder and admonition: "The first job of a politician is to get elected … The second job of a politician is to get, and stay, elected … The third job …" and so on.

"Because if you don't (get elected), then nothing else counts."

Indeed, getting elected is, as they say, the name of the game. It matters not how high the motives, how intense the commitment to public service, how acute the sense of honesty, of integrity, of purpose … All are meaningless, in terms of the exercise of political power, out of power. They are attributes highly to be desired, and as highly valued, in those who hold or seek public office; nor should they be seen as barriers to election, or virtues to be abandoned and laid aside at the threshold on entering public life.

On the other hand, politics is not synonymous with Holy Orders, and becoming involved in it is not to acquire perfection, although the experience can be both exciting and extremely satisfying in terms of the opportunity for public service.

However, the very practical electorate are well aware of all this and in choosing members of the House of Assembly (or other elective bodies) incline to seeking results before virtue. In general, they tend to throw up a cross-section of themselves—hardly better and no worse. And while a few of those they elect may indulge in the self-flattery that somehow they are something special (the temptation to arrogance, and to the assumption of divine right, is not unknown) the brutal truth is that most are pretty average human beings. As is the case in real life, there are those who stand out and catch the eye of party leaders and power brokers. These frequently ascend to greater things, a Cabinet portfolio or some other leadership role.

Nor is there any doubt that politics, being the exercise in human nature that it is, very often is characterized by prejudice and self-seeking. The British parliamentary tradition that we inherit is inspired by the ordinariness of most of its participants, as by the greatness of the few. It is human nature at its best—and its worst. And to attempt to manage it to perfection is to risk destroying it.

In the 1966 General Election, in which the Smallwood Liberals won 39 out of 42 seats in the House of Assembly, there were no saints that I've heard of, though some mighty good candidates were elected—and defeated. The Premier set out to assemble the finest Cabinet lineup in Newfoundland history, his purpose being to provide the Liberal Party with a plenitude of leadership potential: it had become clear he had decided to retire at or before the end of the term. But it was not to be. Defections from the Cabinet and the caucus, challenges from without and within, resignations, retirements, illness, sudden death—all took their toll on a structure painstakingly built. But not being one to accept defeat easily, or to take kindly to attempts to push him out, not only did he contest—and retain—the leadership, but he went on to preside over one more General Election.

However, it is a startling fact that as the October 1971 contest approached, of the seventeen men who sat around the Cabinet table five years earlier, only three remained: the Premier himself, Frederick W. Rowe and James R. Chalker. Gone to retirement were Leslie R. Curtis, Philip J. Lewis, Beaton J. Abbott, Dr. James M. McGrath and C. Max Lane; to be Chancellor of Memorial University, G. Alain Frecker; to be chairman of the Civil Service Commission, Eric S. Jones; to be president of the Canadian Saltfish Corporation, Aiden Maloney; to enter federal politics, Charles R. Granger; deceased, William J. Keough; resigned and left the party, H.R.V. Earle, Clyde K. Wells, T. Alex Hickman, and John C. Crosbie.

Mid-term, and later, replacements included Earl W. Winsor, Edward M. Roberts, John A. Nolan, William R. Callahan, Stephen A. Neary, William N. Rowe, Gerald I. Hill, Harold E. Starkes, Eric N. Dawe, and John A. Mahoney. Brought on board in preparation for the election were Hubert Kitchen, Augustus Oldford, George Warren, Uriah Strickland, Noel. F. Murphy, Melvin G. Woodward, Roy C. Legge, and William G. Adams.

Were change and renewal, in themselves, sufficient to assure re-election, the Liberal Party should have recorded another great victory in 1971. But for the first time since Confederation, a majority of voters—50.9% to be precise—would cast votes for the Official Opposition, signalling that achievements aside, they had decided that twenty-three years of Liberal rule was long enough. Our 44% was the lowest level of support by far in seven trips to the polls over more that two decades.

Yet, in terms of the number of seats won by either party the election, amazingly, was a dead heat. The outcome would be decided by judges of the Supreme Court.

# CHAPTER 4

## THE POLITICS AND THE POWER

*"The Liberal Party belongs to the people. (M)y ambition ... is to settle that ownership so that no selfish interest might gain control of it."*

A few days after the 1966 General Election and the latest smashing victory of the Liberal Party, along with other successful candidates, I headed for Confederation Building. The occasion was the first meeting of the Liberal caucus, and I was anxious to make the acquaintance of my new colleagues.

Some I had come to know previously in the workplace and in the course of my work as a journalist. Others were total strangers. But it would become clear that we were all now blood brothers, thrown together by circumstances that would render our lives out of our control for as long, certainly, as we remained in public life, if not ever afterwards.

The truth is that once publicly identified with a political party a person becomes branded, as it were, with an indelible tattoo. Thereafter every act and opinion stands to be judged—by friend and foe alike—against that background.

Many who have not had the experience of politics may not recognize its tendency to transcend other considerations—age, ability, education, family background, health, religion, social status, personal obligations, personal privacy. In no other context than the human invention of political parties is the competitive instinct, the drive to succeed, more surely at work. And more than education, or personal wealth, or reputation, the attributes of energy, imagination and personal courage play a crucial part.

A committed supporter of the system, I recognize nonetheless that by nature political parties are utterly selfish. However grandly painted, they have one overriding purpose, the quest for and retention of power which, by the same token, is extremely difficult to relinquish. What is done with that power, how exercised and whether to the greatest good of the greatest number of those who confer it at the ballot box, remains the great question.

Attempts to define politics—example, "the art of the possible," or "the constant quest for essential compromise," together with the admonition that "the secret of political power is secret knowledge"—these aim to describe a process that beyond certain formalities is, in effect, a non-process, more often defined by success than how it is achieved. Ethical considerations—truth, honesty, personal and party loyalty, seem ever in peril, and the perversity that the end justifies the means rarely out of sight. Would we be better off without political parties? Some think so; but one of history's most skilled practitioners, the legendary Sir Winston Spencer Churchill, described the British parliamentary system by which we are governed as the world's worst—except for any other. And there is

*PHOTOS CLOCKWISE:*
■ Premier Smallwood launches reorganization of the Liberal Party with speech to a full house of party members in the Grand Falls Armoury (TA); ■ Joey emerges triumphant from 1969 leadership battle (DN/TA); ■ Leadership convention delegates are engulfed by a forest of candidates' stick signs in St. John's Memorial Stadium (DN/TA).

this reality: The House of Assembly is the single most important institution in our province, in that it alone speaks for all of us, or can.

The first gathering of the new government caucus, 39 men and no women, was taking place in the Government Members' Common Room on the east side of the ninth floor, across the corridor from the House of Assembly chamber. Crossing the main lobby, I pressed an elevator "Up" button and almost at once double doors opened to one of the cars. Inside I was joined by a heavy-set, bespectacled individual who seemed vaguely familiar. As the doors closed and the car edged upwards I turned to him and said, "Hello, I'm Bill Callahan … are you Aidan Maloney?"

As my companion took my outstretched hand, shaking his head, I realized my mistake and he said, "No, I'm John Crosbie … But I'm glad to meet you; I recognize you from CJON. You know, Premier Smallwood is getting ready to retire and he asked me to get a committee together to draft a new Liberal Party constitution to get ready for a leadership convention—would you be interested in helping out?"

Would I … ! Setting aside momentary shock at this unexpected, almost casual suggestion of the Premier's intentions—I would want to hear from the man himself—this was the best welcome I could imagine, an invitation to become involved in the inner workings of the party. I seized upon it without hesitation.

"I would be very interested," I replied. "Just let me know when …" The elevator came to a stop at our floor, and we stepped into the exterior lobby of the House of Assembly chamber where other members were beginning to gather, standing round chatting before going into the meeting. Crosbie and I parted, and I have to say that I never again heard of the proposed constitution committee.

The caucus meeting featured a review by Mr. Smallwood of the election campaign, doing nothing to dampen the self-congratulatory atmosphere. There were introductions all around, and contributory comments by some of the veterans. Several holdovers from the former Cabinet were there—the election wiped the slate clean, but the new crew chosen by the Premier and appointed by Her Majesty's representative would include several that I recognized—Dr. James M. McGrath, Minister of Health in the last administration, now moving to Finance; F.W. Rowe, Education; L.R. Curtis, Justice; G.A. Frecker, Provincial Affairs; W.J. Keough, Resources. New MHAs included fresh faces like my own, some of them more than faintly familiar: John Nolan, a friend and former colleague from my days at CJON; Ed Roberts, who had worked as a summer student in the newsroom there and later gained first-hand contact with every reporter as the Premier's executive assistant; Clyde Wells, whom I had known as a lawyer in Corner Brook.

I recognized Steve Neary, very prominent in labour circles, and first elected in 1962 for Bell Island. And I was pleased to meet the ever courteous, thoughtful Aidan Maloney who had come out of the fishing industry to be deputy and later Minister of Fisheries; we were destined to become good friends. He had succeeded my uncle, James P. Rogers, as CEO of the big John Penny & Son operations based in Ramea on the Southwest Coast, where I had visited as a child. My aunt Loretta Rogers was a daughter of plant manager Thomas Vallis, and Marie Smart Penny, wife of company president Senator George Penney, was a close friend of my mother, and my godmother.

This was not only a time to get acquainted, but also for critical information to be passed, not the least when and how we would be paid—an archaic system by which MHAs at that point received half a meagre $6,500 "sessional allowance" the first day the House sat, and half the day it closed months hence. (It would be increased over time to $10,000.)

In fact, "private" members could not survive without a supplementary source of income, and for most it might be accurate to say the allowance itself was an add-on to other earnings. (Days after the election I was back working at CJON Radio and TV as News Director—quite acceptable in those times, but unthinkable today.) Cabinet ministers got along fairly well as full-time "employees," in effect, of the government, receiving a salary of $12,000 in addition to the MHA stipend and a car allowance.

Instructions were given as to MHA behaviour, arrangements for swearing-in, and dress for opening day of the House (formal morning suit complete with top hat.) The question on many people's minds was who would be appointed to the new Cabinet, and to the limited number of House positions with appropriate extra pay—Speaker, Deputy Speaker, and Chairman of Committees, all in the control of the majority government, but in the case of the Speaker, usually made in consultation with the Opposition. There were, as well, the

House Leaders (managers of each party's business in the legislature) and the party Whips (the MHAs charged with keeping track of members, especially ensuring they were present for votes). Obviously, these went to experienced hands.

With a surfeit of 39 members, Mr. Smallwood had the widest choice of any head of government in Newfoundland history. The downside was that with such a large caucus, it would be virtually impossible to keep everyone happy. Cracks would begin to show long before the new government had time to get its second wind.

The main trouble grew out of the new Budget presented on March 29, 1968 in behalf of the government by the new Finance minister, renowned physician and a champion of the war against TB. It exacerbated mounting upset in the Liberal caucus, the attitude of rebellion reflected in simple griping or more serious talk of demanding a showdown caucus meeting—or an undefined "or else."

The Budget, crafted by McGrath so as to spread its effects over as many people as possible but as lightly as possible, had the unintended result of making virtually everyone mad at us. It slashed welfare benefits, tacked five cents onto a gallon of gasoline, increased the retail sales tax, abolished subsidies on municipal water and sewer bills, and hiked the corporation tax. It reduced the subsidy on rural electricity rates, raised liquor prices by ten cents and beer—the so-called "poor man's champagne"—by one cent a bottle, doubled the tax on tobacco products, and placed a levy on insurance premiums.

But worst and most telling of all, it lowered the exemption (or to put it another way, the starting point) for the application of the retail sales tax. Now the government began taxing Cokes and candy bars, the second most popular snack foods among legions of Newfoundland youngsters and their elders after fish and chips with dressing and gravy. Adjustments would be made, but it did little good: the "ragged-arsed artillery," the ordinary people, felt betrayed and we would not be allowed to forget it.

(It was claimed the Budget also abolished free tuition and allowances at Memorial University, the Smallwood concept in practice of equal opportunity in higher education. It did not; rather, it made the program subject to a needs test. On May 23, *The Evening Telegram* denounced editorially what it called "the decision to withdraw this great incentive to higher learning," giving expression to a general, but erroneous, belief.)

That there would be budgetary belt-tightening was not unexpected; for weeks the softening-up process had been underway both in the House and outside.

Officially the whole thing was caused by the situation ongoing in Vietnam. On March 5 *The Western Star* had given top play to a Canadian Press story: "Vietnam War hurts growth plans: SMALLWOOD HINTS GOV'T WILL CUT EXPENDITURES."

Said the Premier, "There has never before in the world's history been a situation as bad as it is tonight," and the government would be "madmen" to turn their backs on it. "We are going to have a pause in Newfoundland this year, a hesitation. We are going to mark time ..."

We backbench members were not so stupid as not to realize tough measures are sometimes required in the management of public finances, or that major world conflagrations such as the Vietnam War inevitably shorten the supply and raise the cost of money that might be borrowed for capital works. But we were convinced that in some respects the Budget had simply gone too far, and in others was downright ridiculous. The real harm lay in the fact that (in keeping with the practice of tight secrecy) we were in the dark as to the range and nature of its provisions, and being left without excuse or explanation, were severely embarrassed before our questioning, demanding constituents.

The Budget added to a growing climate of dissatisfaction that was ready-made for anyone looking to capitalize on trouble in the ranks of the party's ordinary elected members who, of course, outnumbered the Cabinet, and without whose continuing support the government could not survive.

I was at home on May 14, working on district correspondence, when the telephone rang at mid-morning to announce a caucus meeting at one o'clock. There was no time to check around to determine what emergency might be transpiring, but the short notice seemed to render unlikely the possibility it would be the gripe session many of us had been demanding. When the Premier strode into the crowded Common Room, it was to drop a bombshell: two of the government's leading ministers, Crosbie who was then Minister of Health, and Wells who had resigned from Labour but remained as a Minister without Portfolio, were out of the Cabinet. When the House met in a couple of hours they would be sitting across the floor!

The ostensible reason for their departure—disagreement persists three decades later as to whether they jumped, or were pushed—was the matter of $5 million in interim or "bridge" financing for John M. Shaheen's Come by Chance oil refinery. It seemed like a tiny concern, compared to the $200 million price tag on the total project, details of which the two had helped negotiate.

Later, in an ongoing controversy, I issued a statement in which I pointed out the "incredible"—that they had "left the Liberal side of the House over the … (refinery), yet barely 24 hours later Mr. Crosbie expressed the hope that the project would succeed. And then, they declined to vote against it" when the necessary legislation came forward. In my estimation bridge financing was "an obviously lame excuse … (W)hat happened was a grab for power that backfired because backbench dissatisfaction with budget cuts was mistakenly thought to hold the seeds of a wholesale revolt. It was an attempt to split the party wide-open …"—in other words, a bloodless coup!

I was not alone in coming to this conclusion. Many members of the caucus were of like opinion, convinced that being well aware of bruised feelings in the backbench—if not actually encouraging a climate of dissatisfaction—Crosbie and Wells may well have believed and expected that a sufficient number of the private members would follow them so that, either on their own as Reform Liberals, or in alliance with the tiny Tory caucus, they could command a majority of the House and take over the government.

There was no overt attempt, that I was aware of, to co-opt the members of the backbench. But in our own private discussions we were certainly alive to the danger and consequences of wholesale defections. But all but two of us remained firm in our support of the government, the exceptions being Gerald Myrden, the MHA for St. Barbe South, and Tom Burgess, the MHA for Labrador West. Not only did the rest remain where we were, but stood, each in his turn, in a marathon overnight sitting of the House, to speak against and ultimately vote down a Tory motion of non-confidence.

The crisis seemingly over, on Thursday, July 18 readers of *The Daily News* (which then came out about five o'clock in the morning) awoke to the day's lead headline, "Smallwood regroups forces: MASSIVE CABINET SHAKE-UP" and read: "Premier Smallwood brought seven new ministers into his cabinet Wednesday in the most sweeping single cabinet change in the 19-year history of his administration. Three ministers retired in a shake-up designed to give the cabinet a new 'youthful' look.

"Appointed to the cabinet were: Earl Winsor, 49, Minister of Labrador Affairs; Edward M. Roberts, 27, Minister of Public Welfare; John A. Nolan, 37, Minister of Municipal Affairs and Supply; William R. Callahan, 36, Minister of Mines, Agriculture and Resources; and Gerald I. Hill, 49, William N. Rowe, 26, and Stephen A. Neary, 43—all ministers without portfolio."

Meanwhile, Cabinet veteran H.R.V. Earle moved from Public Welfare to Finance, Aidan Maloney assumed the portfolio of Community and Social Development along with his former assignment of Fisheries, and F.W. Rowe would continue in Education, but shed his former responsibilities in Labrador Affairs. The three ministers who retired "for reasons of health" were C. Max Lane, Dr. James McGrath, and Beaton J. Abbott. The newspaper quoted the Premier as referring to the new ministers, all under 50 years of age, as "new youngsters, who are going to put a vigour, thrust and push into the Cabinet that will make us oldsters, and those of us who are not so old, look to our laurels." Mr. Smallwood himself was then heading for his 68th birthday.

As for the Budget, it was probably too late to worry about the 1968 version, but Roberts—erudite, articulate brilliant lawyer and the party's clear-eyed strategist—penned some sage advice grounded in realism to guide preparation of the subsequent edition. Dated by hand 5 February 1969 but evidently written sometime earlier, the memorandum pointed to "a mounting crescendo of criticism" in the two years since the last election:

"In a very real sense," he wrote, "this is inevitable because the pendulum does swing: our overwhelming victory in 1966 had to produce an adverse reaction …"

"Much of the criticism centred and is centering around the theme of financial mismanagement. The report of the Royal Commission on Economic Prospects, the controversy over bridge financing at Come by Chance and the non-appearance of the third and fourth paper mills are all being used with considerable effect as evidence that we have mismanaged the affairs of the Province.

"The 1968-69 Budget, which came in the midst of these events, appeared to lend credence to the attacks. It is of no concern to the people of Newfoundland that every government in Canada faces financial problems. All they know is that last year taxes were increased savagely (our total take increased by some 20% in one year, which is a massive rise), and that this very great increase was accompanied by a withdrawal of Government services. More than any other single event, the Budget seemed to confirm the charges being made by our political opponents."

His advice to Cabinet colleagues: The next Budget—likely the last but one before again going to the electorate—was politically "crucial" and should be viewed as the start of the next election campaign. It must put an end to a "mad" increase in government expenditures, little of which seemed to benefit people directly, and provide for projects that did, such as roads and rural electrification.

◆  ◆  ◆

As the chill winds of autumn 1968 began to whistle through the Exploits Valley and stately birches to turn to flame, Liberals in Central Newfoundland prepared to gather in response to a lengthy summons from the Leader of their party. Certain of its key sections follow:

*Dear Friend:*

*As Leader of the Liberal Party I am privileged to send you this invitation to join with me in an historic meeting to give our beloved Liberal Party a renewal of strength, purpose and direction. The meeting will be held on Saturday, September 28, at Grand Falls. You are one of some thirty active, loyal Liberals that I am inviting from your District to attend this first meeting. Altogether I am inviting more than 1,200 active, loyal Liberals from the forty-one House of Assembly Districts of Newfoundland and Labrador.*

*The meeting is for a discussion of our Liberal Party and its future (and) to re-organize the Liberal Association of the Province, to adopt the Constitution, and to elect a President and above all make plans for the strengthening of our Party in this Province ... I have, as you know, announced publicly my firm determination to pass my leadership of our Party back to the organized Liberals of our Province. I have, in a letter to Senator Petten, declared my intention, before the end of next year, to ask the Liberal Association to hold a Leadership Convention that would receive my resignation and elect a new Leader in my place. In that same letter to Senator Petten I declared my determination to leave behind me a powerfully organized Liberal Party, and to get this noble purpose accomplished before the Leadership Convention is called ... The Liberal Party belongs to the people, and my ambition, in these remaining months of my leadership, is to settle that ownership and control firmly and unshakably in the hands of the people, so that no selfish interests might succeed in gaining control of it. The broader and deeper we can make the foundations the surer the Liberal Party will be to deserve and hold the love and support of our Newfoundland people.*

*Will you help me to accomplish this great and noble purpose?*
*Sincerely yours,*

*JOSEPH R. SMALLWOOD*
*Premier*

As it turned out, some 1,500 women and men were present for the Grand Falls meeting, and almost as many for each of two others in Clarenville and Corner Brook, an estimated 4,500 all told. Many of us who attended these great gatherings had the feeling that with this kind of support, the Liberal Party was destined to remain in office for a long time to come. We would have ridiculed anyone who suggested it would only be for another couple of years!

Officers were elected, and a constitution approved. Next the Premier made good on his earlier announced intention and wrote the new president, John Mahoney, who succeeded former Member of Parliament Richard Cashin in the job and was one of two MHAs for the dual constituency of Harbour Main, the other being Minister without Portfolio Philip J. Lewis, Q.C. Mahoney was asked to call a special leadership convention in order to receive Mr. Smallwood's resignation as Leader and elect his successor.

As far as Mr. Smallwood was concerned, the man best fitted to take over the running of the province was Lewisporte-born Frederick William Rowe, 56, a man with nearly two decades' experience in the House of Assembly and a Cabinet veteran of five major portfolios, who announced his candidacy in January 1969.

But that was before Crosbie—who had returned to the fold in order to be able to attend the party's organizational meetings—announced he also was entering the race with what appeared to be unlimited funds and organizational assistance, and important indirect support as well. It seemed unlikely, for example, that the Crosbie Group in 1968 acquired *The Daily News* and virtually all of the province's weekly newspapers without consideration of what control of so much of the media could do for his leadership bid.

"I soon concluded that my close friend and confidant, Fred Rowe, who had announced his own candidacy for the leadership, didn't have the financial strength or organizing personnel to beat Crosbie," Mr. Smallwood wrote in *I Chose Canada*.

"For years it had been common knowledge in Newfoundland that I had been hoping to see Rowe succeed me in the leadership of our party. I had moved him from one department to another … all part of a deliberate plan to let him become more familiar with the workings of government than any man in our history. He was honoured and respected universally in the province, but he didn't have John Crosbie's grim industry or money. Fred and I talked it over and agreed that he would withdraw, that I would run, and that he would use all his strength to support me. I announced this accordingly."

As might be expected, Crosbie as candidate for Leader had little good to say for the Budget brought down by Earle on April 16, 1969, or much else the government did—or didn't do. The Budget speech was too long for his liking, and spent too much time recounting good things achieved by the Smallwood Liberals. And what must be first and foremost an action plan—the government's annual fiscal report and expenditure blueprint—was criticized for not being what it wasn't supposed to be: in Crosbie's words "an overall plan for the future development of Newfoundland." (It must be said, however, that it necessarily fulfilled that role by providing funding for implementation of ongoing development plans formulated elsewhere than in the normal budgetary process.)

In June, Crosbie Campaign Headquarters issued a typically sensationalist press release that managed to insinuate malfeasance by posing a question: "GOVERNMENT SURRENDERING MINERAL RIGHTS?— CROSBIE: In a blistering attack on the present financial policies of the Smallwood administration, John Crosbie has accused the government of surrendering millions of potential dollars in mineral rights … on the continental shelf." It appears he had made a speech to the Lions Club in Grand Bank claiming the April 16 Budget dismissed untold revenues by conceding the offshore might not belong to this province "in a legal or constitutional sense."

Sheer, total nonsense as Crosbie well knew. In fact this had become the settled law of Canada when the provinces lost out to Ottawa in the Supreme Court of Canada two years earlier. The Premier had helped lead the fight for provincial ownership, but could do little now but express bitter disappointment and press for a political settlement.

As Minister of Mines, Agriculture and Resources I put out a statement accusing Crosbie of "shocking, appalling irresponsibility" that could harm negotiations then underway, aimed at giving Newfoundland "the biggest possible share of revenues from offshore minerals, oil and natural gas." I also recalled the statement of Justice Minister T. Alex Hickman in the House earlier in the year, that despite the Supreme Court of Canada ruling, Newfoundland was prepared to intervene further should any other province take the matter back to Canada's highest court.

On July 3 the Premier, as Leader of the Liberal Party, announced that the leadership convention would take place in the St. John's Memorial Stadium October 30-November 1. Days later he let the province know he would be a candidate, meaning the main event, Crosbie versus Smallwood, was assured. Rowe withdrew to support the Premier, then former ministers Wells and Abbott came out for Crosbie. The battle for delegate support began to be waged in church halls and school auditoriums.

On October 13, with the convention only a fortnight away and most delegates committed to one or the other of the leading candidates, Hickman unexpectedly threw his hat in the ring asking Liberals to "favour me with your support, not as a vote against the Premier but as a vote of confidence in me." He received the backing of Earle and backbenchers Gerald Myrden and Nath Noel.

Hickman pledged, "I assure you that the basic principles of the Liberal Party will be retained, and that I will unite all Loyal and Patriotic Liberals under my Leadership."

There was only one ballot required as Mr. Smallwood emerged with an unbeatable margin, 1,070 to 440 for Crosbie, 187 for Hickman, 13 for Memorial University student Randolph Joyce, 3 for St. John's businessman Peter Cook and 2 for Vincent Spencer, a hotel operator in Windsor in Central Newfoundland.

In the days following the convention Hickman and Earle announced they would join the Tory caucus in the House of Assembly, while Crosbie moved back across the floor to the independent Reform Liberal benches, rejoining Wells. Their numbers were increased by the arrival of Myrden and Abbott.

As a result of the 1966 election the Conservatives held three seats, all in St. John's—Anthony J. "Ank" Murphy in the Centre, Gerald R. Ottenheimer in the East, and Thomas V. Hickey in East Extern.

The following year, Fisheries minister Charles R. Granger resigned and moved to federal politics necessitating a by-election in Gander district; it was won by Harold A.Collins for the Tories, increasing their number to four. It was maintained at this level when Ottenheimer resigned and a by-election in his St. John's East seat was won by William Marshall.

Earlier Burgess had left the Liberals claiming the government was ignoring the needs of Labrador. He announced formation of the New Labrador Party (NLP).

The total effect of these changes and the subsequent defections from the Liberal ranks of Crosbie, Wells, Myrden, Abbott, Earle and Hickman was that, by the end of 1969, the government faced a combined opposition of 11 members—six PCs, four reform "Independent" Liberals and one NLP, compared to just three members in the Official Opposition in 1966.

For what it was worth, a wholesale series of new appointments to the Cabinet had rendered Opposition calls for change—as in the slogan "Time for a change"—somewhat meaningless. The average age was only 48, and members of the "kiddies' corner" who graduated to the inner circle a couple of years earlier were now among the most senior ministers.

## JOEY: HIS LIBERAL HEART "EXALTED"

In contrast to other leadership candidates who presented policy-laden speeches to the delegates gathered in the St. John's Memorial Stadium, Mr. Smallwood first congratulated Crosbie and Hickman who had spoken before him—"We all heard them with interest and appreciation," he said—and then turned to the Liberal Party and its future.

Describing the convention as a great family gathering of Liberals, he told his audience it was just what he dreamed of when he set out a year earlier on a drive to return control of the party to the people.

"This is what I hoped and worked for, and my heart is joyful ... my Liberal heart is exalted. For here we are tonight, the rich and the poor, the high and the low, the great and the humble, the highly educated and the poorly educated, and the few with no formal education at all.

"We are here tonight, fishermen and farmers, miners, loggers, teachers, doctors, railwaymen, clerks and office workers and lawyers, clergymen and writers and legislature members ... all manner of men and women from the north, south, east, and the west ... all of us Canadians, all of us Newfoundlanders, all of us Liberals. There has never been the like of it in this province before."

In The Evening Telegram account he advised Liberals to pay no heed, no attention, to what he described as the "few visionless, timid souls" who had been moaning and wringing their hands because the leadership candidates had been waging vigorous and "sometimes colourful" campaigns.

"Don't let that worry you," he said.

"This is, of course, purely an internal affair, a family affair. Our Tory friends are in for a bad disappointment if they have the vain hope that the momentary divisions, this family quarrel, is anything but a temporary division in our great and historic Liberal Party. What a disappointment is facing them!"

Moments after arriving at the podium for his victory address, Mr. Smallwood was congratulated by opponent T. Alex Hickman, his former Justice minister.

"Mr. Hickman has given me his congratulations … Now I wonder about Mr. Crosbie … will Mr. Crosbie come up and make it unanimous?"

After someone informed the Premier that Crosbie was already heading for the platform, he said, "Mr. Crosbie is trying to get up, he is pushing his way through the crowd."

A few seconds later Crosbie, accompanied by Wells who was his West Coast campaign manager, arrived to shake hands with Mr. Smallwood and congratulate him on his victory.

Although Mrs. Smallwood usually remained in the background, on this occasion she, along with other members of the family, sat in her husband's booth to the south of the podium.

"I feel fine," she commented, after the results were declared by Herman Batten, the former Member of Parliament for Humber-St. George's, who was convention chairman.

"I predicted that he would win three to one, and he didn't do too bad. He almost came up to that mark."

The strenuous business of the leadership campaign and the convention behind him, Mr. Smallwood, who would be 69 in a few weeks, announced that before turning to the demanding job of "tackling the Budget," he might take a holiday "down south."

# CHAPTER 5
## A BURNING IN ST. BARBE

# The Evening Telegram

Volume 94

Number 2

St. John's, Newfoundland Thursday, January 6, 1972

10 Cents

20 pages

## Judges promise quick answer on election

### Hearing marked by heated exchanges

Greene

The Supreme Court hearing of a petition to have the Oct. 28 election in St. Barbe South district declared null and void concluded Wednesday afternoon and the presiding judges have promised a quick decision.

Chief Justice R. S. Furlong

Justice A...

Bennett, according to the official count, contended that the results of the election were not changed by the abo...

or by th...

direction of the court.

the conclusion that this election was ... there are no ...

...petition must be dismissed.

"The ... of Edward Maynard is ...

...action of Edward Maynard, 'to a...

case and decid...

not because b...

the move but ... a partial of ...

doesn't make a...

The PCs won 21 seats in the election, the Liberals 20 and the New Labrador party one. However, Premier Smallwood...

judge who heard the case, Mr. ... ...occurred in the...

## Viets toughen conditions for POWs' release

## St. Barbe South goes to PCs... Moores ready to form government

*Noel responded, "I heartily disagree with Your Lordship." The Chief Justice declared, "I will not tolerate impertinence from ... the Bar."*

For months the Premier had seen trouble looming in Port au Port—trouble to which I had chosen to turn a blind eye—and tried hard to persuade me to switch to the District of St. Barbe South for the 1971 election. No one was better or more favourably known there, he would point out, due to my success in securing the agreement for Gros Morne National Park plus federal development of the historic sites at L'Anse aux Meadows and Port au Choix and the Great Northern Peninsula in general.

He was probably right. Leading Liberals in the area, led by well-known and highly respected Local Improvement District Secretary Henry Payne, had indicated they would welcome me there as their candidate.

"I still thank the Good Lord for a government that has the welfare of all our people at heart, a government trying to drive the best possible bargain (on the National Park) with Ottawa, and a government with the vision to see beyond the selfish ambition of would-be opportunists," Payne wrote me in early 1970.

"We want more than a park to provide jobs and income for a certain segment ... The level-headed folks this way will go along with you and the government. We have sense enough to know that (you) cannot wave a magic wand and presto, there's the park. Good luck and Godspeed in your endeavours."

But stubbornly, and as it turned out perhaps unwisely, I refused to be "driven out" of Port au Port—unless it be through the normal electoral process.

Frankly, I did not feel I could walk out on supporters and friends who worked hard to help me get elected my first time out, and were preparing to do it again—Heber and Bessie Noel, Doug Campbell and George McCormack, Ed Major and Stanley White, Pat and Lillian Hayes, Stan Schumph, Mabel Bungay, Jerry Benoit, Martin McIssac, Phil McCann, Charlie Hynes, Nath Kelloway, and many others. I stayed, and took a licking at the polls on October 28.

During a federal-provincial conference in Ottawa the Premier and I had had one of our last serious discussions on the subject of switching seats. Late one night in his suite in the Chateau Laurier Hotel I refused once again to budge. He threw up his hands:

"You're going to lose in Port au Port, you know ... You're going to get knocked out. I'm telling you, now, I know what I'm talking about. The place for you to go is St. Barbe South. Up there, you'll sweep it."

I replied that I knew what I was about, to which he replied:

"I hope you do ... You have to think of the party, Bill!"

In the event, I could only feel profound regret—more I feel for his sake than my own—when the dust settled and it became clear that in St.

Barbe, I would almost certainly have been elected. We lost by eight votes, and it is no disservice to Trevor Bennett, who stood for the Liberals, to suggest that with a fresh candidate, free of ties to a particular part of the district, but with a strong record in its behalf, the government would have survived. Instead it was ousted after a virtual tie election that the Tories were able to manipulate to seize power after the Supreme Court halted a recount in St. Barbe South, refused a new election, and awarded them the seat in the bizarre affair of the Sally's Cove ballots.

That 106 ballots cast in Polling Station No. 13—tallied election night as 55 for PC Ed Maynard, 50 for Bennett and 1 spoiled—had been destroyed, was discovered during the judicial recount, which was immediately halted. Accordingly, the true, official outcome will never be known.

Canadian National Railways employee Nish Collins, a part-time commentator in verse for *The Daily News*, not unexpectedly had something to say about it:

> *The red-hot stove in Sally's Cove*
> *that caused so much confusion*
> *Was a mistake that made some make*
> *a New Year's resolution.*
> —Rhymes of the Times, Jan. 4, 1972

If the Premier held me in any way responsible for the loss in St. Barbe, he never let on. We remained good friends, and indeed for a time after leaving office on January 18, 1972 he wrote a column for me as publisher of *The News* which, along with a colleague from my CJON days, Jim Thoms, I had acquired from Andrew Crosbie in a deal to buy it out of the profits. (There weren't any profits to speak of, which is a whole other story, but we managed to continue publication of the old paper, started by John Alexander Robinson in 1894, for 15 years longer than Crosbie and almost anyone else thought possible.)

When he decided to launch a political comeback as leader of the Liberal Reform Party, ironically, the same name adopted earlier by dissidents Crosbie and Wells, Mr. Smallwood invited me to stand as a candidate in the General Election of 1975. But I declined and did not hesitate to say why: it seemed to me it could only undermine the real Liberal Party. Although a case may be made, based on actual results, that a unified party led by Ed Roberts would not have won the election anyway, I am not so sure. No one will ever know how many Liberal supporters were driven to the PCs, or stayed away from the polls, because of the split between Liberal and Liberal Reform.

I was glad to attend the December 24 birthday parties at Roaches Line arranged by Steve Neary, Greg Power and other close friends of the former Premier, usually bringing along a bottle of his favourite libation, Harvey's Bristol Cream sherry. I was also a fairly regular visitor to 119 Portugal Cove Road where he threw himself boots and all into his *Encyclopedia of Newfoundland and Labrador*.

"Never could I have won Confederation with Canada without help," Mr. Smallwood wrote me in 1979, a rather formal note suggesting an advertising *contra* arrangement between his latest project and *The Daily News*. "I received the help—and Canada got a new Province. Never, without help, could I hope to have the next greatest accomplishment of my life … I will be grateful for your help." And of course it was done, just as he requested.

When for reasons of inadequate resources and failing health he could no longer pursue the massive project, and the Joseph R. Smallwood Heritage Foundation took over and completed it, I felt especially privileged to be a member of the board of directors and initially of the editorial committee.

One day at his Portugal Cove Road office the man whom critics—notably certain ex-Liberal Cabinet ministers—delighted in branding a dictator regarded me thoughtfully and mused, "You know, Bill, I don't think we have ever had a serious disagreement, you and I … I wonder why that is?"

My response was that as his Minister of Mines, Agriculture and Resources, sometime President of the Treasury Board and acting Minister of Finance, "I always had my homework done—and I believe you always knew that."

The truth is that he could be extremely impatient—to put it mildly—with those who did *not* have their homework done, who were perhaps lazy, or careless, or less than thorough in preparing a matter for the

Cabinet or the House. It certainly was not forbidden to disagree with the Premier; but it was to invite trouble to disagree—or to agree, for that matter—without knowing or having thought through the reasons why. I thank my journalism training for the habit of pursuing a subject to its logical conclusion, having asked all the pertinent questions, the least obvious as well as those that stood out.

In any event, the "dictatorship" epithet often hurled, and picked up and perpetuated by the media (without really knowing why) had little meaning as far as I was concerned. I have seen no reason to change my view that it was an untrue and unfair characterization of the Premier. It was also an undeserved, implied slur upon those who served with him who, it might seem, must have been either supine weaklings or uncanonized saints to endure the alleged terrors associated with membership in a Smallwood Cabinet.

Of course, we were neither. The charges were basically false or self-serving, or both, by persons with a grievance to ventilate or a position to advance or protect.

A major difficulty in defending against allegations of "one-man government" is the fact discussions within the Cabinet are subject to the rule of secrecy—ministers take a solemn oath not to reveal them—so there may be little or no latitude to publicly explain or justify an action or decision, however foolish or unworthy it may be portrayed. Anyone tempted to take advantage of this long-standing convention knows precisely what he can get away with!

The experience of a Smallwood Cabinet minister from the very beginning until his untimely death in March 1971, my friend W.J. "Bill" Keough, a man of unquestioned honesty and integrity and as frank and outspoken an individual as one is likely to meet, is instructive. He wrote:

"I have sat in the Cabinet since its very first meeting. For twenty years I have been a student of the Smallwood approach to the 'art of the possible' ... He has never forced his will upon any Cabinet. Instead, more than once he has set aside a proposal upon which he had set his heart, not because the consensus of Cabinet was against it, but because only one man was strongly opposed." (Keough was given a State Funeral, a measure of the Premier's regard for his old friend, on March 5. Later a bridge in St. Georges District was named for him, and his widow, Gertrude O'Brien Keough, was appointed as the province's first Human Rights Commissioner.)

As for myself, the Premier showed me every consideration and courtesy and supported every worthwhile initiative I proposed as a member of his administration, meeting what I trust was my mature, responsible exercise of ministerial authority with consideration and respect.

At the same time, it is next to impossible to be adequately prepared for an unbelievable range of circumstances that conspire to strain relationships and colour the way people under the perpetual stress of politics must deal with each other. A few extra-Cabinet examples will suffice to illustrate the point:

There was, for instance, no easy way to inform the Premier that I had a report, totally unconfirmed, that a family member intended to appropriate his (Mr. Smallwood's) complimentary caribou licence and might even be preparing to "borrow" a Forest Service helicopter, perhaps to hunt in a closed area. This information came to me one afternoon from a deputy minister who, it seems, received it from a director, who may have gotten it from someone in the government's Air Services Division.

Was it true? True or false, the fact it was raised at all constituted an embarrassment. Could I ignore it, dismiss it as someone's idea of a practical joke, or idle rumour, malicious gossip, perhaps, from a burgeoning bag of political dirty tricks?

As minister responsible for wildlife resources, as well as the government's "air force," I did not think so. And at the risk of offending the Premier and his family, I felt I had no option but to inform him at once and to warn that if it were so and the individual did not desist, my next call would have to be to the RCMP. I was relieved when the matter was taken completely seriously—though with what consequences I do not know. Suffice it to say that the officials who first raised it apparently never heard of it again.

One day the government's environmental agency CAWSA—the Clean Air, Water and Soil Authority—reported to me that the effluent disposal system at the Russwood poultry and livestock barns at Roaches Line threatened to overflow its settling ponds, if it was not doing so already.

Inevitably, unless checked, it would pollute surrounding watercourses. It was abundantly clear that in that event there then would be no choice but to take action, possibly in the courts.

Once again, initial shock subsiding, the Premier unhesitatingly gave the required orders to have the problem dealt with. But even when privately raised, matters of this nature and import are cause for great concern. Quite aside from the potential for harm to the public interest, they demand to be dealt with forthrightly, without delay, to avoid or lessen untoward political consequences. How a genuine dictator might react to the delivery of such news, I cannot speculate. What I do know is that in Mr. Smallwood, I encountered no recriminations, no resort to "shooting the messenger." He never hesitated to do what had to be done, however personally painful it may have been.

Newfoundland's first Premier was a farmer before he became a politician. In politics he chose to pursue his agricultural bent, especially in eggs and poultry but in many other areas as well. Consequently, when as Minister of Agriculture I established the first marketing boards assuring producers of stable prices, common rules and equal treatment, there were immediate cries that he was in a conflict of interest.

It is considerable understatement to say the power of the Newfoundland Marketing Board to set prices and establish production quotas—in the same way, it should be noted, as similar boards in other provinces—was not well received by some of our larger agribusiness operators, of which Russwood Poultry was one.

Invited over for a tour of the sprawling ranch and driving along in his black Chrysler with Mr. Smallwood at the wheel, we came upon (and not, I was certain, by accident) his son Ramsay, the man in charge. He stepped at once to the driver's side window and began to make the producers' case, with which I already was very familiar.

But the Premier cut in, "Now Ramsay, you know there's no point in your telling me—the minister is here and this is your chance to say what you have to say to him." The younger Smallwood then came around to the passenger side, and I listened patiently to his arguments. They did nothing to alter the fact that the producers simply wanted to be able to make all the money their free enterprise could manage, without regulation of any kind—but with all the protections of the marketing "scheme" (unfortunate term, but proper legal terminology!) and especially, its restriction against cheap mainland imports.

"My position is very simply stated," I replied firmly. "Either the producers accept the board's set prices, based on an assessment of costs plus a reasonable profit, or the scheme collapses and you no longer have any protections.

"I'm sorry, Ramsay, but that's the way it is. That's the law." And with that, the Premier and I drove off, he having uttered not another word on the subject. (Two days later, the board's prices were accepted.)

A different kind of issue was what I shall refer to as the incident of the Springdale cutting permit, which provides certain insights into how real politics works, or is supposed to.

In the face of mine closures in the area, I agreed to the issue of a pulpwood cutting permit that would put perhaps 100 men to work during an otherwise lean winter. If I was not aware the applicant company, Pelley Enterprises, was owned by prominent Tory and former election candidate Cyril Pelley, perhaps I should have been—though I'm not sure how much difference that would have made. However, it appears that while I was out of town Green Bay MHA William R. Smallwood, the Premier's son, and Liberal District President Corbin Clarke, prevailed upon the Premier to hold up or even cancel the permit.

Shocked to learn of this on my return, I steamed over to Roaches Line anticipating a confrontation that could even see me out of the Cabinet, voluntarily or otherwise. But it was not to be. The Premier accepted my reasoning that the jobs were vitally needed in the Springdale area, and that a contractor was ready, willing and able to provide them. On the other hand, I learned a valuable lesson about the undoubted right of an MHA to be consulted or at least informed about decisions affecting his or her constituency. The important thing was that the permit was released.

At this point it is useful to ask, are these anecdotes evidences of a reign of terror, of one-man government ruled by fear and dictatorship? I think not!

Years ago, much closer to events, I wrote a brief essay on the subject which reads in part:

"People want strong leaders. They need strong leaders. They are unwilling to confide their governing in political parties whose leadership appears to be weak, indecisive, remote or in doubt. Yet, the strong leader faces certain risks and challenges.

"On the one hand, he may incur the charge of dictatorship; on the other, he is daily faced with the task of holding together a cabinet composed of men whose personalities may be as strong as his own (and) any number of potential successors … anxious to assert their own philosophies and beliefs …

"Time and time again (in the Smallwood Cabinet) I saw issues of greater or lesser importance deferred or dropped because even a single minister had doubts or reservations (or) the Premier himself bring in proposals that subsequently went by the board because they were not universally acceptable to his colleagues …

"How then to explain the accusation of dictatorship, of one-man rule, that formed the core of a campaign of vilification against Joseph R. Smallwood, the likes of which Newfoundland politics has never seen before?"

I went on to apply Churchill's dictum that the Prime Minister (or Premier) is, and must be, "the source and arbiter of public policy"—persuasive in advancing it, fearless in carrying it through, capable of inspiring others to follow.

"We had that once in Newfoundland. If it be dictatorship, let us have more of it. It may well be our greatest need."

There is no question that Mr. Smallwood gave everything he had to the job of governing, literally working night and day, seven days a week, in order to improve Newfoundland's social and economic condition for the sake of the people who live here. There can be no other explanation for his single-minded determination … for decades of unremitting toil culminating in financial bankruptcy.

At the same time, he demanded like efforts from those around him. The reality, however, was that not everyone was similarly dedicated.

## THE THREE-MONTH-LONG ELECTION

It appears just over thirty-five hundred people—3,504 to be precise—voted in the District of St. Barbe South in the General Election of October 28, 1971, but in the end the outcome was determined in the Supreme Court. The far-reaching effect was a change of government, from the Smallwood Liberals, after a 23-year reign, to the Moores Conservatives who would remain in power for the next seventeen.

According to the election night tally, 1,756 voters marked ballots in favour of Conservative candidate Ed Maynard and 1,748 for Liberal Trevor Bennett, a precariously slim margin of only eight votes. However, Bennett claimed his opponent telephoned sometime before midnight to offer congratulations in the belief the Liberal had in fact won by 26 votes.

St. Barbe South was one of five constituencies with differences of fewer than 100 votes and the political parties, as was their undoubted right and responsibility to do, applied for judicial review. The other districts were Bay de Verde, Carbonear, St. Mary's and Labrador South, none of which changed hands as a result of the recounts.

But in the St. Barbe South recount, conducted *in camera* by Mr. Justice H.G. Puddester, a totally unexpected development occurred: 106 ballots previously tallied from the thirteenth of 34 polling stations—55 in favour of Maynard, 50 for Bennett, and 1 spoiled—were missing. It seems that in the election night excitement, following the counting Deputy Returning Officer Olive Payne accidentally threw them in the stove!

Puddester promptly halted the recount, and the Liberal Party, represented by lawyer Nathaniel Noel, himself a future Supreme Court judge, applied to have the election in St. Barbe South quashed and a new one ordered. Quoting various legal precedents to support his argument that an election should be set aside if there was doubt about the outcome, he sought to call Puddester as a witness to substantiate the belief that Maynard's lead had "vanished" at the point the recount was terminated.

Conservative lawyer James J. Greene, former Leader of the Opposition, argued that Noel's precedents had to do with voting irregularities, and there was no evidence that any such occurred before or during the voting in St. Barbe South. Noel maintained that if the PC position was upheld it would be as if a recount was never requested.

However, Chief Justice R.S. Furlong refused to allow him to call Puddester as a witness, stating that it was "not proper" to say the lead was eliminated unless it could be shown by a full recount—which, with the Poll 13 ballots destroyed, was of course impossible. Noel responded,

"I heartily disagree with Your Lordship." The chief justice declared, "I will tolerate no impertinence from members of the Bar."

Furlong and Mr. Justice Arthur Mifflin issued separate but identical judgments awarding the seat to Maynard. With mercurial New Labrador Party Leader Tom Burgess on side—at least for the moment—the Conservatives now had the numbers, if barely, to maintain voting control of the House of Assembly after appointing a Speaker. The election was finally over, nearly three months after it began.

On January 18, the Conservatives having achieved a majority, Mr. Smallwood resigned to Lieutenant-Governor E.J.A. Harnum, professing to be "like a kid out of school." Harnum could now call upon Frank D. Moores to form an administration.

However, on learning he would not get a Cabinet post, Burgess announced he was switching to the Liberals. The Conservatives were saved when former magistrate W.A. Oldford, elected as a Liberal in Fortune Bay, resigned to return to the bench. Next Hugh Shea, elected in St. John's South but miffed as the only city Tory not in Cabinet, decided to sit as an Independent. Then he reconsidered and joined the Liberals.

Once again in a minority position, when the House opened March 1 the Conservatives were saved in the event of a vote by the unexpected absence of Liberal William Saunders, MHA for Bay de Verde, who was said to be feeling unwell. Not a rich man, he thereby forfeited $10,000 of sessional pay and likely his MHA's pension. Some suggested that if he was really ill fellow members would have been glad to carry him into the chamber to be present and receive his due as had been done for MHA Sam Drover from Hodge's Cove, Trinity North years earlier.

In his memoir *No Holds Barred* (McClelland & Stewart, 1997) John Crosbie speaks of the PCs' fear that "Unless we did something right away the Moores government would fall in the first vote in the Assembly ... Were the Liberals about to ooze back into office despite the 52 per cent popular vote for the first Conservative government in the history of Newfoundland?"

He goes on: "Let's not pussyfoot around ... I believe we were justified in doing *whatever had to be done* to prevent the sleazy, discredited, anti-democratic Liberal Party from suborning their way back into power without an election. A way had to be found to foil such foul tactics—and Frank Moores, bless him, found the way." (Italics in original.)

That night the Lieutenant-Governor learned what was going on. Moores came calling, armed with Saunders's letter of resignation to back a demand for dissolution and a new election. He argued that the Liberals under new leader Ed Roberts could no more craft a majority than he himself. Harnum had little choice; the House was dissolved the same day it opened, with all members receiving full sessional pay for their brief attendance.

At *The Daily News*, as our news deadline approached, I received a tip from an unimpeachable source that my old friend and business associate, William MacD. Brown—as strong a Conservative supporter as I was a Liberal—had come in from Corner Brook and been dispatched by the Moores camp on a special mission to Carbonear. He was to complete negotiations with Saunders, his father-in-law, for his resignation from the legislature, and for fair and equitable compensation for the loss of benefits resulting therefrom. In that same telephone conversation I was informed of Moores's after-hours visit to Government House, and the purpose behind it.

Crosbie the author professes not to know "what Saunders got," but the number two man in the Tory administration suggests, "I think it was at least $100,000." He allows, as well, that it may have been his brother Andrew, so recently manager of the Liberals' election campaign, "who secretly raised the money for Frank to give to Saunders" adding:

"As a businessman, Andrew would have known when it was prudent to change sides."

Early on Thursday, March 2, 1972 readers of *The News* received an indication of events to come, which other media picked up and flashed around the province. The main front page headline read: "HOUSE SAID DISSOLVED FOR GENERAL ELECTION."

Newfoundlanders went to the polls again on March 24 and gave Moores a 33-9 sweep. The PCs would own the government for the better part of two decades.

# CHAPTER 6

## TRULY A WINTERS TALE

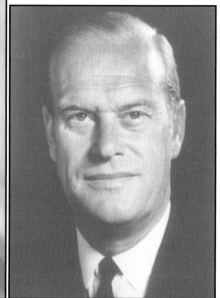

*Winters announced that he, too, was quitting politics and would not "shoot for the … leadership." Suddenly, in March, he was "campaigning (in) the Atlantic Provinces."*

T erm 29 was far from the only source of friction between St. John's and Ottawa during the Smallwood years. Also at or near the top of a long list of federal-provincial issues—hardly surprising in the complexity of shared jurisdictions that is a federal state—was the matter of the ownership of exploitable undersea resources.

Mr. Smallwood had played a significant part in the ascendancy of Pierre Elliott Trudeau as new Leader of the Liberal Party and Prime Minister of Canada. He surely was as dismayed as I myself by Trudeau's bald assertion of exclusive federal jurisdiction over off-shore oil and gas in the House of Commons on December 2, 1968.

It came without warning, preceded just three days by a personal letter to the Premier, taking the position it was "essential" for Ottawa to retain administration and management. Essential? Why essential? I believed we must firmly reject what could only be described as a shameless grab of what rightly were natural assets of the provinces—in Newfoundland's case, certainly—and this notwithstanding the opinion issued a year earlier in the Supreme Court of Canada favouring the federal government.

Founded upon historical evidence relating to the British Columbia continental shelf long before Newfoundland became part of Canada, the facts supporting it clearly did not apply to our situation.

I strongly felt the federal position that "all rights held or acquired by Canada in submerged lands lying outside the boundaries of any province accrue to Canada as a whole," took account of neither the particular history of Newfoundland before becoming a province, nor her acquired constitutional rights over natural resources as a province of Canada. As far as I was concerned it was totally unacceptable, and I so informed my colleagues.

The Premier's response was to set up a Cabinet committee comprising the two most senior lawyers, President of the Council L.R. Curtis and Justice Minister T. Alex Hickman, with myself as Minister of Mines, Agriculture and Resources. Our report confirmed the position rejecting the Trudeau statement, and recommended adoption of the very practical approach of separating the issues of jurisdiction (federal) and administration/ownership (provincial) that I had been pressing.

As well, it recommended acceptance of the eastern offshore boundary proposals (jurisdiction over the Laurentian sub-basin was not then at issue) of the Joint Mineral Resources Committee of ministers of the Eastern Provinces, revenue sharing to be determined.

*PHOTOS CLOCKWISE:*
■ Premier Smallwood, having played a key role in Pierre Trudeau's election as national Liberal leader, joins the charismatic Quebecer on the election trail (MA); ■ The indecisive Robert Winters finished in second place to Trudeau in the leadership race (TA); ■ The Smallwood prediction that Trudeau would attract to the Liberals "a million young Canadians" who otherwise wouldn't bother to vote was borne out in the results of the 1968 federal election (TA).

The Cabinet approved the report, and I could not have been more pleased. At the same time, however, we were engaged in a critical balancing act. The Premier insisted the entire government must remain strongly disposed to cooperate in every way possible with the new Prime Minister in hopes of what his administration of the Queen's government in right of Canada might do for this province.

Much taken by the views and charisma of Trudeau, the little-known, flamboyant federal Justice minister, who turned up for the first time at Confederation Building adorned in trademark leather hat and topcoat, Mr. Smallwood had become a prime mover—perhaps *the* prime mover—in the launch of his leadership bandwagon. He thus abandoned what had been an utterly futile effort to persuade Trade Minister Robert Winters to throw his hat in the ring as a candidate.

As a Member of Parliament, Winters had been one of the first in Ottawa to assist the Confederate leader's pre-National Convention research into the benefits of joining Canada. Then, during a sojourn out of politics, the Lunenburg, N.S. native had become a leading mining industry executive and served as chairman and chief executive officer of Brinco, owner of the Churchill Falls project, advancing critical letter-of-intent negotiations with Hydro Quebec.

Once back in the House of Commons, as Trade minister Winters proved an outstanding member of the federal Cabinet. But concerning the party leadership, he seemed utterly uncertain of his intentions. This became surprisingly evident almost as soon as Prime Minister Lester B. Pearson advised the Liberal Party of Canada in mid-December 1967 of his decision to retire.

The party immediately fixed the place and date of a convention to choose a successor—it would take place in Ottawa in the first week of April, 1968. Shortly, in the Government Members' Common Room of Confederation Building in St. John's, an election was held of delegates and alternates from the provincial Liberal caucus to attend and take part in the leadership process. As a relatively new MHA, I was both pleased and excited to be chosen as a member of our delegation, albeit as an alternate.

A full month after the Prime Minister's retirement announcement, on January 15, 1968, Winters announced he, too, was quitting politics. He was a popular figure in the party and the country, and the decision was devastating to hundreds of friends and supporters whose requests and urgings that he run were summarily dashed. Included in that group was Mr. Smallwood. It was reported from Ottawa that he was actively encouraging Winters to reconsider—but wanted to be "pretty sure" the minister would, in fact, reverse his decision to retire before joining a movement to support him.

But there was no indication Winters would change his mind. To the contrary, he next announced he was planning to step down from the Trade portfolio about March 31, and would not "shoot for the party leadership." Nonetheless, speculation continued that he had changed his mind, or still might.

This caused the Trade minister to insist in Toronto on February 12 that he had not reversed his position and had no intention of doing so. It was now two full months since Pearson's resignation, and with the leadership convention only six weeks off, support was quickly solidifying for other candidates … particularly Trudeau, who had achieved star status at the recent Federal-Provincial Constitutional Conference.

Then, on March 11, a surprising development: *The Evening Telegram* carried a Canadian Press dispatch headlined "Leadership Candidates Stomping (sic) the Prairies," towards the conclusion of which it was mentioned that Winters was "campaigning throughout the Atlantic Provinces …" The newspaper prophesied editorially, and quite correctly, that a decision at this stage to be a candidate after all, following his earlier expressions of uncertainty and subsequent outright denials of interest, "could put the Newfoundland delegation on the horns of a dilemma"—which some members, at least, it surely did.

Obviously taken aback, Mr. Smallwood nonetheless chose to keep his powder dry, refusing to declare publicly for Winters or any candidate. It was not until the Trade minister reached Newfoundland on March 28, the convention only a week away, that the Premier allowed himself to say, "It's (either) Winters or Trudeau."

When the Newfoundland delegation caucused in Ottawa, the position became settled—or as settled as it was likely to be: The Premier announced to reporters waiting outside the Railway Committee Room of the House of Commons that by majority vote, the delegates had decided they would back Trudeau except as individual members were committed to give first-ballot support to other candidates. His own choice he now decided to make public and in doing so said: "What I like about (Trudeau) is that this man will bring to the Liberal banner a million young Canadians who otherwise would not bother to vote."

The Premier had tried again and again to persuade Winters to run. But it took the federal Trade minister two and a half months to finally make up his mind, and in that time he declared more than once that he would not be a candidate. In light of his prolonged indecision many erstwhile supporters had found it necessary to look elsewhere.

But not all Newfoundland's delegates to the 1968 leadership convention were ready to accept Mr. Smallwood's support of Trudeau, or that he was the man to lead the party. It was true that a large majority of the 85 women and men in a rousing pre-convention caucus had voted enthusiastically to follow the Premier's lead. But there were those who insisted that once having encouraged Winters to run, he must now support him, no matter what. Anything less, they argued, was betrayal.

Some of these were among a faction that regarded Trudeau as "an intellectually arrogant, possibly homosexual, French-speaking bastard," and not a few were or would become Crosbie supporters in the forthcoming provincial leadership contest. To them Winters, in contrast to Trudeau, was the model of what they desired in a national leader, as well as a moral English-speaker "just like us."

In the end, the fourth and final ballot announced in the hot, crowded Ottawa Convention Centre that Saturday afternoon gave Pierre E. Trudeau 1,203 votes, Robert Winters 954, and John Turner 195. The decision of not many more than a couple of hundred Liberal Party delegates had made the difference, electing Trudeau as Canada's 15th prime minister. As for Winters, the next year he was dead of a heart attack while playing tennis in Monterey, California.

How well I recall the victory celebration that night in Ottawa's Skyline Hotel. It was as unrestrained an outpouring of confidence in our party's prospects, under an unconventional, charismatic new leader, as any political party ever enjoyed. The era of Trudeaumania was well and truly launched!

Meanwhile, bitter Winters supporters in the Newfoundland delegation burned up the telephone lines between Ottawa and St. John's with lurid, jaundiced tales of dictatorship, back-stabbing treachery and widespread dissension that filled the province's media for days. It was not a useful run-up to a federal election only weeks away.

Pumped up by all the excitement, the Liberal Party nationally surged to a 155-seat majority, but in Newfoundland managed to lose six of the seven seats it held on the eve of election day, holding only that of Don Jamieson in Burin-Burgeo. Mr. Smallwood's public reaction as provincial leader, having presided over every provincial and federal election campaign since 1949, and smarting from his first real defeat in those two decades, was as brief as it was noncommittal: "The Liberal tide," he remarked sadly, almost unbelievingly, "has gone out."

❖  ❖  ❖

Although the Trudeau promise of a "just society" with "fair shares" for all Canadians had been music to the ears of the Premier, leading him to support the urbane Quebecer for the nation's highest position, out of office and looking back on more than two decades of Confederation, Mr. Smallwood made no secret of how he felt.

Momentous improvements in highways and municipal infrastructure and in health and education facilities, all with a generous infusion of federal funds, could not be denied. But more than anything Newfoundland needed, as she still does, a fundamental attack on the problem of economic underdevelopment—real, sustained assistance to overcome the twin burdens of Canada's lowest incomes and highest taxes, and an unemployment rate persistently double the national average.

The frustration that it still had not begun in earnest five years after Trudeau became prime minister on April 20, 1968 is clearly evident in a passage from the Smallwood autobiography *I Chose Canada* which points an accusing finger at "four prime ministers of Canada"—even if he doesn't name them:

"There isn't the slightest doubt that Canada's four Atlantic Provinces"—a term Mr. Smallwood is credited with originating—"are still miles and years behind the rest of Canada. These four provinces have made real progress in the last quarter of a century, but the gap today is wider and deeper between them and the rest of Canada than it was before.

"(If Confederation doesn't mean) Parliament's using its sovereign power to deploy the economic strength and wealth of the nation to raise the standards of the underdeveloped provinces, then Confederation (is) meaningless. The underdeveloped provinces mustn't be just 'colonies' or mere 'markets' for the rest of Canada.

"Will Ottawa ever have the imagination, and the courage, to break the mold that has patterned a Canada of crass provincial inequity?…After dealing with four prime ministers of Canada for twenty-three years, I am convinced that with the exception of a few brave souls, nobody in Ottawa has the slightest belief in the likelihood, or even the possibility, of the four Atlantic Provinces ever being much more than markets or colonies for the rest of Canada. They won't admit this; they'll deny it with vehemence, sarcasm, wit, indignation, and in a variety of other ways, for of course they can't possibly admit it …

"Some day there may come to Canada a government that will brush aside all weasel thoughts of the Atlantic Provinces as Canada's poorhouse; one that will attack the problem with nerve, employing for an experimental period of ten or twenty years the devices that have been condemned in the past, and others that it will think up, to get these four provinces thirty or forty years ahead in the space of a decade or two."

Mr. Smallwood's worst nightmare was out-migration, for which a key, if politically risky, solution—in which Ottawa would join—was to concentrate population in fewer places than the 1,300 or so existing at Confederation. Given more viable communities, closer to jobs and schools and hospitals, people might be less inclined to move away.

This was the resettlement program for which he was the recipient of much criticism ranging to the scorn of opposing politicians, academics, editorialists, and others who had little or nothing at stake—but rarely those who did. The Premier insisted that every community that resettled "did so voluntarily, of their own free will … because they wanted to" and because "the overwhelming majority of people in it were not only willing but anxious to move." There was "no pressure on the people, except the pressure that they put on themselves, and most of that pressure came from the women … It is absolutely false to say that the government suggested to the people of any settlement that they ought to move, or that it would be best for them to move, or that they would be deprived of some official benefit that they were receiving if they did not move."

However, he acknowledged that there were "a few who hated every moment of it … and left only because all their relatives, friends and neighbours were leaving. They were never reconciled (and) practically all the discontent and propaganda came from them"—especially older ones unhappy to be separated from "scenes of their youth."

Education Minister F.W. Rowe, a frequent Smallwood apologist, rejected criticisms of the Premier over resettlement and refuted charges that it was invented by the government of which he was a veteran member. Rather, he told a St. John's Rotary Club gathering in July 1967, it actually was started by outport people: realizing that in their isolation, they and their children would never receive first-class health, education and municipal services, electricity, and transportation, they themselves provided the impetus.

"The government came into the picture," Rowe pointed out, "only when it became clear that people wanted to move, that they were going to move anyway, and that if there was no help or supervision, then the results could be disastrous." (Typical was Woods Island, in the outer Bay of Islands. Parish priest Luke Woodrow, who would leave the Roman Catholic priesthood and become a Tory MHA, successfully led a petition for assistance to move to Benoit's Cove in the inner bay, with road access to Corner Brook.)

In all, in its three phases, some 2,800 families comprising about 12,000 people were assisted to move from mainly tiny, isolated and island hamlets with as few as one, five or ten families. In its major phase, between 1954 and 1965, 115 communities comprising 7,500 people relocated; only a half-dozen had populations of more than 50 people. A young lawyer named Robert Wells, subsequently a member of the Moores Cabinet and still later a justice of the Newfoundland Supreme Court, was on the Premier's staff as provincial economist and asked to take a special interest in the matter. It was said he literally "wrote the book" on resettlement—a pamphlet, widely circulated, that clearly set out the terms and conditions under which people got assistance to move that declared up-front that "the government will not move people, or in any way force them to move." But it would help "if they are absolutely sure that is what they want."

Stated unequivocally was the provision critics would see as subtle intimidation, that the government could not "pay out … money under this plan to any householder, unless all the families in a settlement have decided to move (because) if only some families move, then conditions will be made much worse for the families who are left."

Mr. Smallwood seemed to harbour no doubts whatsoever that his resettlement policy "was right; it was proper; it was democratic; it was and is a great success."

Twenty-five years after the Smallwood Liberals left office, I was in the audience to hear former Cabinet colleague Ed Roberts, who succeeded Mr. Smallwood as party leader, discuss the program at the Newfoundland Historical Society.

It was "endlessly controversial," he acknowledged, in St. John's and in academic circles. But people who were directly involved "to this day will tell you that it was the right choice for them and they are grateful to the Liberal government that helped them do it." The evidence, according to Roberts, is that people in the main resettlement areas in Bonavista Bay, Placentia Bay, the Southwest Coast and White Bay North consistently and almost exclusively had supported Liberal candidates over the intervening years.

"Now what does that prove? It only proves that the people affected by resettlement, that very controversial policy, the one that drew so much odium on Smallwood, those people still stand by it …"

## DREE: THE PROMISE UNFULFILLED

Mr. Smallwood had made it very plain to Cabinet members and all others that a successful "fair shares" strategy implemented by the federal Department of Regional Economic Expansion (DREE) was crucial to the province's interest.

Headed first by Trudeau intimate and former labour leader Jean Marchand (along with newspaper editor Gerard Pelletier, they had entered federal politics as the "Three Wise Men" from Quebec) and later by our own Newfoundland Cabinet representative, Don Jamieson, its success in Newfoundland and Labrador was not to be jeopardized by useless bickering in our own ranks, or squabbling with Ottawa bureaucrats and consultants who seemed to be turning up everywhere.

More easily said than done, however. Appearing to operate on the general, if unspoken, principle that paying the piper they could call the tune, they were seen by some of us to pose a direct threat to the independence of decision and action of the House of Assembly and the government to it responsible. Dark hints surfaced of an unelected bureaucracy not unlike the Commission of Government of unhappy memory.

DREE was just the latest in an alphabet soup of not very successful bootstrap programs—the Atlantic Development Board (ADB) and Fund, the Agriculture and Rural Development Act (ARDA), the Fund for Rural Economic Development (FRED), the Area Development Agency (ADA), and the Regional Development Incentives Act (RDIA). Before it, too, sank into oblivion in the 1980s, falling far short of vaunted development objectives, DREE designated "special areas" where roads and high schools, water systems and sewer lines, industrial parks and housing subdivisions were funded, largely to accommodate the centralization of people from isolated rural communities. (A new but very different incarnation is ACOA—the Atlantic Canada Opportunities Agency—which can claim, at best, a spotty record of success.)

No doubt all were sincere efforts to redress regional disparity. Unfortunately, hardly a dent was made in the long-suffering Newfoundland economy which continues to drag along as Canada's weakest—and never mind those spurious claims of prosperity based on shiploads of crude oil sailing off unprocessed to fuel economies elsewhere and leaving behind minimal royalty revenues.

We are still the province plagued by the nation's highest unemployment, lowest personal incomes and highest taxes, still sending thousands of our people to Ontario or Alberta in search of jobs and a decent living, and encouraged and almost blackmailed by mainland economists and editorialists to send still more. Either they do not comprehend that this is our lifeblood, as a society, spilling out across the Cabot Strait, or else they do comprehend, like what it's doing for them, and covet even more of it.

# CHAPTER 7

## THE ROAD TO CHURCHILL FALLS

# Churchill Falls deal: Everyone's a winner

By JOHN CARTER
Telegram Staff Writer

Fears that Newfoundland came out on the short end of the stick in the agreement to develop Churchill Falls appear to be unnecessary.

In fact, Newfoundland seems to have fared very well under the agreement, although on the surface it might appear otherwise.

The agreement, signed between Churchill Falls (Labrador) Corporation and Hydro - Quebec, assures that the mighty Churchill Falls in Labrador will be developed, bringing into being the world's largest hydro - power project.

Now, Quebec gets the power it needs so badly and gets it at a very reasonable cost; Newfoundland gets the honor of having the world's largest source of hydro - power, a guaranteed income, enough power to care for Labrador's needs, plus being able to develop 3,000,000 additional horsepower for her own use on the lower Churchill

be looked in favor of Quebec, but a close study gives it a new light.

There is, perhaps, one point in the contract that could pose some legal problems in the future. It is the delivery point of the power, mile 143.8 on the Quebec Northshore and Labrador rail line, just over a mile inside the Newfoundland border.

While the delivery point is inside Newfoundland and not Quebec, as demanded by Mr. Lesage, province of the contract that makes Hydro - Quebec totally responsible for the line, its maintenance and liability to a third person from the point of delivery, could in years to come, give Quebec an argument that it has administered the line inside the border and therefore exercised control over that portion of the land.

The contract, according to very reliable sources, is essentially the same as the letter of intent signed in October, 1966. However, the letter of intent has never been made public and Mr. Smallwood declined to table it in the Legislature.

Incorporating a host of federal and provincial initiatives there emerged, in the fifth year of our mandate, a development "master plan" that should have been just about the biggest, most beneficial package of economic and social improvements ever to have descended upon rural Newfoundland in particular.

At least a year and a half in preparation, its imminence had been signalled by Premier Smallwood in the House of Assembly the previous spring. Now the details were revealed to representatives of the province's educational, social and economic interest groups during a largely attended Development Conference that took place in the St. John's Arts and Culture Centre at the beginning of February 1971.

For three days, before some 1,200 delegates from all over the province, the Premier and various ministers—myself, John Nolan, Ed Roberts, Bill Rowe, Steve Neary, Harold Starkes, Fred Rowe, Eric Dawe, Earl Winsor—laid out our plans for future development of the province. It involved resources and the economy in general, health care, community futures, social programs, highways, education, municipal affairs, and fisheries, literally hundreds of millions of dollars worth of development.

Provincial government objectives on the table, a trio of federal ministers came forward to express their involvement and support—the product of long and arduous negotiations: Don Jamieson, the Transport minister, Fisheries Minister Jack Davis, and Jean Marchand, minister for DREE. It was inescapable that the detailed presentations—product of the very planning, short-term, medium-term and long-term, that we were often accused of not doing—would be seen as cut and dried election bait. It was hard to miss overtones of skepticism in the discussion and the questions of delegates.

Media responses ranged from the "Dull, unrevealing and uninteresting" headline in *The Evening Telegram* to musings in *The Daily News* that perhaps the conference marked "the grand opening of the Liberal election campaign."

On its face, however, Mr. Smallwood had reason to be pleased. We were in the final lap of the overwhelming mandate given by the people in 1966, and a general election must be held before the year was out. Rather shallow commentary aside, the blanket coverage given the conference by all media was extraordinary.

Nevertheless, the Premier appeared restrained and cautious, seemingly unconvinced that the ostensibly good news coming out of the three-day exercise would, in fact, translate into renewed support for his administration. Simply put, there seemed little confidence that the DREE program espoused by the Trudeau government would achieve its high promise for Newfoundland.

Hope lingered however, that in keeping with his often declared dedication to equality and fairness, Prime Minister Pierre Trudeau would personally help ensure that the province got fair treatment in the Churchill Falls hydro deal with Quebec. By refusing to allow energy from the project to be transmitted across its territory, Trudeau's home province had grossly violated the constitutional foundation of the Canadian common market.

Unfortunately, the belief that Trudeau might, indeed, make a difference was proving no more than a false hope that foundered on the rocks of a worsening climate of separatism in Quebec. It had climaxed in the FLQ (Front de Liberation du Quebec) crisis three or four months earlier in which, it may truly be said, the nation lost its innocence, if not its nerve. The consequence for Newfoundland was perpetuation of one of the most shameful episodes in Canada's history—blatant economic victimization of one province by another, to the tune of perhaps some $20 billion so far—while federal politicians in Ottawa and Canadians everywhere studiously looked the other way.

In the early morning of October 5, two armed men kidnapped the United Kingdom trade commissioner, James Cross, from his home in Montreal's exclusive Westmount district. He would be held prisoner until December 3 and then released physically unharmed. But five days after the Cross abduction, members of another FLQ cell seized provincial Labour Minister Pierre LaPorte. After a week they murdered him, stuffed his body in the trunk of an abandoned car, and called a radio reporter to say where it could be found. A far cry from earlier vague threats and mainly nuisance activity!

The upshot was imposition of the War Measures Act by which the Prime Minister, in response to the plea of a terrified Premier Robert Bourassa, sought to meet head-on an apprehended insurrection in Quebec, and—who knew?—perhaps elsewhere in Canada. The sight of armed troops in the streets, and hundreds of civilians arrested without charges, left a lasting scar on Canada as a free and democratic society.

Mr. Smallwood was acutely conscious of the implications for Newfoundland, and for the Churchill Falls project, of what was happening on the other side of the wide-open—and from the point of view of many in Quebec, historically and politically obscene boundary by which, they insisted, Labrador was stolen by Newfoundland in 1927. Nor could he erase the knowledge or discount the seriousness of Quebec Energy Minister René Lévesque's well-publicized warning earlier that unless that province controlled the output of Churchill Falls, it would never flow across its territory: "The people of Quebec would not allow (the hydro towers) to stand." Sabotage, then, was a credible threat, if not a real possibility. This was the future Premier and apostle of nationalization who, according to journalist Peter Desbarats—after Geoff Stirling started up a popular English-language radio station in Montreal—declared: "We are on the road to becoming a second Louisiana … Good God! We've been colonized by Newfoundland! At least being colonized by the United States is semi-respectable."

The chilling sabotage remark was strikingly reflective of concerns expressed by Prime Minister Lester B. Pearson to Mr. Smallwood during a secret meeting in Ottawa before he retired to be succeeded by Trudeau. Guessing correctly that the Newfoundland leader, frustrated by Quebec's attitude and the slow pace of negotiations, was about to present a formal demand for federal intervention to force a power corridor across Quebec—a demand both knew Ottawa constitutionally could not easily refuse, if at all—Pearson convinced the Premier it could be the trigger that would plunge the country into deep crisis, a crisis it might not survive, and one that could be even more harmful to the fledgling province of Newfoundland and Labrador than any other.

Accordingly, he asked him, in the name of Canadian unity, not to force Ottawa's hand. And Mr. Smallwood—despite receiving earlier the Newfoundland Cabinet's formal consent, in the form of an Order in Council, to request Ottawa "to declare the development of Churchill Falls to be in the national interest"—complied.

"I wasn't fooling myself, or my colleagues," he wrote in *I Chose Canada*. "How safe would a transmission line built through Quebec by Brinco be in that case? For most of its distance it would go through wild, uninhabited wilderness. A well-placed bomb here and there would put the line out of commission for days at a time, and Brinco could be led on a merry chase restoring the destruction … Not for a moment did I suppose that designation of the project as national would be a solution of itself."

(Even had Ottawa been willing, it is unlikely the billion dollars needed to build the huge project could have been raised without Quebec's willing participation, as well as other hundreds of millions for a redundant high-voltage transmission system, duplicating Quebec's own, that might have been blown up as soon as it was erected. It does, however, raise the question of federal compensation to Newfoundland. For more than three decades this province has carried alone the tremendous financial and economic consequence of having protected Canada from civil war—or worse, total disintegration.)

Meanwhile, concerned that the terrorist activity in Montreal might be replicated in this province, the Premier ordered that plainclothes police in unmarked cars take up station outside the homes of Newfoundland Cabinet members. And after an executive visiting from outside the province reported he accidentally intercepted a Premier's Office call in his room in nearby Holiday Inn, indicating a serious breach of telecommunications security, ministers and senior officials were provided with evil-looking "scrambler" telephones in their offices and residences.

In Ottawa, federal Cabinet members came to be protected around the clock by Armed Forces personnel. Going to a meeting with Don Jamieson in his Transport minister's offices on O'Connor Street, just down from Parliament Hill, I was stopped on the sidewalk for an identity check, then escorted into the building, by a soldier in full battledress. Later when Jamieson and I left for a conference elsewhere, the escort saw us to the ministerial limousine which came equipped with an identical, battle-ready Armed Forces member in the front passenger seat. The implications for disaster for a Churchill Falls power project independent of Quebec participation seemed grave indeed.

◆  ◆  ◆

In their anxiety to hold him personally, and even solely, responsible for any shortcomings of the Churchill Falls deal—and really there is only one of significance, the absence of a provision requiring Quebec to share profits on the resale of power—Mr. Smallwood's critics, more than three decades after the fact, show little appreciation of the complexity of the matter, and seem largely ignorant, if not extremely careless, of the historical record.

They seem incapable of understanding that the global explosion in energy values had not yet come to pass and plainly was unanticipated. Price escalation, therefore, was a non-issue when the contract was signed. Else it must be asked why nobody—in particular, the lawyers who left the Smallwood Cabinet over a matter of infinitely less consequence, John C. Crosbie and Clyde K. Wells; the leading lights of the opposition Tory party, men like James J. Greene, Gerald R. Ottenheimer and W.J. Browne; and other persons prominent in public and business life—raised or pursued this issue. There simply is no evidence that anyone saw it as a major concern, if at all, either during or for years after the conclusion of nearly two decades of negotiation of the Churchill Falls deal of which *The Evening Telegram* declared, in a feature article on May 30, 1969 reviewing the sales contract and negotiations leading to it, "Everyone's a winner."

The reality is that Quebec, by agreeing to purchase virtually its entire output, effectively financed the huge undertaking seen in some quarters as a less-than-prudent investment. ("Lack of Interest Shown in Falls Corp. Shares," reported *The Daily News* in September 1967, reflecting "cool" reaction to a proposed $37.5 million issue—so cool, in fact, that it caused Brinco to decide it would best be delayed.)

Furthermore, only Hydro Quebec's advanced technical capacity made long-distance transmission of high-voltage electricity feasible; and only its financial strength made the massive project possible. Why would it offer or agree to share windfall profits that no one anticipated or demanded?

Occasionally the suggestion is made that Mr. Smallwood unwisely rejected Quebec's demand to oust Brinco and pursue the project with a Newfoundland Crown corporation equivalent to Hydro Quebec. But driving out of this province a consortium of major international investors holding statutory rights—while perhaps serving Quebec's interest—would have constituted reckless bad faith, an action highly prejudicial to Newfoundland on the part of the government that invited them in. It is easy to see how it might have led to crippling lawsuits and possibly prolonged, further delays.

The Churchill project was born in 1961 legislation that was given unanimous approval by the House of Assembly, governing Liberals and opposition Tories alike. This legislation granted the British Newfoundland Corporation (Brinco) exclusive rights to develop and market the hydro resources of the Churchill River watershed and the Labrador plateau. Consequently Brinco's negotiations with Hydro Quebec, carried on by its subsidiary, Churchill Falls (Labrador) Corp. (CFLCo.), were entirely between a private company, acting entirely in its own right, and a Crown corporation of another province.

It is true that Newfoundland's Premier (as did, indeed, a succession of Quebec leaders) pursued the negotiations with the tenacity of a sheepdog herding the flock, pressing and prodding, arguing and cajoling interminably to get the huge project going and to secure the best possible advantage for his province from the biggest civil engineering undertaking in North America at that time.

But Mr. Smallwood did not, as is sometimes claimed, either negotiate or sign the 65-year, $5 billion purchase-and-sale agreement. The signatories, in Montreal, were CFLCo. President Donald J. McParland and Vice President of Finance Eric Lambert, and for Hydro Quebec, President Jean-Claude Lessard and General Manager of Operations and Sales Yvon de Guise.

And for those who harbour the belief the development was somehow rushed and thus ill-considered, the date was May 14, 1969—seventeen years after the Premier's fateful meeting in London, England with Prime Minister Winston Churchill. That meeting directly led to formation of the British Newfoundland Corp. and its "bridling" of the mighty Labrador river that came to bear his name.

The Newfoundland government was not party to the contract, and had no right to interfere—so long as Brinco followed the Newfoundland law establishing the company's waterpower rights and providing for power recall for this province's use. There was and is a serious issue as to whether Brinco complied fully with this law, but any chance of doing something about it was foreclosed when the Moores government, during the period Crosbie was energy minister, incurred the single biggest charge ever against Newfoundland's credit, without prior warning or public consultation, to nationalize the Churchill Falls project.

Their original plan was to take over Brinco as the owner of the project, but its main shareholders, some of the biggest and richest corporations in the world, would have none of it. To save political embarrassment, Moores conceived the alternative of acquiring the shares of Brinco's subsidiary, Churchill Falls Labrador Corp. (CFLCo.) The cost approached $400 million, but with debt service—the money had to be borrowed—is estimated to have grown to far exceed $1 billion, about enough, at one stage, to finance the Lower Churchill!

Although critics hold Mr. Smallwood accountable for the huge inequity that Newfoundland suffers from the deal Brinco signed with Hydro Quebec, the Moores government had the potential remedy in their hands and mindlessly traded it away, since nationalization took Brinco off the hook for alleged failure to satisfy the requirements of its statutory lease. (A satisfactory explanation for the move has never been forthcoming. There was muted speculation about wanting to replace Brinco with either Franklyn D. Roosevelt Jr.'s Atlantic Energy and Development Corp.—AEDC Newfoundland director Burf Ploughman denies it absolutely; Roosevelt himself is on record as claiming the right to a sales commission if ever Churchill River electricity was sold to PASNY, the Power Authority of the State of New York—or John Shaheen's energy conglomerate, Shaheen Natural Resources Inc.) Whatever the case, the takeover surely ranks among the worst commercial and economic blunders in Newfoundland, and perhaps Canadian history.

It has caused a quarter of a century delay so far in the development of the Lower Churchill, with the loss of many billions of dollars in electrical production value, the huge flow of water running away uselessly to the ocean, and who knows what spinoff industrial activity. It almost certainly has denied the people of Labrador the economic and social advantage of a concomitant fixed-link connection across the Strait of Belle Isle.

But more consequentially, it provided an easy way out for Brinco and its shareholders who might have been held liable for substantial damages for allegedly concluding an agreement in violation of the statutory waterpower lease, and responsibility for getting it fixed. Meanwhile, the province through its Crown corporation, Newfoundland and Labrador Hydro, had to assume the huge, costly burden of owning and operating the Churchill Falls facility.

The law required that CFLCo. reserve some 500,000 horsepower of electricity for Newfoundland's use, and that it have prior claim on an unspecified block of power whenever demanded, provided it was "feasible and economic" to accord it priority. However, it appears the contract with Hydro Quebec did not contain the same provisions. It was speculated that if Newfoundland, as the new owner, had required CFLCo. to comply with these terms, the company—in effect, the province itself—might have been subject to an expensive, seriously damaging, breach-of-contract suit by Hydro Quebec.

In the fall of 1976, as the province tried and failed to enforce its rights in the courts, Crosbie admitted in a *Daily News* interview that the government was alleging the Newfoundland recall provision was violated by Churchill Falls (Labrador) Corporation while it was still a Brinco subsidiary, by virtue of its contract for the sale of power to Hydro Quebec. The recall clause was "the meat … the nub" of the province's case, he explained. The government was suggesting that "the contract … made inadequate provision for Newfoundland consumers, and thus violated the lease provision."

In the period after it occurred Mr. Smallwood blasted the "incredibly wrong and stupid act of the Moores administration" in taking over CFLCo. He blamed Crosbie's "powerful animus (which) has put the province in debt … interest-bearing debt" in an amount even then close to a half a billion dollars—"and this without adding one solitary horsepower of electricity to the millions of horsepower generated by the great pioneer developers, Churchill Falls (Labrador) Corporation." (*The Time Has Come To Tell*, Newfoundland Book Publishers [1967] Ltd., 1979)

Having performed the "astonishing" feat of completing the "awesome" development of the Upper Churchill ahead of schedule and under its $1 billion budget, he pointed out, Brinco's "superb planning, engineering, construction and management team … was about ready to develop the Lower Churchill when the whole enterprise was nationalized." The result was that the team disintegrated and the Lower Churchill development was indefinitely delayed, its cost escalated by several hundred percent, and a proposed major aluminum smelting industry for the Lake Melville area was lost.

"Oh, yes, John Crosbie, with his iron will in the weak Moores Cabinet, was the most expensive Newfoundlander of all time. Newfoundland is doomed to go on paying—and paying—and paying for many long years to come."

Like scores of resource development companies, big and small, once it acquired its legal rights Brinco had set about doing the studies, conducting the negotiations and assembling the complex plans and qualified personnel for one of the world's greatest engineering and construction undertakings.

It had all begun in London, England in August 1952 when Mr. Smallwood regaled the British prime minister with the impressive catalogue of the resources of Newfoundland, and in particular Labrador. The idea of assembling a consortium of world-class British companies to undertake their development—and in the bargain, revive the United Kingdom's flagging entrepreneurship in the wake of the spiritually, physically and financially exhausting Second World War—clearly seized Churchill's interest. He pronounced it "a great imperial concept" and with his encouragement Brinco was born.

It carried out a plethora of resource studies and investigations and also did considerable mining in the province, but the prospect of a huge hydro development on the Hamilton (later Churchill) River became its main preoccupation.

The detailed story is told elsewhere of the largest construction project undertaken in Canada at that time. Suffice to say that when the regular supply of electricity began flowing into the Quebec grid at 6:47 P.M. St. John's time on December 6, 1971, it was just eight months short of twenty years since those fateful talks in London; it was two and a half years from the day Brinco and Hydro Quebec signed the $5 billion, 40-year, take-or-pay power contract, renewable for a further 25 years. The delivery of electricity was nearly six months ahead of the contract requirement; and the whole thing had been achieved on or slightly under budget.

In the interim Sir Winston Churchill had passed on; Brinco chairmen Donald Gordon and Robert Winters had died; and CFLCO head Donald McParland and several key members of his team perished when the company jet crashed in Labrador. As for Trudeau, and whether he could be looked to for an injection of equity into the deal, by the time the FLQ crisis subsided, the contract was signed and it would all be a matter for the courts.

Having blatantly refused to allow Brinco to build transmission lines across its territory or to "wheel" power to customers beyond its borders, Quebec had gotten what it wanted—a huge, captive supply of electricity for its own use or resale. Brinco was relieved, following a nerve-wracking period of not knowing if it would ever realize on or recover its considerable advance expenditures, to obtain a deal that allowed it to amortize the nearly $1 billion project cost, and provide a satisfactory return on its shareholders' investment. From the corporate perspective, a long, hard negotiation had concluded in a thoroughly respectable business arrangement.

Newfoundland had realized one of the world's mightiest hydroelectric developments—it was said only two in the world ranked with it, Krasnoyarsk in the Soviet Union and Grand Coulee in the United States. It had seen 12,000 of its citizens, few of whom likely expected ever to find work in the interior of Labrador, participate in the development of its resources on a grand scale. In addition, impoundment of the waters of the Labrador plateau to feed into a single river had created the potential for further, massive hydro developments downstream, with the possibility of supplying the Island of Newfoundland as well as Labrador, and even justifying a bridge or tunnel connection across the Strait of Belle Isle to physically unify the province for the first time.

But for all that, for Newfoundlanders the outcome is one of maddening frustration and disappointment, and it must be clearly stated that this story is far from over. The Churchill Falls contract was negotiated and signed by Brinco under duress, both economic, and by virtue of the threat of destructive violence, culminating directly in violation of the cardinal principle of the Canadian common market that goods—of which electrical energy is surely one, and one of the most important—pass free and freely across provincial borders, and ultimately the loss of enormous economic rents.

There was in the air at the time an overriding, paralyzing fear for the future of Canadian unity—or better said, an unreasoning desire to avoid at any cost the risk of civil unrest. This caused Ottawa to prevail on Newfoundland to refrain from pressing its undoubted right to export electricity for fair return, as it might oil, or gas, or fish, or lumber, or iron ore—across adjacent Canadian lands, being the territory of another Canadian province or provinces, to the nearest receiving market.

We cannot, we must not, abandon our striving for justice in this matter, not only for Newfoundlanders but for all Canadians, for it remains an issue with profound national implications.

## LAYING DOWN THE LAW

It is unlikely that anyone will ever know how long—months certainly, perhaps years—that the incomparable Clerk of the Executive Council, James G. Channing, had held in a safe place in his desk at Confederation Building a draft of the invitation to the ground-breaking ceremony for the huge Churchill Falls development, waiting for the red-letter date to be determined.

When finally it arrived, given the uncertainty of weather, the large number of guests (about 500, plus media), the restriction on the size and type of aircraft able to use the nearby Twin Falls airstrip (twin-engine, propeller-driven DC-3s), and the absence of conventional accommodation (only construction trailers on site), it presented a logistical nightmare to challenge a less cool head.

But Channing was, as usual, unflappable. With the deal finally made and construction about to get underway, he could now send out the invitations. Dignitaries on the international guest list would be flown into the Labrador wilderness in stages and put up on two overnights in U.S. Air Force bachelor officers' quarters (BOQs) at Goose Bay, the so-called Goose Hilton.

"Guests wishing to attend this Ceremony," he wrote on June 12, "will be flown from Montreal (in the case of mainland residents) and St. John's (in the case of residents of the Province) to Goose Bay, Labrador, on Sunday 16th July and to Twin Falls and on to the site of the ceremony on Monday, 17th July. Guests will be returned to their point of embarkation on Tuesday, 18th July. Aircraft between the points mentioned above and accommodation in Labrador will be furnished."

This was the occasion of the Premier's famous "This is our land" speech in which he first expressed gratitude to those who had fostered and led the project, from Sir Winston Churchill to Brinco President Donald McParland, and then proceeded, as Philip Smith described it in *The Story of Churchill Falls* (McClelland and Stewart, 1975) to "lay down the law."

Those of us who were present on that occasion in 1967 will never forget the electric moment. The hairs stood on the back of my neck as Mr. Smallwood's voice, roughened by a sore throat, rose until he was almost literally shouting:

"This our land. This is our province. This is our river. This is our waterfall. And we will forever make sure that it is developed, and when developed will operate primarily, chiefly and mainly for the benefit of the people of Newfoundland. Let there be no mistake about that."

Having corrected federal Energy Minister Jean Luc Pepin's assertion that all power from the project would go to Quebec, the Premier declared the entire output of the Lower Churchill (at that time seen as phase two of the overall development) would in fact stay in this province. Brinco was reminded that "all the work on this job—all of it—shall be done by Newfoundlanders" so far as the province could provide the workers.

He emphasized: "Number one is Newfoundland. Number two is Quebec. And number one is ahead of number two, and don't you forget it."

# CHAPTER 8
## THE KITCHEN CABINET

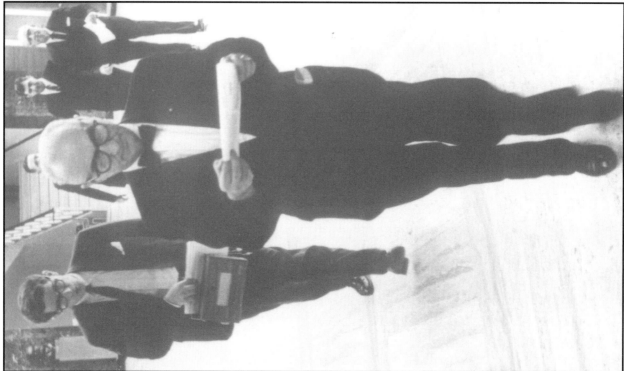

One Sunday morning in the spring of 1970, just as my wife Daphne and our six children and I were about to leave for ten o'clock Mass at our parish church of Corpus Christi, in the West End of St. John's, a most unusual thing happened. The telephone rang and it was a very senior civil servant—they were still called that, and many proud of it!—wanting to see me on an urgent personal basis.

I informed the caller (who, out of respect for his request at the time for confidentiality, shall continue to be nameless) that we were literally going out the door. But he insisted he could be at our home at 15 Cowan Avenue in a matter of minutes. Reluctantly I agreed, and we resigned ourselves to attending a later Mass.

The man was, indeed, on our doorstep in quick time, by taxi, and since he lived in the East End, I concluded he had called from a pay telephone en route. In our dining room, behind a closed door, he delivered an agitated message.

He was privy, he said, to certain conversations. He had overheard certain of my ministerial colleagues express alarm about some of the things I had been attempting to do since joining the Cabinet, and the attendant publicity thereby generated. One possible conclusion: that it was seen as evidence of leadership ambition on my part—and, consequently, a threat to their own.

Nor might it be any accident that this was happening at about the same time the Premier added me to his lengthening list of publicly proclaimed potential successors.

My visitor warned of what he believed was or would become a systematic campaign to undermine what I was attempting to achieve regarding offshore resources, the environment, agriculture, forestry, a solution to a horrendous health problem in the St. Lawrence fluorspar mines—and in particular, negotiations for Gros Morne National Park.

He emphasized the very real danger that my detractors (whom he did not name) were gaining the ear of the Premier, so as he saw it, my efforts were in danger of being totally frustrated.

The man's concerns did not lack some logical base. The department of which I was minister encompassed all the province's major resources except ocean fisheries. It was inevitable that I would be much in the public eye. As most politicians understand, whether favourably or otherwise seems to make precious little difference.

In the meantime, the potentially grave risk this career employee of the government was taking in coming to me in this way was immediately obvious, lending great weight to his concerns. Given the strict rule then existing against civil servants becoming in any way involved in the political side of government, depending on how I responded and how I used his information, his job could very well be on the line.

I concluded—correctly, I believe, though he was reluctant to say—that my visitor had recently been a guest, perhaps more than once, at the luncheon table of the "kitchen cabinet." This was the daily informal lunchtime gathering of the Premier and certain ministers in the private dining room on the South Wing, Main Floor, of Confederation Building.

With Mr. Smallwood presiding, and Economic Development Deputy Minister O.L. Vardy as a kind of regular *maître d'*, it was usual to have guests who might well include other ministers (such as myself) who were not regular members, senior civil servants, businessmen and entrepreneurs negotiating or proposing projects for support of the government, and prominent visitors (especially federal or other provincial ministers) from outside the capital or outside the province.

No doubt a valid, useful purpose was served; entertaining such personages elsewhere would require special arrangements to be made, often at very short notice. Ministers and others would have to get themselves to a commercial location—hotel, or restaurant, unless the more private Green Room of the Arts and Culture Centre was available. There would be inconvenience, very likely the disturbance of other plans or appointments, and a most important consideration, the likely absence of privacy, not to mention substantially higher cost.

There was a quite serious downside, however, namely that the "kitchen cabinet" operated almost as an unofficial inner cabinet where all sorts of business might be concluded, minds quite possibly be made up, decisions taken, long before it ever got to the real Cabinet table and thus the majority of ministers. Those who were not regulars clearly faced a serious potential disadvantage in terms of being denied timely input into discussion of matters currently at issue. These could even include their own departmental programs, objectives and concerns.

Neither a member nor having any serious desire to be, I could nonetheless see that it might have certain advantages. But among other concerns, I found "kitchen cabinet" sessions time-consuming, tending to be long, and expensive, with regulars personally assessed for the costs including wines, liqueurs and chef services. I preferred a light lunch at my desk. As well, as an occasional guest, I found the gossip-club atmosphere somewhat disconcerting.

Seemingly it was in this context that my Sunday morning visitor was shocked to hear his minister become the object of loose speculation and outright criticism. Rather than raise the matter in the precincts of officialdom in my Confederation Building office, which I judged he would consider thoroughly inappropriate, after worrying over it for several days he came to my home on a private, personal basis.

I thanked him warmly for his concern and he left. Except for family and one or two close friends, the fact of the Sunday morning visit and its subject matter have never been discussed, between us or otherwise, until this moment, at least by me. But forewarned is forearmed; I decided to govern myself and my activities accordingly.

I began at once to accelerate the implementation of policies to enhance the value of agriculture in the province—e.g., a much more aggressive position on coordinated marketing, and the provision of new storage and processing facilities, expansion of Farm Products Corporation operations to Corner Brook, and introduction of the province's first program of crop insurance, all with the Premier's support.

Negotiations with the federal government to help fund inventories of forest and mineral resources were stepped up. Added emphasis was placed on opportunities awaiting the province in offshore oil and gas, pressing even more strongly our claim to ownership of those resources. I took immediate steps in Ottawa and in St. Lawrence to deal with heightened concerns regarding the health problems of miners affected by radon gas contamination in the Burin Peninsula fluorspar mines.

No doubt my most effective, and personally most satisfying undertaking, was a "white paper"—technical term for an important government policy proposal or set of them; it actually had a green cover—setting out detailed development proposals for the fantastic Gros Morne area, most of which would become reality. The National Park's focal point is Bonne Bay, on the Gulf of St. Lawrence, but in fact it extends from the Trout River tablelands just beyond Bay of Islands and Corner Brook to the spectacular beaches of Shallow Bay on the Great Northern Peninsula.

Discussion of the possibility of creating a Provincial Park in the area of spectacular Western Brook Gorge had begun in the Department of Mines, Agriculture and Resources in the 1950s. Then in 1965 the Smallwood government asked Ottawa to undertake studies to determine the potential for creating the province's second National Park there.

However, on taking over the file in 1968, I decided that rather than simply handing over a vast area of some 1,500 square miles of Newfoundland territory with all its resources to be locked up forever, mainly to become a federal wilderness preserve, and in the process permitting the forced shutdown of a dozen or more communities—a large, unnecessary resettlement of people—we must first know precisely what we would be giving up. Then we could begin to bargain for commensurate benefits for residents of the area, in particular, and the province in general. This set off a virtual war with Ottawa, fuelled by opposition Tories and disaffected Liberal MHAs who joined with a few environmental purists to howl for my scalp.

But I believed I had the Premier's support and set to work formulating a proposal that would include major improvements in transportation infrastructures for the Great Northern Peninsula and southern Labrador, in addition to and based upon the National Park. I believed I could strike a deal for the federal government to develop the unique historical resources of L'Anse aux Meadows (the Viking site is now a huge international attraction) and Port au Choix (where archaeological work continues) all connected to the world by a 300-mile, all-weather St. Barbe highway. The proposal became a smashing success.

If there was ever any doubt about the regard in which I was held by the leader of the government, it was utterly erased with my delivery into his hands of the document that I had entitled "The Historic Coast—A Proposal for Integrated Development on the Great Northern Peninsula," product of an intensive research-and-writing marathon. (For the final writing stage, armed with files and other materials provided by departmental staff, I locked myself in a room at the Holiday Inn in Clarenville, and stayed there until it was done. Once again my journalism experience had served me well!)

The Premier praised the plan in the House of Assembly and pretty well everywhere else. Copies were printed for distribution to households throughout the region and around the province, accompanied by a letter in which he announced to householders of Humber East, White Bay North, Labrador South and St. Barbe North and South in particular:

"We are very proud of (the proposals) in the government, and we are thankful to Hon. Mr. Callahan and his officials for a good job well done. Help us get this big plan carried out. Support it. Back it. It will be good for you."

Cynics remarked that although the election might be a year away, it seemed it was never too early to begin—especially after a lengthy broadcast interview in which the Premier undertook to describe the plan in superlatives, as in the following: "In my opinion this is the most important White Paper that has been put to the House of Assembly, I think, since the coming of Confederation." A transcript of the interview and a reprint of a long, detailed very favourable report by the resident Canadian Press correspondent, Ed Walters, were included in the householder package.

The proof of the pudding, as always, is in the eating. Following a series of complex negotiations in which I was given my head to carry them on, played out against an unbelievable barrage of political carping and criticism both in the House of Assembly and outside, I was ready to sign a Memorandum of Agreement with Ottawa barely two years after taking over a file that had been activated more than a dozen years earlier.

The federal Minister of Indian Affairs and Northern Development at the time was Jean Chrétien who would go on to become Prime Minister of Canada. On October 30, 1970, following discussions in St. John's, we flew together to Corner Brook for the formal signing—but en route, made a significant diversion to Bonne Bay by Forest Service helicopter.

On top of Gros Morne we alighted to admire the magnificent scene below. Any woodland caribou, Arctic hares or pine martens lurking in the tuckamore must have been startled to see men in dark business suits, clearly ill-equipped to be out in the Western Newfoundland wilderness on the eve of November, strolling around the summit!

Later that lovely fall day with the Premier, Newfoundland's federal minister Don Jamieson who had moved the massive file along in Ottawa, and some 250 guests from many areas of the West Coast present in the Corner Brook Arts and Culture Centre, the MOU was signed and witnessed by prominent residents of "The Forgotten Coast" as Canon John Thomas Richards, a former rector of the Anglican mission of Flowers Cove, once described it.

◆ ◆ ◆

It was during a meeting of an expanded "kitchen cabinet" towards the end of September 1970 that the single most important decision affecting the future of the 23-year-old Smallwood regime was arrived at. It would have literally life-and-death political consequences.

To the uninitiated it might appear a simple matter, deceptively so—whether to ask Lieutenant-Governor E. John A. Harnum to grant dissolution of the House of Assembly for a trip to the polls before Christmas, which by all the rules, if asked, he was bound to do. The reality was that it had implications that were simply enormous, consequences that would be nothing less than cataclysmic.

The alternative was to wait, which for several very practical reasons could mean the election might not be held until the fall of 1971, forcing us to the absolute end of our constitutional five-year mandate. In that event, we would voluntarily have donned an electoral straitjacket, leaving absolutely no room to manoeuvre, come what may. Yet despite the obvious danger, the potentially disastrous consequences that all could visualize, that is exactly what we did.

Of the 15 or so men who were present, armed with the best advice of the Liberal Party's favourite pollster, political *guru* Martin Goldfarb of Toronto, only one, Municipal Affairs Minister Eric Dawe from the District of Port de Grave, stood against it. He argued that delay could mean disaster, the very real chance of electoral defeat. Although to my knowledge he has never claimed the power of prophecy, Dawe's dire prediction turned out to be spot-on. Over the following months, concerns he voiced that day were borne out with depressing regularity.

On the other hand, he pointed out, in going to the polls now, in the fall of 1970, we would be dealing with known quantities—including a Tory Party still in the throes of basic organization, and weakened (and much more, in fact, than Liberals knew) by divisions and bloodletting in the wake of the leadership contest a few months earlier.

Only one ballot had been required as Frank Duff Moores won in a 425-vote landslide over Hubert Kitchen 91, Walter Carter 50, John A. Carter 41, Joseph Noel 2, Hugh Shea 2, and Howard Rose 1. But Kitchen, former PC president, was soon drummed out of the party. He switched to the Liberals, and then was invited into the pre-election Smallwood Cabinet. Meanwhile, Moores would barely escape a plot to dump him in the uncertain period following the deadlocked 1971 election. One of its leaders was Crosbie, the Tories' so-called "indispensable man"; the other, John A. Carter, would survive briefly as Education minister but was jettisoned along with Aubrey Senior, the Community Development minister, before the year was out.

As well, the PCs were split on the emotional resettlement issue—the official position was that rural residents who "freely" wanted to move should continue to be assisted from public funds to do so. Nor could their convention delegates agree on the Smallwood decision to change the name of the province to "Newfoundland and Labrador," some claiming it "tended to separate the people of Labrador from their fellow Newfoundlanders."

By all the evidence unprepared for an early election, with few candidates lined up and fundraising in its earliest stages, and their new leader in and out of trouble with the party, at this point the Tories could be considered extremely vulnerable. However the Premier, the reputed "dictator" whose sole decision it was to make, bowed to the overwhelming sentiment at the fateful strategy session: The election would be delayed until the following year.

Cynics might suggest we fell victim to our own propaganda, and they might be right. Certainly, it made sense to think all those DREE dollars announced at the Development Conference would kick in during the months ahead to sweeten the disposition of the voters towards our election candidates. It would not be quite that simple, however, and the decision to put off the election until late 1971 not only sounded the death knell of the administration of which I was proud and happy to be a member, but sent the Liberal Party into the political wilderness for a very long time.

We could have won an election in the fall of 1970. No doubt it might have been a hard fight, and we might well have sustained a few casualties. But we could have done it, managing yet another majority government. It would have been Mr. Smallwood's seventh in a row, and provided him with the opportunity for the honourable, orderly retirement that he so richly deserved.

The proof, if it may be called that—circumstantial evidence, perhaps—is that despite having chosen to remain for the full five years of our mandate which expired September 8, 1971 (thereby telegraphing to the world that we were, perhaps, desperate and running scared, afraid of an election) and despite giving the Tories an additional 12 months to organize and prepare (a full year during which nearly every fortnight brought some new political disaster that might have been avoided) we nonetheless managed a tie election on October 28, 1971. Calling it a night, The Canadian Press reported the election standings as Liberals 18, PCs 18, New Labrador 1, and doubtful 5—the latter, all too close to call, to be decided by recounts. Down by an aggregate of fewer than 400 votes, had these few Liberal candidates polled an additional 200 or their PC opponents 200 fewer, then with the right distribution, the government might have survived with seats to spare.

Now the "fun" began—the wheeling and dealing, the to-ing and fro-ing, as political opportunists played for advantage on either side. October turned into November, then December, then January. A week to the day after the Supreme Court awarded the St. Barbe South seat to the PCs on January 11, 1972, Mr. Smallwood tendered his resignation to the lieutenant-governor, ending an unprecedented tenure in Newfoundland as the Queen's First Minister. He recommended that His Honour call upon Moores to form a new administration.

Moores opened the House of Assembly at 3:00 P.M. on March 1, but a few hours later sought and obtained dissolution for a new election. Mr. Smallwood would not be a candidate, though he would come back three years later for a last hurrah—as leader of a newly organized Liberal Reform Party.

On March 24, 1972 the PCs scored their first general election success since Confederation, defeating the Liberals led by Ed Roberts 33 seats to 9.

## THE SMALLWOOD COURAGE

Far too little is made of the physical courage of Newfoundland's longest-serving Premier who, certainly in his earlier years, was by no means a big man. In fact, the "little fellow from Gambo" sobriquet that followed him (and that he did little to discourage) reflected accurately that he was short of stature, and at least into his forties, of relatively modest girth.

Biographer Richard Gwyn describes a young man who, as a journalist, was "thin to the point of emaciation (resembling) an inquisitive but aggressive grasshopper," while Harold Horwood has the younger Smallwood "lean, sparrow-like ... (He) might have been a Jewish intellectual," and, indeed, may have been taken as such by Jewish acquaintances in New York, including relatives of his friend Lillian Zahn.

Yet, he seemed utterly unintimidated by the challenges, whether physical or intellectual, that life and circumstance might bring—of which Confederation itself was by far the greatest. Witnesses to a disagreement with the rotund Major Peter Cashin, when the pair scuffled and crashed to the floor of a National Convention committee, were said to fear Mr. Smallwood, by far the smaller of the two, might be seriously injured. (Although Cashin was then his most bitter political rival, after the First World War hero lost a bid for federal politics in 1953 and perhaps faced a bleak future, the Premier who couldn't hold a grudge appointed him Director of Civil Defence, and kept him in the sinecure well past normal retirement age.)

In plenary debate, he once challenged fellow Convention delegate Pierce Fudge, who was about his own size, to "go outside" to settle an argument, but nothing came of it. Their disagreement did nothing to encourage the Corner Brook labour leader to support the early Smallwood attempt to persuade the Convention to seek preliminary terms of union from Canada, or later, to have Confederation placed on the referendum ballot.

A leading supporter of the Squires administration, in 1932 a diminutive Mr. Smallwood had pushed his way into a huge anti-government protest meeting staged by the Conservative Opposition in the Majestic Theatre in St. John's. Demanding to be allowed to speak, he was tossed, body and bones, into the street and was attempting to make his way back inside when a friend dissuaded him. The meeting presaged the riot at the House of Assembly during which, along with Prime Minister Sir Richard Squires, his MHA wife Lady Helena, St. John's West MHA Joseph FitzGibbon, and others he found himself under siege by a surging mob bent on causing maximum destruction to the building and throwing Squires in the harbour. Evidently the future Premier took charge of the situation and assisted the Prime Minister and his wife to escape. The entire group were considered fortunate to emerge unscathed.

For a man who allegedly hated the sea, Mr. Smallwood seemed quite at home on the water, fair weather or foul. His brother Reg, in the slim volume *My Brother Joe* (Jesperson, 1995), describes a summer spent on the rigged schooner *Margaret P.* that the older sibling had purchased for use in his organizing efforts among Bonavista Bay fishermen, there being no roads to speak of and no other way to get around.

En route from Bonavista to Greenspond in heavy weather, Reg recalled:

"Joe came on deck. I asked him what he thought of the storm. 'What storm?' he asked. I don't know if he was kidding, but I doubt that he could sleep through the storm—but maybe he did ... We travelled the Northeast Coast for about two months, visiting almost every town. Between 1932 and 1935 Joe enlisted 8,500 fishermen in the union."

As a newspaper reporter, Mr. Smallwood did not hesitate to inject himself into potentially hazardous situations, whether hitching a ride in a small, primitive airplane—one of the first Newfoundlanders to sample this emerging form of transportation—or finagling passage on board the Royal Navy cruiser HMS *Cornwall* sailing for Flat Islands, B.B., with an armed force to quell expected rioting. A journalist's propensity to turn up in dangerous places where news so often happens prepared him well for political life and the hazards of the campaign trail, whether fighting the battle for Confederation or for House of Assembly majorities at literally hundreds of frequently uproarious political meetings.

As the minister responsible for Forestry, I accompanied the Premier to what reporter Vic Parsons of *The Daily News* reported from Happy Valley as a "wild and woolly" public meeting in Happy Valley, Labrador in January 1969. It proved a fine example of his lifetime habit of facing challenges, including physical ones, head-on. Parsons wrote that Mr. Smallwood took on "a hostile audience of about 1,100 persons and apparently convinced a majority of them of the wisdom of the changes in plans for the Melville Pulp and Paper Company linerboard mill."

The main headline in the province's only morning paper on Monday, January 13 read: "From jeers to cheers, JRS triumphs in Happy Valley."

The "changes in plans"—monumental understatement—were dictated by the belated realization on the part of John C. Doyle and his officials that Labrador's ice-shortened shipping season made location of a promised $18 million wood-chipping plant there a risky proposition. Instead, it would be built as an integral part of an estimated $136 million linerboard mill at Stephenville. As a consequence, plans for two 77,000-tonne vessels to carry chips to the Island were scrapped, which meant, as well, that a $20 million improvement in harbour facilities at Goose Bay would not be required. Alternatively, a number of smaller, shallow-draught ships would carry unprocessed logs to the mill pond on St. George's Bay.

Labrador residents were outraged. Led in an outpouring of anger by Deputy Mayor Patrick Vickers of Happy Valley, Hank Shouse, chairman of the Northwest River Community Council, Edward Hollett, chairman of the Labrador Development Committee, and Labrador West Liberal MHA Tom Burgess, many declared that although the loss of industry was bad, a greater sin was the fact it was announced on Christmas Eve!

For days feelings had been whipped up by the media, but as Parsons reported it, the Saturday night crowd made up of "the curious, the hecklers (and) those who wished to be informed booed and hooted ... at the start of the four-and-a-half-hour meeting but seemed satisfied as, at the finish, they greeted the speakers with applause." Actually, the only speaker of consequence—excepting Labrador MHAs Earl Winsor and Gerald Hill, who offered obligatory greetings, and Doyle whose brief remarks were greeted with respectful silence—was the

Premier, the usual bundle of energy despite the fact he was now in his seventieth year having celebrated his 69th birthday three weeks earlier. Mercifully I was not called upon, nor was the other member of our party, Economic Development Deputy Minister David Butler.

Arriving at the meeting location, Mr. Smallwood led the way, sweeping into an already jam-packed high-school auditorium promptly at 7:00 P.M. to encounter a solid wall of human-ity. Eventually, RCMP officers formed a flying wedge and forced a path through the boister-ous, chanting crowd, many all too obviously fortified by alcohol.

The meeting got underway, and Parsons described a "seemingly untiring Mr. Smallwood, drenched with sweat, (who) faced the crowd alone for about three-quarters of the encounter." He had begun fully attired in a dark, three-piece business suit, but as the temperature soared, from my location directly behind him I could plainly see rivulets of perspiration gathering at the ends of his greying hair and dropping onto his collar and the shoulders of his jacket. In a short time, off came the jacket; then the vest; the shirt sleeves were rolled up and the tie loos-ened; and with each action the audience, beginning now to enjoy the spectacle, roared and cheered and clapped.

As he had gotten up to speak, a voice in the crowd yelled "We don't love you any more!" to which the Premier replied, "You will ... Now, who wants the truth, and who wants lies? Those who don't want to listen, leave now, please. I invited you to this meeting to give you the lowdown, the truth and nothing but the truth ..."

Happy Valley, he promised, would still become "the biggest logging town in eastern North America"—which it might have, had the plan to provide a year-round wood supply to Stephenville been adhered to following the 1972 change of government. (In addition, a plan to export 300,000 cords of peeled wood to Europe, to bring the total woods labour require-ment in eastern Labrador to some 1,500 jobs, was abandoned.)

The Premier proceeded, in the hot and steamy auditorium, to review efforts to get Labrador development, pointing principally to the iron ore mines in Labrador West and the Churchill Falls project. However, as he was telling the audience about future employment prospects in the area, fuses for the stage lights and amplifiers blew repeatedly, due appar-ently to an overload caused by the lights of a CBC television camera. Exasperated by the repeated interruptions, he ordered the cameraman to "Turn that damn thing off!"

Getting to the politics of it all, he assured the crowd there would not be a general elec-tion for a couple of years, but when there was "I will get every vote in Happy Valley ... All Lake Melville will vote for Joey!" (In the General Election of October 1971 his candidate in Labrador North, Melvin Woodward, won by some 300 votes over Herbert D. Brett of the New Labrador Party and about 1,100 over third-place Arthur D. Hale of the Progressive Conservatives.)

Two or three inebriates near the middle of the hall had been carrying on a raucous, running commentary interspersed with insults and bursts of drunken laughter. Suddenly, Mr. Smallwood stopped dead in the midst of a declaration, in response to expressed concerns, that he would "fight to the last drop of my blood against Quebec getting one inch of Labrador ... no ... no ... no ... !" and invited them onto the stage.

"Come on ... Come on up here, where everyone can hear what you have to say!" he insisted, and they reluctantly and somewhat sheepishly advanced to the podium, left little choice now by the jeering crowd.

Only one man actually approached the microphone, mumbling "This was all made up before we were invited up here ..." But the protest was drowned out by a chorus of boos and catcalls as the crowd now turned on him and his companions. The man went on inaudibly for a few seconds before giving it up for a bad job, whereupon the Premier shook his hand and offered the poor fellow congratulations on his "great speech."

That was the end of the heckling, and Mr. Smallwood now had the full attention of the audience and, in the end, their appreciation as well.

In a lead editorial entitled "Confrontation at Happy Valley," The News observed: "Even his bitterest opponents will agree that Premier Smallwood has never run away from a fight. He probably suspected that he would be involved in a tough confrontation when he went to Happy Valley. But he had every right to expect a more courteous reception than was given him by a belligerent and noisy minority who did not advance their cause by their behaviour.

> "If the real issue was the relocation of the chipping mill, the Premier was able to convince the majority of his audience that what they would lose by that would be made up many times by what would be gained from the increase in logging and ancillary operations. That ought to be self-evident ...
>
> "What was more likely the issue was the desire of the people of Happy Valley to have assurance that the Melville project is moving well towards the start of construction. Ventures of this kind take time to plan and underwrite. That is particularly true in the kind of money market that has prevailed during the past two years. But the indications appear to be that the last obstacles have been cleared. It is certainly to be hoped that this is the case, in which event a good deal of activity may be expected with the opening of navigation."

Precisely three months short of his 85th birthday Mr. Smallwood suffered a stroke that robbed him of his greatest asset, his voice. Severely impaired as well was his ability to read and write. He thus was rendered physically incapable of completing his major literary/historical project, the five-volume *Encyclopedia of Newfoundland and Labrador*, with only two volumes published.

A year and a half later the Ontario-based printers of the work, which now seemed to be in grave danger of never being completed, sued for their unpaid bills in an amount exceeding $170,000. His son William stepped into the breech, pledging his home in support of a settlement amount.

The TV image of the frail former Premier, styled (but never by himself) as "The Only Living Father of Confederation," and his elderly spouse, in an encounter with the sheriff, raised hackles across Canada. Among those who saw and were stirred by the telecast was country singer Tommy Hunter who resolved to organize a benefit concert in St. John's to assist the project.

It served to kick-start the launch of the Joseph R. Smallwood Heritage Foundation which, under a succession of excellent chairmen—Campbell Eaton, Moses Morgan and Paul Johnson—set out to raise the $2.5 million required to get the work completed, and succeeded with room to spare. Memorial University's Smallwood Institute of Newfoundland Studies would benefit from any excess.

Mr. Smallwood took no small pride in his long-lived ancestors, notably "the champion"—his grandfather's great-aunt, Catherine Brown, in Prince Edward Island. "... As my grandfather David often told me, (she) danced the Highland fling on her one-hundredth birthday. I don't know what she did on the last day of her life, eleven days before she was 111 years old, but she was still able to read with her one eye almost to the hour of her death."

However, for a man never seriously ill in his life—repair of a detached retina at St. Michael's Hospital, Toronto in the late 1960s hardly qualifies—his health was now in rapid decline with frequent bouts of pneumonia. Travel to Ottawa for investiture as a Companion of the Order of Canada was considered out of the question, so Lieutenant-Governor James McGrath presided at a ceremony that was transferred to Government House in St. John's.

One of Mr. Smallwood's last public appearances was a banquet in Conception Bay North—in his wife Clara's hometown of Carbonear, actually—to celebrate the 40th anniversary of Confederation, on March 31, 1989. He did, however, go out a few weeks later to vote in the general election of April 20 when his old nemesis, or one of them—Clyde Kirby Wells—led the Liberal Party back to power after nearly two decades in the political wilderness with a convincing 10-seat majority, 31-21. I feel sure he marked his "X" to favour the Liberal candidate and Port de Grave's favourite son, John Efford.

He could take satisfaction in the fact it was one of his staunchest supporters from the earliest days of political success, indeed throughout his career, Joseph D. Ashley, who started the ball rolling to launch the Liberal revival. But it is hard to imagine that he did not also savour the irony that in 1989 it was a junior in Wells's former Corner Brook law firm, Tory Lynn Verge, who sent him down to personal defeat—recalling the time more than two decades earlier that he and Crosbie, as relatively new members of the Cabinet, attempted to unseat Mr. Smallwood. Wells's embarrassing loss occurred in the same Humber East district in which the new Premier first entered politics in 1966 as a Smallwood Liberal. He was forced to arrange a by-election in adjoining Bay of Islands district, where newly elected MHA Eddie Joyce resigned to allow his leader to secure a legislature seat.

◆ ◆ ◆

It is a sad duty to write a friend's obituary, but that is what I found myself doing the night of Tuesday, December 17, 1991 after learning with shock and surprise that the former Premier had slipped away. I could have assigned it to someone else, but I *wanted* to perform this last service myself … perhaps *needed* to do so.

It may not be the best thing I have ever written; as he would understand better than most, there is precious little time or opportunity to consider, sort out and prioritize the doings, the achievements, of the greatest Newfoundlander of us all, in the face of a late-night newspaper deadline. A portion follows. I trust it is better than adequate—and that were he here he would say so:

# JOEY SMALLWOOD DEAD AT 90

*STATE FUNERAL MAY BE HELD FOR PROVINCE'S LONGEST-SERVING PREMIER*

### BY WILLIAM R. CALLAHAN, TELEGRAM MANAGING EDITOR

Joseph Roberts Smallwood, architect of Newfoundland's entry into Confederation with Canada and the province's longest-serving Premier, in office nearly 23 years, died Tuesday night at his home in Roaches Line, Conception Bay.

He would have been 91 years old Christmas Eve.

The former Premier's son Bill told *The Telegram* the only living Father of Confederation passed away peacefully just before midnight.

Mr. Smallwood had been in and out of hospital several times over the past couple of years, the latest time in November with a lung infection. His health deteriorated steadily following a stroke in 1984 that robbed him of his speech.

The former Premier is survived by his wife, the former Clara Oates, another son, Ramsay, and a daughter, Clara Russell. There was an indication funeral services could be held as early as Friday, but this could not be confirmed. Premier Clyde Wells told *The Telegram* the province would arrange a state funeral if the family wished.

"Joey" Smallwood, as he was known far and wide across Canada, was born December 24, 1900 in the Bonavista North lumbering community of Dark Cove, Gambo, the first of 13 children of Charles W. Smallwood and Mary Ellen Devanna. His father held a temporary job there as a woods surveyor. However, the family soon moved to St. John's where Charles went to work in his father's boot factory.

By his own later-life description an "educational cocktail," Joey attended a series of schools from British Hall operated by the Church of England, to the Methodist Centenary School, to the Roman Catholic Littledale School run by the Sisters of Mercy, and finally the Church of England Bishop Feild College.

An aspiring journalist, his first job at 14 was as a printer's devil for the newspaper *Plaindealer* at a salary of $1.50 a week. He subsequently worked for *The Daily News* and *The Fishermen's Advocate* before becoming a full-time reporter on *The Evening Telegram*.

After a brush with political organizing in St. John's, he set out for New York and a stint of labour organizing and reporting for the Socialist newspaper *The Call*, working en route on the Halifax *Chronicle-Herald* and Boston *Herald-Traveller*.

Returning to Newfoundland in 1925, Mr. Smallwood became an organizer for the Pulp, Sulphite and Paper Mill Workers Union which formed locals in the newsprint mills at Grand Falls and Corner Brook, and later helped found the Newfoundland Federation of Labour.

After a brief stay in England, he returned to Newfoundland to get married, settle in Corner Brook and begin raising a family. He also started a weekly newspaper, the *Humber Herald*, and published his second of many books, *The New Newfoundland*, an exercise in future-gazing. The first was *Coaker of Newfoundland*, a biography of the 20ᵗʰ century politician and fishermen's union organizer. These were followed by the first two volumes of *The*

*Book of Newfoundland*, replete with contributed articles on the history, culture and social development of the country.

Next Mr. Smallwood developed a newspaper column that evolved into a popular nightly radio broadcast, "The Barrelman, Making Newfoundland better known to Newfoundlanders." He became involved in pig farming in Gander, one of many sides of his agricultural bent.

He was in Montreal in 1946 when he heard the news that the British government would permit a referendum on the future of Newfoundland.

"My heart leapt," he recalled afterwards, and he made the fateful decision to launch the campaign to bring Newfoundland into Canada, whose living standards and social welfare system he saw as the answer to his people's needs … *(With files from The Canadian Press)*

# CHAPTER 9

## MY CABINET AGENDA

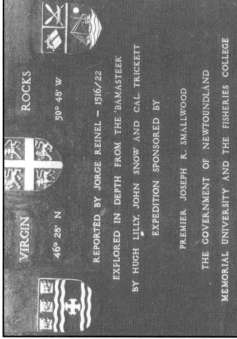

VIRGIN ROCKS

46° 28' N    50° 48' W

REPORTED BY JORGE REINEL – 1516/22

EXPLORED IN DEPTH FROM THE 'BAMASTEER'

BY HUGH LILLY, JOHN SNOW AND CAL. TRICKETT

EXPEDITION SPONSORED BY

PREMIER JOSEPH R. SMALLWOOD

THE GOVERNMENT OF NEWFOUNDLAND

MEMORIAL UNIVERSITY AND THE FISHERIES COLLEGE

JUNE 1964

THE WEATHER
ALL OF NOVA SCOTIA
CLOUDY, SNOWFLURRIES
(See Details Page 2)

# THE CHRONICLE-HERALD

VOLUME 10, NUMBER 266    HALIFAX, CANADA, WEDNESDAY, NOVEMBER 8, 1967    48 PAGES

# OFFSHORE MINERAL RIGHTS RULING IN FAVOR OF OTTAWA

## Gas Trace Found On Sable Island

By ERIC DENNIS
Ottawa – Copyright

The federal government yesterday won the important opening round – and possibly the full final count – in its long dispute with the provinces over offshore mineral rights.

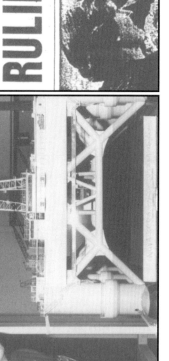

*It was clear on
every important count
...that development
of the oil and gas
on the Grand Banks
had to be our
number one priority*

In July 1968 I was invited by Mr. Smallwood to become a member of his Cabinet in the back-breaker portfolio of Mines, Agriculture and Resources—the tip-off being that it required not one, not two, but three deputy ministers for its day-to-day administration. He provided me with three magnificent public servants, respectively, Frederick Gover, Gerard O'Reilly and Gerald Malone to assist with the task, and so I set about at once to deal with a veritable blizzard of heavy-duty files, including:

- Forestry—in particular, at the peak of the forest-fire season, major and minor crises on the Island and in Labrador. There was controversy over aerial spraying to combat tree-destroying insects. A lasting wood supply for paper mills, versus sawmillers and domestic wood-burners, was one of the principal considerations before a Royal Commission already in existence, headed by Dr. L.Z. Rousseau, retired federal Deputy Minister of Forestry. The possibility surfaced of reacquiring extensive forest holdings granted the Reids decades earlier in return for pushing the railway across Newfoundland.

- The proposal for the Gros Morne National Park, on the books since the mid-fifties.—It had been going nowhere fast, mainly because the federal government was demanding too much Newfoundland territory (as much as 1,500 square miles of the Great Northern Peninsula) with dire consequences for the people living there. Serious issues around Crown lands use in general would require new planning initiatives.

- Rationalization of the government's fleet of owned and leased aircraft, and future operational and maintenance protocols.—Based on a study already in hand, should we or could we continue with Crosbie-owned Eastern Provincial Airways operating and/or supplying fixed-wing aircraft (helicopters were otherwise supplied) on a multi-million-dollar annual contract without public tenders being called?

- Offshore oil and gas.—Jurisdictional/ownership issues remained unsettled, and if anything the federal government was tightening its grip on these resources. The continuing provincial-federal dispute had left prospects for their exploitation, so vital to the province's economy, clouded in uncertainty, and placed a damper on necessary exploration.

- Issues around the presence of cancer-causing radon gas in the fluorspar mines at St. Lawrence.— How to reduce the incidence to safe levels, plus the type and reliability of monitoring to ensure the safety of workers in future? There was also the matter of the final closure of the Bell Island iron ore mines, together with the economic impact on the community and the means of alleviating it, if any. Each was a matter of economic, social and political urgency, and certain of my colleagues let me know they were less than reassured by the government's handling of them.

- The environment.—There was need for government to become proactive in the burgeoning area of environmental issues and concerns. These included the virtual explosion in the numbers of all-terrain vehicles and their effect on natural areas and wildlife. There also were concerns over the growing problem of industrial effluents, both from existing plants such as the pulp and paper mills and mining operations, and new activities in Long Harbour and Come by Chance, and the effects on air and water quality.

- Resource development.—Federal funds would be required to boost the search for minerals on land which, in the same way as exploration for oil and gas offshore, was the first requirement for the development of new mines. However, it would require change—"refinement" was the term I used—in the province's existing concession system, which federal officials regarded with suspicion, favouring open staking. (In an effort to make up for lost time and lagging development compared to the rest of Canada, major companies had been given rights to large areas in return for guaranteeing large exploration expenditures, much as is done today in the offshore.) Despite the implied criticism of his past policies, Mr. Smallwood agreed to go along.

- The broad and thorny issue of agricultural marketing boards.—In operation for many years in other provinces, and considered life and death protection of their producers in key agricultural sectors, our farmers had absolutely nothing to compare. There was need for expanded inspection, processing and storage of agricultural produce to assure quality and continuity of supply for Newfoundland and Labrador consumers. And we had dire need for crop insurance programs, so far unknown in this province.

- Wildlife resources and parks.—There were increasing demands on the range of resources managed and administered by the department in support of the tourist industry, referred to as the tourist "plant" (i.e., provincial parks and wildlife and to some extent, inland fisheries, as well as Crown lands for summer cabins and commercial development.) With completion of the Trans Canada Highway and other roads, both the mobility of our own people and the annually increasing number of visitors to the province from all over the world were creating an unprecedented demand and making upgraded and improved facilities and regulations significant issues.

I also was acutely aware, as a former journalist, of continuing Opposition and media criticism of the absence of a daily verbatim, printed report of House of Assembly debates. A touchy subject to be sure; the Premier bristled at suggestions he was "afraid" to allow an official record to which he could be held, yet refused to be "forced" to bring in the reform. I soon advanced a proposal, which he readily accepted, to research practice across Canada. After visiting the Clerk of the House of Commons, Alister Fraser, to observe the federal system, I recommended a similar setup here. Cabinet approved it in October 1968, and the daily *Hansard* was forthcoming at the next legislature session.

In the British parliamentary system that we have inherited every minister, by virtue of the great principles of cabinet solidarity and joint responsibility, is accountable equally with every other for every government decision. Furthermore, each is bound to support publicly the administration and his or her colleagues, or resign. Therefore no minister, not even the Premier, acts totally on his or her own, but assumes at least tacit approval by his/her Cabinet colleagues for whatever is done in the government's name. Accordingly, it is important for every minister to study carefully the proposal papers circulated by colleagues, recommending policies and decisions with which they might or might not happen to agree, or wish to be party.

It was within this broad context that the Premier (who by tradition, as "source and arbiter of public policy," had the right to determine the Cabinet agenda) and his ministers considered how the Department of

Mines, Agriculture and Resources proposed to deal with issues facing the people and the government of the province, insofar as they fell within jurisdiction granted to the department by the sovereign legislature. And it was, of course, to the degree that my colleagues agreed to and supported the department's proposals, that these then became part of the province's public policy.

◆  ◆  ◆

It was clear that on every important count—in particular the provision of needed and high-paying employment, and substantial direct revenues to the government enabling broad support for the range of public services—development of oil and gas on the Grand Banks had to be our number one priority. We could not drop everything else; but we knew that just as in Norway, our offshore resources promised the biggest, most immediate payoff, and therefore should command a large, if not the largest share, of our attention.

The issue of Newfoundland's ownership of the wealth beneath the ocean floor was far from a new one for Mr. Smallwood. The Terms of Union by which he steered the province into Confederation with Canada provided that after the marriage Newfoundland would comprise "the same territory as at the date of Union." Furthermore the British North America Act, supreme law of Canada, now recognized that "all lands, mines, minerals, and royalties belonging to Newfoundland" before 1949 would continue after Confederation to belong to the new province.

By simple logic, since the vast offshore territory of Newfoundland's Continental Shelf did not and could not belong to Canada before union, so it could not belong to Canada afterwards except as an extension of the land mass of the new province. And then only insofar as necessary to the integrity, and the exercise of various international responsibilities, of Canada as a nation to which Newfoundlanders had chosen to become part.

The offshore lands became Canadian territory, yes; and the waters overlying them became Canadian territorial waters, yes. However—and this is the critically important consideration that has tended to be over-looked in the negotiations and the litigation that have occurred over subsequent decades—the constitutional division of powers in Canada is such that *natural resources belong to the provinces*. The position I advocated, consequently, was that exploitable resources lying beneath the waters of Newfoundland's Continental Shelf *belong to this province and it alone, just as the oil and gas lying beneath the Canadian territory known as the Province of Alberta belong to that Western province.* The federal government should be unimpeded in carrying out its responsibilities for navigation and shipping, pollution control, defence, seabird protection, and fisheries management (although this should, I believe, be a shared or concurrent jurisdiction with the province), including the area inside the headlands of our great bays, some of which are themselves virtual oceans.

The proposition of provincial ownership had been advanced—and rejected by the Supreme Court of Canada—as recently as 1967. Mr. Smallwood had selected one of Canada's most distinguished lawyers, Hazen Hansard of Montreal, a former president of the Canadian Bar, to lead Newfoundland's case in which it joined others to challenge the federal claim of jurisdiction. In their behalf constitutional expert Gerald V. LaForest of the University of New Brunswick, a future justice of the nation's highest court, argued that the right of seacoast provinces to exploit the resources of the Continental Shelf descended from pre-Confederation claims that were made on their behalf by England during the colonial era. (Landlocked Saskatchewan and Alberta were not involved; Quebec "stood aloof.")

However, on November 7, 1967 The Canadian Press flashed to newspapers and radio and TV stations across the nation the following:

> *"OTTAWA (CP)—The federal government was dealt an ace Tuesday for its next round of bargaining with the provinces on offshore mineral rights. Strengthening the Ottawa hand will be the unanimous opinion of the Supreme Court of Canada that natural resources under the territorial sea and on the continental shelf on the West Coast are the sole property of the federal government."*

Disappointed in the ruling, which was deemed to apply everywhere in Canada, but unwilling to rail against the Supreme Court, the Premier returned to advocating that Ottawa cede ownership of offshore resources to the provinces. The 1967 court reference, he maintained, was "mainly a legal exercise" and solved nothing: "When the matter was brought up (at the last Federal-Provincial Conference) it so happened that I was the one who spoke in behalf of all the premiers and argued with the Prime Minister, Mr. Pearson, that this matter should be settled not in the courts, not on a legal or constitutional level, but rather at the political level," he told *The Daily News*.

But its legal and constitutional rights confirmed, he hoped Ottawa now "might be willing to step aside and let the provinces concerned possess and exercise these rights."

Growing out of this position, I set about developing a strategy whose basis was separation of federal oceans jurisdiction from *de facto* provincial ownership of oil and gas. As chairman of the Joint Mineral Resources Committee for the five eastern provinces, I advanced a proposal for shared jurisdiction to then federal Energy Minister J.J. Greene. In a communication in mid-September 1971 he gave some appearance of being prepared "to review (the provinces' position) again." Unfortunately he suffered a stroke while on a trade mission to Japan, was forced from active political life, and died soon after. The prospect of early political settlement based on joint or shared jurisdiction, recognizing provincial ownership of seabed resources, unfortunately died with him.

I reported to the eastern premiers on September 13 that the matter of offshore mineral rights appeared to be entering "a critical stage" with the prospect that it would probably wind up back in the courts—which for Newfoundland, in time, it did under the Peckford Tories, but certainly with no discernible advantage to this province. As well, I recommended a full-scale conference of Premiers, Resources and Economics/Finance ministers to devise strategy for the future, but I am not aware one was ever held.

On October 28, the very day of the election that would put us out of office, Justice Minister John Turner resurrected an earlier federal offer of an advisory committee on which the provinces would be given representation. But he made clear that joint administration was "not contemplated by the federal government."

In time, a youthful Tory leader named Joe Clark would offer provinces like Newfoundland ownership of offshore resources, but when Prime Minister (albeit for only nine or ten months) failed to deliver on the promise. Later still, being "unafraid to inflict prosperity" upon Newfoundland, Prime Minister Brian Mulroney gave us the Atlantic Accord—little more (if not less) than a Tory version of the proffered Liberal advisory committee by another, if glitzier, name.

Nothing has occurred in three decades and more to alter the validity of our position adopted in the 1960s, except to strengthen the conviction that Canada's so-called "have-not" provinces will never become equal partners in Confederation until they own and fully control all their resources. They will never achieve the fiscal capacity to achieve economic independence within Confederation, and never escape the colonial bondage Mr. Smallwood spoke about, until—like Alberta in 1947, when oil gushed forth at Leduc No. 1— they can count their own cash flowing into their own bank accounts, free from devastating, impoverishing, and constitutionally illegal federal clawbacks.

Notwithstanding the legal uncertainty as to which level of government owned the resources, within the first decade after Confederation oil industry interest had begun to heat up in the potential for resource wealth offshore. The Smallwood administration proceeded to enter into provisional agreements and to issue permits for Grand Banks exploration, including the area containing the huge Hibernia field. By the 1960s some fifteen companies were active offshore. In light of the federal-provincial jurisdictional dispute most, if not all, covered themselves by obtaining both provincial and federal permits.

One of the Premier's inspirations was to send a dive team representing the province, Memorial University and the Fisheries College to undertake a "voyage to the bottom of the sea" and affix a bronze plaque to the Virgin Rocks to underscore Newfoundland's claim to ownership of seabed resources. Hugh Lilly, John Snow and Cal Trickett "explored in depth" walking on the floor of the Grand Banks southeast of the Avalon Peninsula on June 23, 1964. The date itself was significant—the eve of the 467th anniversary of John Cabot's voyage of discovery.

In the spring of 1971 Mr. Smallwood personally led a delegation of government and private industry (including fisheries) representatives to Morgan City, LA, centre of Gulf of Mexico oil and gas operations. There we observed first-hand the magnitude and complexity of offshore exploration and production, including effects on the ocean environment. Around the same time I took a group of Mines Branch and Workmen's

Compensation Board (as it was then called) officials to Halifax to inspect the *SEDCO 706*. The giant semi-submersible owned by Southeast Commonwealth Drilling Co. Inc. was being readied for the first major exploration program on the Grand Banks.

Our purpose, certainly, was to learn first-hand what we could in advance of the complex and unbelievably costly exploration work about to commence in the North Atlantic—a far more hostile environment than waters off the southern United States—and to determine the likely effects, good or bad, on the fishing industry. But we also had deep concerns for the safety of workers offshore. These would tragically be borne out in the February 15, 1982 loss of the *Ocean Ranger*, the world's largest deep-sea drilling rig. The Peckford administration's admission that it had been ill-equipped either to do anything to prevent the sinking, or to protect the lives of the 84 men who perished that wild February night, shocked many who had relied on earlier assurances that all was in order.

However our immediate interest at the time, in all the clambering on and off helicopters, service boats and oil rigs, was to show the flag—to demonstrate the claim of the province to ownership of the tremendous resources of oil and gas offshore.

One of the more exciting development proposals to surface around this time was that of Pan-Maritime Shipping and Maritime Fruit Carriers of Haifa, Israel to take over and develop the Marystown Shipyard into a facility capable of building VLCCs—very large crude (oil) carriers, and "reefers" or refrigerator vessels, of which, at the beginning of the 1970s, there was a perceived, widely forecast world shortage. The negotiations, which continued for many months, unfortunately ran into the 1971 provincial election and subsequently were abandoned by the Moores administration. (In the end, the Israelis took their business and hundreds of millions of dollars in shipbuilding orders to the United Kingdom, as *Time* reported in March 1973, "the largest transaction from a single customer in British history.")

The talks with Pan Maritime took a Cabinet committee, headed by the Premier, to New York where we put up at the Americana Hotel. However, the business meetings took place at the posh Waldorf Towers, and were both friendly and constructive, but were doomed by the outcome of the election. "I will always regret deeply the failure of that great project," Mr. Smallwood later wrote.

During the New York visit I was treated to a personally conducted walking tour of locations from his earlier life as a youthful journalist in "The Big Apple." We visited familiar (to him) landmarks, including park benches on which he had slept, winding up at the New York Public Library. Then there was a long lunch of excellent goulash and Bock beer in an unimposing Hungarian restaurant that must have been all of a half-dozen yards wide, but extended back 100 feet or more from the sidewalk, somewhere near Times Square.

This was the opportunity to float my ideas for the coming Budget, which as acting Minister of Finance and President of the Treasury Board I would have a strong hand in formulating. It was also my chance to press the issue of university programs "beyond the overpass," and to suggest the time was right to pursue the concept of a polytechnical institute coordinating various programs of the university, the Fisheries College and the College of Trades and Technology (as they then were known).

As well, I wanted to advance the merits of creating one or more wildlife parks, in eastern and western Newfoundland and possibly in Labrador, both as tourism attractions and as centres of environmental education and appreciation for our students. This would result in establishment of the tremendously popular Salmonier Nature Park, opened, however, after we were gone out of office. (Here I must acknowledge Premier Moores who not only sent me a personal invitation to the official opening, at which he presided, but in his speech credited my effort and initiative in getting the popular facility established.)

In the meantime, good progress was made on most, if not all the major elements of my departmental agenda.

In the Resources area, I was blessed to have the support and guidance of Deputy Minister Gerry Malone, reassigned by the Premier from the Labour department at my request. First off we had to deal with the loss of Chief Forester Ed Ralph, who had gone to pursue a doctorate at Harvard University. (Re-emerging as a consultant, he represented the Reid interests, offering to sell back to the government their vast forest holdings together with the wildlife contained therein—every moose, caribou, partridge, rabbit, and beaver, perhaps even federally introduced shrews, for $46 million. Wildlife Director David Pike couldn't quite believe it; I, too, managed to restrain my enthusiasm! Sometime later Ralph lost his life in a tragic canoeing mishap.)

Creation of the Newfoundland Forest Service as a vital arm of the department had obviated the need for the Newfoundland Forest Protection Association (NFPA) in which the government and the forest industries had cooperated in fire prevention and suppression. It fell to me to signal an end to the arrangement, making the industries more responsible for protecting their own limits. At the same time, it was necessary to negotiate with the newsprint companies annual cost-shared contracts for aerial spraying of insecticides to combat a variety of voracious pests—the spruce budworm, the larch sawfly and other more exotic species that made no distinction as between Crown and company-held forests. The multi-million-dollar contracts invariably went to experienced companies from New Brunswick whose Second World War-vintage spray planes become a familiar sight in many areas of the province.

Ralph's deputy, John Munro, and Director of Forest Resources Al Brennan, were highly qualified, youthful administrators of the complex woodlands resource responsible to respond to all Island users—including a big new one, the proposed Shaheen paper mill for Come by Chance (the linerboard plant at Stephenville was to be fed from Labrador.) It was a major challenge for the Rousseau Royal Commission, which sought a cure in the device of a coordinating Commercial Forests Corporation in which various ownerships (including Crown) would be vested, and users would draw down annual requirements via a wood-fibre "budget" based on the total allowable cut for the province. The first original idea in decades for comprehensive forest management might possibly have worked, but newsprint companies were wary, we were soon out of office, and the Moores government didn't push it.

Details of the Gros Morne National Park negotiation are given elsewhere. But it should be noted that the controversy that surrounded the dealings with Ottawa *grew out of the refusal of the province to blindly turn over a huge area of the Great Northern Peninsula—some 1,500 square miles!—virtually without any quid pro quo.*

In retrospect, it seems very nearly incomprehensible that it should have been so in a province in which the complaint is so often heard that we habitually "give away our resources," but the fact is that the pressure to do so was on from the Opposition in the House of Assembly, from environmentalists and academics, from influential members of the media. The federal parks administration wanted unencumbered ownership, in perpetuity, of a huge slice of Newfoundland territory nearly half the size of the province of Prince Edward Island, and we should just hand it over, no questions asked.

And never mind that the people in twenty-one or twenty-two communities would be forced out. That fishing and landing rights along the coast would be lost. That lumbering and pulpwood harvesting would no longer be permitted. That hunting and angling would be stopped. That minerals and oil and gas known to exist in the area—but never properly or adequately assessed—would be locked up forever, denied to the benefit of Newfoundlanders. It didn't happen, of course. In the negotiation the 1,500 square miles was reduced to about a third, and no communities forced to resettle. Fishing and landing rights were protected, and domestic firewood harvesting. Hunting would be curtailed, angling allowed only under licence, and the mineral, oil and gas potentials we gave up—but the "commensurate benefit" included a magnificent national park complete with the heated swimming facilities I wanted, no longer a source of amusement!

The golf course I demanded was not built in Gros Morne, but Ottawa agreed to put it in Terra Nova National Park in Central Newfoundland. (I continue to believe Gros Morne would be a magnificent site, and that an 18-hole course would greatly enhance the park as a world-class tournament site as well as a tourist destination.)

We also got federal development of the 1,000-year-old Viking site at L'Anse aux Meadows, which like Gros Morne has since been declared a United Nations World Heritage Site, and a 300-mile all-weather highway from Wiltondale to St. Anthony.

On the surface it appeared that the Newfoundland government directly operated an "air force" consisting of a dozen or so workhorse airplanes—*DMR*, the Twin Otter that doubled as an executive aircraft flying the Premier and Cabinet around the province, and frequently as an air ambulance; up to a half-dozen PBY

Canso water bombers; plus "straight" Beavers, Cessnas and Super Cubs that were the backbone of the Forestry and Wildlife divisions; and helicopters as required.

In fact they were operated by contractors for the government, the majority by Eastern Provincial Airways. Typically the government purchased or leased aircraft, and turned them over to EPA. The airline leased them back complete with crews, supplies and maintenance, a lesser segment of its overall operations in Gander.

I was concerned that we were not getting the best deal from EPA, and although the meetings with the company president, James Lewington, and other senior officials were friendly enough, they refused to improve the arrangement. The consequence was that we decided to go to public tenders, with the successful bidder being Atlantic Aviation of Montreal, its manager former Newfoundlander Victor Bennett. An undesirable fallout was that with the government's hangar facilities located on the Torbay side of St. John's Airport, it was inevitable that the new Air Services Division, with Atlantic providing operational oversight, would be located there rather than at Gander.

In a completely separate arrangement, but with an eye to what was about to transpire, I hired the incomparable Capt. Ted Pearcey away from EPA to be the government's chief pilot. Soon after becoming minister of the department, while flying with the Premier and other ministers to Central Newfoundland on *DMR*, I was startled (to put it mildly) to discover a lone pilot in the cockpit. If anything happened to Pearcey, I pointed out to Mr. Smallwood, half the government could be wiped out! Furthermore, I felt that as a matter of principle, the pilot charged with flying the Premier and his ministers should be the government's man. Thus Pearcey came on the payroll and made his choice for co-pilot, fellow EPA employee Wayne Tuck.

Early one beautiful morning, soon after the 1966 General Election, I stood on the beach near Mount Arlington Heights, Placentia Bay with the MP for St. John's West, Richard Cashin, and the MHA for Placentia East, George Alain Frecker. We gazed across the smooth, blue waters of the bay at the site chosen for a big, new industry. The government had secured a $40 million investment by a company that would build a factory at Long Harbour to produce elemental phosphorus for the food processing, agriculture and detergent industries. We were full of hope for a signal advance in the desperate struggle to create a new economy—in the Placentia area, offsetting the inevitable closure of the U.S. Naval Station, and in general, the catastrophic loss of thousands of Newfoundland civilian jobs at U.S. Air Force bases at Pepperrell, Harmon, Goose Bay, and lesser military sites.

Over some two decades the Electric Reduction Company (ERCO) would employ up to 450 people with spending on local payroll and purchases in the range of $23 million annually. However, it would also prove a harbinger of alarms being sounded the world over about industrial pollution. Soon all Newfoundlanders, but Placentia Bay fishermen especially, were shocked by the appearance of red fish— gills damaged and hemorrhaging from the effects of chemical effluent—leading to closure of waters near the plant. As well, the effects of stack emissions were clearly evident in damage to vegetation in the area, raising concerns about potential impacts on human health. After the world energy crisis destroyed the basis for its cheap energy contract with Newfoundland Hydro, forcing the quadrupling of the rate, in the 1980s the plant closed.

But the pollution problems of its early life served as a wake-up call. Where for decades paper mills at Corner Brook and Grand Falls had daily poured tons of sulphurous exhausts from the pulping process onto those communities, and daily discharged millions of gallons of industrial liquors into Humber Arm and the Exploits River, the high price of industrial employment now came into question. Where since the 1930s miners of fluorspar in St. Lawrence had gone underground day after day, year after year, to breathe air laden with radon gas, and surrounding communities paid the price in a virtual epidemic of cancer deaths, the cost became no longer acceptable.

When the new, modern asbestos mining and milling operation at Baie Verte was shown to hold the seeds of deadly lung lesions in workers, and its fire-retardant and insulation products fell under suspicion as cancer-causing virtually worldwide, the industry went out of business.

The paper mills would literally clean up their act, in the first place switching to thermo-mechanical pulping processes based on heat and high pressure, rather than cooking with huge amounts of sulphuric acid.

Treatment of liquid effluents to avoid fouling fish habitats such as the Exploits River and Humber Arm was demanded by the federal Fisheries and Oceans department and achieved with financial assistance from Ottawa.

But regarding the safety of the St. Lawrence mines, which eventually ceased operation for economic reasons, a much more complex problem demanded attention. As in other mineral resources and Crown lands matters—both on land and under the sea—I had the invaluable, impeccably professional advice of Mines Deputy Minister Fred Gover, Director of Mineral Resources John McKillop, and Chief Engineer Fred Lukins. The fluorspar mines were extremely wet, the result of groundwater continually flowing over radioactive fields down the slope of the Burin Peninsula. The solution recommended included a more adequate ventilation system to eliminate cancer-causing radon gas freed by aeration as the water ran down the walls of the mines. It would be backed by a more intensive company inspection process aimed at ensuring that the ventilation system was doing its job. The company inspection system would be overseen by a government monitor.

All the evidence was that these measures would be successful. However, it was only when I could demonstrate, following on-the-spot meetings with the miners' union and the town council in St. Lawrence, that they agreed to the department's proposals, that my Cabinet colleagues would approve them.

Bell Island was another story. The decision to shut the operations had been made long since by the Dominion Steel and Coal Company (DOSCO), and provoked a highly emotional and politically partisan response. My unpleasant chore was to see to the actual disposal of the assets, including mine machinery and equipment and a large stockpile of ore that nobody wanted because of high phosphorous content. The last I remember it was valued on the market at much less than $1 a ton—hardly worth the cost of transportation. Opposition carping aside, the disposal was carried out under contract by a reputable national firm, based on public tenders, and monitored by the Auditor General.

In the vanguard of the environmental revolution was CAWSA—the Clean Air, Water and Soil Authority—its title somewhat unwieldy, but it meant precisely what it said. In setting it up, I secured the agreement of the Premier to have one of the province's most respected public servants as chairman in the person of Clarence W. Powell. Back home to Newfoundland from Alberta I welcomed a first-class petroleum engineer to be general manager, in the person of Kenneth Oakley.

We began to establish, for the first time as a province, comprehensive levels and standards of industrial behaviour, cutting clear across the corporate spectrum. But CAWSA went much further, drawing attention to the least desirable habit of generations of Newfoundlanders of dumping almost anything, anywhere—often just by the side of the road: all manner of unwanted, used-out possessions, including wrecked cars, old tires, bedsteads and mattresses, stoves, refrigerators, toilet bowls and cisterns, and mounds of tin cans, bottles and other containers, bagged and not, which scarred the outskirts of communities. Even with a massive program of community incorporations and the designation of scores of landfills the habit was hard to break.

The agency made a good beginning in this whole broad area. Teams of summer students were sent out to identify areas needing cleanup—hard to do in the winter, in any event—and inspectors were not shy in tracking down sources of illegally dumped garbage and car wrecks based on discarded envelopes, invoices and the like, and vehicle serial and licence plate numbers. They employed their legal authority to require remedial action where water supplies were endangered.

Eventually, jurisdictional lines began to be drawn as the federal government asserted responsibility in respect of ambient air quality, as well as fisheries habitat. It was, of course, in a much more favourable position to back its proscriptions with financial incentives. (After we were gone from office the Moores government, which never liked CAWSA, killed it.)

It is no exaggeration to say the opportunity afforded me to advance the cause of Newfoundland agriculture translated into something close to obsession. I had long believed that as a province, we could do much better than supply ourselves with 20 per cent, perhaps less, of the produce we consumed. My Harbour Grace area forebears had managed to feed themselves, and I was aware of my own father's efforts to organize, in effect, a marketing co-op—the idea being for farmers to jointly rent railway boxcar space to transport vegetables to market.

My predecessors in office, William J. Keough and C. Max Lane, had persuaded the House of Assembly to pass legislation to enable the establishment of agricultural marketing boards, but no further action had been taken. However, I was certain that a marketing framework backed by legal sanctions was essential to success in developing the agrifoods industry, and my Cabinet colleagues agreed.

With the advice and support of experienced, dedicated public servants like Deputy Minister Gerry O'Reilly, Director of Agriculture A. Clarence Badcock, and his deputy A.J. "Gus" Hutchings, and field staff that included men like the legendary Rupert Wood in Central Newfoundland and Patrick Griffin on the West Coast, I waded into the so-called "chicken-and-egg wars." Ottawa was well on the way to deciding the only provinces that should be producing eggs and broilers were those that had "comparative advantage"—this was the operating principle—of being large producers of animal feeds. If allowed to proceed, the policy could eliminate us from whole segments of the livestock industry, and perhaps entirely.

For even greater danger loomed: once this principle was accepted, they could begin picking and choosing in the application of various federal agriculture programs (e.g., crop insurance, Farm Loan Board services) making them apply only to those same "advantaged" provinces. The whole approach, I believed, was discriminatory and *ultra vires* of the British North America Act (which still served as the Constitution of Canada) in the sense that provinces were entitled to equal treatment in the development of their resources—in this instance, their agricultural land base and its potential uses.

Thus in meetings of provincial ministers, negotiations with the federal minister, at that time Bud Olsen from Alberta, as well as before the House of Commons Agriculture Committee, I made a case sufficiently strong that comparative advantage—at least as an all-encompassing, and arbitrary, federal *modus operandi*—was set aside. Instead, a national egg marketing agency was established in which all provinces had equal rights, honouring the principle of constitutional equality that we had fought so hard to uphold and setting a precedent for other areas of agrifoods. (The interesting outcome was that the Newfoundland Marketing Board as a provincial overseer agency, and commodity boards set up under its authority, were less than favourably received by some of our own producers, and despite the fact their party had approved the foundation legislation, some Tory politicians.)

My agriculture agenda didn't stop there. With the Premier's active support and encouragement we expanded Farm Products Corporation operations to Corner Brook, built public farm storage in a dozen or so communities across the province, and took steps to introduce crop insurance. We established a model farming settlement named for fieldman Wood—Wooddale, just east of Grand Falls, but had to refuse demands for a freeze on non-farm development on agricultural lands in the St. John's area because funding for a proper land-bank system was not then available.

The biggest challenge was to change the perception—unfortunately and tragically wrong, in my judgment—that due to climate and soil conditions, this province is unsuited to have an agrifoods industry. Good progress was made in this direction, though admittedly not enough. However, it is encouraging to see exciting growth and diversion occurring, such that in the year 2000, according to government papers, industry output was worth some $500 million, including secondary processing, with about 4,000 persons employed.

The only major resource—it is our greatest, historic, economic mainstay—that was not included in my portfolio was ocean fisheries, but that did not prevent me from actively supporting the Premier's varied approach to fisheries development. As well, I openly encouraged the new fishermen's union started up by boyhood chum Fr. Desmond McGrath while parish priest at Port au Choix, pressed for free collective bargaining for people in the industry, and made what I consider one of my better speeches in the House in support of the setting up of the Canadian Saltfish Corporation.

The persisting myth is that Mr. Smallwood strove mightily to kill the fishing industry, advising fishermen to "burn your boats" and get into some other area of economic activity. As a matter of demonstrable history, he did just the opposite.

He appointed his most articulate confederate associate, William J. Keough—he of memorable turns of phrase, e.g., "the last lonely fisherman on the bill of Cape St. George"—to be his first Minister of Fisheries and Cooperatives. (Keough was close friends with confederate Roman Catholic Bishop Michael O'Reilly who, as a parish priest on the Port au Port Peninsula, had promoted fisheries cooperatives as early as the 1920s.)

Fisheries experts were sent around the world to observe and report on the latest fishing techniques and technologies. The government set up the Fisheries Loan Board and the powerful Fisheries Development Authority, pouring tens of millions of dollars into building and modernizing fish plants, and stimulating development of multi-purpose fishing vessels destined to become cornerstone of a greatly diversified industry. The first "longliners" began to appear in 1951, a fleet which would approach a thousand vessels with values up to and exceeding $1 million not uncommon.

The Premier appointed three special inquiries into critical aspects of the fishing industry—Royal Commissions headed by Sir Albert Walsh, John T. Cheeseman, and the Labrador Fisheries Development Commission led by Harold A. Dawe, general manager of the Fishermen's Protective Union. Ottawa was pushed to hold a national conference on the fisheries that had important results, the Marystown Shipyard was created, mainly to build and maintain a fleet of steel, deep-sea fishing vessels, and the Fisheries College was instituted. A subsidy program was set up for ships taking salt fish to market, and although severely cash-strapped, when it divested the 127-year-old Newfoundland Savings Bank in 1962, the government devoted the proceeds ($2.5 million, a huge sum in its time) to a gear acquisition program for inshore fishermen.

Clearing the decks for a General Election on November 19, 1962, the Premier sought the voters' support for an unprecedented initiative: *The Daily News* reported he "would ask the voters for a mandate authorizing his government to go ahead with a $50 million fisheries development program." Was this encouragement to "Burn your boats"?

The people knew what they wanted and gave him a huge response: 34 seats for the Liberals (versus 7 PCs, 0 NDPs, 1 Ind.) and 58.3 per cent of the popular vote.

# CHAPTER 10

## A BALANCING OF THE BOOKS

The Premier:

"The public debt is in three forms: There is the direct funded debt. Secondly, there is the direct unfunded debt. Thirdly, there is the indirect debt, the contingent liabilities, the indirect, guaranteed debt which is not our debt at all but is the debt of others ... (I)f you put it all together you get the indebtedness of Newfoundland's people."

# PREMIER SMALLWOOD'S SPEECH

Delivered In The House of Assembly On June 1st 1964

ON THE SUBJECT OF THE BUDGET SPEECH

AND ESPECIALLY ON THE SUBJECT OF THE

# PUBLIC DEBT

The Premier:

The Budget Speech should provide "a balance sheet of the financial year just past ... (but also) an account of the Province's economy as a whole; not merely how the government is faring, but rather how is the economy doing? Not merely the treasury ... but whether the trade and commerce and industry, the income of the people, the economic situation in general, are doing all right ..."

A couple of years ago, in a display of extremely questionable news balance, CBC Radio in St. John's invited a couple of guests into the studio to analyze and discuss the Liberal provincial government's Budget, brought down that day.

The principle of balance was abused because both happened to be former Conservative ministers of Finance, John C. Crosbie and H. Neil Windsor. As it turned out, they were only mildly critical of what then Finance Minister Paul Dicks had wrought. Instead, the main castigation was saved for "poor Mr. Smallwood" (predictably, Crosbie's phrase.)

Mr. Smallwood had left office all of three decades previously, and was deceased nearly ten years. Nonetheless the message, stated or implied, was that the first Premier of Newfoundland had bankrupted the province forever, and was the author of whatever problems, budgetary and otherwise, it might be grappling with on the eve of the 21st Century. It is high time this particular nonsense was finally put to rest.

One thing to be noted is that Mr. Smallwood's several administrations between 1949 and 1972 employed the traditional system of government accounting, segregating capital from current account.

It only made sense. Capital account referred to expenditures on assets of lasting value, such as buildings, roads, bridges, etc. These were financed mainly from borrowed funds, raised by selling the province's bonds on international money markets. Allowing only for normal depreciation, these assets maintained their value over time, and, highly appropriately, were paid for over time—and at least in part by future users.

Current account was a very different matter. It referred to day-to-day operational expenditures such as salaries, light, heat, paper and paper clips, pens and pencils and other consumables, and general maintenance—all paid for out of day-to-day revenues, mainly tax collections and transfers from the federal government.

From this same source came "sinking funds," monies put aside for orderly repayment of capital account borrowings as they came due. It was quite proper, I believe (certain current opinion notwithstanding) for excess monies in the sinking fund account—usually unanticipated earnings from higher-than-expected interest on investments—to be returned to current account for general purpose spending.

Virtually every Newfoundland family with a mortgage on their home operates on this basic system, which probably means 99.9 per cent of them. Few people have the cash to put down for a house, fully paid up, so they "borrow" it by way of a mortgage secured by the property and can have a decent roof over their heads while they pay it off over 25 or 35 years.

*PHOTOS CLOCKWISE:*
■ Premier Smallwood's major address to the House of Assembly "on the Subject of the Budget Speech, and Especially on the Subject of the Public Debt" was both a primer on the province's system of public finances, and a concise history of Newfoundland's fiscal performance both before and after Confederation. The series of file photos is from the Tower Archives (TA).

It may be popular to pander to public misunderstanding of the matter, but "pay-as-you-go" is just not economically or socially viable except for day-to-day spending for heat, electricity, the telephone and general upkeep.

It is not going too far to say Mr. Smallwood had an absolute fixation on the health of the public purse. I have reason to know this first-hand, having not only served in his Cabinet as Minister of Mines, Resources and Agriculture, but concurrently as acting Finance minister (dealing, among other things, with preparation of the 1971 Budget) and Treasury Board President.

The fact is that within the capital-versus-current account structure, successive Smallwood administrations had, for all practical purposes, a balanced Budget in every year that he was Premier.

The question to be asked and answered is whether or not, during those years, the province was safely and comfortably able to service the public (i.e., capital account) debt. The answer is a resounding yes, no doubt about it. Nonetheless, the Tories painted a lurid picture of the alleged perilous state of the Treasury at the hands of the Liberals that was manufactured into a major issue for the watershed 1971 election. It was either a completely incompetent reading of the facts or a bare-faced, deliberate lie, and not even a clever concoction. But many in the media swallowed it hook, line and sinker. And not only with regard to government finances, but also the Newfoundland and Labrador economy in general.

The new PC leader, fish merchant Frank Duff Moores, had spurned an opportunity to run in a St. John's East by-election for a seat in the House of Assembly. While still federal MP for Bonavista-Trinity-Conception and national PC Party president (as well as provincial leader) he set about carrying his gloom-and-doom message to every bay and inlet. He had the complete freedom, the time, and the money to do it during nearly two years available to organize and prepare for a classic confrontation in the fall of 1971, beginning with his landslide win in the PC leadership in May 1970.

As nearly 2,000 Liberal delegates prepared to head for St. John's to choose the man who would lead them into the next election, Moores was stumping Central Newfoundland. Pledging to provide "an honourable government" in place of "political gamesmanship (that) cannot be tolerated," he painted Mr. Smallwood as "a dishonest little man with a mighty ego … and a cunning political instinct."

*Evening Telegram* reporter Randy Joyce had been a Memorial University student radical and received 13 votes (out of 1,705 cast) as a Liberal leadership candidate in 1969. He was the author of a 1977 newspaper series on "How the Tories wooed and won Newfoundland and how they hope to hold her."

"Newfoundland is a sick, sick mess," he quoted the PC leader as saying after the convention at which the Smallwood leadership was overwhelmingly reconfirmed. "It is frightening, the province is so near to bankruptcy. It is a billion dollars in debt, with no way to pay it off … Newfoundland will need austerity to straighten out this mess. The next government of Newfoundland will have a thankless job."

Moores spent his time condemning the strenuous efforts to encourage major industries to employ Newfoundlanders in their own province and offset out-migration.

"Our best possible role in the future may be as the home for cottage industries," the millionaire businessman intoned. "Newfoundland is going to have to develop excellence in what we do know and what we can be better at—everything from logging, mining, fish processing, to sheep raising, rather than … heavily industrialized plants."

In this context the Come by Chance oil refinery—which as head of a Tory government he would later support, and agree to support another three times its size—was described as "the worst deal ever perpetrated on a free people in a civilized land." Moores's alternatives to create employment included a system of selling fish by auction, and a Crown corporation to develop the resources of Labrador strikingly reminiscent of Mr. Smallwood's Newfoundland and Labrador Corporation (NALCO) or even Brinco. Neither Moores proposal survived the Tories' accession to power.

Was Newfoundland really in the financial mess that Moores claimed, a billion dollars in debt and no way to pay it off?

Whenever the government goes to the bond market to raise money it must make full public disclosure of the province's fiscal and economic condition, everything that might affect its ability to repay. This may occur several times in a single year, depending on need and strategy. The formal document in which such disclosure is made, its correctness certified by the Minister of Finance, goes by the technical name *prospectus*—a Latin word meaning, as might be expected, a detailed, descriptive outline of the province's financial and economic condition and—what else?—its realistic prospects. As a public disclosure document, it dare not be "cooked."

Five years after the Moores government came to power—a reasonable period, I believe, for the purpose of judging the performance of both the present and immediate past administrations—Finance Minister C. William Doody issued a *prospectus* in support of the sale on the New York market of $50 million in Newfoundland government 10.5 per cent sinking fund debentures. From this sale, after paying out underwriting discounts and commissions, the Treasury expected to realize $49,437,500.

A key section of this document, Table VIII, entitled Provincial Debt Position, disclosed the "Total Debenture Debt" (direct debt) of the province in 1971, last year of the Smallwood administration. The figure was $535.7 million, or little more than half the $1 billion referenced by Moores!

To be fair, because government fiscal years run from April 1 to March 31 and therefore overlap calendar years, a small portion of the following year's (1972) debenture debt could have belonged to the Smallwood administration. This was reported in the *prospectus* at $594 million—still a far cry from the Tory leader's estimate. Time would prove Moores some kind of prophet, however. His predicted austerity had still not appeared, but by 1975, after only three years of his administration, the "Total Debenture Debt" had soared to $1,104.7 million, exceeding the billion-dollar level for the first time in Newfoundland's history.

There is more to the province's debt obligations than debenture borrowings. They include, as well, the "floating" debt made up of accounts payable, bank overdrafts, accrued interest and other miscellaneous short-term amounts. Then there are the "contingent liabilities"—sums guaranteed in behalf of private entrepreneurs who are responsible to pay them off, and Crown corporations and municipalities, which in 1971 amounted to $383.8 million, bringing "Total Provincial Obligations" to $919.5 million. But against all that, sinking funds: loans, advances and mortgages receivable; investments; other assets; and self-liquidating guaranteed debt; these reduced the actual net debt, when the Smallwood Liberals left office after 23 years, at $363.3 million.

Comparable figures for the Moores administration after just five years: Total provincial obligations of $1,774 million (or one and three-quarter billion) and a net debt of $709 million, each roughly double that of "the previous administration!"

There is one other set of figures that is of interest, namely the per capita debt. When Mr. Smallwood went out as Premier in 1972—following what must have been by far the biggest, sustained development boom in Canadian history—he could take satisfaction in the construction of 5,000 miles of highways, including the Trans Canada; a network of new and expanded hospitals; Memorial University; the College of Trades and Technology and 17 vocational schools; dozens of regional and local day schools; Confederation Building; the Arts and Culture centres and dozens of libraries; various airstrips; dozens of Provincial Parks; water and sewer systems and street lighting in nearly 300 municipalities. The people of the province, theoretically at least, shared in the cost of all this to the extent of $1,761 dollars each, but a net obligation of $740.

By 1975, under the Moores regime, the gross per capita obligation had nearly doubled: at $3,231 for every man, woman and child in the province, or a net of $1,289. This question must be asked: with most of the major provincial infrastructure already in place when Moores took over, what was there to show for this huge increase?

Meanwhile, the total public sector debt continued to soar, due largely to borrowing for the takeover of Churchill Falls Labrador Corp. and subsidies to the Stephenville linerboard mill, and the aborted scheme to punch a tunnel under the Strait of Belle Isle—an expensive piece of play-acting for the purposes of the 1975 election. It increased from just under two billion dollars—$1,961 million, to be precise—in 1976, to $2,239 million in 1977, to $2,398 million in 1978, to $2,603 million in 1979, the year Moores resigned.

At the end of the Peckford administration's first year, March 31, 1980, as reported by Finance Minister John F. Collins, it was closing in on three billion dollars—$2,747 million, to be exact. And when

Premier Brian Peckford resigned in 1989 the total public sector debt stood at $4,844 million. Within the year it would edge past five billion dollars!

There is an interesting sidelight to this particular discussion, something that occurred in Corner Brook in June 1979. The city's most prominent lawyer, Clyde K. Wells, wrote a long letter to the editor of *The Western Star*, which may not in itself be noteworthy. But what he wrote must have made more than a few people take notice.

The newspaper had published for "The Peckford Team" a full-page advertisement in advance of a General Election only a few days off. Except for "mug shots," as the media call them—standard facial photographs—of Peckford, Prime Minister Joe Clark, and Tory candidates Lynn Verge, Ray Baird, Luke Woodrow and Wallace House, it consisted of an editorial reprinted from *The Star*'s June 12 edition, reproduced in extra-large type, bearing the headline: "We have to back Peckford." The quite lengthy editorial started out by stating that despite the paper's traditional practice of staying out of partisan politics, it felt "a duty to the people of Newfoundland to choose sides in the June 18 provincial election." Then it went on to say that the Conservative government "despite earlier shortcomings, deserves the backing of Newfoundlanders to administer the affairs of the province for the next five years."

Wells, along with Crosbie, had split with Mr. Smallwood in 1968, due ostensibly to the government's financial and economic shortcomings. Departing from the Cabinet—but unlike Crosbie, who joined the Tories, choosing to leave public life—Wells appeared to support the PCs electorally in the early 1970s but now was identified in an editor's note as "a Liberal campaign worker in Western Newfoundland."

His letter first castigated the newspaper itself for failing to meet standards of objectivity and fairness, charging it had pointed out what it called Peckford's good points "but ignored completely … the very substantial record of faults and failures" piled up by the Conservatives. However, concerning Liberal leader Don Jamieson, he said the paper had "pointed out all of the faults and failures you believed him to be responsible for and … none of his good qualities." In addition, Wells wrote, some of the paper's criticisms of Jamieson were "factually wrong."

He was also critical of the *The Star's* coverage of a Liberal Party rally a couple of nights earlier. He declared speakers had made "too many detailed criticisms of the faults and failures of the Conservative government … to believe very easily that the failure to report a single one of them was due to accident or incompetent reporting." Then, lawyer fashion, he got down to cases:

"1. The Conservatives campaigned in 1971 and 1972 on the basis of the most severe, and probably unjustified criticism, about the level of the public debt in Newfoundland. At that time it was $900,000,000.* In less than eight years the Conservative government of which Mr. Peckford was a part and is now the Leader, tripled this to more than $2,700,000,000.
   (*See "Total Provincial Obligations." above—Editor)

2. The personal income tax rate in Newfoundland in 1972 was 33 per cent of the basic federal tax. In 1958 it was 58 per cent of the basic federal tax. To be fair many of these increases were made coincident with decreases in the federal tax so that the total tax burden in most years did not vary very much. Nevertheless the personal income tax rate in Newfoundland remains the highest in Canada by a substantial margin.

3. The retail sales tax was increased from 7 per cent in January 1972 to 11 per cent in 1978. This amounts to an increase in the rate of tax of 57 per cent and the Conservatives, instead of working towards a reduction, have stated their intention of freezing the retail sales tax at an unbearably high rate.

4. The unemployment rate in the years before the Conservatives came to power was generally in the area of 9 per cent or so. In recent years under the Conservative government it has averaged closer to 18 per cent.

5. The Conservatives campaigned in 1971 and in 1972 primarily on the basis of a promise to provide good, clean and honest government and to rid government forever of scandal and corruption and patronage. But in less than 8 years the reputation of that government was as bad or worse than any government in Newfoundland's history.

6. Immediately before and during the 1975 election campaign the Conservative government spent approximately $100,000,000 in an effort to persuade the electorate that work had indeed started on the Lower Churchill hydro project and then stopped work when the election was over.

7. The Conservative government led by Mr. Peckford was grossly irresponsible in calling the election for a date that was 2 1/2 months after the start of the fiscal year without bringing in a budget to set financial and public works policy for that year."

Wells's strong, wide-ranging criticism included, as well, the fact that Peckford, "without regard to the best interest of the province," called the 1979 election to be held three weeks before a Liberal leadership convention in the hope that the electorate "would have no choice but to vote for him and his party." (And vote for him they did, delivering an increased Tory majority and electing the entire "team" pictured in the newspaper ad.)

Wells's intervention had little effect on the election outcome, but it signalled that he had not, after all, abandoned all interest in Liberal politics. Indeed, some people remembered that he had renewed his party membership in January 1972—ironically, in the same week as the final demise of the Liberal government of which he had been a member, and had helped defeat. "They have seen the light and issued me a card," he had told *The Daily News*, confirming that he was "again a card-carrying Liberal."

Nearly another decade would pass before a search committee, growing out of meetings of party activists, of which I was one, organized by Smallwood friend Joseph D. Ashley and his son-in-law, former party president Aidan Hennebury, would recruit Wells (he had moved his law practice to St. John's) as the top candidate for Liberal leader.

Peckford resigned in early 1989, admitting he could no longer be sufficiently "ruthless" to function as Premier, and was succeeded as PC Leader and Premier by former Liberal Tom Rideout. He called a snap election and lost the government to Wells's Liberals after only 44 days in the Premier's chair. Wells led the Liberals to a second majority in May 1993, and two days after Christmas 1995 resigned as Premier and party Leader to be succeeded in turn by Brian Tobin and Roger Grimes. He would be appointed to the bench of the Supreme Court and later Chief Justice of Newfoundland by the federal Liberal government of Prime Minister Jean Chrétien.

Fiscal standing, in particular existing debt obligations, is only one of the major elements that are considered in depth in the province's bond market *prospectus*. The other is broad economic performance—the gross provincial product or GPP, the sum total of goods and services produced; the condition and performance of particular industrial sectors; employment and unemployment numbers; and the labour force participation rate. Clearly, a healthy tax regime rests mainly, in the end, on the ability, not to say willingness, of individual citizens to provide the government with the monies it needs to function and repay borrowings. Those who invest in the province by buying its bonds need to know they will get their money back, plus dividends.

As he travelled the province prior to and during the 1971 election campaign, Moores was incessant in his attacks upon the Liberal government's economic record. Joyce, in his *Telegram* series, has the Tory leader telling people in Trepassey, "You have to decide whether you want planning and action, or the dreams of one man and promises which are to be broken." At a rally in McIver's, during a tour of Bay of Islands, the Tory leader promised to loud applause, "After this election, there'll be no more Doyles or Shaheens"—clear reference to the Stephenville linerboard mill and the Come by Chance refinery.

And in Humber East, headquarters of the biggest private sector employer on the West Coast—speaking, as it happened, of political organization, but the intent of the remark unmistakable—"Of course, a do-it-yourself kit is pretty effective, if you have a Lundrigans Meccano set to do it with!" (Joyce noted the irony of Moores subsequently hitching a ride to St. John's on the Lundrigans executive jet.)

An excerpt from Moores's leadership convention speech in May 1970 projects an attitude of mind that is more than simply critical—brimming at once with bitterness, even hatred of all things Liberal, together with a surprising tinge of political idealism:

"To some extent I could even accept the government's incompetence in the handling of Newfoundland's affairs if I could find in them some sense of democracy or care for the people, but I cannot. Its practice of democracy is shameful and, coupled with its record, this leaves little it can stand by except the Premier's endless promises—empty promises—of better things ahead when this is built or that is enacted. The old issues are no longer relevant, and (the Premier's) style of cunning political gamesmanship cannot be tolerated."

Together with the Tories' preference for "cottage industries ... rather than putting up industrialized plants," such references were intended to discredit Smallwood development policies. Were these policies, then, such outrageous failures?

A likely place to find an answer (a surprising answer, surely) is a speech Crosbie gave in St. John's—apparently with a completely straight face—on October 5, 1972 to the Data Processing Association. The Moores administration, of which he was the chief minister, was barely six months old. The speech was long and detailed, so I will only provide highlights. I have attempted to bridge the nearly 30-year time gap by means of minor updating, but this has not materially changed Crosbie's own words.

As well, it is useful to bear in mind that very little of what was going on in the province at the time—whether bad or good—could be laid at the doorstep of the new government, in power only six months. Virtually everything referenced, therefore, must be attributed to the Smallwood administration:

- Unlike the national economy, the provincial economy had not undergone a recessionary period in the past several years. In each of the past three years from 1969 to 1971 the gross provincial product of Newfoundland had grown by over 10%. Even when allowing for inflation the real growth rates had been in excess of 6% which was impressive by any standard.

- The government of the province had a relatively larger impact on the economy than was true nationally and therefore the economic growth in the province was being maintained because of large government expenditures over the past two years ... increasing from $76 million on capital account in 1969-70 to $222 million dollars last year, an increase of almost 200%. Total government expenditures (including debt service and retirement) increased from $307 million dollars in 1969-70 to $400 million dollars in 1971-72, an annual average of 26.4%. Because of this the province did not have a recessionary period.

- The population statistics were of great interest. Since the census date of June 1971 the population of the province had increased by 10,000 to June of 1972. This was a 1.9% increase in one year. For comparable periods in 1970 and 1971 the rates of increase were 0.6% and 1.0% respectively. It appeared that more people were staying in the province because of improved job opportunities.

- Although the unemployment rate in the province was the highest in Canada this could, in part, be attributed to the rapid increase in the labour force. In the last year the labour force in this province had increased by 7.8%. *This compared with an annual average increase of only 3.0% in the past 10 years.* (Ital. in original.) In the past year the number of people employed increased by 7.3% or over twice the national rate of 3.2%. However, unemployment continued to increase; the annual average unemployment rate in 1972 was forecast at about 12%, and would remain the central problem facing the economy over the next few years.

- Personal income in Newfoundland had grown by over 10% in the past three years. Personal income in 1971 reached just over $1,000,000,000 and should be in the vicinity of $1.1 billion dollars in 1972. Average weekly wages and salaries had also increased by over 9% in the first five months of this year.

- After-tax income in 1972 had grown even more because of income tax reductions, especially for lower-income people, and because of higher unemployment insurance payments. *Unemployment insurance payments in the first five months of this year are 91 per cent higher than during the same period last year.* (Ital. in original.)

- With more disposable income available and generally improving economic conditions, consumer demand in our province has been very strong. In the first half of 1972 total retail sales are 15% higher than the same period last year. New car sales are extremely strong for the second year in a row. The number of new cars sold increased by 28.6% in 1971. This rate of increase has been surpassed so far in 1972 as the number of cars sold in the first six months is up by over 30%. In value terms the retail value of cars sold up to June of this year is up by 45%. Such strong consumer demand is certainly surprising, given the persistent high unemployment ...

- In general, the economy was moving ahead at a good pace but unemployment and renewed fear of price inflation continued to cause concern. The economy was once again expected to grow by approximately 10% in 1972 although a larger proportion of this would be due to inflation than was the case in 1971. (The Minister of Finance and President of the Treasury Board also discussed the fishing industry which, based mainly on cod, he said was "a failure" in the first half of 1972 with the value of landings cut in half.)

- The minister covered the forestry sector, citing strong recovery in newsprint, and said the new government was "determined to assist in the establishment of a viable sawmill industry." The Stephenville linerboard mill, he said, was "scheduled to be completed in November 1972"—the following month—but might not get into full production until early 1973. (It actually did not commence turning out product until 1974.)

- Crosbie talked about the construction industry which, he said, for the second consecutive year "performed strongly" in 1971 but would not do as well in 1972 because "capital expenditures in most areas of activity had levelled off."

- In mining, production would be down "considerably"—in iron ore because of strikes in Labrador against both Wabush Mines and the Iron Ore Company of Canada. Production values for all other minerals were down 20% in 1971 from the year before, mainly because of strikes in Buchans and St. Lawrence, but were expected to recover in 1972.

- Offshore exploration for oil had "greatly intensified" during the past two years, and 1972 expenditures were expected to "again increase substantially."

- Before concluding Crosbie again turned to "vastly increasing expenditures" of the provincial government that he said were "a very significant feature" of the economy which would only be securely based when government activity became "a less important and significant factor." He said it was the hope of the new administration that "with proper planning, with hard work, with the reversal of harmful policies of the past 10 years, with the overcoming of the problems left by the past administration ... we can develop in this province a rounded approach to business and industrial activity that will lead to increasing prosperity and less dependence on the government."

I believe it important to provide detailed references to this Crosbie speech in order to show, from the lips of the most powerful minister in the Moores administration, what was the real economic condition of the province in 1971-72—in direct contrast to the Tories' election rhetoric.

Secondly, the combined evidence of the Crosbie speech, together with authentic financial reports—those presented to the House of Assembly in official papers of the Moores government, as well as information disclosed to the investment world in various issues of the financial *prospectus*—is more than adequate to demonstrate that contrary to Crosbie's allegation that "poor Mr. Smallwood" had put Newfoundland on the rocks, and Moores's election rhetoric, in all-important fiscal and economic terms the province's affairs were being very well managed up to the time the Tories took over.

It is clear that the Moores administration, and the Peckford administration that grew out of it, took Newfoundland farther and faster down the road of public indebtedness than any other in this province's, or perhaps all Canadian history. And this while adding precious little to infrastructure and industry already in place. In his political autobiography *No Holds Barred* (McClelland and Stewart), Crosbie asserts that probably the greatest achievement under Moores was "to put honesty back into government," and that it was "very much a reform" administration—claims that fall far short of universal agreement. But he also paints Moores as a playboy who "always enjoyed the good life, the high life ... and as little work as possible," remarking that this "didn't change by one iota" after the fishing industry scion became Premier.

"People said government was a game to Frank," according to Crosbie, for the most part avoiding direct criticism of his leader who was "content to let me run (it) in most day-to-day matters." But he allows there was no doubt that the public was seized with a belief that the government wasn't "doing any-thing." He stops short of admitting that perhaps they were right!

After repeated threats to resign over the way Moores infringed or interfered with his functioning as a minister, in 1975 Crosbie made his decision to leave: "I knew I'd gone as far as I could in Newfoundland politics, and frankly, I was tired of playing second fiddle."

So he resigned from the Cabinet and House of Assembly, ran successfully in a federal by-election, and entered the House of Commons as M.P. for St. John's West. There is an inescapable conclusion from all this, namely that Newfoundlanders did themselves no great favour in electing the Moores government; that on the other hand, with Joseph R. Smallwood as Premier, the Tories' election propaganda notwith-standing, the people's affairs had been entrusted to exceptionally good hands!

# CHAPTER 11

## THE PERILS OF DEVELOPMENT

*It would take
capable promotors
who knew where
investment funds could
be raised—even some
seen as unworthy of the
priesthood of high
finance.*

M r. Smallwood was never happier, never more gratified, than to be able to boast about local enterprises succeeding and employing Newfoundland workers—with generous government support if and as required. This was how to "grow" Newfoundland, to maintain its population. This, in practice, was his "develop or perish" philosophy.

Anyone in the audience who did not know and understand the intensity of the Premier's feeling on this most basic issue must have been surprised, perhaps even shocked—as some clearly were—at the outburst that occurred at the official sod-turning at the site of the huge Churchill Falls development on July 17, 1967.

Pent-up anger from nearly two decades of frustrating negotiations came spilling out, touched off by reports of Newfoundland workers getting short shrift on the project.

There was also the appearance of a fleet of yellow Quebec school buses, wearing French-language "Ecoliers" signs, to ferry important guests to the ceremony from the Twin Falls airstrip. And he was upset, to put it mildly, over the snub to Tom Burgess, the MHA for Labrador West, who was not provided a place on the platform for the ceremony.

This, then, became the occasion of the famous "This is our land!" speech, a not-very-subtle reiteration of the Premier's characteristic insistence on recognition of the rights and dignity of Newfoundlanders.

His basic, unfailing instinct, feeding his deliberate and directed efforts, was constant and single-minded—things had to be made better for Newfoundlanders now, in the present!

Not that he was unmindful of the future world of his grandchildren and great-grandchildren; not that he was against long-term planning … But he very well knew that if the present was taken care of, with the people healthier, better educated, living in better conditions, in a cleaner environment, and gainfully employed at good wages, then the chances of the future being a better place would be enhanced immeasurably. Else many would not—could not—remain in Newfoundland, and for them, at least there would be no future in Newfoundland and Labrador.

I think it was Robert F. Kennedy who observed that there is nothing so perilous, and so uncertain of success, as to initiate a new order of things. Mr. Smallwood very well knew this too. He also understood, and would often remark, that "If you want to change a man (or a society) you must begin with his grandfather."

No one will seriously challenge that as Newfoundland firms, Lundrigans and Crosbies were favoured instruments of growth and development in the Smallwood years. They were not alone; the government's "Newfoundlanders First" local preference policy meant scores of existing and many new ones were born or expanded to match the vast upgrading of public services after Confederation. Yet the realist in Mr. Smallwood recognized, clearly better than most, that not all growth and development would or could be provided by homegrown Newfoundland companies, and that is the other side of this story. He realized it would take shrewd promoters who knew where investment could be found, even some regarded in so-called respectable, blue-chip circles as unworthy of the priesthood of high finance and economics.

Principal players in this group (but by no means the only ones) from outside the province were John M. Shaheen and John C. Doyle who together brought close to $1 billion of investment to the province and some 2,000 or more of its best-paying industrial jobs. It should also be said that Lundrigans and Crosbies between them added possibly another 5,000. The irony is that all four companies, as they were then known, have disappeared—even if what they built in the way of mining, oil refining, paper-making and various service sector enterprises lives on.

In the meantime, a large book could be filled with the names of dozens and scores of smaller firms, many of them newly sprung-up—architects, engineers, contractors, suppliers, subcontractors, and specialist firms engaged in various aspects of general construction, road building, shipbuilding, and other activities spotted around the province, and all participating in a huge wave of progress. Nor is this in any way to disparage firms and industries that were operating here before Confederation—the pulp and paper mills, the sawmilling and mining companies, and of course, the fishing operations that had sustained Newfoundlanders, in good times and bad, for 500 years.

It must be acknowledged, however, that native Newfoundland enterprises that grew from nowhere or from modest circumstances to employ as many as 2,000 and more people have been few and far between. One of these was founded by William James Lundrigan, a native of Blaketown, Trinity Bay. Like tradesmen from every corner of Newfoundland (of whom my own father was one) he made his way in the 1920s to Corner Brook where construction of a huge newsprint mill was underway to fulfill Sir Richard Squires's promise to put a "hum on the Humber."

Lundrigan found work in the Newfoundland Power and Paper lumberyard, later opened a general store, then a meat market, and still later a sawmill high up on the West Side of Corner Brook, and another on the railway line near Stephenville Crossing. He was on the spot when the American military needed a large supply of lumber to build Ernest Harmon Air Force Base at Stephenville, as a result of which W.J. Lundrigan Ltd. became a major player in the West Coast economy virtually overnight.

After the Second World War, Newfoundland's entry into Canada touched off spectacular progress in the provision of public buildings and infrastructure of every kind. Directed by the eldest son, Arthur, Lundrigans soon branched out into road building; heavy construction; ready-mix, pre-stressed and pre-cast concrete; gypsum products; polystyrene products; prefabricated homes; building supplies; and automobiles. It constructed schools, hospitals, industrial and commercial buildings, the Holiday Inns across the Island, the Golden Eagle oil refinery at Holyrood, and components of the Shaheen refinery at Come by Chance. It built and paved highways and constructed bridges.

Its own payroll grown to more than 2,000 employees, and having won contracts in such far-flung places as Saudi Arabia and Bermuda, Lundrigans acquired Comstock International, a large Canadian company specializing in mechanical and electrical construction, which employed some 3,000. A survivor of the horrific 1942 sinking by a German submarine of the Newfoundland Railway ferry SS *Caribou*, William J. Lundrigan died in 1986 when he was 85 years old, mercifully unaware of the impending disaster about to devastate what he spent a lifetime building. (Arthur followed a few years later after a debilitating stroke.)

In 1992 I wrote about it in my column in *The Evening Telegram* under the headline "Failure of Lundrigans (a) Newfoundland Tragedy"—that in the existing state of business in Canada, more especially in Newfoundland, the Corner Brook firm "like scores and hundreds of companies big and small, has had to sell off parts of its operations to reduce debt load, a situation not helped at all by an unproductive investment of $8 million in an unsuccessful bid for Hibernia heavy construction …"

I reported that divestiture had been underway for some time, starting with the sale of Comstock International, and went on: "You have to ask: If this well-organized, well-connected, well-run firm can't make it here, who can? And the obvious second question: Is there a message in this for others in Newfoundland, or those who might consider investing here—that no matter what government economic development experts tell you about opportunities for entrepreneurs to invest and make their fortune in this province, the truth is the prospects are mighty slim?"

◆   ◆   ◆

The opposite number to Lundrigans—rival might be too strong a term—were the Crosbies whose foundations as a major Newfoundland business enterprise were set much earlier after the tradesman son of a Scottish immigrant family, George Graham Crosbie, arrived in the bottom of Conception Bay from New Brunswick in the late 1850s.

Trained as a plasterer, he married Martha Chalker, a cooper's daughter, and settled in her home community of Brigus. Some years later he purchased from a man named Samuel Knight what would become known as the Central Hotel at 173 Water Street, St. John's. This prosperous business fell victim to the Great Fire of 1892, which razed most of the city. Undaunted, Crosbie rebuilt on a new site what would be the capital's principal hostelry and bear the family name. The Crosbie Hotel on the north side of Duckworth Street, west of Prescott, opened in December 1894 and stood for 100 years.

He died suddenly a few months after it opened, and responsibility fell on his widow and teenage son, John Chalker Crosbie, who was forced to leave school to help with the family business. According to a sketch of the family's affairs in Volume 5 of the Smallwood *Book of Newfoundland*, at only 24 he established a fish exporting business that became Crosbie & Co. He started up a coastal mail service, a fleet of ships in the foreign trade, a large insurance business, and in 1925 "astounded critics by launching a margarine manufacturing business in the face of heavy competition."

Invited by Sir Edward Morris to contest the district of Bay de Verde in the 1908 election he won the seat, was re-elected in 1909, and at 33 became a member of the Cabinet. He was created a Knight of the British Empire "for outstanding service as a Minister of the Crown" through the critical years of the First World War and when Sir John died in 1932, at the age of 56, he left "a record of business development, political service and philanthropy that has set the standard for Crosbie operations ever since."

Chesley Arthur Crosbie "took over the administration of the Crosbie interests" after his father died and in a "remarkable" 30-year period until his own death in 1962, at 57 years of age, "developed the business to embrace a diversity of activity in Newfoundland commercial and community life."

His brother Percy succeeded as chairman of the Crosbie Management Group, and his son Andrew, as president, became responsible for its sprawling organization, development policy and program direction. Twenty companies operated under its banner, employing some 2,200 people in project design, engineering and development, light and heavy construction, manufacturing, sales and services, insurance, shipping and land transportation, hotel and fishing lodge operations, offshore services, printing and publishing, and aircraft operation and servicing.

Mr. Smallwood got "particular pleasure" recalling "the phenomenal rise of Eastern Provincial Airways" which old friend Ches Crosbie and family, with his government's support—major contract work, and financing to the tune of $5-6 million—built from a bush operation into Canada's third-largest airline flying Boeing 737 jets.

Andrew Crosbie died tragically of lung cancer in January 1991 at the young age of 58. His business empire, like that of Lundrigans, suffered badly in the recessionary, high-interest period of the 1980s. He was forced to sell Eastern Provincial, lost the major downtown development Atlantic Place after Canadian National Railways backed out of a deal to construct a hotel tower on top of the office-shopping complex, and endured the bankruptcy of Crosbie Offshore, set up to catch an offshore oil and gas boom that did not occur when anticipated. The final blow came when he and partner Richard Spellacy were charged with defrauding German associates in the offshore firm of $1 million. Crosbie died before he could go to trial; Spellacy was sentenced to eight years.

New entities bearing the Crosbie name soon began to spring up—and new Lundrigans activities too—out of the ashes of what their forebears built. Younger generations began to take their place at the forefront of Newfoundland business and enterprise, following in the footsteps of fathers and grandfathers, and hopefully with longer-lasting success.

◆ ◆ ◆

It was obvious that construction of the Trans Canada Highway and several thousand miles of secondary highways and other roads would mean an explosion in the number of cars, trucks and other motor vehicles requiring substantial, ever expanding supplies of fuel. The same was true of electrical generation and industrial operations.

Mr. Smallwood concluded early that security of supply of gasoline and other fuels, and price levels and stability as well, meant the province should have its own oil refinery, which would also provide an important expansion of manufacturing capability and the employment that goes along with it. However, approaches to refiners such as Imperial Oil, British-American, Irving and others elicited little or no interest.

Then Arthur Lundrigan introduced the Premier to John Michael Shaheen, native of Lee County, Illinois and decorated U.S. war hero (Navy Silver Star and Air Force Legion of Merit). Shaheen had served with the Office of Strategic Services (OSS), the wartime spy agency, in Europe and the Pacific before retiring with the rank of a naval captain.

In May 1960 it was announced that Golden Eagle Refining Co. of Canada, headed by Shaheen, would establish a refinery on tidewater at Holyrood, Conception Bay, as it had already done in Panama and California before merging with Ultramar of England of which Shaheen was the main shareholder. The Holyrood refinery opened December 1, 1961 following expenditure of $20 million of private capital for the plant, wharf facilities, storage tanks and two railway spur lines. Production peaked at 15,000 barrels a day, supplying government petroleum requirements under a 20-year exclusive contract guaranteeing tank-car prices equal to Halifax, the nearest terminal supplying the province. (The Peckford government would not renew it and in 1983 the refinery closed.)

In Mr. Smallwood's description Shaheen "performed admirably" in relation to the Holyrood refinery, keeping "every syllable of his word." Thus the government "had good reason to be confident" in him when he proposed in 1965 to build a much larger refinery at Come by Chance, Placentia Bay. This was to be a 100,000-barrel-a-day plant, programmed to expand in time to 600,000. It would become the foundation for a world-class petrochemical industry, and located beside it would be the long-talked-about third paper mill to supply, among others, Shaheen's own proposed daily newspaper, the *New York News*. The whole would help provide employment for Newfoundland's burgeoning population, a need never more obvious than on July 30 that year when the birth occurred of Bernard Joseph William Hynes at Twillingate. It raised the number of people ordinarily resident in Newfoundland and Labrador—only 340,000 at Confederation, 15 years before—to the 500,000 mark.

Unfortunately, the refinery project was in difficulty from the start. Apparently under pressure from petroleum industry lobbyists, the Government of Canada changed its rules to exclude from tax-free status provincial Crown corporations that private interests had been given an option to purchase—in the case of Come by Chance, 15 years in the future, after Shaheen had paid off all its debts.

Next, two of the Smallwood government ministers who had negotiated details of the $200 million project agreement with Shaheen, Health Minister John C. Crosbie and Minister without Portfolio Clyde K. Wells, decided they would not go along with the advance of $5 million "bridge financing" against a government-guaranteed $30 million loan that Shaheen was to raise. They not only left the Cabinet but, sitting across the House of Assembly and joining in common cause with the Tory opposition, spearheaded an all-out attack on the government and on the project that they had, in effect, fathered.

(However, when time came for the House to finally decide, they did not vote against it.)

This could not have come at a worse time. A federal general election, Pierre Trudeau's first as Prime Minister and Leader of the Liberal Party, was only days away. There is little doubt the Come by Chance fiasco played a significant part in the outcome in Newfoundland. On June 25, 1968 the Liberals went into the election holding seven parliamentary seats and emerged with only one, Don Jamieson's in Burin-Burgeo.

Undaunted by delays and difficulties, Shaheen secured a contract with British Petroleum for a 10-year supply of crude oil, and take-or-pay contracts for the purchase of more than 70 per cent of the refinery's output. Then he obtained, at long last, from a reluctant federal government a commitment to build a wharf and docking facilities to cost $20 million which the project would repay. Most important of all, a British banking consortium having agreed to put up the major financing, in August 1970—five years almost to the day after the proposal was first advanced—a contract was signed with Procon Limited of Great Britain, a major engineering and construction firm. It would build the refinery itself for $155 million.

Procon arrived on the 330-acre site in Come by Chance early in 1971. By the time the government changed hands in the spring of 1972, with the Conservatives taking over, construction was well underway. In a speech to the St. John's Lions Club on February 10, 1972, Crosbie said the Moores government would likely permit the refinery project to continue—but it might take over the Stephenville linerboard mill.

On October 10, 1973 the world's most luxurious ocean liner, the 66,851-ton RMS *Queen Elizabeth 2*, steamed up Placentia Bay bringing some 1,000 international guests—who could not otherwise be accommodated in the tiny outport—to Come by Chance for the dedication of the refinery. Six weeks later it would be in production, having survived nearly a score of costly work stoppages on site that put completion back six months, and labour problems in Britain that delayed delivery of essential components.

The Moores government, which on the campaign trail had condemned the quest for major industry—the Premier proclaimed repeatedly that "the day of the billion-dollar project is over"—now reversed itself and came very much on side. Having already announced that a second refinery would be built on the site to produce 300,000 barrels a day, thus advancing Mr. Smallwood's original plan, the Premier was unstinting in his praise of Shaheen. In a letter that was made public Moores wrote:

"Congratulations to you and your staff … We are pleased with the excellent rapport that has characterized the relationship the personnel of Shaheen Natural Resources has with our government and we look forward to further co-operation in the construction and operation of your second refinery in Newfoundland."

Shaheen and his key people were experienced petroleum refiners. To ensure the soundness and the success of the project they selected well-known, reputable industry consultants, contractors and suppliers. However, incessant political attacks and industrial intrigues served to impair confidence and retard progress. Construction delays drained working capital, and following startup it was found key sections of the plant supposed to produce higher-value products were failing to operate to design specifications, reducing anticipated revenues significantly. Funds were unavailable for critical redesign and reconstruction. The operation was reported to be losing up to $10 million a month.

As if this were not enough, renewed troubles in the Middle East, source of the crude oil supply, led first to an embargo on 1973 deliveries to the U.S. (where Come by Chance product was mainly intended to sell) and then to huge price increases—several times the level of cost upon which Come by Chance was predicated. Its cumulative debts in the range of $500 million, a bankruptcy was inevitable, reputedly the biggest to that time in Canadian history.

Seven years later, following numerous efforts to reopen the refinery—among them several re-acquisition attempts by Shaheen—it was purchased in a fire-sale by Petro-Canada for $10 million with no obligation to operate, and promptly mothballed.

Shaheen died in New York on November 3, 1985 when he was 70 years old, and with him his dream of a core chemical complex, a paper mill and a great daily newspaper in New York.

The following year, with demolition looming, his refinery was sold for $1 to a Bermuda-based company, Newfoundland Energy Processing Ltd., owned by Cumberland Farms Inc., a large Massachusetts-based convenience-store chain. The plant was refurbished and got back in operation with some 200 people on the payroll nearly 15 years after the bankruptcy. In 1994 it was acquired by Vitol Holdings, a Texas-based world oil trader, and at this writing operates under the name North Atlantic Refining. It claims to employ more than 700 Newfoundlanders in the plant and external operations.

◆ ◆ ◆

In a column in *The Daily News* in early 1972 Mr. Smallwood wrote, "When all the hatred dies down … (John Christopher Doyle) will go down in history as one of the great industrial promoters in North America, and perhaps the greatest that Newfoundland has ever known."

This much is certain: no other person in all our long history produced a mining development, or perhaps any other, of the size and commercial importance of Wabush Mines, and a modern community in the Labrador wilderness to go along with it, and then turned around and launched a giant forest-based manufacturer, Javelin (Melville) Forest Products Ltd.—altogether worth perhaps a half-billion dollars of investment.

Wabush Mines, of course, is a great and continuing success. It may be argued that the industry that has turned the Stephenville area from a threatening poorhouse into perhaps the most prosperous, on balance, in the province, is a very different one from that which Doyle had in mind. But like Sir Richard Squires's "hum on the Humber" that went broke before it turned out a single roll of paper, and has changed hands no fewer than four times—from Newfoundland Power and Paper, which built it, to Armstrong Whitworth which seized it on a mechanic's lien, to International Pulp and Paper which sold it to Bowater's, to Krueger which operates it now—but remains the sparkplug of the Corner Brook economy, the mill on the shores of Bay St. George, despite its birthing pains, wouldn't be there if Doyle hadn't put it there.

And there are those like myself who, having known the tough and determined Doyle, believe that left to his own devices, he surely would have made it into a profitable enterprise or found a competent operator who would do so.

Ironically, Tory politicians who decried Mr. Smallwood securing an option on the Corner Brook mill, a well-established going concern, while seeking an operator to replace Bowater's who meant to withdraw, did not hesitate to wade into Doyle's unfinished project.

While negotiating to buy out his interest for a stated $5.1 million, and estimating the mill's finished cost at $130 million, the Moores government obtained House of Assembly approval in May 1972 to nationalize the industry, to be run by a Cabinet committee. Created as a Crown corporation to complete and operate the mill, Labrador Linerboard Limited was nonetheless set up in the manner of a private company, a most unusual arrangement. (Documentation in the Registry of Deeds and Companies dated December 31, 1974, but filed April 18, 1975, lists John C. Crosbie as chairman of the board, together with Cabinet ministers C. William Doody and Ed Maynard and company officials Howard E. Ingram (president) and Robert Kraft as directors. Total debt of the company was reported as $178,622,000.)

When construction was completed in 1973, the cost was reported to have swelled to $155.4 million, some $25 million over estimate. However, commercial production did not commence for still another year, the delay attributed to "initial production runs to iron out minor technical difficulties." Next the government complained of a recession in the industry resulting in excess capacity and weak prices—a claim hardly borne out by market reports—and in 1975 there were "serious labour problems" that forced a shutdown for 109 days.

In April 1979 the government disclosed that in operating the company for four years, it had had to cover losses of $142.3 million. A statement revealed that by March 31, 1978 the province had "guaranteed indebtedness or provided advances … in excess of $300 million," by far the biggest drain on Newfoundland's finances ever incurred in all our long history. Other sources put the losses close to a disastrous $450 million, all of it borrowed, and like the bill for nationalization of Churchill Falls, subject to annual debt charges, year after year after year. (Neither figure could be verified. Listed in the Registry of Deeds and Companies in the manner of a private company, Linerboard was never subjected to the scrutiny of the Auditor General.)

Shocking though it may have been, by the time the extent of the losses was revealed it had, at best, only historical value. The government announced that production at Labrador Linerboard Limited had officially been terminated as of August 26, 1977. On November 16, 1978 the company was sold for $43.5 million to Abitibi Paper Company which converted it to the manufacture of newsprint.

Whatever else may be said of Doyle—and it would be hard to find another in Newfoundland's often turbulent history of development politics who has been more vilified—he was not a man to do things in half-measures, or to be satisfied with less than the best. This applied equally to his taste for fine living, as to his selection of the designers (the Canadian firm E. & B. Cowan), and the builders (British Walmsleys/Sir Robert McAlpine) of the linerboard mill, probably the best in their fields in the world. He also had top managers, exceptionally experienced men, to run the mill and its critical woods operations in Labrador, respectively H.Y. Charbonnier, an executive with the big Union Camp Co. in the U.S., and Henri Geoffrion, a highly respected Canadian forester.

To provide reliable transportation of wood supplies to Stephenville he settled on the excellent U.K./Norwegian firm Tennax, and to market the linerboard product a European sales agent of international repute, Heintzel A.G. of Vienna, Austria.

The Moores Cabinet committee could not do much about the designers and builders chosen by Doyle. But they soon got rid of his plant and woodlands managers, cancelled the pulpwood shipping contract, and found a new but inexperienced sales agent. By the government's own admission these would turn out to be the areas in which the huge, unprecedented operating losses mainly occurred.

Interestingly, they kept the consulting engineers the Smallwood government had appointed to monitor construction and installation—and whose very existence Crosbie had so often denied, Donald D. Dick Limited of Toronto. They retained, as well, the original auditors, Peat, Marwick & Mitchell.

Amid charges of graft, corruption, waste and mismanagement sprinkled through the *Hansard* record of House of Assembly debates, the words of the new Premier in 1979, Brian Peckford—a minister in the Moores Cabinet from 1974, with no inkling of his own Sprung Greenhouse disaster to come—hit close to the truth:

"(The) mistake," he said, "was in government trying to run an industrial enterprise of that magnitude … given very little experience, and in running linerboard mills none at all …

"We started to lose money badly, the taxpayers of Newfoundland started having to pump twenty and thirty and forty million dollars a year into that enterprise. For whatever reasons, there was a lot of, I agree, inefficiency in the operation, not only at Stephenville but more particularly in Happy Valley-Goose Bay … (T)here was a lot of inefficiency in the system, no question."

As for Doyle, who died of leukemia in Panama City on May 31, 2000 at the age of 85, the so-called "evil genius" of scores, perhaps hundreds of media reports—as lurid and libellous as reporters chose to make them, safe in the knowledge he was indeed "a fugitive from justice" and could not easily strike back—never admitted to wrongdoing.

In 1963 in the U.S. he had pleaded guilty to a misdemeanour—the influential financial weekly *Barrons* referred to possibly "a short jail term for mail fraud"—namely sending unregistered stock in the mail, not an offence in this country. Apparently anticipating a fine, Doyle was taken aback when what came down was a three-month prison sentence. Claiming he had not been personally responsible for the breach of securities law, and unwilling to serve time while awaiting the outcome of an appeal, he jumped bail and headed for Canada, his other home.

Doyle had been born in Chicago, IL of Canadian parents, and served with the U.S. Army Engineers in North Africa, Sicily and Italy during the Second World War, rising to the rank of captain. He apparently had some responsibility for fuel supplies management in the Mediterranean theatre.

After the war he was involved with coal mining and marketing and invested in and became president of Canadian Javelin Foundries, a small manufacturing concern, in Joliette, PQ, just north of Montreal. Soon Javelin began buying up shares in Newfoundland and Labrador Corporation (NALCO), the former Crown development agency then being traded publicly. However, what Doyle intended—the takeover of NALCO—was frustrated when Javelin was de-listed by the Montreal and Toronto stock exchanges for alleged share manipulation.

On a plane to Newfoundland on a routine selling trip, Doyle's seat-mate was a government official who happened to mention that the Iron Ore Company of Canada had just handed back—the technical term is "shedding"—as of little value a large portion of the 10,000 square miles of territory to search for minerals granted to its predecessor, Labrador Mining and Exploration Company, by the Commission of Government.

Once in St. John's, the 37-year-old promoter headed straight to the Premier's office, and Mr. Smallwood recalled: "He came to ask me if his company, Canadian Javelin of Montreal, could have a mineral concession in Labrador … Doyle wanted a concession in Labrador? All right, see what he could make of the apparently useless Wabush Lake territory! I took the matter to Cabinet, we passed the necessary order, and Doyle went off with his concession of several thousand square miles of allegedly mineralized territory."

He made quite a lot of it, as it turned out—producing the $300 million dollar Wabush Mines development and the city of Wabush. And when the Iron Ore Company saw what Doyle was about, it followed suit and developed the neighbouring Carol Project with its support community, Labrador City. It might be only fair to give Doyle a little credit for that too: his coal industry background had provided an understanding that low-grade, pit-run ore of about 35 per cent iron content around Wabush Lake could be upgraded—the technical term is "beneficiated"—to around 70 per cent, then pelletized for easier shipping to steel mills in Canada and beyond.

Remarked the Premier, "It was a billion-dollar idea; and as far as I know, Doyle was for a time the only man in Labrador to think of it."

In time Doyle bought out NALCO. Writing in *The Evening Telegram* Harold Horwood, in his trenchant "Political Notebook" column, allowed: "(His) record suggests that he may not be the very best person to whom we could entrust virtually all our remaining mineral lands"—a columnist's hyperbole, surely!—"but on the other hand, Pickands Mather & Co. and the Steel Company of Canada have become associated with Mr. Doyle, and the Wabush Iron Co. has been formed, with Stelco as its main shareholder. This could mean that Canadian Javelin, after its dubious beginnings, is on its way to becoming both reliable and respectable ..."

In a further comment on Javelin's takeover of NALCO Horwood wrote: "(This) may be an excellent move. And Javelin would not be the first small company to rise, after doubtful beginnings, to a position of power and respectability in the mining world."

Wabush Mines became Javelin's main revenue source, a reliable cash cow producing to the tune of millions of dollars a year—more than enough to fuel a never-ending round of conflicts and schemes to gain or maintain control that kept Doyle and Javelin in the civil courts of Newfoundland and Quebec, and made lawyers rich.

Much more seriously, in December 1973 Doyle was arrested in Montreal, transferred by the RCMP to St. John's, and charged with defrauding Canadian Javelin of 49,000 shares worth $540,000, Javelin Forest Products of $2,000, and two counts of breach of trust involving a pair of vacant buildings in Stephenville, purchased as the sole bidder in response to a public tender case. Charged as co-defendant in the latter action was former Deputy Minister of Economic Development O.L.Vardy, alleged owner of a company, Engineering Services Limited, that was said to have received a kickback from the purchase.

But Vardy had already departed for Florida, never to return. Free on $75,000 bail but with his passport confiscated, Doyle languished in St. John's for a few weeks, then persuaded the courts to let him travel in Canada while reporting regularly to the RCMP. In the fall of 1974, his passport returned, he left for his second home, Panama City.

He did not go quietly, however, and for more than two decades carried on from afar a campaign against what he considered the corruption of the Newfoundland justice system by politicians. Operating from the penthouse suite of the El Panama Hotel, he doggedly fought off attacks by unfriendly Javelin shareholders and Canadian prosecutors while alleging that the Newfoundland department of Justice systematically interfered with his right to counsel by appointing no fewer than four of his defence lawyers in turn to positions as Crown prosecutors, of whom at least three later became judges. He was left no choice, he insisted, but to forfeit the $75,000 bail and leave Newfoundland for good.

"I did not feel I could receive justice there."

# CHAPTER 12

## HIS MONUMENTS ARE EVERYWHERE

> *"I became a Confederate when I discovered that (it) would give our people a half-decent chance in life...and remove some of the millstones that hung around their necks."*

Acknowledged as Britain's greatest architect, Sir Christopher Wren died on February 25, 1723 at the great age of 91 years. He had served as Surveyor General under five sovereigns, and was buried in St. Paul's Cathedral, London, his greatest work.

There, in Latin, his well-known epitaph is found: *Si monumentum requiris, circumspice*—which means, "If you seek his monument, look about you."

It is no exaggeration, and indeed highly appropriate, to say the same of Newfoundland's greatest political, social and economic architect who, like Wren, also lived to be nine years—less a few days—short of a century, Joseph Roberts Smallwood. His monuments are everywhere in the province—from the Trans Canada Highway and connecting roads that ended the ancient isolation of hundreds of communities, to Memorial University and scores of modern school and college buildings in every region, to the Health Sciences Centre and the Janeway Child Health Centre in St. John's and many regional hospitals, to the Memorial University Medical School, and the dozens of libraries and Arts and Culture Centres and recreation facilities that underpin the cultural life of Newfoundland and Labrador. There are, as well, the National and Provincial Parks that provide the opportunity for recreation and enjoyment for residents and visitors alike, and are the backbone of the tourist industry.

The population passed the half-million mark during his premiership, most in nearly 300 organized municipalities assisted to provide their citizens with the amenities of modern living—electricity, town planning, paved roads and streets, street lighting, water and sewer and garbage disposal systems, and firefighting and police services. That these things simply did not exist in the lifetimes of many Newfoundlanders still alive today, that their absence or non-existence was the norm, seems all but impossible. Then Mr. Smallwood came along and talked his fellow citizens into accepting a new form of democratic existence, with all the benefits Canadians had long enjoyed.

During the 23 years he held office, from 1949 to 1972, Newfoundland's first Premier laboured unceasingly at the self-imposed task of building virtually "from scratch" the broad infrastructure of Canada's newest province. The task was formidable.

In 1949, the population of only 340,000 lived in more than 1,300 settlements, and perhaps as many as 1,500, most of them, in his description, "cut off from each other, unconnected, unreachable, except for the ocean." Before the Second World War municipal government existed only in St. John's; by the time Newfoundland became a province a bare handful of communities had any semblance of local administration. For hundreds of them electric lights were still in the future.

At Confederation there were barely 100 miles of paved highways in the entire province, out of a total mileage of approximately 2,100, and the number of passenger cars and commercial vehicles was about 15,000. By the 1970s highway mileage was nearing 6,000, half of it paved, with vehicle registrations nearing 125,000—a veritable explosion!

Health care depended largely on a scattering of tiny cottage hospitals and a handful of rural physicians and public health nurses. It was not possible to acquire a university degree in medicine or anything else except by going "up to Canada," to the U.K., or to the "Boston States." The small few who did is sure testimony to the small few who could, mainly rich men's sons, or poor students sponsored by the church.

One of the first acts of the Smallwood government, announced in the Throne Speech opening the House of Assembly on July 13, 1949, was to ask the legislature to pass a law raising Memorial University College to the status of a degree-granting institution. Subsequently there were added Schools of Medicine, Nursing, Pharmacy, Engineering, Music, and in a regional college at Corner Brook, a School of Fine Arts. As registration grew towards 17,000, Memorial became "the largest university in Atlantic Canada" and many would say it stands as Mr. Smallwood's greatest achievement.

Construction of a network of district vocational schools ensured the availability of post-secondary education in the trades and technologies in every region of the province for the first time. It was complemented by the provision of dozens of new regional and central high schools; overall the number of schools more than doubled in the first 15 years to 1,250, the number of students went from 75,000 to 146,000, and the number of teachers from 2,500 to over 5,700. Spending on education soared: from $31.5 million in the entire 15 years of the Commission of Government, to $242.7 million in the first 15 years of Confederation.

Creation of the Medical School at Memorial University not only attracted scores of highly skilled specialists to the province to be teachers of new doctors, but as well, provided a broad range of specialist services to the people, services that could hardly become available otherwise. It reflected a central thrust of the Smallwood government's attack on the most serious of all the challenges it inherited, namely the poor health of the people, and especially the children.

At the end of the Second World War, which provided many thousands of adults with the unprecedented health and nutritional advantages of working on or living near well-supplied U.S. and Canadian military bases, the general health of Newfoundlanders had improved tremendously. The general death rate was now 10.4 per 1,000 of population compared to Canada's 9.4. But infant mortality remained among the highest in the world—73.8 for every 1,000 live births, versus Canada's 47.0. That grim statistic was enough and more to spur Mr. Smallwood to introduce a series of programs aimed specifically at improving children's health—and inferentially, their later health as adults—such as the Children's Health and Dental Plans.

Of course, children also benefited from general improvements in health care, including expansion of the cottage hospital system and subsequently, construction of new regional hospitals, provision of a fleet of medical boats to serve isolated coastal communities, air ambulances, development of mental health services, and unbelievable increases in the numbers of doctors, nurses and medical technologists. It culminated in a partnership with Ottawa: the Medical Care Program (MCP), also known as Medicare.

The picture would not be complete without reference to the ultimate success during the Smallwood years of the war on tuberculosis, eradication of such deadly afflictions as meningitis, diphtheria and polio, once of epidemic proportions, and the conclusion of the federal-provincial agreement that saw development of the Health Sciences Centre as the heart of health care and specialist referral in the province.

The spectacular success of the effort to improve people's health is reflected in the fact—crowning result and glory of the epic Confederation struggle—that in the Smallwood era there occurred rapid, comprehensive improvement in all aspects of health and health care to the result the average life expectancy of Newfoundlanders was raised from abysmally low levels—some estimates put it as low as 45 years—to be brought up to or near the Canadian average … and the population exploded to far exceed 500,000 residents. This, indeed, may be his greatest memorial!

In the two decades after union about 200 of the smallest isolated villages, many with a dozen families or less and not a few on completely isolated offshore islands, were assisted to relocate to places with easy access to schools, hospitals and in many cases jobs. The much-maligned Resettlement Program became an emotional platform from which to launch political attacks upon the Smallwood government—notwithstanding surveys showing most people who moved were glad they did, but about which a few poets and songwriters continue to romanticize today.

The truth is that relocation of people from isolated, ill-served and economically distressed communities to places that offered a better life for themselves and their children was and is nothing new to Newfoundland, Canada, or other lands. These, surely, were principal factors in the migration of our ancestors across the oceans to this place, and even within the Newfoundland context account for the growth and development of such modern communities as Corner Brook and Grand Falls, Gander and Marystown, Mount Pearl and Happy Valley-Goose Bay and Labrador City-Wabush, none of which existed as a major centre at the turn of the century or even much later.

My own forebears were part of this experience. Having arrived in the late 18th or early 19th Centuries from England and Ireland, on one side they relocated from the Northeast Coast to Conception Bay, and regularly "stationed" on the Labrador, later moving on to Grand Falls and Corner Brook in search of opportunities for a better life. Or, it was leave St. John's for work in the mines of Tilt Cove-Betts Cove, or the developing fisheries of the Southwest Coast.

A lot of moving around, and on its face hardly conducive to comfort and stability and the accumulation of family assets—but what choice if the stakes are a better job, a better education for the children, and better health care?

In 1939 William Bernard and Alice Marie Rogers Callahan decided that as a family, we were unlikely to find a better life than in Corner Brook. Accordingly, as the Second World War was breaking out, we left St. John's for the West Coast—first Petries Crossing, later Corner Brook West. But times were hard; three of their seven children did not survive childhood, and my father himself fell victim to the tuberculosis pandemic in 1945 at the young age of 44. A few years later my mother met and married another wonderful man, architect Michael J. Downey.

A skilled machinist, my father had travelled and worked in both Canada and the United States, and in the face of temporary layoffs at the Bowater's paper mill found employment in booming, wartime Gander and Argentia, and Louisburg, N.S. He was acquainted with Mr. Smallwood in cove meetings of St. John's unemployed in the 1930s, and they sometimes sharing a "makings" of Bugler tobacco. Each knew firsthand the wrenching family hardship occasioned by lack of a steady job, and the future Premier became determined to see to it that his fellow Newfoundlanders fared much better. Not for him the attitude that it is not government's task to find people work!

Concerning resettlement, if there was a difference in the Smallwood era—and history must recognize a huge difference—it was that in the 1960s and 1970s people moved with government assistance and support. They were enabled to relocate to places of considerable permanency, where government had begun to provide a level of town planning, hydro, water and sewerage, roads, schools, and hospitals or access to them, and as far as it could do, new and expanded employment opportunities.

Mr. Smallwood realized, perhaps better than anyone, that Newfoundland would never be able on its own to provide its citizens with social safety nets comparable to those Canadians enjoyed—unemployment insurance, family allowances, decent pensions for the elderly, and a reasonable level of social assistance for thousands of families who, with the war over, were or soon again would be staring poverty in the face. There was but one alternative, and that was to become part of Canada.

Confederation came, and the number of occupied communities in the new province declined as scores of isolated hamlets were abandoned. At the same time, the number of places persuaded to organize into city, town, community and rural district councils ballooned. Under the Smallwood government's direction, town planning became the norm with introduction of the Urban and Rural Planning Act. Serious and successful attempts were made to correct higgledy-piggledy development, and new, modern subdivisions to rival the best in North America began to spring up. Establishment of the St. John's Metropolitan Area Board and amalgamation of four towns to create the city of Corner Brook were important milestones in the development of forward-looking local government.

While streets were paved and lighted, water and sewerage installed, garbage disposal instituted and volunteer fire departments set up and equipped, the province's first Premier was seized by something even more fundamental: This was the urgent need to spur economic development—"to make two blades of grass to grow where one grew before." And of course, to employ Newfoundlanders doing it.

This was his principal dedication, just as his worst nightmare was that once Confederation opened wide the doors to Canada, large-scale depopulation would occur as Newfoundland's people, and especially its young people, moved away looking for work they could not find at home.

Hence the slogan—uniquely Smallwoodian, and admittedly politically risky—of "Develop or Perish":

"I worried about the danger of losing our population. I knew, even before Confederation Day, that somehow I had to inspire the Newfoundland people with new faith in their prospects. I had to persuade them that Newfoundland was a place with a bright future; a place to stay in; a place ... (to) get married, raise a family, and enjoy a good life—that there was no need to go rushing off to Toronto ...

"But we had to develop. We had to develop our resources. We had to develop everything we had in Newfoundland and Labrador. The price of failure would be disaster ..."

How well he succeeded is clearly illustrated—briefly noted earlier—in the fact that during the years he was in office, the Newfoundland population (instead of suffering the massive decline that he feared and strove to avoid) in fact increased from 340,000 to well in excess of a half-million, in 1971 standing at 522,102, to be precise.

Critics of his development efforts care to remember, and ridicule, a plant to manufacture rubber boots (plus a range of other products) that should have been a "natural" in a place whose main industry was the fisheries, and a candy factory whose confections were in fact of excellent quality. Unfortunately, neither could compete with established big-name brands.

But there was much more—investment, as well, from the Commission of Government's surplus, in factories that would manufacture most of the Portland cement and fire-retardant gypsum wallboard used in the province's huge post-Confederation building boom, and continued five decades later. There was a plant to make birch-veneer and plywood, and another to make birch flooring from the province's underutilized hardwood stands; a plant to make particle board; a boot and shoe factory that prospers in a 21st Century reincarnation; together with a tannery, plants to manufacture leather goods and clothing and knitted goods, each unfortunately with a foreshortened lifespan; and an automotive battery factory that was only temporarily a success.

Two wartime plants constructed at Clarenville by U.S. interests, one to manufacture asphalt for road paving and another to treat rail ties, utility poles and wharf piles, had closed. The government acquired and successfully reactivated them.

More than two decades after the New Industries Program was launched Mr. Smallwood, now retired, reported that nine of the original 20 plants were operating as they did when first started up, two had converted to a different kind of production, and "strenuous efforts" were being made to give new life to another.

Looking at it from "a narrow, orthodox, private enterprise, balance-sheet point of view, over half of them have been losers," he admitted, but "the fact is that from the province's point of view they have, taken as a whole, been a profit-maker." Substantially more had gone back into the economy in wages and other disbursements than the government invested, and a lot more would—and this even before the costs of unemployment, both fiscal and human, had been calculated.

The Premier's overriding attention to the economy, to the pressing need for industrial development as if little else mattered, did not by any means end with the New Industries Program. To the contrary, he continued literally to scour the globe in the search of industries to employ Newfoundlanders, contribute to government revenues, and stave off the ultimate failure and tragedy of large-scale depopulation.

Hand in hand with meeting the need of hundreds of communities that still depended on the kerosene lamp, Mr. Smallwood had seen the impossibility of acquiring modern industrial development, or development of any kind, without large-scale provision of electrical energy. This led him to creation of the Newfoundland Power Commission, forerunner of today's Newfoundland and Labrador Hydro Corporation, which undertook the Bay d'Espoir hydroelectric development and various lesser projects which remain the mainstay of domestic and industrial energy supply. It built the backup oil-fired thermal generating station at Holyrood, created the standardized 60-cycle provincial electrical power grid, and eventually would assume ownership and control of the Churchill Falls (Labrador) Corporation.

Among its innumerable social and industrial benefits, principally the extension of electricity to the communities of rural Newfoundland and Labrador, energy development permitted wholesale transformation of the fish-processing industry from a largely salt-fish base to the range of fresh-frozen products the markets now demanded. In direct contradiction to charges that his government wrote off the fisheries, favouring instead heavy industrialization—the spurious "burn your boats" accusation—major emphasis was placed on modernization of the ancient industry. Assisted by the newly created Fisheries Loan Board and the work of the Fisheries Development Authority, well-equipped inshore and near-shore harvesters delivered their catch to modern processing plants provided with direct government support in the tens of millions of dollars.

Many of the new steel deep-sea vessels that enabled mainly southern plants to operate year-round were constructed in the purpose-built Marystown Shipyard, like the Bay d'Espoir hydroelectric generating station an outcome of the Smallwood-appointed South Coast Royal Commission. At the same time, in a score of smaller yards and marine haulouts established around the province, the inshore and near-shore fisheries saw creation of a fleet of hundreds of multipurpose vessels and longliners, with safe places to maintain and store them.

Reference must be made to Director General of Economic Development Alfred Valdmanis, recommended to Mr. Smallwood by no less than officials in the office of Government of Canada economic czar Industry Minister C.D. Howe, perhaps even the great man himself. Valdmanis, who sought to line his pockets while ostensibly negotiating for new industries for Newfoundland, wound up in prison for four years for fraud. Subsequently, having served his time, he moved to Western Canada where he met his death in a highway smash-up.

The Valdmanis bombshell in 1954 (he personally turned in the multi-talented Latvian to the RCMP) "was a shattering experience," the Premier admitted.

"I confess that I felt bitter (towards him) … I had defended and praised him (and) went so far as to say that I wouldn't want to continue to be Premier without him …"

But continue he did … for nearly another two decades.

◆　◆　◆

Perhaps some media wag came up with it—the idea of combining the initial letters of the Corner Brook firm of Lundrigans Limited together with the surname initials of John M. Shaheen and John C. Doyle to create a rather derisive acronym, "the LSD boys." The purpose, presumably, was to invoke an unsavoury image suggestive of the most popular, yet most dangerous, hallucinogenic of the era.

Opponents and critics of the Smallwood government may even have believed that, somehow, it reflected discredit on the administration, and perhaps in some minor degree it did. (It failed, however, to take into account the other chief partner in Mr. Smallwood's province-building efforts, the Crosbie Group of Companies.)

Taken together these firms, working in collaboration with the government, created economic activity of staggering proportions—building mills and mines and refineries, fish plants, shipyards, public buildings, schools and colleges, hospitals and highways, one of the nation's largest universities, even a major Canadian airline. They may never have sat down together to plan the dimensions of it, but what they accomplished came about in a much shorter time frame than any other agglomeration in the province's history, before or since, might have hoped to do.

At one point, the Premier calculated that he had taken "an energetic part"—profound understatement!—in getting some $4 billion in industrial capital invested in the province. He included a half-billion in electrical development and fisheries, as much again in oil, and a billion dollars each in mining and Brinco. At that point he counted some 97,000 jobs that did not exist before, "new jobs … the creation of which, directly or indirectly" resulted from his government's policies. On closer analysis and some years later this was revised upward to138,000, including 25,000 "multiplier" jobs.

Looking back over it all in later years, Mr. Smallwood acknowledged both failures and successes during his more than two decades of striving to build up the new province, and rendered this judgment:

"Some of these accomplishments of Confederation are very great, but ... the greatest is the disappearance forever of the old benumbing sense of inferiority that had Newfoundlanders in its grip for so long. We have a new sense of pride and confidence.

"Bigness of concept frightens us no longer ... Newfoundlanders now demand, and will never again be willing to do without, constant, unending development and advance.

"I tried, in the long years before Confederation, to propagandize our people into that frame of mind, that habit of thought; but never did I think that I would live to see it become a fact of life in Newfoundland.

"And this is Confederation's greatest glory."

## JOEY'S "OTHER PUBLIC LIFE"

The story of Joey Smallwood's "other public life ... not his term as the radio Barrelman, or his career as a journalist, or his stints as a labour organizer, but his exciting 30 years domination of the public policy debates of the Methodist College Literary Institute" was detailed in a letter I received from my old friend F. Burnham "Burn" Gill in December 1991. (The MCLI was, of course the leading public forum and platform for thrashing out issues of Newfoundland national importance, especially during the period while the democratically elected House of Assembly was silenced by the Commission of Government dictatorship between 1934 and 1949.)

The retired Provincial Archivist and long-time journalist and his wife Mary were spending the Christmas holiday period in Naples, Fla. with their daughter and her husband, Elinor and Edward Ratcliffe, when "the sad news was received that the former Premier and my good friend had passed away."

Gill went on: "Despite the fact that I knew before leaving home that his condition had worsened and he was nearing the end, I felt a certain emptiness within over the demise of this great man whom I had known and respected for so many years."

Gill examined the records of the MCLI, "that great cultural organization where so many prominent citizens ... assembled on one evening a week to debate important topics of the times.

"(The) Institute spawned many leading politicians and prominent businessmen. I mention the names of Winter, Outerbridge, Currie, Curtis, Hickman, Bennett, Soper, Herder, Pratt, Peters, Carew, and many others who comprised the social Who's Who of the city.

"And of course there was Joey Smallwood, the great debater. The records show that from 1919 when he was just 19 years of age, to 1959, when he was not out of town or out of the Island, Joey was in there for every debate, taking on premiers and other politicians and businessmen and usually ending up on the winning side."

Gill found in the minutes of the MCLI meeting of February 6, 1919 the notation that "young Smallwood, not long out of Bishop Feild College, had applied for membership. He was confirmed and signed the roll on February 13 along with William Howell, George F. Taylor and Graham Freeman." At the same time, he joined C. Bowden on the Committee of the Methodist College Home.

The retired Provincial Archivist referenced many debates in which Joey played a "very active role" and made a list of "some of the more important topics that were debated" during the first years of his MCLI membership, giving the names of participants:

**January 6, 1921. "That the fishery regulations have been an unjustifiable restriction of trade."** Affirmative, Capt. A. Kean, Capt. George Whiteley, E.F. Peters. Negative, R.F. Horwood, William White, J.R. Smallwood. Won by Negative.

**January 13, 1921. "That the United States was justified in rejecting the Treaty of Versailles and in refusing to join the United Nations."** Affirmative, W.H. Jones, Ray Gushue, J.R. Smallwood. Negative, I.C. Morris, G. Bursey, G. Freeman. Won by Negative.

**February 10, 1921. "That the adoption of the Referendum and the Recall in Newfoundland would result in better government."** Affirmative, A.E. Parkins, J.R Smallwood, A.E. Hayward. Negative, J.A.W. McNielly, S.R. Penney, J. Moore. Won by Negative.

**January 26, 1922.** "That the nationalization of the fishery of this country is both feasible and advisable." Affirmative, George Soper, J.R. Smallwood, A. Pelley. Negative, William Drover, C. Bowden, F. Moore. Won by Negative.

**February 23, 1922.** "That women be admitted to ordination in the Methodist Church." Affirmative, A.W. Mews, J.R. Smallwood, G. Giles. Negative, Rev. T.B. Darby, A. Soper, William White. Won by Affirmative.

**March 30, 1922.** "That adequate food supplies for her population can be produced in Newfoundland." Affirmative, A.E. Parkins, R. Herder, J.R. Smallwood. Negative, Richard Cramm, J. Moore, W.H. Peters. Won by Affirmative 13-4.

Gill reported that on April 13, 1922 John Puddester and J.R. Smallwood were commended for the excellence of their report on the 1921 activities of the MCLI, and despite his busy life as a journalist in Newfoundland, Canada, the United States and England, his activities as a union organizer and his early years in politics, Joey always found time to attend the MCLI when in St. John's. The records show that during the period 1923 to 1959 he took part in more than 60 debates.

Some of the topics debated during those years—not a few "obviously thought out in the keen Smallwood brain"—included: "That labour's rooted suspicion of the employing class is historically justified" ... **"That all goods imported into Newfoundland be subject to duty"** ... **"That the 1926 Alcoholic Liquors Act is inadequate"** ... "That the resources of **Newfoundland lie more in the land than in the sea"** ... "That advertising is an economic **waste"** ... **"That Britain's industrial life is imperiled by the demands of labour for larger wages and shorter hours"** ...

(Gill notes that Joey's Negative team defeated this latter motion.)

In 1932 the Smallwood team defeated the motion **"That capitalism is sound in principle"** and won the argument **"That co-operation has contributed more to human welfare than has competition."**

It is clear, Gill concluded, that Mr. Smallwood not only persuaded the MCLI to debate topics that would permit him to expound his own philosophy, "but in a master stroke of near-genius manoeuvred leading citizens of the time into participating with him and many others—prominent politicians, and other high-ranking members of the community—into listening to him speak for hours at a time.

"Strange to say, even though many of them disagreed strongly with him, they nonetheless came back to hear him, week after week, month after month, and year after year."

As a member of the MCLI executive, according to Gill, Mr. Smallwood also made his voice heard in the management and general administration of the organization.

"Once he opposed the expenditure of $100 for the purchase and installation of curtains on the windows of the meeting place at Pitts Memorial Hall. He suggested that the sun be permitted to pour in and some way should be found to trap the energy and put it to useful purposes. He was dead-on—but some years ahead of his time."

Gill remarks that during the first years of Commission of Government it was quite apparent that Newfoundland was being subtly prepared for the Second World War, the proposal for the airport at Gander being the most obvious sign. It was during this period, in 1935, that Mr. Smallwood was on the losing side debating the topic **"That pacifism is unjustifiable"** against a Negative team led by his lifelong friend, N.C. Crewe, just as in 1940 friendship played no part as another friend and mentor, former prime minister Sir Richard Squires, emerged the victor on the Smallwood resolution **"That private profit should be abolished."**

Mr. Smallwood had an opportunity to vent his dislike for the Commission system of government, debating the issue **"Dictatorship or Democracy."** It became, the records note, "a speech ... a brilliant lecture (after which he) replied to questions put to him."

There is a certain irony in the future "Barrelman" arguing—and winning—the resolution **"That this House approves the proposals outlined by the Commissioner for Finance for broadcasting in Newfoundland"** which in time would bring him success as a radio personality ... and in the future Premier, who would build the Trans Canada Highway, losing to a team led by H.J. Russell, the general manager of the Newfoundland Railway and father of a future Lieutenant-Governor, on the proposition **"That the construction of a highroad from St. John's to Port aux Basques ... would be of substantial benefit to Newfoundland."**

Commented Gill, "We now know that in real terms, Mr. Smallwood eventually won that argument—and sadly, Mr. Russell's railway is no longer with us."

As well, there is an element of the prophetic in a brief record of a meeting of the MCLI on March 31, 1947 which reads: "Pitts Memorial Hall debate ... **"Newfoundland should federate with Canada"** ... Affirmative, J.R. Smallwood, H.B. Snelgrove, R.W. Bartlett ... Negative, E.G. White, D.W.K. Dawe, P. Forsey. The Affirmative won both votes."

"Some people might argue," Gill noted, "that given the political atmosphere at the time, the slate of debaters contained little or no opposition to the topic."

Put another way it seems, at least in retrospect, that both sides of the debate were laced with Confederates!

JOSEPH ROBERTS
# SMALLWOOD

JOURNALIST, PREMIER,
NEWFOUNDLAND PATRIOT

# PART TWO

## THE WORK OF BUILDING
## A PROVINCE

# CHAPTER 13

## THE GREATEST GIFT UNDER GOD

Members of the National Convention elected in 1946: First row - Capt. W.G. Warren, Secretary, Joseph Fowler, F.J. Ryan, Assistant Secretary, Prof. Wheare, Technical Advisor, K.M. Brown, Mr. Justice C.J. Fox, Chairman, J.R. Smallwood, Rev.L.L. Burry, A. Watton, F.G. Bradley, I. Newell, M.F. Harrington; Second row - C.A. Crosbie, E.C. Cranford, C.H. Ballam, E.L. Hickman, T.G.W. Ashbourne, R.B. Job, R.G. Stokes, M.J. McCarthy, W.P. Crummey, C.G. Jones, A.E. Penny, J.A. Hannon, A.B. Butt; Third row - K.M. MacDonald, M.L. Hollett, R.T. Vardy, C.L. Bailey, J.T. Spencer, J.J. MacCormack, D.L. Ryan, W.J. Keough, F.D.F. Fogwill, E.P. Reddy, L.J. Miller; Fourth row - E.L. Roberts, P. Figary, D.I. Jackman, G.F. Higgins, D. Hillier, W.J. Banfield, W. Dawe, P. Fudge, A. Northcott, A.J. Goodridge, Maj.P.J. Cashin, S.F. Vincent, T. Kennedy (MA).

# Newfoundland Confederate Association

## Head Office: Lyon Building, 158 Water St., St. John's

### OFFICERS

#### PRESIDENT
F. GORDON BRADLEY, K.C., LL.B. (Bonavista)

#### VICE-PRESIDENTS

| | |
|---|---|
| Claude E. Dawe | St. John's |
| J. M. Duggan | St. John's |
| Michael A. Foley | St. John's |
| William J. Frampton | St. John's |
| S. J. Hefferton | St. John's |
| J. S. Kelley | St. John's |
| Capt. Bert King | St. John's |
| Dr. William Roberts | St. John's |
| F. W. Rowe, B.A. | St. John's |
| Dr. S. P. Whiteway | St. John's |
| Stanley Sullivan | Pouch Cove |
| Max V. Hutchings | Bell Island |
| Bernard Downey | Bell Island |
| Nathaniel Mugford | Port de Grave |
| Ernest Lear | Hibbs' Cove |
| George Mackinson | Clarke's Beach |
| A. A. Keefe | Coley's Point |
| Capt. Leonard T. Stick | Bay Roberts |
| James Holmes | Shearstown |
| Solomon Gosse, J.P. | Spaniard's Bay |
| William Clarke | Victoria |
| George Thoms | Freshwater |
| Jesse Butt | Western Bay |
| Edgar B. Case | Lower Island Cove |
| Enos Benson | Grates Cove |
| John Noah Barrett | Old Perlican |
| Lewis N. Piercey | Winterton |
| James Callahan | New Perlican |
| Evan Pugh | Heart's Content |
| A. W. Smith | Markland |
| Solomon Drodge | Little Heart's Ease |
| Capt. George Dalton | Little Catalina |
| William Davis | Musgravetown |
| Hfbert Davis | Port Blandford |

#### VICE-PRESIDENTS

| | |
|---|---|
| I. T. Samson | Sandringham |
| Capt. James Blackwood | Glovertown |
| Thomas Goulding | Dark Cove |
| John Robertson | Gander |
| Capt. Peter W. Carter | Greenspond |
| Capt. Charles Downer | Greenspond |
| Capt. Chesley Dyke | Pool's Island |
| Capt. Herbert Bown | Badger's Quay |
| Capt. Garland Gaulton | Brookfield |
| Capt. Thomas Wimsor | Wesleyville |
| Capt. Harry Andrews | Wesleyville |
| S. F. Vincent | Pound Cove |
| Capt. Charles Dowling | Pound Cove |
| Capt. George Melendy | Templeman |
| Capt. Joseph Parsons | Newtown |
| Capt. Alex Perry | Newtown |
| Bert Vincent | Pinchard's Island |
| Cecil Hann, J.P. | Cape Island |
| Garfield Parsons | Cape Freels |
| Alfred Robbins | Lumsden |
| Andrew G. Toope | Lumsden |
| Archibald Mills | Joe Batt's Arm |
| Thomas G. W. Ashbourne | Herring Neck |
| Capt. John White | Twillingate |
| John Walker | Twillingate |
| Philip J. Ryan | Point Leamington |
| Frank I. Robertson | Grand Falls |
| Capt. W. J. Pittman | Buchans |
| Capt. Peter Parsons | Pilley's Island |
| Jacob Churchill | Lush's Bight |
| Capt. J. H. Wiseman | Springdale |
| William Rowsell | Little Bay Islands |
| J. R. Bartlett | Rattling Brook |
| R. G. Starkes | Burlington |
| | Nipper's Hr. |

#### VICE-PRESIDENTS

| | |
|---|---|
| Bert Thoms | LaScie |
| Leander Rowsell | Englee |
| Horace M. McNeill | St. Anthony |
| Samuel D. Grant | Battle Hr. |
| Henry Genge | Flower's Cove |
| A. S. Darby | Port aux Choix |
| Austin House | Bellburns |
| Edgar L. Roberts | Bonne Bay |
| Henry N. Payne | Cow Head |
| John J. St. George | Deer Lake |
| Harry Oxford | Corner Brook |
| Baxter Fudge | Corner Brook |
| F. G. Matthews | Corner Brook |
| Charles H. Ballam | Curling |
| Kevin J. Barry, LL.B. | Curling |
| Percy Figary | Port aux Basques |
| Aidan Maloney | Ramea |
| John T. Spencer | Head D'Espoir |
| Alan Jensen | Belleoram |
| William J. Banfield | Bay L'Argent |
| Capt. Eli Antney | Garnish |
| Howard Patten | Grand Bank |
| Fred. M. Tessier | Grand Bank |
| Aubrey Lake | Fortune |
| Daniel Hillier | Lamaline |
| Arch Edwards | Lawn |
| Frederick J. Edwards | Lawn |
| Philip Slaney | St. Lawrence |
| Frank J. Brenton | Burin |
| Thomas F. Murley | Marystown |
| F. W. Diamond | Flat Islands, P.B. |
| Ernest Stacey | Sound Island |
| Gerald Healey | Argentia |
| Carl Hollett | Jersey Side |

### Teachers' Advisory Committee
Frederick Kirby, Chairman

Woodrow Hunt
T. J. Serjeant
Raymond Curnew
William Porter
Roy Saunders
Philip Forsey
Byron March
J. R. Courage

### Labour Advisory Committee
Harold Horwood, Chairman

Bernard Saunders
Clarence Hardie
Irving Fogwill
William Jenkins
John J. Lewis
Gregory J. Power
Frank J. Brenton

### Veterans' Advisory Committee
C. F. Garland, Chairman

James McGrath

George Cooper

#### FINANCIAL SECRETARY-TREASURER
C. F. GARLAND

#### GENERAL SECRETARY
J. R. SMALLWOOD (Pro Tem.)

#### CAMPAIGN DIRECTOR
J. R. SMALLWOOD
GREGORY J. POWER (Asst.)

*Enroll now! Take your place in this People's Crusade for a better Newfoundland*

This advertisement inserted for by a Newfoundlander who believes in Confederation

*Mark Your X For The One in the Middle* CONFEDERATION

# THE CONFEDERATE

*Mark Your X For The One in the Middle* CONFEDERATION

Vol. 1     Published weekly by Newfoundland Confederate Association, 118 Water Street, St. John's, Newfoundland, Monday, May 31, 1948     No. 8

# WATCH FOR A LANDSLIDE!

## CONFEDERATION IS SWEEPING THE COUNTRY

### BRADLEY AND SMALLWOOD GIVEN GREAT RECEPTION

Grand Falls, Windsor, Bishop's Falls and Botwood gave Confederation a wonderful welcome last week.

So did Corner Brook, Humbermouth, Curling, Buchans, Twillingate and Change Islands.

The plane taxied up to Ashbourne's wharf, which was gaily decorated with flags and bunting. A big crowd was gathered on the wharf and cheered Mr. Smallwood as he stepped ashore.

Mr Ashbourne greeted him and Mr. Vincent, and the group then drove by motor-car to the centre of the town, where the whole population had gathered. There was a thunder of cheering, and the gunfire became louder

### Let Us Settle It Now!

Do you want another referendum to be held after the one on June 3rd?

Do you want another big political campaign after this one?

Do you want another National Convention 3 or 4 years from now?

### A QUEER FISHERMAN!

## NATIONAL CONVENTION

## SMALLWOOD RESOLUTION

### To Send a Delegation to Ottawa

Resolved that the National Convention desires to send a delegation consisting of the Chairman and six other of its members to Ottawa to ascertain from the Government of Canada what fair and equitable basis may exist for federal union of Newfoundland and Canada; and

Resolved that the National Convention requests His Excellency the Governor in Commission to ascertain whether the Government of Canada receive such a delegation for the purpose stated; and

Resolved that should the Government of Canada be willing to receive such a delegation, then the said delegation shall be elected forthwith by secret ballot, and shall proceed to Ottawa so soon as possible after the Convention shall have received from His Majesty's Government in the United Kingdom that Government's replies to the questions adopted by the Convention pursuant to Mr. Hickman's resolution of even date, but not before.

Smallwood.

Feb. 28/47

"Confederation with Canada," Premier Joseph R. Smallwood never tired of proclaiming, during 23 years at the helm of Newfoundland's government and ever afterwards, "is the greatest gift under God ever bestowed on our people … the greatest single event that has happened to us since our Island was discovered" in the distant past.

"One casts one's mind over the five centuries of our recorded history and finds nothing so great. Nothing, that is, that was particularly Newfoundland in character."

While two World Wars were huge events in the world, and had far-reaching effects on Newfoundlanders as on all peoples, Confederation "reached deep into the life of every Newfoundlander, young and old, then and now … as no other event has ever done, he wrote in the *Book of Newfoundland*.

"It stopped our history dead in its tracks, and set it on an altogether different course." Indeed, it was "a revolution"—no mere palace revolt, street insurrection or squalid riot that would be over in an hour or a week—"that so far from showing signs of subsiding (was) actually gathering momentum even more now than at its outbreak."

The Premier continued: "The biggest thing to happen to us since the coming of Confederation is the emergence of Labrador, and its recognition as the greatest storehouse of undeveloped natural wealth on the North American Continent.

"Churchill Falls, Upper and Lower, with its 10,000,000 horsepower of hydroelectric power now being 'bridled,' as Sir Winston Churchill wanted it to be, is only the first of a number of great potential sources of power in Labrador, and power is only one of the many huge natural resource on the Peninsula.

"Every particle of greatness in our people is challenged by the opportunity and call of Labrador, and if we are worthy of our destiny we will build a brilliant future there."

In the meantime, no part of North America could equal "the incredible acceleration in the tempo that we have seen, and continue to see, in education progress. We have built a thousand new schools, a new University, a new College of Fisheries, and eleven magnificent Vocational Training Schools. A month before Confederation we had only fifty-seven teachers with degrees. Today you find more teachers than that with degrees in any one of fifty schools."

Best of all, perhaps, Newfoundlanders' historic isolation—"the curse of curses"—was ended.

"In 1,300 little coastal settlements we lived, cut off from each other, unconnected, unreachable except by the ocean. Newfoundlanders didn't know each other; they never met. Many of them were foreigners to each other; to the people of the Southwest Coast, Newfoundlanders along the Northeast Coast might just as well have lived in Finland for all the people of the south knew about them, and vice versa.

"How could there be a Newfoundland spirit? How could the hearts of Newfoundlanders beat in unison on anything? How could anything more than a purely local patriotism develop?"

All this, Mr. Smallwood declared, was swept away with the coming of Confederation and the building or rebuilding of more than 4,000 miles of roads that Confederation made possible.

"Six hundred settlements have been connected by road to the main road system of the Island, and 200 more of them have closed down as the people were encouraged and helped to move to larger places.

"Miracle of miracles," he exulted, then approaching two decades in office, "you can drive now from Trepassey to St. Anthony, from St. Anthony to Port aux Basques, from Port aux Basques to Bonavista, from Bonavista to Lamaline. There are only two or three places in the whole of Green Bay not connected by road."

And on top of all that, diseases that had "racked our people" had been brought under "normal control."

New hospitals had sprung up, and continued to spring up all over the province, with the new Janeway Child Health Centre, in Mr. Smallwood's words, "one of Canada's best." Still to come under his direction were the Medical School of Memorial University, and the ultramodern Health Sciences Centre in St. John's for which the funding agreement with Ottawa was negotiated while he was still in power.

"These are breathtaking changes indeed," the province's first Premier declared.

## "MY HEART ALMOST STOPPED ..."

For Joey Smallwood, what would develop into the greatest challenge of his lifetime appeared with breathtaking suddenness—and not in Newfoundland, but in Montreal, Quebec as he was on the way home to Newfoundland from a business trip to Ontario.

The former journalist, author and broadcaster, in Canada "looking at some pig farms," was heading for Gander where he operated a large hog-raising establishment, in conjunction with the Royal Air Force. It was 8:00 A.M. on December 12, 1945 when he stepped down from the overnight train from Toronto, and made his way to the Ford Hotel on Dorchester Street. He registered, sent up his suitcase, and made for the dining room.

And that's when it happened. As the waitress took the breakfast order, he picked up his copy of the *Montreal Gazette*: "My heart almost stopped when I saw the headlines. They had to do with Newfoundland, and few Newfoundlanders away from home can ever see without excitement any reference to their Island home ... and these headlines were sensational indeed!"

The newspaper story originated in London, England. It proclaimed, "SELF-RULE IS PLAN IN NEWFOUNDLAND: Colony Soon to Have Own Government After 12 Years of Commission."

It would not be quite as simple or straightforward a proposition as might have seemed the case, based upon the news report from Reuters, which tended to suggest that the country was "set back on the path leading to self-government." But the British government had signalled commencement of a process by which it was ready to permit Newfoundlanders to "elect a National Convention (to make) recommendations as to the possible forms of future government which will be submitted to the people ... at a subsequent referendum."

It was enough, and more than enough, to set Mr. Smallwood's mind racing.

"The news that so many of us wanted," he recalled, "came now with complete unexpectedness and in complete surprise. I do not imagine that even one Newfoundlander (unless it chanced to be the Newfoundland members of the Commission of Government who might have been given a few hours' notice by the British government) had the slightest whisper of the news before it broke upon the world ...

"After reading and re-reading the news from London I ate very little breakfast, but got up and went out onto the street. I walked the streets of that part of Montreal for a large part of the day (and) my thoughts began to take firm shape."

He knew there was widespread respect in the outports for the Commission of Government which people felt was "the best government that they had ever known." At the same time, there was precious little desire for a return to Responsible Government, which had been officially condemned as corrupt and incompetent by the Amulree Royal Commission.

Yet for all that, Mr. Smallwood considered it "unthinkable" that the people of Newfoundland should continue much longer under the unelected Commission system which "left them voiceless in their own land." So if not Responsible Government, and not continuation of Commission of Government, then what?

"The thing became crystal clear before the day was over: Confederation with Canada. I was not a Confederate. To that moment I would have counted myself as an anti-Confederate, though not a violent one or even a very confident one.

"The simple truth is, I didn't know what Confederation was. I didn't understand it or how it worked ... The result of this 'soul-searching' that day in Montreal was a decision to keep the promise I had made to Gordon Bradley and to myself: I would find out what the Confederation thing was all about. That night I sought out a fellow Newfoundlander, Ewart Young, a journalist. I found that he was already a convinced Confederate, and we talked until past midnight."

Mr. Smallwood returned to Gander, which would become the *de facto* birthplace of the Confederation movement. He decided he would offer himself as a candidate for election to the National Convention, while continuing to gather information on the Canadian system of government. That process included writing letters to prominent persons, beginning with "The Prime Minister of Canada, Ottawa, Canada."

Gradually, the sought-after information accumulated "... and the thing began to take shape in my mind. I began to understand what Confederation was, and how it worked."

And in the end to conclude that, as old friend Gordon Bradley had frequently argued, becoming part of Canada's Confederation was Newfoundland's "only hope, our only salvation!"

Getting into pig-farming in Gander in partnership with the R.A.F. was a most fortunate thing for Mr. Smallwood and for Newfoundland. He would have had little chance of being elected to the National Convention as a known Confederate in St. John's. But Bonavista Centre—which included both the area of Gander where he was now resident, and Gambo, his birthplace—was another matter entirely. The rules for the election required that candidates seek election in the place they ordinarily lived.

"We might or might not be a province of Canada today had not (R.A.F. Group Capt. David) Anderson insisted on my living in Gander, or had the Commission of Government not inserted the residence qualification ... Gander itself was to be the birthplace of the drive to unite Newfoundland and Canada as one country."

The election of the 45 members was held on June 21, 1946 with Mr. Smallwood winning a "comfortable" 89 per cent majority, 2,129 votes to 277 for his opponent, Kitchener Pritchett. It was the largest majority of any of the members, whose task was to assist the people of Newfoundland to arrive at "a free and informed decision as to their future form of government."

Their Terms of Reference were succinctly stated:

> "To consider and discuss amongst themselves as elected representatives of the Newfoundland people the changes that have taken place in the financial and economic situation of the Island since 1934, and bearing in mind the extent to which high revenues of recent years have been due to wartime conditions, to examine the position of the Country and to make recommendations to His Majesty's Government as to possible forms of future government to be put before the people at a national referendum."

The members were sworn in and the Convention opened by Governor Sir Gordon MacDonald on September 11, with Mr. Justice Cyril J. Fox in the chair. The member for Bonavista Centre sized up the situation as follows: He could count on the support of 16 members for a resolution to seek proposed Terms of Union from Canada. There was the possibility of support from seven others, and a "fighting chance" of support from two more, but 11 were definitely opposed, and nine were uncommitted.

"In a Convention of forty-five members," he recounted in *I Chose Canada*, "I didn't have a chance: I would be voted down, and Confederation would die there on the floor ..." His calculations were borne out on November 5 when the Convention rejected his first attempt to get a Terms resolution approved. The vote was 25-18.

He had no thought of stopping there, however, and decided the Confederation idea might not die "if I could get it out of the hands of the forty-five and into the hands of the Newfoundland people."

This was achieved in large measure when the government-owned Broadcasting Corporation of Newfoundland brought in its microphones and announced it would carry the entire Convention proceedings daily on the radio—a decision of which Mr. Smallwood insisted he knew nothing "until the moment I walked into the Chamber on opening day and saw them in place." But he was, needless to say, "profoundly happy" with the development: as one of the very few members to have ever spoken into a "mike" and owner of perhaps the most recognizable voice in Newfoundland as a result of his long-running "Barrelman" radio program, both he and the cause of Confederation had been handed an enormous advantage.

Eventually, on the following February 28, the Convention accepted his resolution to send a delegation to Ottawa to determine "what fair and equitable basis may exist for federal union of Newfoundland and Canada." A similar delegation went to London with clearly unsatisfactory results. A third resolution to send a delegation to the U.S. was approved by the Convention, but the Commission of Government disallowed it.

From June to September, the Newfoundland representation of seven members headed by Bradley, who had succeeded as Convention chairman on the sudden death of Fox, held discussions with a committee of the Canadian Cabinet in Ottawa. Then, on October 27, a statement of terms that the government there would be prepared to recommend to Parliament, contained in two so-called Black Books, was forwarded to the Governor of Newfoundland for consideration by the Convention.

After protracted debate the Convention, on January 27, 1948, rejected by a vote of 29-16 Mr. Smallwood's motion to recommend to the government of the United Kingdom that Confederation with Canada be placed on the referendum ballot. The following day, it voted 45-0 to give Newfoundlanders two choices only—restoration of Responsible Government as it existed prior to 1934, and retention of the Commission system.

The Convention met for the last time on January 30.

Unwilling to accept the decision of "twenty-nine dictators" who refused to allow Confederation on the ballot, and thus cheated the people of that option, Mr. Smallwood prepared a radio address for Bradley. It called upon Newfoundlanders to express shock and anger at this denial of the opportunity "to exercise their own judgment about the future of their own country."

They were urged, "If you think that Confederation should be placed on the ballot paper, so that people can vote for or against it according to their own free and independent will, send instantly your telegrams demanding that Confederation be put on the ballot paper, and your demands will be delivered to the British government." In just a few days, nearly 60,000 people registered their disapproval. A few weeks passed, then on March 2 London responded: His Majesty's government did not think it right to deny Newfoundlanders the opportunity to pronounce on the option of Confederation. Therefore, it would be on the referendum ballot.

Mr. Smallwood was ecstatic: "We had won! Glory hallelujah!!"

# CHAPTER 14

## THE RETURN OF DEMOCRACY

# The Evening Telegram

VOLUME 71  16 PAGES  PRICE 5 CENTS  ST. JOHN'S, NEWFOUNDLAND, THURSDAY, FEBRUARY 17, 1949  PRICE 5 CENTS  NUMBER 39

# UNION BILL IS APPROVED

*New Peace Hopes in China War* | FINAL ACT OF LEGISLATION FOR

# SMALLWOOD IS PREMIER

## BRADLEY SECRETARY OF STATE

### NEW PROVINCE'S FIRST CABINET WILL CONSIST OF TEN MEMBERS

Smallwood, Quinton, Pottle, Curtis, Forsey, Winter, Ballam, Keough, Sinnott and Hefferton Nominees

J. R. Smallwood was called on today by the Lieutenant-Governor of Newfoundland, Sir Albert Walsh, K.C., to form the interim cabinet, to act as the government of the Province of Newfoundland until such time as a provincial election can be held, probably in late May or early June.

The Cabinet will be: J. R. Smallwood; L. R. Curtis, K.C., prominent St. John's lawyer; S. J. Hefferton, St. John's school teacher; Philip Forsey, St. John's school teacher; M. J. Sinnott, O.B.E., magistrate; Dr. H. L. Pottle, past Commissioner for Home Affairs and Education in the last Commission of Government; H. W. Quinton, C.M.G., past Commissioner for Public Health and Welfare; Gordon A. Winter, prominent St.

#### Closer News Relations

REGINA, March 31 (CP) — Closer news relations that will prevail between Canada and Newfoundland was favorable comment today during a telephone conversation between R. B. Herder, Director of the Evening Telegram of St. John's, Newfoundland, and D. B. Rogers, Editor of the Regina Leader-Post.

Mr. Rogers, as President of the 1950 Canadian Managing Editors Convention, phoned Mr. Herder to welcome the Managing Editors of the Evening Telegram and the Daily News of St. John's to attend, next June.

### BRIEF CEREMONY TODAY UNITES NEWFOUNDLAND AND CANADA

Sir Albert Walsh Sworn in as Island's First Lieutenant-Governor

The final act in the confirmation of union with Canada took place this afternoon in the drawing room at Government House when Sir Albert Walsh, K.C., was sworn in as first Lieutenant-Governor. The ceremony, which was broadcast, was attended by about 100 invited guests.

At 3.35 the guests, who had assembled in the ballroom, were admitted to the drawing room, where at one end of the room at a table flanked with flowers were the Excellency the Administrator, Sir Edward Emerson; col. the Hon. Colin Gibson, K.C., Secretary of State for Canada, for Albert Walsh and Capt. Gordon Warren, O.B.E. administering.

The ceremony opened with the oath to Newfoundland by a chaplain. Mr. R. McLeod, Mr. W. J. Carew, C.B.E., then read the oath...

### THE KING GIVES HIS BLESSING TO NEWFOUNDLAND-CANADA UNION

Message Read From His Majesty by Governor-General During Ceremony at Ottawa

OTTAWA, April 1— (CP)—The King, in a message conveyed by Viscount Alexander, to-day gave his blessing to Confederation between Canada and Newfoundland. "May the union that is now complete continue, under God's guidance, to grow in strength, prosperity, happiness, and may it bring new benefits to its people from sea to sea," His Majesty said.

The message was read by the Governor-General before the throne that gathered in Parliament hall to witness ceremonies marking the historic union between the old British Colony and Canada.

#### Sundry Items Discussed at Council Meeting

*There could be
no more convincing
demonstration...
(The) majority...had
accepted Confederation
and Smallwood's
leadership.*

It is 1949, and the people have spoken. Half a year ago, Confederate forces led by Joseph R. Smallwood emerged victorious from the decisive segment of an historic, two-stage referendum on the nature and form of Newfoundland's future governance.

By a margin of almost 7,000 votes, 78,323 to 71,334, the people had voted against a return to Responsible Government "as it existed in 1934"—a form of semi-independence, with ties still to the apron-strings of Mother England but the right to elect their own Prime Minister and government. Newfoundlanders chose instead to join Canada as that nation's tenth province. In so doing, they certainly regained as great a say in their own, local affairs as was forfeited without a struggle in 1934, and I would argue considerably more.

Confederation would, in fact, confer a form of Responsible Government with a restored, elective House of Assembly. In place of the arbitrary veto-wielding bureaucracy of far-off Whitehall, there now would be inviolable provincial rights according to the powers-sharing provisions of the Canadian Constitution, and direct representation in the Canadian Parliament, House of Commons and Senate. Moreover, Newfoundland won constitutional equality with the other provinces of Canada, and for our individual citizens, there would be full and automatic entitlement to a broad range of social programs and public services, arguably the most generous in the world.

Seemingly starved for a return to democratic politics after 15 years of Commission of Government-by-edict, on July 2, 1948 just short of 85 per cent of the eligible voters went to the polls in the second leg of a two-stage referendum to unmistakably and finally indicate their choice. This compared to slightly more than 88 per cent in the initial phase of the referendum a few weeks earlier, on June 3, when the option of continuing with the British-appointed Commission came in a poor third and was dropped from the ballot. The final outcome: 18 electoral districts in favour of Confederation to 7 for Responsible Government—in conventional electoral terms, a substantial victory.

But the referendum on the future of the Old Colony marked only the beginning of the process leading to Confederation with Canada. Next, the Terms of Union must be finally negotiated, and for this purpose a delegation led by Commissioner for Justice Albert J. Walsh, a former Speaker of the House of Assembly, arrived in Ottawa on October 6.

Two months and five days later, on December 11, the Terms were signed in a formal ceremony in the Senate chamber. Legislation to give effect to the negotiated agreement, together with a draft petition to King George VI for enactment by the United Kingdom Parliament of a measure confirming the proposed union, passed the Canadian House of Commons on February 16, 1949 and the formality of the Senate the following day. The Canadian Press reported the package "was sent on its way with the singing of God Save the King" after Chief Justice Thebaudeau Rinfret, in the stead of Earl Alexander of Tunis, the last British Governor General in Canada, gave Royal assent to the acts of the Canadian Parliament and signed them into law.

The lead story in *The Evening Telegram* on February 17 bore the headline "UNION BILL IS APPROVED." One subsidiary headline read, "Final Act of Legislation for Canada-Newfoundland Union Passes by Vote of 140 to 74," but a second related, "Progressive Conservative and Social Credit Parties Oppose Measure on Constitutional Grounds." George Drew, Leader of the Official Opposition, said the PCs objected to the request to amend the British North America Act—legislation of the United Kingdom Parliament that would continue to serve as Canada's Constitution until 1982—without consulting the existing provinces. Prime Minister Louis S. St. Laurent, well aware of the opposition of Quebec politicians, in particular, to Newfoundland's entry as finally closing the door on latent claims to ownership of the huge Labrador territory, retorted that if a majority in the House took the attitude represented by Drew, there would be no union with Newfoundland.

Within days, in London, the measure amending the B.N.A. Act was approved by the British—on March 3, *The Telegram* carried a dispatch from Reuters news agency indicating "Nfld. Bill Passes 217-15 in U.K. Commons." In St. John's the Commission of Government, still the legal custodian of power and authority, followed suit to set the stage for Newfoundland's entry into the Canadian union, and its own demise, on March 31, 1949.

Now the challenge was to recreate the Newfoundland House of Assembly and to put in place a government to implement the referendum decision, tackling the myriad issues, many obvious and some not, that would be involved in the integration of the new province into the Canadian family.

In the first instance this would be accomplished by means of a General Election on May 27, but first a major difficulty must be overcome: Newfoundland's political parties existing prior to the institution of Commission of Government 15 years earlier had effectively disbanded. They were officially dead. Yet Canada's parliamentary system, based on the British model, rests solidly upon the foundation of political party practices and traditions. It would be highly impracticable to try to hold an election, if not impossible, until and unless the party structure was brought back to life.

In the meantime, the formal process of reinstituting a functioning democratic government for the new province, in keeping with the fundamental nature of Canada as a constitutional monarchy, required the appointment of a vice-regal representative. Walsh, lately recipient of a knighthood, was named Lieutenant-Governor and he, in turn, called upon Mr. Smallwood to form an interim administration.

Sworn into office as Premier at 11:00 A.M. on April 1, the 48-year old journalist and latter-day pig farmer, although a keen professional observer of the governmental process and close associate or acquaintance of some who had been involved in it, had himself no elective political or parliamentary experience, except for membership in the National Convention. Other than Herman W. Quinton (who had handed him what would be the only personal defeat of a long political career, in a House of Assembly election in Bonavista South in 1932) and Herbert L. Pottle, both former members of the Commission of Government, neither did other members of his first administration, a mixture of Confederate activists, professionals and businessmen. These ministers, or most, would become of necessity the nucleus of a reborn Liberal Party with Mr. Smallwood as Leader.

As Premier he chose for his first, appointed Cabinet Leslie R. Curtis, Minister of Justice and Attorney General; H.W. Quinton, Minister of Public Health; Herbert L. Pottle, Minister of Public Welfare; Gordon A. Winter, Minister of Finance; William J. Keough, Minister of Natural Resources; Michael J. Sinnott, Minister of Public Works; Charles H. Ballam, Minister of Labour; Samuel J. Hefferton, Minister of Education; Philip S. Forsey, Minister of Home Affairs; and Addison D. Bown, Minister of Supply.

In the election soon to follow, the first since 1932, Curtis, the Attorney General, would be successful, as would Quinton who moved to Finance to replace Winter who chose not to run, and Pottle. Keough moved to Fisheries and Cooperatives, to be succeeded in Natural Resources by Edward "Ted" Russell. Ballam, Hefferton and Forsey also won election, the latter moving to Supply in place of Bown who didn't. The originals were joined by Edward S. Spencer as Minister of Public Works, replacing Sinnott who went down to defeat; James R. Chalker succeeded Quinton in Health; and James J. Spratt became Minister of Provincial Affairs.

Meanwhile, adherents to the Responsible Government League, many of whom had supported the pre-Commission Conservative Party, formed the Progressive Conservative Association, choosing as their first leader First World War veteran and prominent insurance agent Henry G.R. Mews, a St. John's city councillor and future mayor.

To prepare for the election, Mr. Smallwood organized, with the help of F. Gordon Bradley, Harold Horwood, Gregory Power, Charles Garland, Fred Kirby and others, a founding convention of the new Liberal Party. It was held April 28, 29 and 30 in St. John's where between 1,200 and 1,500 delegates took part, many brought in from around the Island by a specially chartered train. Returning to their homes they carried with them the spirit of a new beginning and the names of candidates they would support, and encourage their neighbours to support, at the polls.

"For three days," Mr. Smallwood later recounted, "we met in the big C.L.B. Armoury, and there, after speeches by Bradley and me, we constituted the Liberal Party.

"Nominations were asked from the floor for the positions of the Leader of the Party federally and the Leader of the Party provincially. Bradley was elected to the former and I to the latter ... We then split up the big meeting into many smaller ones, so that I could tell the individual constituencies who their candidate was to be."

In *I Chose Canada*, the 1973 autobiography published by Macmillan, he explained how he "followed the normal Newfoundland practice and selected every candidate in every constituency in every provincial General Election" while he was Leader, and with only two exceptions, every federal candidate as well.

"Sir Richard Squires, Lord Morris, Sir Robert Bond and Sir William Whiteway had all done precisely the same in their time, and the Tory leaders did it too, before and after Confederation. Unless he was a fool, the Leader would seek advice and guidance in most of the constituencies; in some of them his own knowledge would be so extensive and sure that he could act without consulting anyone."

And so it was in the case of the General Election of 1949 in which 22 Liberal Party candidates were successful, the Progressive Conservatives elected five members (Mews was not among them), and one Independent won his seat—arch-anticonfederate Major Peter Cashin, who stood in the District of Ferryland. In Labrador, which was given representation for the first time, the election had to be deferred because of bad weather until July 25 when Horwood emerged the winner under the Liberal banner.

Mr. Smallwood was elected in Bonavista North where he received 87 per cent of the votes, 4,215 to 637 for Progressive Conservative J.M. Way.

Writing about it years later in *Joey: The Life and Political Times of Joey Smallwood* (Stoddart, 1989) Horwood, who broke with and then became a stern critic of his former leader as *The Evening Telegram*'s political columnist, pointed out that overall the Liberals received more than 65 per cent of the popular vote. The PCs got less than 33 per cent and Cashin, running as an independent, was the only opposition candidate elected with more than a slim majority.

"The Progressive Conservatives came within inches of being wiped out altogether," Horwood recalled.

"There could be no more convincing demonstration of the fact that ... the overwhelming majority of Newfoundlanders had accepted Confederation and Smallwood's leadership."

# THE SMALLWOOD LETTERS

It was the most natural thing for Joseph R. Smallwood, former journalist, who understood better than most the vital importance of propaganda—in those days, the word was more acceptable, perhaps, than today—to turn to the medium he knew best to get the Confederation campaign off the ground. The one-time newspaper reporter told the story in *I Chose Canada*:

"On March 1, 1946 I launched my campaign for Confederation. I did it by writing a series of eleven articles that I took in to St. John's to the Hon. John S. Currie, editor of *The Daily News*, asking him to publish them.

"He was strictly anti-Confederate, but a personal friend of mine and a man of fine spirit.

"'Yes, Joe,' he said. 'I'll publish them, but I would prefer to have them appear as letters to the editor from you. If I publish them as articles, it will look as though I had commissioned you to write them, and that would suggest that I favoured or our paper favoured Confederation with Canada.'

"'That's all right with me, but will you publish them daily without interruption, so they will appear as an unbroken series constituting one whole?'

"He said yes, and so they appeared. Except for one or two gaucheries, the eleven letters, and two or three others that I added in reply to real or fancied objections raised to them, were truthful, accurate and for many readers a great revelation of what Confederation would mean, or do, for Newfoundland.

"Having nailed my colours to the mast as a staunch Confederate (always provided that Canada would offer us acceptable terms and conditions of entry) I now took my second step. This was to embark upon a speaking tour of Bonavista Bay ... These meetings were not only to convert the people to Confederation, but to persuade them to elect me as their representative to the forthcoming National Convention.

"'Don't vote for me,'" I pleaded at every meeting, 'unless you want to be represented by a man who will fight to get Canada's terms and conditions of Confederation. Somebody else will be asking you to elect him (I could change that tense whenever that opponent appeared at the same meeting) and if he is against Confederation, I plead with you to vote for him, not for me, if you don't want to be represented by a man who'll fight to get Canada's terms of Confederation.'"

When Confederation came, Mr. Smallwood recalled, the Liberal Party was not alone in its lack of organization in Newfoundland—others were in the same position. In 1934 existing political entities, such as they were, had disappeared along with the House of Assembly and the elected government. (In reality they were merely groups of elected Members of the House with not even the vestigial signs of political organization.)

William Ford Coaker's Fishermen's Protective Union, strictly speaking not a political party, was neither tightly nor efficiently organized in any case. It had supported Coaker candidates along the Northeast Coast, but virtually disappeared even before the legislature was dissolved to make way for the Commission of Government. In the fifteen-year period between 1934 and 1949 there had not been even a sign or a token of political party organization in the country. This, then, was the scene as the man who would become Premier laid his plans for the organization of a political party as the vehicle for future electoral activity.

Mr. Smallwood was an unabashed Socialist, no doubt the result, or largely so, of his years in New York associating with left-wing politicians, journalists and labour organizers. Socialism was his "basic philosophy, if so grand a word may be used," he wrote in *I Chose Canada*. However, in his politics "I was a Liberal, because I felt that Liberalism in Newfoundland, with its roots set deeply down in the fishing, and working classes generally, and its honourable record of taking always the side of the people, was as close as it was reasonable or practical to think the Island could get to Socialism."

It was Liberalism, he wrote, that "through the great Dr. William Carson waged the original battle for the right merely to live in Newfoundland, to enclose a piece of land, to put a chimney in your house; the historic fight to make the English-appointed Governors of Newfoundland live on the Island all year long; the fight to force the Governors to have a small advisory council of local people; the fight for sweeping reform of the Supreme Court; the fight for Representative Government.

"It was Liberalism that brought in manhood suffrage and the secret ballot. It was Liberalism that had built the railway across Newfoundland; Liberalism that had built the great pulp and paper industry at Grand Falls, and again at Corner Brook.

"All down through the years, it seemed to me that Liberalism had done the things Socialism would have done, except for the impossible socialization of industry. I found no difficulty whatsoever, as a Socialist, in being a Newfoundland Liberal, and indeed a Canadian Liberal when I became a Canadian."

Hardly surprising, then, that the first thing he set out to do, after taking the oath as Premier, was to found and organize a new Liberal Party.

"I could have done this easily and cheaply by emulating Sir Richard Squires: in 1919 he had held the famous 'cock-loft meeting' to found his Liberal Reform Party. The meeting took place in the unused attic of his *Daily Star* newspaper building, and Squires invited fifty or sixty friends to attend, a few of them undoubtedly Liberals of the old school.

"They adopted a resolution constituting the Liberal Reform Party and making Mr. Squires its Leader. And thus was born the party which claimed the mantle of the old Whiteway-Kent-Shea-Carson Liberal Party. I don't suppose that meeting cost Squires more than a hundred dollars.

"I might, at little more expense, have splurged as Walter S. Monroe (the Leader of 'the first true Tory party in Newfoundland'—Ed.) did a few years later: through his friends, he organized a public meeting at the old Casino Theatre. The CLB brass band was hired for the night, the speeches were eloquent, and a resolution was adopted asking Mr. Monroe if he would please become the Leader.

"John T. Meaney, who organized the whole thing, told me about it years afterward. He was behind the platform, his eyes on the audience and his ears on the telephone receiver, giving Mr. Monroe a running account of the meeting and then telling him when he should hurry to the theatre to receive the tumultuous greeting of the carefully selected audience.

"I chose otherwise. I invited 1,200 or 1,400 to come to St. John's to form, or reform, the Liberal Party of Newfoundland and Labrador. We chartered a train to cross Newfoundland from Port aux Basques, taking delegates aboard from every sizeable place across the Island. Others poured into St. John's by regular trains, truck, bus and a few by private car. For three days we met in the big CLB Armoury ..."

In fact, the foundations for the modern Liberal Party were laid in the launch in 1948 of the Newfoundland Confederate Association at a meeting on March 26 in the ballroom of the Newfoundland Hotel. A few weeks later it began publishing its own newspaper, *The Confederate*, to promote the cause of union with Canada. Its president, Frederick Gordon Bradley, was a St. John's-born lawyer and veteran MHA and Cabinet minister. First elected as a Monroe Conservative, he later sat as an Independent, and then as a Squires Liberal who opposed establishment of the Commission of Government. After winning a seat in the National Convention he served for a time as its chairman, and led terms-seeking delegations to London and Ottawa. He was one of the signers of the final Terms of Union with Canada. First Newfoundlander appointed to the Canadian federal Cabinet, as Secretary of State, he wound up his political career in the Senate.

General secretary, campaign manager and all-around sparkplug was Mr. Smallwood, who recruited over 100 vice-presidents of the association from all over the Island and Labrador. Gregory Power became deputy campaign manager, Charles Garland financial secretary-treasurer and chairman of a war veterans' advisory committee, and Fred Kirby and Harold Horwood were named chairmen for teachers and labour respectively.

On January 5, 1949 the association held a celebration dinner in the place of its founding, the Newfoundland Hotel Ballroom, and there was much to celebrate: The difficult referendum battle had been won, and Terms of Union, much improved over the original Canadian offer, successfully negotiated. Messrs. Bradley and Smallwood were presented with engraved silver cups to commemorate the momentous victory.

The next item on the agenda would be appointment of the interim government sworn in on April 1 a few hours after Confederation took effect just before midnight on March 31. This would be followed by the Liberal Party's founding convention which opened on April 28 and immediately launched preparations for the province's first General Election on May 27.

# CHAPTER 15

## THE ECONOMY MEANS EVERYTHING

*"I worried about ...*

*losing our population ...*

*(W)e had to develop*

*everything (and the)*

*price of failure*

*would be disaster,*

*and so our slogan had to*

*be 'Develop or Perish!'"*

PHOTOS CLOCKWISE:
■ Fisheries development was high on the agenda in the Smallwood years, such as the opening of a modern processing plant near Marystown (MA); ■ The Premier taught legions of children to spit on their hands before grasping his sod-turning shovel to help launch dozens of new industries and facilities (MA); ■ On the leading edge of development was construction of some 6,000 miles of highways and the building of hundreds of bridges (TA); ■ Development means employment and prosperity for the people, evidenced by the many modern housing developments in every area of the province (TA).

The state of the economy—that is to say, the level of productive, job—and wealth-generating activity—means everything to the people of this or any province or country. On it depends whether they have employment—job permanency or the lack thereof; the levels of wages and salaries; the levels of taxation people are able to pay to various governments; and as a consequence of all this, the availability as well as the quality of public services. The adequacy of health care, of education at all levels, of the so-called social safety net, of highways, of recreation and cultural services, of police and fire protection, of drinking water supplies and water for industrial and other uses, of safe disposal of liquid and solid wastes—these and the many other requirements of a modern and progressive society come at enormous cost that only a buoyant, developing economy can support.

In the end, these also are the considerations that mainly determine whether Newfoundlanders and Labradorians—especially the young people—will remain here to build a satisfying life and career, or move elsewhere.

And this precisely was the overriding concern harboured by the first Premier of the province, having led the former British colony into Confederation and contemplating all the while the open-door consequence of the political union: No longer would there be anything—certainly no political or geophysical barriers—to stop Newfoundlanders from leaving in droves for other, more prosperous areas of their newly adopted country, and beyond.

"I worried about the danger of losing our population," he recalled, reviewing the progress the province had made in its first 25 years in Canada—a period during which, rather than a net loss, the number of people residing in Newfoundland and Labrador actually increased by some 160,000 or nearly 50 per cent.

"I knew, even before Confederation Day, that somehow I had to inspire the Newfoundland people with new faith in their prospects. I had to persuade them that Newfoundland was a place with a bright future; a place to stay in; a place ... (to) get married, raise a family and enjoy a good life—that there was no need to go rushing off to Toronto."

He continued: "But ... we had to develop. We had to develop our resources. We had to develop everything we had in Newfoundland and Labrador. The price of failure would be disaster, and so our slogan had to be 'Develop or Perish!'"

His efforts were crowned with much success. They included the much-reviled New Industries Program which sought to diversify and renew the economy by developing manufacturing and other opportunities for employment, using funds from the Commission of Government nest egg—he put it at $45.5 million—to do it.

"… (W)hat we were free to spend amounted to two-thirds of the total, and besides we had certain physical assets that we could turn into cash … I was irrevocably committed to a policy of economic development of the province, and I was happy to be Premier because of the opportunity it gave me to initiate that development."

Accordingly, the Liberal manifesto for the first provincial General Election was titled "Ahead—or Astern" and declared: "Newfoundland can not stand still. We must go ahead … We will put into this work of developing Newfoundland the greatest drive that (it) has ever seen." It sought a mandate to proceed accordingly, and the public response was overwhelming—in that election, and in others to follow.

Mr. Smallwood realized that the fisheries alone could not support a healthy, expanding population, even if a majority of young people, in particular, would be satisfied to work in it. There were also the province's forests and minerals, waiting for further development. And there were other abundant resources, from hydroelectric potential to offshore oil and gas, to southern ice-free harbours, and global strategic location, the latter best realized in the recent experience of the Second World War.

Despite long-standing mythologies, the drive to build a manufacturing base involved much more than a rubber-boot plant and a chocolate-bar factory and a facility to manufacture eyeglasses—all, it now appears, slightly ahead of their time. Portland cement and gypsum board and hardwoods and second- and even third-generation versions of oil refining, linerboard and shipbuilding, boot-making and broiler chicken-raising, continued to employ thousands of people five decades later.

His conviction that Newfoundland and Labrador's offshore oil and gas must be processed here, giving the province a lucrative petrochemical industry, remains as an unfulfilled challenge to policy-makers and industry alike.

There can be no doubt that Confederation has had a profound beneficial impact on Newfoundland and Labrador. Some of the evidence is found in statistical indicators. For example, when Newfoundland first became a province of Canada personal per capita income was measured at only 51 per cent of the level enjoyed by other Canadians. Today it advances beyond 80 per cent. Another measure of progress in developing the economy of the province and raising the standard of living: after adjusting for inflation, real incomes of Newfoundland and Labrador people are more than five times higher today than in 1949. This was accompanied by vast improvements in health care, municipal services, income support, education, highways and air and water transportation, fisheries infrastructure … over time, assisted by the federal government in the billions of dollars.

It is also recognized increasingly that Newfoundland and Labrador is an important contributor to the Canadian economy on both a per capita and a total value basis. With less than two per cent of the country's population, the province accounts for more than 50 per cent of Canada's iron ore shipments, 19 per cent of fish landings, 8 per cent of newsprint shipments, 7 per cent of hydroelectric power generation, and in prospect, one-third of the nation's production of light crude oil.

According to recent provincial government economic reports, speaking of Newfoundland and Labrador's contribution to the federal Treasury, "revenues from the province in recent years have been in the $1.8-$2.0 billion range."

In 2001 employment grew by 3.3 per cent to reach a record high of 211,300, and in 2002 was expected to grow by 1.4 per cent to 214,200. The unemployment rate in 2001 was 16.1 per cent, the lowest level since 1989, and forecast to drop further to 15.7 per cent in 2002. Real Gross Domestic Product for 2002 was forecast at 3.7 per cent, strongest of all the provinces—the third time in five years that the province would lead all Canada in terms of real GDP growth.

At the same time, Mr. Smallwood's number one concern—the bleeding of population—remains, despite the fact that in 1992 and 1993 the number of persons resident in Newfoundland and Labrador was the highest in our history—a record 580,200. However, in the wake of the northern cod moratorium steady decline took place so by July 1, 2001 the population estimate was 533,761, down eight per cent from 1993.

There is room for optimism, to be sure. The annual shrinkage has begun to slow in correspondence to expansion in the provincial economy, largely due to spinoffs from offshore oil. According to provincial government figures, net out-migration at 3,608 in 2001 was 7.5 per cent lower than 2000 and more than 62 per cent lower than 1998.

◆ ◆ ◆

Hand in hand with development of the economy must go the building-up of local communities, upon whose prosperity ultimately depends the ability of the province, its residents and business and industrial enterprises, to carry a tax burden adequate to provide the range and quality of services people require and demand.

Accordingly, one of Mr. Smallwood's major concerns was encouragement of the spread of local government organization throughout the province. His determination in this regard led to an almost unbelievable expansion from a small handful of organized communities in the 1940s to some 300 cities, towns and local service districts.

Before the Second World War, St. John's, whose citizens had enjoyed limited say in the selection of municipal councillors as far back as 1888, was the only incorporated municipality, although a few places had managed to set up rudimentary and partial water systems. This meant that as late as the 1950s few places had been organized to provide their residents with safe drinking water, effective sewage and garbage disposal, and streets that were much better than cowpaths or muddy tracks. Almost none had firefighting services, snowclearing or street lights. A thin layer of policing was provided by the government in St. John's.

Legislation to provide for the encouragement of local government had been passed by the Commission of Government, but bureaucratic red tape, combined with people's concerns about the burden of local taxation, and the possibility higher government might in time unload upon those progressive enough to become organized the responsibility for services otherwise provided, all had a dampening effect.

At long last, the town of Windsor (formerly Grand Falls Station, where my father's father, Edward Callahan, was the railway freight agent) became incorporated in 1942, with an elected council succeeding a board of management set up four years earlier to help overcome unplanned development and the absence of water and sewer. The West Side of Corner Brook followed, and for the same reasons, then Grand Bank, Harbour Grace, St. Anthony, Wesleyville, Channel-Port aux Basques, Belleoram, Lewisporte, Fortune, Curling, Fogo, Carbonear, Corner Brook East (Humbermouth) and Englee. Rural district councils were formed in Placentia, Springdale, South Brook, and Badger's Quay-Valleyfield-Pool's Island, fewer than two dozen places in all.

It was following Confederation in 1949, after the Smallwood government brought in a new Local Government Act, that the dam broke. Removing the requirement that each incorporation, however small the community, be subject of a special act of the legislature made the process easier. New forms of local government were created, and emphasis began to be placed on town planning in order to get rid of higgledy-piggledy development. A new term, land assembly, entered the local government lexicon as the Newfoundland and Labrador Housing Corporation, building on Sir Brian Dunfield's St. John's Housing Area model, extended its influence across the province.

Incentive grants, which the Commission of Government had tried without much luck, began now to have an effect, e.g., $2 provided by the province for each $1 collected in local taxes up to a certain level, as well as the guarantee of bond issues and bank loans for water and sewer and street paving.

By the mid-1950s there were more than twice as many incorporated areas as only five years earlier—two cities (St. John's and now Corner Brook), 40 towns, six community councils, one local improvement district, and one rural district council. By the end of the decade, the numbers had grown to two cities, 62 towns, 74 places governed by community councils, 10 local improvement districts, and four rural councils.

The Smallwood government established the St. John's Metropolitan Area Board to coordinate development in the province's most populous area, with emphasis on land use and zoning and regional services. The overall level of activity province-wide led to creation in 1964 of the Newfoundland Municipal Financing Corporation. Its purpose was to undertake all debenture borrowing in behalf of municipalities with the exception of St. John's. In time the extent of financing required by local governments raised concerns with regard to their future viability. The result was the appointment in 1972 of a Royal Commission that recommended a series of changes in the local government system. A new Municipalities Act provided for the development of regional government, but little progress has been achieved in this area. However, the foundations of municipal government had been well and truly laid, and it would take a cataclysm of historic proportions to shake them. The northern cod moratorium imposed in 1992 was that instrument. It effectively shut down an industry worth some $700 million a year in an estimated 250 rural communities, with a devastating effect on many of them. It led to curtailment of services ranging from pumped water, to street lighting, to street and road maintenance, to snowclearing and fire protection, as populations dwindled and tax revenues dried up.

Individual fishers and plant workers were sustained by subsidy programs—N-CARP (for Northern Cod Adjustment Recovery Program) and TAGS (for The Atlantic Groundfish Strategy)—as they waited and hoped for the recovery of cod stocks, but an uncertain future led to substantial out-migration to larger communities and other provinces. Slack was taken up by explosive growth in shrimp and crab and development of other, less traditional fisheries, but benefits were less well distributed leaving many formerly prosperous towns in difficulty.

Latterly, an infusion of post-TAGS funds under an $81 million federal-provincial agreement assisted attempts by newly formed zonal development boards to revitalize hard-hit fishing areas.

The systemic effects could only translate into mounting pressure at the level of the provincial government. As the century turned, the combination of cumulative debt load and cuts in federal payments under the Canada Health and Social Transfer, as the Chrétien Liberals beat down the $45 billion annual deficit inherited from the Mulroney PCs, made life increasingly difficult for both politicians and their electors.

The cruel, unfortunate reality is that despite glowing forecasts—borne out, in some arcane sense, by results—of record economic outputs, the "Rock on a roll" national newspaper headlines mask massive exports of our non-renewable petroleum resources to fuel (no pun intended) growth and development elsewhere.

The cruel, unfortunate reality is that the province with, allegedly, Canada's hottest economy continues to limp along at double the national rate of unemployment, with the lowest per capita incomes, the highest levels of taxation, and a fiscal position growing more difficult by the day.

The cruel, unfortunate reality is that Ottawa's perverse clawback of the bulk of provincial earned revenues, mainly from non-renewable resources, renders economic development efforts, as the source of significant Treasury receipts, maddeningly futile.

Billions of dollars worth of crude oil being taken from the Newfoundland Grand Banks, and the province receiving a paltry few million in net royalties: The same stands to happen with Voisey's Bay and every other major development. It is an unspeakable, reeking scandal before which colonial practices of the distant past pale into insignificance.

Against that, it is an unalterable historical fact that four men, each of whom was then or would become Prime Minister of Canada—Pierre Trudeau, Joe Clark, Brian Mulroney and Jean Chrétien—gave the most solemn assurances that the development of offshore petroleum resources (why not all provincial resources?) would be permitted to transform Newfoundland and Labrador to "have" status as a province.

Trudeau promised, "… (F)or as long as it takes Newfoundland to reach the ranks of Canada's 'have' provinces, (she) will obtain the maximum benefit from these finds." It simply is not happening.

Clark declared that the province "should own the minerals of the Continental Margin off its coast ... as if these resources were located within the boundaries of the province," equal with, say, Alberta. But as Prime Minister he did nothing to enable it.

Mulroney delivered the Atlantic Accord, hailing it as "the end of 'have-not,'" and confirmed that the province would be "entitled to establish and collect revenues from (offshore) resources as if these resources were on land ... (T)his agreement is about dignity for Newfoundland and Labrador, long a 'have-not' province (and) reflects important Newfoundland values and accommodates legitimate provincial aspirations in a generous Canadian prospective." But the fine phrases are now shown to be meaningless.

Chrétien committed that Newfoundland would receive "the lion's share of the revenues" from the offshore, and notwithstanding the equalization principles, held out the prospect that "provincial revenues from Hibernia might be large enough to make Newfoundland a 'have' province within five years..." But the reality is otherwise.

It is clear that these repeated assurances were worth very much less than the paper they were written on. If you cannot depend upon the word of the Prime Minister of Canada, irrespective of political party stripe, what can you depend upon? It is clear that there exists a most serious breach of trust for which successive governments of Canada must be held accountable, and which demands to be reversed ... with interest!

In the meantime, Newfoundland and Labrador sinks deeper into debt and deficit, prevented from using what rightly are its natural resources—natural resources, which the Constitution of Canada wisely assigns to the jurisdiction and ownership of the province—to the benefit of its people.

A few years ago I suggested to, no, virtually pleaded with the present Prime Minister—an outstanding Canadian, a man for whom I have great respect, and whom I have been proud to call friend (I managed, and very successfully too, his original leadership campaign in Newfoundland and Labrador) to take radical actions to deal with this blatant injustice, which for us is at the root of regional disparity, but unfortunately to nil effect. My concerns and suggestions were not ignored; they were passed to various ministers of the Crown, and elicited litanies of tired platitudes in praise of the existing system.

What follows represents the substance of that proposal:

## THE GREAT CANADIAN CAPTIVITY
### HOW THE SO-CALLED "HAVE-NOT" PROVINCES ARE KEPT IN PERPETUAL ECONOMIC BONDAGE

As Canada enters the 21st Century, the greatest challenge to our country remains the glaring economic and social inequalities that divide constituent parts of the nation and the people who live in them. Clearly, the problem of regional disparity has not been resolved; far from it.

Large areas of this country and many Canadians remain hostages of this cruel phenomenon, in perpetual bondage imposed by a legislative and economic system that is heavily weighted in favour of the centre. It should not be beyond the wit and the wisdom of political leaders who care about the future of the land to give them freedom at last.

No matter how much we may want to believe that Canadians are born equal, and enjoy equally the benefits of living in "the best country in the world," the truth is that millions of our people are, in a real sense, second-class citizens ...

Canada, it is clear, requires a New Charter of Development and Prosperity that not only will encourage economic renewal in the so-called "have-not" regions, but also will remove penalties and disincentives to progress—in particular the equalization clawback that virtually guarantees that less-developed provinces are kept that way. It constitutes the worst form imaginable of economic bondage, the very antithesis of the enlightened policy that equalization pretends to be ...

A New Charter of Development and Prosperity: Could there be a more appropriate or exciting way to celebrate the Millennium and launch Canada's New Century?

Its cornerstone, if justice and fairness prevail, will be the release of offshore oil and gas resources to ownership and control of contiguous provinces, particularly Newfoundland and Labrador which brought them into Canada.

"Have-not" must be banished from this nation's lexicon. It is time.

# CHAPTER 16

## HEALTH CARE: A GREAT LEAP FORWARD

e Home of the New Janeway
Children's Health and Rehabilitation Centre

JANEWAY
CHILDREN'S HOSPITAL FOUNDATION

*Not only ... startling reduction in diseases of children, but average life expectancy ... raised to 65 years from as low, perhaps, as 45 in the Great Depression.*

Successive Smallwood administrations set in place the foundations for Newfoundland and Labrador's presently existing health care system, enabling a "great leap forward," as it were, in all aspects of hospital, medical and nursing practice.

This included the development of medical and dental plans for children, the introduction of Medicare, the establishment of the Janeway Child Health Centre, building and refurbishing and/or enlarging some two dozen other hospitals, and planning, negotiating financing with Ottawa, and launching development of the Health Sciences Centre in St. John's. In many respects the centrepiece, critically important to the success of the entire health care enterprise, was creation of the Memorial University Medical School, followed by Schools of Nursing and Pharmacy.

The Medical School decision, which gave most young Newfoundlanders their first, best chance in history of becoming physicians, led directly to the St. John's General Hospital becoming a teaching institution, relocating to the university's North Campus as part of the Health Sciences complex. It was the primary recommendation of a Royal Commission led by Lord Russell Brain, the British peer and medical expert chosen by Premier Smallwood to recommend a course of action that would radically change Newfoundland health care for the better.

"I brought the great medical leader ... from England to advise us on the question of establishing a medical college at the university," Mr. Smallwood wrote. "He and a number of other authoritative voices advocated its establishment, and we went forward with the plan, at pretty shattering cost. The first medical doctors were graduated from Memorial in 1973."

However, for their own reasons, the Newfoundland medical establishment—as they would again when the Premier proposed the establishment of the Janeway Child Health Centre—threw cold water on the idea. "For a long, lonely time," he recalled, "the only supporter I had for my proposal to start the medical college (besides Health Minister Dr. James McGrath and other members of the Cabinet) was Dr. Gordon Thomas, chief of the Grenfell Hospital at St. Anthony."

The Brain report and recommendations were accepted by the Cabinet. The Commission reported in 1966, proposing that rather than continuing to depend on importing physicians from elsewhere—principally, from England and Ireland—the government, through the university, should commence training its own. The province thus would be assured, as it never could have been otherwise, of a continuing supply of specialist medical personnel, both locally trained, and recruited from around the world to be both teaching staff and to provide clinical expertise in Newfoundland's main referral and treatment centre.

Lord Brain also recommended that Memorial University begin offering a degree program in nursing, and called for the establishment of medical rehabilitation facilities. As soon as practicable, the former General Hospital was converted into a major medical rehabilitation facility for adults, and named to honour Newfoundland's longest-serving Deputy Minister of Health, Dr. Leonard A. Miller. The vacant American high school at the former Pepperrell Air Force Base became the Children's Rehabilitation Centre.

When Newfoundland became part of the national Medicare program proposed by the federal government, it meant significant expansion of the federal-provincial hospital insurance plan the province had joined in 1958. Under the new arrangement, which the Smallwood government financed from general revenues rather than impose user fees or premiums, people received medical treatment and hospitalization free of charge. The government established the Medical Care Commission to administer the new program. It issued each citizen an identity card that was all that was required in order to access medical treatment, or receive institutional care.

Earlier programs instituted by the Smallwood government, and believed to be among the first of their kind in North America, such as the Children's Hospitalization Plan and the Children's Dental Plan, were simply absorbed into the new Medicare program. The results of these programs, together with the general improvements in health and nutrition, became quickly evident … most notably in the marvellous smiles of so many children with healthy teeth.

Not only was there startling reduction in the incidence of diseases of children, but by the time Mr. Smallwood left office after 23 years, average life expectancy of Newfoundlanders had been raised to 65 years—very close to the Canadian average—from as low, perhaps, as 45 in the worst days of the Great Depression.

Writing in the 1960s about the myriad benefits of Confederation, the Premier was able to proclaim that diseases "which racked our people" for decades had been brought under "normal control … Tuberculosis has been all but wiped out. All contagious and infectious diseases have been reduced to negligible proportions."

The contrast with earlier described conditions was nothing less than dramatic. Issued in 1950, a Canadian Government publication describing "Newfoundland, Canada's New Province" had gone into considerable detail concerning the state of public health in the new province. At the time of joining Canada, it reported, Newfoundland had higher death rates than the rest of the country "from tuberculosis, puerperal causes, congenital malformations and diseases peculiar to the first years of life, diarrhea, senility and pulmonary infections." On the other hand, "deaths from cancer, intercranial lesions, diseases of the heart, nephritis and accidents were, on the whole, lower than in other parts of Canada."

But by far the worst menace to health was identified as tuberculosis, which accounted for 12.5 per cent of all registered deaths, and between the ages of 15 and 44, more deaths than any other single disease and for more than half the total deaths from all diseases. It was estimated that at least four per cent of the population of 340,000 had active TB and that 75 per cent had been exposed to it.

"The records indicate that the disease increases in times of depression and declines in periods of prosperity, and the Public Welfare Committee of the National Convention emphasized in its report that although treatment and preventative measures were of great importance, the real cure for tuberculosis was a satisfactory standard of living." It was further, if unintended, support for the Smallwood emphasis on economic development, for lacking a high level of development, discussion of a high standard of living would be so much idle chatter.

The death rate from tuberculosis in Newfoundland in 1946 was elsewhere reported at 122.0 per 100,000 of population, versus 47.4 in Canada and 36.4 in the U.S.

Miller, who had been Director of Medical Services under the Commission of Government and became the first Deputy Minister of Health in 1949, reported on the vast improvement in Newfoundland public health after 15 years of Confederation:

- The general death rate had declined 25 per cent, infant mortality 40 per cent, and maternal mortality 80 per cent.

- Mortality from tuberculosis and diphtheria had each fallen 95 per cent.
- The number of working doctors had increased from 150 to 330, and working nurses from 350 to 900.
- Total annual expenditures by the Department of Health had increased from $4,904,142 in 1949 to $25,939,700 in 1964.

## FOCUS ON PROBLEMS OF CHILD HEALTH

The most exciting improvement in Newfoundland public services following Confederation took place in the area of child health, which would reach its apex in creation of the Janeway Child Health Centre.

Around the time of Union with Canada, Newfoundland's general death rate was 10.4 per 1,000 of population, compared with the Canadian rate of 9.4. But our rate of infant mortality was among the highest in the world—in 1946 standing at 73.8 for every 1,000 live births, compared to Canada's 47.0.

Statistics like these help explain the single-minded determination of Premier Smallwood to bring in a series of health care innovations aimed specifically at children that, notwithstanding the province's "have not" status—rather deplorable, inadequate terminology destined to come into general use—would match or exceed anything in the country: the Children's Health Plan in 1957, covering all hospitalization and medical costs for Newfoundlanders under 16; and following this, the Children's Dental Plan, a comprehensive system of dental care for the youngest groups of schoolchildren.

Of course, children also benefitted from the general improvements in health care—expansion of the cottage hospital network, new regional hospitals, provision of a fleet of floating medical clinics to offer care in places unconnected by roads, the introduction of air ambulances, improved mental health services, increases in the numbers of doctors and nurses. Helping families relocate to places where health care would be accessible was critically important.

Then along came Dr. Clifton Joseph Joy, native of Port au Port, graduate of St. Bonaventure's College and St. Francis Xavier, Dalhousie and Harvard Universities. From 1954 to 1966 he engaged in general pediatric service in St. John's, meanwhile winning election to the House of Assembly as a Liberal in the District of Harbour Main in 1962.

As a consultant in pediatrics to the Department of Health, he produced in 1958 an analysis of child health conditions that described infant mortality rates as still frightening a decade after Confederation, much higher than any other province. There was only one way to overcome these terrible, shameful deficiencies, he argued, and that was the establishment of a centre dedicated solely to the health of children, and staffed by doctors, nurses and other personnel especially trained to care for sick children.

His recommendation: convert the vacant military hospital at the former Pepperrell U.S. Air Force Base to this purpose. The Smallwood government accepted the recommendation, notwithstanding the daunting cost: an estimated capital expenditure of some $7-8 million. (A rule of thumb was developing that the annual operating cost of hospitals and like institutions would come to equal and then exceed the capital cost after a few years. Indeed, by the time the Janeway became part of the Health Sciences complex in the 1990s, its annual operating cost had grown to exceed $35 million.)

The Janeway proposal stirred great controversy, being opposed by the Newfoundland Medical Association as too idealistic and too expensive. Instead, the NMA called for the addition of a pediatric wing to the existing St. John's General Hospital, which was already proving inadequate for its own purposes, and would soon be abandoned.

After extensive investigation, the government engaged Dr. Charles A. Janeway of Harvard University, physician-in-chief of the Children's Hospital Medical Centre in Boston, Mass., to advise in the matter. He confirmed Joy's recommendation, which was endorsed as well by Lord Russell Brain, the Royal Commissioner who had authored the landmark report on health care in Newfoundland.

Considered "the father of the Janeway," Joy helped get it off the ground operationally as acting chief of staff during the first two years of its existence.

A tremendously important adjunct to basic health care is occupational safety and accident prevention, a particular concern of workers' organizations.

Mr. Smallwood had served as editor of the Newfoundland Workers Association newspaper and as early as 1925, as organizer for the Pulp, Sulphite mill union in Grand Falls, led efforts to establish a Newfoundland Federation of Labour. They would bear results a decade later under Alphonsus Duggan, founding president of the same union.

Early after the Smallwood government came into power, it set out to reform and update existing labour legislation, introducing important reforms. Among these was a system of no-fault insurance for men and women injured on the job. There had been workplace health and safety legislation on the books since 1906, targeted mainly at mine workers. Broadened two years later, it had a significant flaw: to obtain compensation, workers had to sue employers in the Newfoundland Supreme Court.

The complications—the difficulty facing an individual or family in mounting a case, the time involved, the inability of many employers to pay if a worker managed to sue and win, the blacklisting of those who did, made it a completely unsatisfactory system. These were essentially overcome when the Smallwood administration, during the first year of its life, passed legislation entitled "An Act Relating to Compensation to Workmen for Injuries Suffered in the Course of their Employment" which came into force in 1951.

Its principal effect was creation of the Workmen's Compensation Board (today known as the Workplace Healthy, Safety and Compensation Commission) as an autonomous authority over all aspects of workplace safety and compensation. Its first chairman was labour activist and committed confederate Irving Fogwill, who had been assigned by Mr. Smallwood to research compensation laws elsewhere, borrowing the best for the Newfoundland legislation.

The revolutionary legislation protected not only workers, but employers as well. For one thing, it eliminated the disruptive, time-consuming and expensive burden of lengthy court proceedings which might not, in the end, give a worker or his or her family relief.

Now employees needed to be little concerned about reaction to the filing of claims that the employer did not have to pay, since compensation came out of a general assessment on all employers in the province. Claims were investigated by compensation board staff and awards paid directly out of its own funds.

# CHAPTER 17

## ELIMINATING THE "CURSE OF CURSES"

FIRST OFFICIAL MOTORCADE

St. John's to Port aux Basques

Nov. 14 - Nov. 16, 1958

Joseph R. Smallwood
Premier of Newfoundland
Gregory J. Power Min of Highways
Mrs. William R. Smallwood
William R. Smallwood M.H.A. Green Bay District
Ramsay Smallwood
Bernard J. Kenney C.B.C. St. John's.
Charles W. Bursey - Doyle News Bulletin St. John
Doug. Bigsby C.B.C. St. John's
Jim M Butler VOCM St John's
Bill Squires VOCM St Johns
Harold N Butler VOCM St. John's
Nelson L Squires CJON-T.V. St Johns
Noel J Vinicombe Daily News
Don Fisher Adelaide Motors (St Chanel Motors)
Tommy J Rogers Dept of Highways
W L Callahan CJON

*When Confederation came there were barely 100 miles of paved highway ... It is unlikely that more than 300 of the 1,300 towns and villages had connections to the outside world.*

Newfoundland 19th Century historian Moses Harvey declared over 100 years ago that in no other country than his own had "the material and social advancement of the people been so seriously retarded" for the want of roads. It would be hard to find anyone who agreed more strongly than Joseph R. Smallwood, who had walked across the Island in the 1920s along the railway track—there was no other way; besides, he was organizing railway workers engaged in a wage dispute—and well knew the isolation of the people. The future Premier branded it "the curse of curses."

He would point out, looking back over two decades of Confederation progress, that before 1949 most Newfoundlanders lived in some 1,300 communities that were "cut off from each other, unconnected, unreachable, except for the ocean." People wanting or needing to travel had, of necessity, to go by boat. But now, in the decade of the Sixties, at least 600 places had been joined to the rest of the province (some 200 others, mostly on islands and unable to benefit from highways development, had been or would be abandoned, many of their residents with government assistance, and many remained to be "connected up").

Nonetheless, in just a few years the centuries-old curse of isolation had been or was in the process of being broken for tens of thousands of people.

The Premier's words are worth repeating. "Miracle of miracles," he exclaimed, "you can now drive from Trepassey to St. Anthony, from St. Anthony to Port aux Basques, from Port aux Basques to Bonavista, from Bonavista to Lamaline. There are only two or three places in the whole of Green Bay not connected by road!"

Up to and during the time of the Commission of Government the emphasis in road-building was almost entirely on local roads maintained by a handful of local roads boards or by private interests such as the pulp and paper companies. Historically, the *Encyclopedia of Newfoundland and Labrador* suggests, because residents of John Guy's 1610 settlement evidently employed the horse and carriage for their transportation, it made sense to believe that crude paths and trails developed in and between adjacent communities, notwithstanding the anti-settlement laws of the 17th and 18th Centuries. However, aside from roads built by the military and the efforts of individuals, little was done prior to the arrival in 1825 of Governor Thomas Cochrane.

His desire was to open up the country for development, while providing employment for the able-bodied poor—perhaps the first example on record of "make-work" projects. People were provided with food (e.g., the staple Indian meal, or corn meal) in return for their labour. The Indian Meal Line, linking Portugal Cove with Torbay, got its name from this practice.

Under Cochrane's administration Newfoundland was granted Representative Government in 1832 and in its first session the new House of Assembly voted 2,200 pounds stirling for roads and bridges. The first formal roads built were those that extended 14 kilometres out of St. John's to Portugal Cove and 19 kilometres from the capital to the Topsail area. However, as late as 1877 Alexander Murray, head of the Geological Survey of Newfoundland, reported the roads system was in an "embryonic" state with only "a few miles of road in the peninsula of Avalon and around the shores of the southern bays."

There is some irony, perhaps, in the fact that the single greatest impetus to the development of roads generally across the Island came from completion in 1898 of the Newfoundland Railway: it created a demand from communities along its route to be connected to it. Interestingly, too, the first automobile to appear in Newfoundland was a Rolls Royce imported by railway head Robert Gillespie Reid in 1903.

The first department of the Newfoundland government created to be responsible for road construction was established in 1925 by the Highroads Commission Act at a time when barely 1,000 motor vehicles were registered. But it had hardly cast its sights beyond the Avalon Peninsula before it died an untimely death in the austerity of 1933 that presaged the suspension of Responsible Government.

In the 1930s, a proposal to build a trans-insular highway foundered after some 80 kilometres were pushed through between Grand Falls and Hall's Bay—the infamous Hall's Bay Line. Then the Second World War came, bringing United States and Canadian forces who built roads in various locations in Newfoundland and Labrador to satisfy the need for ready access to communications sites and other remote military installations and assets.

An important stretch of road in Central Newfoundland joined Grand Falls to Gander and Gambo, and travellers will recall "Joe Hampton's ferry"—a rudimentary flat-top barge that for years transported vehicles across the Exploits River, being replaced in time by the Sir Robert Bond Bridge on the Trans Canada Highway at Bishop's Falls. Secured to a steel guide cable stretching from bank to bank to prevent it from being swept down the fast-flowing river, the conveyance was propelled by the two-stroke engine of the fisherman's punt lashed to its side. Capable of taking only two vehicles at a time, it presented both a convenience and a bottleneck on the increasingly busy road.

Farther to the east, a train-car ferry for some years bridged the highway gap between Clarenville and eastern Newfoundland and the expanding central area road network. Motorists drove their vehicles onto railway flatcars and rode themselves in attached day coaches on the journey between Clarenville and Gander.

The newsprint industry in Corner Brook and Grand Falls, already linked by road to power development at Deer Lake (International Power & Paper and Bowater's) and shipping facilities in Botwood and mining activity at Buchans (Anglo-Newfoundland Development Co.), pursued expansion of a growing network of roads for pulpwood harvesting incorporated, in time, into the public highways system. Elsewhere, in the 1940s, pioneer motorists braved a newly constructed but narrow, dusty Cabot Highway to reach the Bonavista Peninsula in season, and the Avalon and Burin Peninsulas were similarly linked by a rudimentary dirt road from Goobies.

With all this, when Confederation arrived there were in all barely 100 miles of paved highways. As well, it is unlikely more than 300 of the 1,300 towns and villages in the Newfoundland of 1949 had road connections to neighbouring communities, or access by road or rail to the outside world. By the end of the Smallwood era there were some 6,000 miles of highways and secondary roads, and half of it paved.

The Commission of Government, on the road, so to speak, to establishing a cash surplus in excess of $40 million, spent $1.5 million on roads in 1940, rising to a peak of $1.9 million by 1945. The new provincial government that took office in 1949 doubled this expenditure to $3.9 million in its first year, and increased it to $12 million within five years. By 1960, it was devoting in excess of $22 million annually to roads and highways, about 10 times the Commission's highways budget when the government changed hands.

But this was merely the beginning. The year before Newfoundland became a province of Canada, the federal Liberal government of Prime Minister W.L. Mackenzie King introduced in Parliament legislation providing for a national highway of consistent standard from the Atlantic to the Pacific. The Smallwood government lost no time pursuing the matter of an agreement for construction of the Trans Canada Highway in Newfoundland, the cost to be shared by the federal and provincial governments.

In 1950, only a year in office, it introduced legislation that would establish the standard to be met in constructing the highway, framing the intention in a formal resolution presented to the House of Assembly for what would be the single largest construction and public service project in Newfoundland history:

> *"Whereas, the Government of Canada and Newfoundland agree that the completion of a Trans Canada Highway is necessary to assist in creating a better means of connection between all provinces of Canada, and in promoting the economic development of Canada generally; and Whereas, it has been agreed by the said Governments that the construction of that portion of the Trans Canada Highway within Newfoundland should be undertaken by Newfoundland, and that the cost of that construction should be shared by Canada and Newfoundland ..."*

At first, the sharing split was to be 50-50 with completion from St. John's to Port aux Basques scheduled for 1956. But it soon became obvious that it would be impossible for the new province, considering demands for local roads and secondary highways, to take full advantage of the deal.

Accordingly, a new agreement was negotiated, signed and completed with Ottawa meeting 90 per cent of the cost for construction of 10 per cent of the total distance of 565 miles. Originally, the first phase of construction was to have been followed by a new arrangement similar to the first, based on 50-50 sharing of cost, but with a completion date of 1963. However, it was clear that this proposed deal was equally as unrealistic as the first, even if the province was hard-pressed to refuse it.

Finally, the new administration of the federal government under Prime Minister Lester B. Pearson agreed, on January 28, 1964, to pay 90 per cent of all Trans Canada Highway construction between April 1, 1963 and December 31, 1967.

A furious and determined construction drive ensued that resulted in the highway across the Island of Newfoundland being completed well within that time frame, the first all-weather highway in its history. Rather than the shortest distance between two points, it was routed deliberately to link up or come within reasonable proximity to dozens of communities that otherwise would have remained isolated. This was particularly noticeable in Terra Nova National Park, where the highway not only "made the rounds" of the communities, but because it was what it was—a federal park—Ottawa agreed to meet 100 per cent of the cost.

The total expenditure on the Trans Canada on its completion in 1965 was $120 million, of which some $92 million was provided by Ottawa.

Mr. Smallwood had gotten what he wanted, and devised a slogan to give credit where credit was due: "We'll Finish the Drive in '65—Thanks to Mr. Pearson!" There was an official opening marked by a giant motorcade across the Island (not to be confused with the Premier's Land Rover safari in 1958, the first crossing of the Island by motor car). A three-day celebration culminated in the unveiling by the Prime Minister of a memorial shaft emblazoned with a large "Pearson Maple Leaf" to honour the man who also had given the country its distinctive flag. The location, the halfway point of the highway, just west of Grand Falls, was dubbed "Pearson's Peak."

Meanwhile, rapid progress was taking place in the development of secondary highways and local roads, which led to the disbandment of dozens of local roads boards that were no longer needed. (According to the *Encyclopedia of Newfoundland and Labrador*, in 1956-57, some 540 roads boards operated throughout the province serving some 740 settlements. In 1964-65 a reclassification of local boards led to the cancellation of about 220 of them. In 1974 a similar reclassification led to further cancellations when all local roads boards having highway connections with the main highway system were cancelled. By 1962 fewer than a score of local boards remained.

In 1957 the first provincial Department of Highways was created to take over construction and maintenance of roads and bridges from the Department of Public Works. It also would become responsible for other transportation areas—ferries and ferry terminals, airstrips, and soaring motor vehicle registrations along with inspection and licensing. This occurred with negotiations about to get underway for a new equal-shares arrangement with Ottawa. The Roads to Resources Agreement, signed on December 15, 1959, provided for $18 million to be expended on nearly a score of roads projects and a dozen bridges.

In the late 1960s, Ottawa created the Department of Regional Economic Expansion (DREE) to replace the former Atlantic Development Board and to launch new programs that included industrial incentives, rural development, social adjustment, and infrastructure assistance. Under DREE, highways and forest access roads valued at some $65 million were negotiated for designated Special Areas of the province with Ottawa meeting the total cost for about one third of the mileage. Prominent among these projects were the Burin Peninsula, Bay d'Espoir and Great Northern Peninsula Highways, the latter growing out of the Gros Morne National Park agreement.

In the St. John's area, the $52 million project to build the Harbour and Crosstown Arterial Roads, to create smooth flow of traffic from the Trans Canada to the inner city, began in 1971 with Ottawa agreeing to contribute $37 million under DREE. (The new regional water supply for the St. John's area was developed with a $20 million grant from the agency, which also provided $22 million to fund the Newfoundland and Labrador Development Corporation, an initiative of the Smallwood Liberals that achieved fruition after we had gone out of office.)

Meanwhile, in sparsely populated Labrador, the curse of isolation was also being erased, if slowly. Linking the ancient communities of the Coast, and providing the resource-rich areas of Central, Eastern and Northern Labrador with connections to the outside world, would constitute a major challenge.

However, the economic foundations had been laid in the huge iron ore developments at Wabush and Labrador City, and the giant hydroelectric project at the Upper Churchill. It seemed inescapable that major transportation initiatives—including the Strait of Belle Isle tunnel to carry a power infeed to this Island and an electric railway, as proposed by Mr. Smallwood and Churchill Falls president Donald McParland as long as four decades ago—would, in time, come to pass.

# CHAPTER 18

## ENDING THE ERA OF THE OIL LAMP

The day Newfoundland became a province of Canada, only half the population of 340,000 enjoyed the convenience and security that electricity brings. For every larger community whose residents, or many of them, had entered the era of the incandescent light bulb, a dozen smaller ones remained tied to the oil lamp; for every Newfoundlander enabled to work or study or relax in the relative comfort of artificial daylight, another was condemned to the dim, flickering shadows of the kerosene lamp.

Electricity to light homes, shops and streets in Newfoundland's capital was first generated in October 1855. That's when Alexander M. MacKay launched the St. John's Electric Light Company, which started up a generating plant on Flavin's Lane, just south of Rawlins Cross.

Next, in the 1890s, the railway-building Reid family established the St. John's Street Railway Company to build and operate a transline service in the capital. It was driven by energy from Newfoundland's first hydroelectric generating station at Petty Harbour, which began operating in April 1900.

This company began selling surplus power for domestic and commercial use, and soon purchased the assets of MacKay's firm. By the 1920s the St. John's Light and Power Company had been formed to operate the system separate from other Reid interests, and in 1924 was itself sold to Royal Securities and its subsidiary, Montreal Engineering Company. The local company then became known as Newfoundland Light and Power Company Limited.

In the meantime, the United Towns Electric Company was formed in 1902 to supply electricity to residents of the Avalon Peninsula outside the St. John's area, in the Trinity-Conception towns of Harbour Grace, Carbonear and Heart's Content, and on the Burin Peninsula from Newfoundland's second hydroelectric generating station at Victoria, Conception Bay. In time it acquired ownership of Wabana Light and Power, set up a subsidiary, West Coast Power, to serve the Port aux Basques, St. George's and Port au Port areas, and bought out the rival Public Service Electric Company selling power in Harbour Grace, Carbonear and Heart's Content.

While all this was happening, the Fishermen's Protective Union founded by William Ford Coaker was busy promoting an electricity company to supply the towns of Trinity, Bonavista and Catalina and to be the industrial "heart" of its own model town of Port Union. The Union Electric Light and Power Company was founded in 1916 and in time would serve virtually the entire Bonavista Peninsula.

In addition, the two existing paper mill companies, Bowaters in Corner Brook and Anglo-Newfoundland in Grand Falls, had their own

*For every Newfoundlander that electricity enabled to work, study or relax in relative comfort ... another was condemned to the dim shadows of the kerosene lamp.*

PHOTOS CLOCKWISE:
■ The Smallwood government established the Newfoundland Power Commission - later Newfoundland and Labrador Hydro - and through this agency built the Bay d'Espoir generating station to be the heart of the island electric energy system (GN); ■ The objective: to eliminate the kerosene lamp (centre) upon which half the population depended (TA); ■ Next, the thermal generating station near Holyrood was provided as the backup for Bay d'Espoir and a supplementary power source (TA); ■ Meanwhile, Premier Smallwood battled a succession of Quebec leaders to get Churchill Falls project going, starting with Premier Jean Lesage (TA); ■ By this time, Hydro transmission towers were bringing electric power to some 800 communities in Newfoundland and Labrador (TA).

electrical generating facilities. They supplied their particular industrial needs and the commercial and domestic requirements of the surrounding areas, as did the Ministry of Transport in Gander and the towns of Lewisporte and Springdale.

This hodgepodge of inadequate services not only imposed a hardship on tens of thousands of individuals and businesses, even whole communities, but constituted as well a serious detriment to economic development.

Persisting into the post-war era and the early years of Confederation, it led the government of Premier Joseph R. Smallwood to create a central authority, the Newfoundland Power Commission, headed first by George H. Desbarats, later (and through most of its spectacular development phase), by George P. Hobbs to begin the massive task of bringing electrical service to hundreds of unserved rural communities and tens of thousands of unserved households. A significant start on the Rural Electrification Program (it would come to serve 100,000 people in rural areas) was made in Labrador in 1958 with the installation of a 200-kilowatt diesel generator at Happy Valley. By 1972 the entire program was complete, and every community with a customer population of 15 or more had service available.

In the meantime, Canada's fastest-growing provincial population was not only creating increasing demand for electrical service, but once free from the restriction of the oil lamp tended to consume maximum, rather than minimum, quantities of power. The "Domestic and Farm Customer Population" exploded from 28,725 purchasing 31,906 kilowatt hours in 1949 to 149,366 customers and 1,642,134 kilowatt hours in 1979.

Among its innumerable social and industrial benefits, electrification of rural Newfoundland, and eventually Labrador, permitted transformation of the fishing industry from a salt fish base to production of the fresh-frozen products the marketplace was now demanding. (In direct contradiction, indeed, to charges the Smallwood government had written off the fisheries, giving preference instead to heavy industry—essentially, the "burn your boats" accusation—major emphasis was placed upon revitalization of the fishery enterprise that was in dire straits at the end of the Second World War.)

In 1965 the power commission, in future to be known as Newfoundland and Labrador Hydro, was reorganized and given the task of developing the province's first major, publicly owned hydro generating station at Bay d'Espoir. It would also build an Island-wide high-voltage transmission grid to interconnect the various public and private generation facilities—in the process, rationalizing technical differences in the British-standard systems at Grand Falls and Corner Brook—and providing the province with security of supply by constructing a backup oil-fired thermal generating plant at Holyrood. As well, new hydro generating plants were constructed at Cat Arm, Hinds Lake and on the Upper Salmon River.

Construction of the provincial grid greatly facilitated amalgamation of the many diverse elements that made up the electrical generation industry. In 1966 shareholders of Newfoundland Light and Power, Union Electric and United Towns voted to form a single entity. It was reported in 1985, 100 years after MacKay launched the St. John's Electric Light Company to turn on a handful of customers and half a hundred street lights, that in two decades since total amalgamation the number of accounts had increased from 88,951 to 169,071 and annual sales from approximately 500 GWh (gigawatts, a unit of power measurement equal to one billion watts) to in excess of 3,000 GWh. The private company then claimed it was providing "efficient and dependable service to 85 per cent of the population."

Hydro became operator of the Churchill Falls (Labrador) Corp. (CFLCo.) generating plant, one of the world's largest, and custodian of the province's majority interest, after the company was nationalized from British Newfoundland Corp. Ltd. (Brinco) in 1974.

Construction of the largest civil engineering project undertaken to that time in North America was begun in Central Labrador in 1966 by CFLCo., then the hydro subsidiary of Brinco. It held a statutory lease on development of the Churchill River watershed granted by unanimous vote of the House of Assembly in 1961. A search had been underway for a dozen years for potential markets for power from the project, principally in the New England states, but Quebec consistently refused to permit transmission lines to be built across its territory or to permit CFLCo. to "wheel" the power to market and in the end became, in effect, the sole customer.

# IN THE NATIONAL INTEREST

The original legislation by which the British Newfoundland Corporation (Brinco) was brought to life was given approval in the House of Assembly, without a dissenting vote, on March 31,1953.

Ten years later, the effort to locate customers for the electricity that the company proposed to generate from the fall of water at Churchill Falls on the mighty Labrador river formerly known as the Hamilton or Grand, was finally showing important results: Consolidated Edison, one of the world's greatest utility companies, had expressed interest, thus giving credence to Mr. Smallwood's long-ago prophecy that Labrador power would one day light the streets and run the subways of New York.

The big question was, how would the power get to New York? The practical, and perhaps only realistic answer, was by transmission across the territory of Quebec. But as the Premier of Newfoundland realized perhaps better than anyone, under the imperious Premier Jean Lesage and the mercurial Energy Minister René Lévesque, Quebec "had not the least intention" of allowing a company—especially a private company chartered by the legislature of Newfoundland—"to do any such thing." This was underscored when the Quebec government "suddenly, with scarcely an hour's warning, nationalized virtually all power production and transmission" in that province.

Mr. Smallwood also recognized that property and civil rights, under Canada's written constitution, "are of exclusive provincial jurisdiction. Accordingly, Quebec would be within its rights to forbid the use of its soil for a transmission line (but) it became perfectly obvious to me, and to my colleagues in Cabinet, that Quebec was taking an altogether selfish view."

The government there, he wrote, "believed, in the first place, that Newfoundland was a usurper in Labrador; that Labrador rightfully belonged to Quebec ... In the second place, Quebec was implacably set upon using Labrador power for its own purposes. Labrador power, Quebec was convinced, couldn't be used within Labrador, and couldn't be used anywhere else unless it went through Quebec. Where did that leave Newfoundland? It left us at the mercy of Quebec. Our people's heritage could be developed only if Quebec consented, and it would consent only if it got its own way."

Finally, all efforts to change Quebec's position by negotiation having failed—specifically at this point, refusal to sign a Letter of Intent—the Premier decided to formally request federal help. A late 1966 diary entry helps tell the tale:

*"September 12. Cabinet at my request passed order that on 23rd we'll ask Ottawa to declare the Churchill to be in the national interest if by then Quebec has not agreed. J.W. P(ickersgill) to lunch—told him, and he phoned Ottawa to tell them ..."*

The Premier, although acknowledging the principle of provincial jurisdiction, went on to point out that "there is an overriding principle that allows the Government of Canada to declare something to be in the national interest, and in that case the federal authority is paramount (but) not for a moment did I suppose that designation of the project as national would be a solution of itself. The threat might, however, be more effectual than the reality ..."

In the meantime, in a provincial General Election, the Lesage Liberals had been narrowly defeated by the Union Nationale party, and new Premier Daniel Johnson's administration appeared to be split on the deal. Mr. Smallwood flew to Montreal, bringing with him a letter to Prime Minister Lester B. Pearson based on the Cabinet order. There he met with CFLCO President Donald McParland and other Brinco officials who, having read the letter in confidence, "pleaded with me not to deliver it ... and delivered a message that Johnson had sent me through them, asking me to wait until October 6. I appeared to consider the request (and after some time alone) agreed."

In *BRINCO: The Story of Churchill Falls* (McClelland and Stewart, 1975) author Philip Smith states that McParland reported following a meeting with Johnson that the new Premier appeared satisfied with the economics but wanted more time to deal with political opposition to the proposed development. However, he warned that the Newfoundland Premier's plan to seek Ottawa's intervention would "slam the door" on the project.

According to Smith: "Dubiously, Joey permitted himself to be persuaded to hold off for another week. But he said he was not going to fool around any longer; if Johnson had not fulfilled his promises by October 7, Churchill Falls would be taken out of the hands of Brinco and Quebec and would become a national project." To underline that he meant business, according to Smith, he left the letter to Pearson with Attorney General Leslie R. Curtis to be mailed if the decision went against the scheme while he was overseas.

Within days, by this story, Johnson gave his government's approval and Hydro-Quebec and Brinco signed the Letter of Intent allowing the project to proceed.

Several years ago, in a nationally published article in the *Globe and Mail*, St. John's lawyer and businessman Cabot Martin, former senior policy advisor to Premier Brian Peckford, wrote that Mr. Smallwood told him Smith had it all wrong, that in fact he travelled from Montreal to Ottawa by car so no one would know to deliver the letter personally to the Prime Minister.

"… (B)efore I could say a word," Martin quoted him as saying, "Mr. Pearson said, Joe, I know why you are here and if you ask me I'll have to say yes, otherwise we would not really have a country. But I'm asking you not to ask me because we will not be able to keep the towers up.'"

Then, according to Martin, the former Premier paused, looked at him as if to demand what he would have done, and concluded: "So I didn't ask him."

In 1963, by now having many millions invested, and therefore little choice in the matter, Brinco began negotiating the sale of power directly to Hydro-Quebec which had the technology for extra-high voltage transmission over long distances. Talks broke down in 1964, but resumed the following year after a proposal to bypass Quebec and proceed by means of undersea cables via the Island of Newfoundland and Nova Scotia and on to the United States—the so-called "Anglo-Saxon route"—was shown to be feasible, if expensive. Once the Letter of Intent was signed it was, of course, no longer necessary to be considered.

The Letter of Intent between Hydro-Quebec and Brinco, providing for the purchase and sale of all available power surplus to the needs of Newfoundland, was issued in October 1966. Two and a half years later the parties concluded a 40-year agreement, renewable at Quebec's option for a further 25 years, and estimated at the time to be worth $5 billion. The documents were signed in Montreal on May 14, 1969 by Donald McParland and Eric Lambert for Brinco and Yvon de Guise and Jean-Claude Lessard for Hydro-Quebec.

It had been six years since a Crown corporation of the Quebec government and a subsidiary of Brinco, an international consortium, had begun negotiating together, and seventeen years since Mr. Smallwood had called on British Prime Minister Sir Winston Churchill in London on August 14, 1952 to propose the "bridling" of a great Labrador river, and to make the first moves that resulted in creation of Brinco mainly for that purpose.

In time, in the absence of a formula or agreement to equitably split windfall profits on the final sale of power, rapidly rising world energy prices would see Quebec realize huge, unforeseen revenues in the hundreds of millions of dollars annually in which Newfoundland does not share. On the other hand, escalating costs of maintenance and upgrading of facilities give rise to concerns that the project could get into serious operational, as well as financial, difficulty—a matter of overriding concern to Newfoundland and Labrador Hydro, as custodian of the province's interest majority in the Churchill Falls (Labrador) Power Corp. since nationalization in the mid-1970s.

On the 25th anniversary of first power from the project, December 6, 1991, the then Premier of Newfoundland and Labrador, Brian Tobin, told the House of Assembly the government was "steadfastly committed … to ensure that (the people of this province) receive their fair share of the benefits of this great development."

# CHAPTER 19
## DYNAMIC CENTRE OF LEARNING

*Unlikely prophecy
as the "Dirty Thirties"
loomed, he foresaw
"a large university," and
the development of
"technological colleges."*

PHOTOS CLOCKWISE:
■ The sprawling main Memorial
University campus, comprising the
second largest community in the
province - up to some 30,000
persons on a daily basis - stands as
the greatest physical and cultural
achievement of the Smallwood
years; at right is the familiar façade
of its Grenfell College in Corner
Brook (MA); ■ Academic procession
marking opening of the new
campus included Smallwood
ministers (foreground, l-r) L.R. Curtis,
E.S. Spencer, C.H. Ballam, P.J. Lewis,
F.W. Rowe, and M.P. Murray among
hundreds of dignitaries and invited
guests (TA); ■ Other areas of post-
secondary education and training
were not forgotten; architect's
rendering shows Corner Brook District
Vocational School (now part of the
College of the North Atlantic) typical
of facilities established in nearly a
score of communities (GN); ■
Pictured in academic dress is
Premier Smallwood, moving force
behind the creation of Memorial,
today Atlantic Canada's largest
university, as a degree-granting
institution (TA).

A
ppropriately, it was the first significant legislation brought by the Smallwood government to the reconstituted House of Assembly in 1949—a Bill to provide for raising Memorial University College, established in 1925 in memory of Newfoundland's war dead, to the status of a full-fledged, degree-granting university.

This had been just one aspect, albeit an important one, of "The New Newfoundland" about which youthful journalist Joseph R. Smallwood had been writing with unbounded optimism fully two decades earlier.

Indulging in what must have seemed like extremely unlikely prophecy, given the condition of the country on the threatening edge of the "Dirty Thirties," he foresaw that Newfoundland would have one day "a large university in St. John's." Moreover, education would be free and compulsory, illiteracy would be abolished, and there would be "technological colleges" established.

Now, as the first Premier of a new Canadian province, he would have the opportunity to make these prophecies come true.

The Speech from the Throne outlining the policies of the new government to the resurrected legislature on July 13, 1949 had Lieutenant-Governor Sir Albert Walsh (who would become first chairman of the new university's Board of Regents) announce to the newly elected Members and the world:

"It is considered that Newfoundland should have her own degree-conferring University and you will be invited to consider legislation which would confer upon the Memorial University College the status of a university. It is planned to widen and improve the functions, and thus improve the public usefulness of this institution created originally in honour of our illustrious dead of the First World War."

"A Bill, An Act Respecting the Memorial University of Newfoundland," was given Royal Assent on August 13, exactly one month to the day after the House opened.

The Board of Regents (i.e., board of directors) and the Senate (the academic authority embracing representatives of various faculties) were inaugurated in May, 1950 and the first Convocation was held the month following, when the first degrees were awarded.

During the debate on the legislation, Mr. Smallwood promised the new university would be "a dynamic centre of learning, culture and research of which every Newfoundlander can be proud." As well they might. In the intervening years, some 65,000 degrees have been awarded, and many other thousands of Newfoundlanders, who otherwise might not have had the chance to attend university or obtain courses, earned diplomas and certificates.

Memorial has expanded from some 300 students attending in 1949, to an enrolment that in 1992-93 peaked at 18,632 full- and part-time. (In 2001-02 there were 16,156 including 12,237 undergraduate and 1,687 graduate students, and 2,057 part-time. There were 1,012 full-time students and 5,295 part-time at the Marine Institute, the former College of Fisheries, Navigation, Marine Engineering and Technology, also founded by the Smallwood government, that became part of the university in 1992.)

Originally the university offered courses in only two faculties, Education and Arts and Science. However, a period of rapid development generously funded by the government included expansion to six faculties—Arts, Science, Education, Medicine, Engineering and Business Administration, and seven Schools—Graduate Studies, Nursing, Physical Education and Athletics, Social Work, General and Continuing Studies, Music, and Pharmacy. In 1975, there was established a West Coast campus at Corner Brook, named for the medical missionary who pioneered medicine in Northern Newfoundland and Labrador, Sir Wilfred Grenfell. Grenfell College offered a full range of university-level courses leading to B.A. and B.Sc. degrees, and also became the home of degree programs in Fine Arts.

As well, the university developed an immersion program in the French language on the island of St. Pierre, the French territory off the South Coast of Newfoundland. Institut Frecker was named for the late former Chancellor of Memorial and Newfoundland Minister of Education, G. Alain Frecker, who was born in St. Pierre.

In addition to all this, in the interests of broadening the scope of its activities and meeting specific needs of the province, the university established over the years some three dozen special divisions, among them the Art Gallery of Newfoundland and Labrador, the Botanical Garden, the Centre for Fisheries Innovation, the Centre for Cold Ocean Resources Engineering, the Centre for Management Development, and the Maritime History Archive. There is also the Smallwood Foundation for Newfoundland and Labrador Studies, substantially endowed by the Joseph R. Smallwood Heritage Foundation on its winding up following completion of the *Encyclopedia of Newfoundland and Labrador*.

In 1966, the Board of Regents approved establishment of a residential campus at Harlow, Essex, England. The campus provides accommodation for students and academic staff of Memorial while they gain field experience in the United Kingdom and Continental Europe, and also acts as a base for teaching credit courses and for academic seminars and conferences.

## ON RAISING MEMORIAL COLLEGE
## TO UNIVERSITY STATUS

### Newfoundland National Convention, May 26, 1947

Mr. Smallwood: Mr. (John G.) Higgins's resolution is the one before us. It is a resolution which, if passed, would put this Convention on record as being in favour of turning the Newfoundland Memorial College into a university, into an institution that would confer degrees. I am in favour of that, and that is why I seconded the motion. I have looked up some facts concerning nearby parts of the world, those nearest to Newfoundland—Nova Scotia, New Brunswick, and Prince Edward Island. The population of Newfoundland, with Labrador, is about 320,000. In Nova Scotia, with a population less than twice the population of Newfoundland, they have eight degree-conferring educational institutions. In the city of Halifax alone there are five ... In New Brunswick, with less than 200,000 more than our own population, they have five degree-conferring institutions ... and in the tiny province of PEI, with only 95,000, they have one ... We have not got even one. Not one in all the island, where a Newfoundland boy or girl, young man and young woman can attend and take sufficient training to lead to the conferring of a degree. This motion is to the effect that, in the opinion of the Convention, not that we can do anything about it, the Memorial University College ought to be raised to the status of a degree-conferring institution.

I am no authority on education but I am fully agreed that from a purely educational standpoint, the Memorial College ought to be raised to that status, but there is another side to it, another angle that interests me a great deal. In this country of ours we have had 450 years of a very remarkable history—perhaps the most remarkable history of any part of the western half of the world. This is a country in which we have developed very distinctive peculiarities. We have our own traditions. We have our own folklore. We have our own folk music. I remember on one occasion in London going to talk to Miss Maud Karpeles, perhaps one of the world's greatest authorities on world folk songs, and her telling me that in Newfoundland there had been discovered some of the most interesting folk songs anywhere on this side of the Atlantic. We have got a distinctive culture all our own, and yet we have nothing ... with the exception of the O'Leary poetry award which is given annually, we have nothing, nor have we had anything to foster and encourage the development and growth and recognition of a distinctly Newfoundland culture. And one of the most attractive possibilities of the Memorial University, if it became a university, would be that of having the university become a dynamo, a powerhouse, in the inculcation and dissemination and encouragement of a distinctly Newfoundland culture, because mark this—whatever form of government we may have in the future ... remember this, that we Newfoundlanders must never for a moment forget or neglect or turn our backs on our own distinctive Newfoundland outlook on life, our distinctive Newfoundland culture. I go a step further; in the case of our deciding some day this fall, perhaps, in the national referendum, to link this country with another country, in such a case it will be more important than ever to see to it that our Newfoundland culture is preserved and encouraged and fostered and developed, and in no way can that be done better that through the creation of a Newfoundland university. I wanted to make that point. It is not a new point, I have been making it for many, many years, and I want to associate myself very heartily indeed with the motion ...

*(The first session of the Newfoundland House of Assembly after Confederation was convened on July 13, 1949, with Lieutenant-Governor Sir Albert Walsh reading the Speech from the Throne in which the new administration of Premier Joseph R. Smallwood declared that Newfoundland should have her own degree-granting university. Members were advised that they would be invited to consider legislation to quickly bring this about. Just under one month later, on August 9, "A Bill, An Act Respecting the Memorial University of Newfoundland" received First Reading, in effect notice the legislation was about to be presented. It was given Second Reading, debate on the principle, on August 11, followed by Third Reading, clause-by-clause examination and final approval, on August 12. Royal Assent and proclamation into law occurred on August 13, 1949.)*

Among the principal ambitions of Newfoundland's first Premier—hardly less important, on his scale of priorities, than university education—was to raise significantly the levels of literacy and trades skills of his countrymen and women.

As a journalist, public speaker, debater and publisher of books Mr. Smallwood had no equal. In his writing, he foresaw the day when university and college education would be made available to every young person, and some not so young, regardless of economic circumstances or where they live in Newfoundland and Labrador. It was typical of the man that once given the opportunity, he did not hesitate but would bend every effort to bring this about—and Confederation provided that opportunity.

The results of his ambition in addition to Memorial University, were the College of Trades and Technology and a network of District Vocational Schools—in the 1990s, amalgamated into the multi-campus College of the North Atlantic, testimony to his determination to give young Newfoundlanders with the skills and knowledge to make their way in the world.

Senator Frederick W. Rowe had a distinguished career in education before serving two decades in Smallwood Cabinets, including several years as Minister of Education. In his authoritative history of *Education and Culture in Newfoundland* (McGraw-Hill Ryerson, 1976) he wrote of the irony that "from the first days of organized educational activity ... the need for developing vocational and technical opportunities was stressed over and over," yet next to nothing was ever done about it.

"The one-sidedness of Newfoundland's emphasis on academic education was obvious ... but in view of the prevailing poverty" and insistent demands for ordinary school facilities, neither governments nor denominational authorities "cared to assume the staggering financial burden ..."

This condition prevailed until, thanks to Mr. Smallwood's energy and drive, Confederation came along, and the infusion of Canadian federal resources "made possible a radical and spectacular departure."

In 1950 came the Vocational Schools Assistance Agreement, under which the province could receive 50 per cent of the cost of approved capital projects. This was followed in 1960 by an even more generous arrangement, Ottawa paying 75 per cent, which enabled the Smallwood government to build what would become known as the College of Trades and Technology on grounds adjacent to Confederation Building. At the time the largest structure in the province, with a floor area of 262,000 square feet, it was completed in early 1963 at a cost of $8 million and opened almost immediately. By 1971-72 it had an enrolment in excess of 4,000 full- and part-time students.

However, Mr. Smallwood realized in building it that it would do little for young people in distant areas of the province, outside the St. John's area. Therefore he set out, under the terms of a revised 1960 agreement with Ottawa, to build 11 modern trade schools at Corner Brook, Grand Falls, Burin, Gander, Bell Island, Carbonear, Port aux Basques, Stephenville Crossing, Lewisporte, Clarenville, and Seal Cove, Conception Bay. A few years later this building program was followed by a new one calling for doubling of the size of the school at Seal Cove, a second storey at Gander, and the installation of "portables" to expand capacity at Corner Brook, Grand Falls, Gander, Burin and Clarenville.

Even more significantly, additional schools would be built at Happy Valley, Labrador, at or near St. Anthony, on the Baie Verte and Burin Peninsulas, and at Springdale and Placentia. The expanded program would further ensure that youth living in the far reaches of rural Newfoundland and Labrador would be provided with the same advantages as those in larger, more urban centres.

All told, by the 1970s, there were in operation 17 modern trades and vocational schools in the province, plus the Stephenville Adult Centre, where none had existed previously. Some 5,000 students were registered at any given time, and as they graduated from high school, a waiting list of at least 1,000 more. Never before in our history had anyone dared to contemplate education and training Newfoundlanders on the scale and in the variety of technological and other skills to which young people could now apply themselves … and if not in Newfoundland and Labrador, then anywhere they chose to go in the world. In the meantime, if the economists were right, as they surely are—that a skilled workforce is the single more important concomitant of economic development—then this was the way to do it.

Moreover, it was a far cry from the jack-of-all-trades experience acquired in the fishing boat and on the head of the wharf that for most had been the limit of ambition only a few years before.

That said, it is clear that the post-secondary education enterprise—the university, the vocational network—would be nothing without the solid foundation of a competent day-school system, preparing Newfoundland's children adequately to take advantage of higher education.

In all the years since the Church of England's Rev. Henry Jones launched the first formal school in Bonavista in the 1720s, hundreds of millions and perhaps even billions of dollars have been spent providing our young people with the most basic necessity, next to life itself, required for survival in an increasingly demanding North American, and indeed, global industrial society. Most of this effort has been expended in the past five decades.

When Newfoundland became a province of Canada in 1949, the school population stood at approximately 75,000 students, instructed by some 2,400 teachers in 600 schools that in most cases were small, ill-equipped, and lacking both indoor plumbing and central heating, only a few with electric lights. The Commission of Government budget for teachers' salaries amounted to $2 million, on average quite less than $1,000 a year for each of the men and women in charge of the classroom.

In the first fifteen years of the Smallwood government—and of course, it did not end there—the number of students nearly doubled to 146,000, and the number of teachers more than doubled to more than 5,700. Their salary budget had increased almost 900 per cent, to approximately $18 million a year. The number of schools increased to 1,250, virtually all of them brand new and complete with modern amenities—indoor plumbing, adequate heating and lighting, and many of them served with a brand new phenomenon: a fleet of some 200 school buses that was sure to grow.

During the 15 years of the Commission of Government, from 1934 to 1949, total expenditure on education was $31.5 million. Between 1949 and 1966 the education budget swelled to $242.7 million, spectacular growth during the Smallwood era of some 800 per cent!

# CHAPTER 20
## THE FLOWERING OF THE ARTS

WINNING ENTRIES IN THE GOVERNMENT
ARTS AND LETTERS COMPETITION 1966

SPONSORED BY THE GOVERNMENT OF NEWFOUNDLAND AND LABRADOR

*The Confederation years would see flowering of the cultural expression of Newfoundland and Labrador ... out of all proportion to size and population.*

A major concern harboured by many serious-minded Newfoundlanders concerning Confederation with Canada was that a unique culture and history might become lost ... submerged ... swallowed up ... in the diversity of the much larger partner in the proposed union. Prominent among them was none other than Confederation's main proponent, Joseph R. Smallwood. As a delegate to the National Convention, he had cautioned that in the event it was decided in a national referendum to link Newfoundland to another country, it would be "more important than ever to see to it that our Newfoundland culture is preserved and encouraged and fostered and developed."

He went on to point out that at the time, with the exception of the Newfoundland Poetry Awards offered by F.M. O'Leary Limited, sponsor of his former radio program "The Barrelman," there was "nothing to foster and encourage the development and growth and recognition of a distinctly Newfoundland culture." He argued that the principal means by which this might be achieved was the creation of Memorial College into a full-fledged university—which occurred, of course, as soon as Mr. Smallwood became Premier.

Greatly to the contrary of the expressed concerns, the Confederation years would see the flowering of the arts, as the cultural expression of Newfoundland and Labrador, on a scale and depth no one could anticipate. The evidence is on every hand—in music and dance and other elements of stage performance; writing, mainly biography but with a good deal of historical work, and much fiction as well; and painting and sculpture. Never before have they achieved such prominence, not only in the province but across Canada and beyond, and out of all proportion to our size and population.

Consequently, it has long since ceased to surprise that entertainers Ron Hynes, the Ennis sisters, and Great Big Sea, successors to Mademoiselle Toulinguet, Emile Benoit and Rufus Guinchard (neither any longer with us) and the Wonderful Grand Band and Figgy Duff with their repertoire of traditional music and Celtic rock, are sought-after performers, not only in North America, but in Britain, Ireland, Continental Europe and far-off Japan.

Newfoundlanders and Labradorians—the arts community, and the community in general—accept with total equanimity that this province's visual artists, led by David Blackwood, Christopher and Mary Pratt and Gerry Squires, are among Canada's most important.

They have become used to the fact that classical musicians like Marina Piccinini, Thomas Yee and Joanne Hounsell, and the Newfoundland Symphony and Holy Heart choirs, all products of a broadly based system comprising both regular school and private instruction and Memorial University's School of Music, are leading performers in Canada and elsewhere.

Novelists Kevin Major, Wayne Johnston (who received basic training as a reporter at *The Daily News* during my time as publisher), Bernice Morgan, Ed Riche, Gordon Rogers and Donna Morrissey, and Helen Porter, Michael Crummey and Earl Pilgrim, are filling up the formerly lonely landscape of Margaret Duley, Percy Janes, Cassie Brown and Harold Horwood.

Newfoundland actors Gordon Pinsent, Robert Joy and Natasha Henstridge and comedians Andy Jones, Mary Walsh, Rick Mercer and Shawn Majumdar (to name a few) have made their mark on film and/or television.

How is this broad artistic awakening explained? And what public policy part did Joseph R. Smallwood and his colleagues in the Newfoundland government play in fostering and encouraging it?

First, it is important to consult some history. In an incisive article in *The Book of Newfoundland* (1967) Rae Perlin, a visual artist in her own right and prominent arts critic for *The Daily News* and the *Newfoundland Herald*, raised this question: "If the art of a country in some measure reflects its history, one may wonder why Newfoundland, which has had so much history, should have produced so little art."

Suggesting a clue could be found in the history itself, she turned to contemporary educator and historian Helen Louise Whiteway (1901-82) who had written: "The early settlers led a poor, scrambling, tormented existence, subject to tyranny, corruption and violence; between attacks from abroad, rioting, mutiny, epidemics of smallpox and cholera and other disasters at home, there could be little leisure and opportunity for the arts."

Perlin herself commented: "Add to this the Island's isolation from mainland centres and within its own borders. Scattered settlements, separated from one another and from the capital city, were virtually cut off in the wintertime and some could be reached only by steamer in the summer; only in recent years have routes been opened up to provide contact by road between smaller and larger centres."

The sparseness of local artistic output seems obvious as she refers to the fact that for "centuries" the work of early cartographers and topographers had been in evidence. Judge D.W. Prowse's *A History of Newfoundland* (1895) was "profusely illustrated with drawings and watercolour sketches by both professional (often military) and dilettante landscapists"—but most likely from away. Mention is made of *A View of St. John's* dated 1798, by H.P. Brenton, in the British Museum, and an even earlier landscape by the Dutch artist Gerard Edema of *Fishing Station, Newfoundland.*

"It is tempting," Perlin wrote—and immediately succumbed to it—"to mention the work of what is probably Newfoundland's first known native artist, a Beothuck girl (Shawnadithit) whose maps, illustrating the last tragic episodes of Beothuck history, and drawings of the house in St. John's, her last residence, as well as of spearhead designs and food utensils used by the Indians ..." were reproduced in James P. Howley's *The Beothucks or Red Indians* (1915.)

By the early 19th Century "schools were scattered about the Island (and) sporadic private academies" but the purpose seemed to be more to "round out an education than to develop special talents in the individual arts." In the 1860s the various denominational schools took "the teaching of music and art seriously enough to acquire a number of qualified teachers from abroad," and in particular those administered by the Sisters of the Presentation and Mercy Congregations.

"Some Newfoundlanders had, by the turn of the century, already left to further their art studies abroad. The most famous, Maurice Cullen (1866-1934) went to France, where he was greatly influenced by the Impressionists. When he returned to Montreal (he became) one of the strongest influences leading to a purely Canadian (as against European) art, leading to the work of the Group of Seven. "

In the 1920s, Newfoundland "perhaps was not too different from other, more advanced centres, in regard to favouring a conventional art," Perlin allows, and in the 1930s "painting ... took a second or third place to theatre and music, which being more outgoing activities probably attracted more people to them." But it appears music education and performance also suffered during this period and it was not until the new Memorial University was established with its degree—granting School of Music that solid improvement occurred.

In 1949, the editor of *Canadian Art*, Robert Ayre, "defined the art situation here to the effect that Newfoundland had left the painting of her 'rugged landscape to outsiders, and amateurs.'" He said it had produced no outstanding painters except Cullen and his stepson, Robert Pilot, both of whom had earned Canadian rather than Newfoundland reputations. (Harold Goodridge was credited with some "vigorous watercolours" but "such sculpture as existed was by outsiders," e.g., the War Memorial, the Fighting Newfoundlander, Peter Pan. He had favourable judgment for J.R. Ewing's profile of Capt. "Bob" Bartlett ... "impressive in its native simplicity and dignity."

Perlin recalled that Ayre summed up this way: "While Newfoundland has dozens of dabblers and hundreds go to see their exhibitions, the lack of an art school, and of a public gallery or any proper place to hang pictures, has hindered the development of painting beyond the dabbling stage."

At this point the St. John's Art Club presented a brief in 1950 to the Royal Commission for the National Development of the Arts. It was quite possible, it declared, "for a Newfoundland schoolchild to leave school without ever having heard of the great names of art." And it judged that the public taste was aesthetically undeveloped "because there are few opportunities for placing before the people the best of the world's achievement in the fine arts."

Such comments were not lost upon Mr. Smallwood, well established as writer, historian and broadcaster-folklorist. Within the year after becoming Premier his government announced inauguration of the Newfoundland Arts and Letters Competition "as an endeavour to broaden the scope of activities and develop a greater interest in the arts and letters" on the part of Newfoundlanders generally. Perlin noted that "by far the most popular section for the public was the visual arts ..."

Cash awards and subsequently medals were offered for the best historical account of neglected periods of Newfoundland history; the best short story; the best portrait, landscape and mural; the best musical or literary script for broadcast; the best play written and/or produced. Categories and rewards were changed and/or broadened over the years, but there is general agreement that thousands of Newfoundlanders had their artistic and literary talents awakened and developed as a result of this initiative. The *Encyclopedia of Newfoundland and Labrador* lists "several ... who later received acclaim in their fields"—Gregory J. Power, Christopher Pratt, David Blackwood, Michael F. Harrington and Gary Saunders.

Senator F.W. Rowe, writing from the vantage point of lengthy careers in education and politics, wrote in his *History of Newfoundland and Labrador* (McGraw-Hill Ryerson, 1980) that "the material prosperity that followed (Confederation) ... helped to make possible a cultural flowering that has received national recognition."

Moreover, the upsurge of interest in drama, music and artistic expression in general—in which, no doubt, the Arts and Letters Competition played a part—had "increased the desire of many people to have facilities where cultural activities could be reasonably well-housed." Thus was the Smallwood government, which provided its entire Budget, influenced to support the development of programs at Memorial University to encourage interest in arts and culture, and in time to create a network of centres where exhibitions and performances could be properly accommodated.

It began with the $8 million St. John's Arts and Culture Centre, the province's major project honouring Canada's 100th birthday, concerning which Rowe remarked that there were "a few who thought that, with so many other needs, such centres were a luxury the province could not afford."

Next came the Corner Brook centre in which Lundrigans Limited and Bowater's Newfoundland Limited participated, followed by centres in Grand Falls and Gander constructed from sections of the Czechoslovak pavilion from Expo 67 in Montreal. A new structure was erected in Labrador West, and a former USAF building at Stephenville would be converted for the same purpose.

As indicated, the provision of facilities underlay unprecedented activity and growth in the cultural industries. For example, Rowe reported that by the decade of the 1970s, there were 16 bands and orchestras and 250 glee clubs and choirs where only a small handful had existed before. In St. John's the Kiwanis Music Festival Association, most prominent of community organizations involved in encouraging music participation, had 1,400 participants in its first year, 1952, but two decades later there were 12,600 and by 1979 the number had grown to 20,000. At the same time, the St. John's (later Newfoundland) Symphony Orchestra was formed, along with the Memorial University Extension Choir, both under the tutelage of Ignatius Rumboldt, which along with a number of school and community choirs began to win national acclaim.

The Smallwood government's interest in fostering the arts and culture was not limited to building buildings. It also, in Rowe's phrase, set out to "remedy the vandalism of the Commission of Government which had destroyed Newfoundland's national museum" in a burst of misguided fiscal austerity in 1934. In 1957 the institution was reopened, the government providing a staff to assist Curator L.E.F. English to restore, so far as possible, what had been scattered and lost.

In 1956 the Newfoundland Archives was established at Memorial University. When the legislature was relocated to its new home in Confederation Building four years later, the government reassumed responsibility for the archives and turned the now vacant Colonial Building to that purpose. In 1959 it introduced legislation to formally establish the Newfoundland and Labrador Archives. The Historic Objects, Sites and Records Act provided for the "safekeeping, classification, indexing and calendaring" of public documents and materials considered to be of historical importance.

Of a succession of directors, the Provincial Archivist who perhaps contributed most importantly to archival development was ex-newspaperman F. Burnham Gill, under whose stewardship public interest in historical/cultural resources was raised to unprecedented levels.

"One of the great defects in Newfoundland's educational and cultural services prior to 1949," Rowe pointed out—without question, it may be said, contributing to a high rate of illiteracy—was the limited number and the poor calibre of "libraries and related services." By the 1970s the annual government expenditure on libraries had reached $1 3/4 million, some 20 times the provision of $80,000 before Confederation, and the number of libraries in existence had been increased from 25 to 104.

A strong case may be made that, far from destroying or damaging the innate Newfoundland talent for art and performance or obscuring our history and culture, by rolling back the ancient isolation and providing substantial new enabling and sustaining resources, Confederation opened the new province to the nation and the world with largely unanticipated, but tremendously beneficial results.

# CHAPTER 21

## WHO SAID TO "BURN YOUR BOATS"?

*"Do you sincerely believe that I was such a chump, such a jackass, such a traitor to Newfoundland ...? For the record, I never said it..."*

In all the years since Confederation, in newspaper columns and letters to the editor, in biographies and treatises on political economy, on the political stump, and still today on the *Open Line* shows, the myth survives: Joey Smallwood advised Newfoundland fishermen to "Burn your boats."

In other words, the first Premier and his government wrote off the fishing industry. Consigned it to the dustbin of history. Made the cold, unblinking decision that it would not figure in their plans for the building-up of Newfoundland and Labrador.

Is it true? And if it is, where and what is the evidence?

It was nothing new, he recalled; enemies spread the falsehoods that Sir Edward Morris had "promised" to make the Southside Hills white with sheep; that Governor Sir Ralph Williams had condemned Newfoundlanders as being "dirtier" in their ways than the Boers, at a time when the bitterness of the South African war was still current; that Sir William Coaker had vowed to "make the grass grow on Water Street"; and that Nova Scotia-born Sir Alfred Morine had ridiculed our people as being "too green to burn."

He would pay scant attention to this very similar allegation, and for two decades maintained the determination not to issue a denial. His reasoning: "Friends don't need it, and enemies won't believe it."

"I suppose," the Premier guessed at one point, "that I have had more slanders, more falsehoods, invented about me, and with great determination spread around, than any other public man for a long time in Newfoundland. I dare say that there were (and perhaps still are) slanders that I never even heard of, for that's the way of slanders ... Clever, I admit it was; unscrupulous, yes; politically, just about the most damaging rumour about me that could have been spread amongst the fishermen: 'Smallwood said that the fishermen should burn their boats!'

"I waited until May 30, 1977 (quarter of a century after the lie was launched) to nail it," he wrote in *The Time Has Come to Tell* (Newfoundland Book Publishers Limited, 1979).

"I did it in the very last speech I ever made in the House of Assembly on our fisheries."

It seems best that he speak for himself to debunk the obvious canard.

The speech was a lengthy one, sprinkled with grim, sardonic references—e.g., advising Walter Carter, then Tory Minister of Fisheries, to not do "everything in his power to develop (the industry), to initiate, to introduce, to finance fishery development; and having done that, contradict it all by telling the fishermen to burn their boats ..."

- He went on to name "fifty-eight settlements on this Island (where) my administration built or financed, or helped to build or helped to finance, sixty-three fish plants, most of them frozen fish processing plants, but some of them salt-fish processing plants … Mr. Chairman, what monumental inconsistency in the one breath to build sixty-three fish plants, costing tens and tens of millions of dollars, and on the other hand, in the other breath, call on all the fishermen to burn their boats!

"In those sixty-three fish plants over twenty thousand fishermen and plant workers got their living. Now, if you take a multiplier of only two to one that would mean a total of sixty thousand jobs arising out of fishery development …

"From 1950 to the end of last year those plant workers had received a grand total of about $185 million in wages—$185 million! And the shore fishermen and the dragger fishermen dozens of millions of dollars in addition to that. That was simply appalling inconsistency. No premier, no government, should spend tens of millions of the public money to build fish plants while at the same time they are enjoining, they are coaxing, almost ordering and certainly advising the fishermen to burn their boats.

"That is what I warn the minister against, inconsistency. Build all he can, get all the money from the Treasury that he can get to develop the fisheries, but do not tell the fishermen to burn their boats or the plant workers to burn their plants or their homes, because that is not consistent," Mr. Smallwood went on.

He outlined a long list of actions taken under his leadership giving "at least some … evidence of our having some little interest in the fishing industry":

- Appointment of the Southwest Coast Fishery Royal Commission headed by John T. Cheeseman;
- Appointment of the Labrador Fishery Development Commission, led by H.A. Dawe of the Fishermen's Protective Union;
- Appointment of the Royal Commission on Fishery Development, headed by Sir Albert Walsh, in which Ottawa took an active part;
- The holding of a national, or international, fisheries conference—"the most famous in Newfoundland's 500 years of fishing history"—with harvesters from around the entire province, leading fish merchants, all the exporters, trade representatives from both sides of the Atlantic and the Caribbean, the governments of Newfoundland, Nova Scotia, New Brunswick, Quebec and the Government of Canada, the theme of which was that from Ottawa "there had to be (support) for the fishing industry … under the various headings, capital aid, crop failure, harvesting, marketing, under all the headings, exactly what they had been doing (for agriculture) … And we did win that battle."

It was "no accident," he insisted, that Canada now poured "tens, scores, and hundreds of millions of dollars" into support of the fisheries, "so I resent bitterly a contemptuous remark that I heard in this House that (this) great conference was useless or futile. It was anything but …"

It also set the stage for the 1962 General Election, called to get a mandate to invest $50 million in a giant fisheries development program—the single biggest direct public investment ever made in any sector of the Newfoundland economy.

- Missions were sent "around the world" with men like Colin Story, Donald Andrews, Harold Dawe, Capt. Matthew Whelan and Rupert Prince visiting Iceland, Scotland, Norway, Germany and Japan "to find out what they were doing in their fisheries that we might imitate …" Fishery representatives were appointed in the Caribbean and West Indies, and the Spanish, Portuguese and Italian markets, and a shipping subsidy inaugurated to make salt fish exports easier;
- The Premier named a succession of strongly pro-fisheries Fisheries ministers—William J. Keough, "famous co-op worker among fishermen"; Max Lane, "a born fisherman … from

Salvage," later head of the big new fishermen's union; John T. Cheeseman, a future Royal Commissioner who was "in the fish trade all his life"; Capt. Earl Winsor—"He and his family for nearly 300 years had been engaged actively in the fisheries of Newfoundland, before she was a province and after. And then I chose … a man who had been running a big fish plant on the Southwest Coast, who is today the head, the active manager, of the Canadian Salt Codfish Corporation that markets all the salt cod that is produced in Newfoundland, all the salt cod, Aidan Maloney, Minister of Fisheries."

- Encouraged by the Premier in a province-wide broadcast, there was formed "a solid, power-ful" fishermen's union (the Newfoundland Federation of Fishermen).

Invited to gather in St. John's for the purpose "they poured in here … This was after they had burned their boats, of course. They had nothing else to do so they came in to celebrate the burning of their boats!" Mr. Smallwood continued:

"I suggest to you, Mr. Chairman (the House was in Committee of the Whole, with the Chairman of Committees, rather than the Speaker, presiding) that these actions of mine do not square with my alleged advice to the fishermen to burn their boats. They do not jibe. They do not fit together. They contradict each other."

- The Premier recalled that at one point he made a speech in the House that was its longest on record, a speech on the fisheries—"eloquent testimony to my indifference, my lack of interest. It lasted five days, the longest speech in Newfoundland history. Five days I spoke on the Fisheries. That must have been the time I was advising (fishermen) to burn their boats, perhaps the Committee might think."
- The MHAs were reminded, as well, that it was the Smallwood administration that introduced the idea of community stages—about 100 communities had them, some financed entirely by the provincial government, some entirely by the federal government, and some jointly. It also brought in the innovation of marine service stations, obviating forever the need for Newfoundland longliner fishermen to get boat service in Nova Scotia—"a magnificent program that is surely one of the best that Newfoundland has ever seen, surely one of the most useful things ever done for the fishermen of this province, and the country before we were a province."
- Mr. Smallwood now turned to one of his achievements in which he took the greatest pride, the College of Fisheries, Navigation, Marine Engineering and Technology. In the dozen years after it was established in 1964 in the building on Parade Street that formerly was home to Memorial University, it "passed through its hands 34,572 persons both inside its walls, and in its exten-sion work out in the field, with a faculty of ninety-five (and) a staff of fifty-six … Outside of Japan and the Soviet Union, Newfoundland's College of Fisheries is the world's greatest, and students have been coming to it from all points of the compass …"

When he became Premier, he remembered, "there were still a few schooners fishing the Labrador. We still had a dory, a bank fishery, not very much, and what little we had was disappearing fast. We had an inshore fishery, such as it was, run on eight and ten horsepower make-and-break engines … In fact, when we took office, when Confederation came, the fisheries of Newfoundland were just about at death's door, and what happened after that was the gigantic task, which is still going on, of rebuilding them, bringing them back to be a great part of our economy."

- It was the Smallwood administration that introduced longliners to Newfoundland "and in every way helped to develop the longliner and helped fishermen to get longliners." The Fisheries Loan Board that it created for the purpose enabled fishermen to get, up to the end of 1967, 722 of these vessels, and other boats besides: trap-skiffs, combination trap-skiffs and longliners, "and still other boats ... 1,254 other boats that we enabled fishermen to get ... A total of 700 and 1200, 1,900 boats, of course, that we advised them to burn ..."

- "Then, Mr. Chairman, there were engines. The loan board that I created—when I say 'I' you will understand that I am speaking as leader of an Administration; I did not do it on my own. I was not a dictator. I had to bring it before my colleagues in Cabinet. Cabinet had to make the decision (and) to the end of 1966-67, the loan board that we created had advanced just under 3,000 engines—3,000—that is, engines for the boats that they were to burn, obviously. The exact number was not 3,000, it was 2,937; that was from the inception of the Fisheries Loan Board to the end of last financial year, 2,937 marine engines for the boats that I am said to have advised the fishermen to burn ..."

(The Fisheries Loan Board operated in concert with the three-member Fisheries Development Authority, consisting of Ross Young, Harry G. Dustan, and Harry Winsor. Men with fisheries and/or financial backgrounds, their mandate was to investigate and recommend specific projects and to give continuing advice to the government on the course fisheries development should take.

The Premier might also have made mention of fishermen's unemployment insurance. A broadening of the existing federal UI program, it was introduced in 1957 in response to demands arising from two gatherings of fishermen that were organized by the provincial government, the Northeast Coast and South Coast Conventions.

However, credit for forcing it through the federal bureaucracy, where there was little sympathy for the move, must go to his influential friend John Whitney Pickersgill. Once Ottawa's chief mandarin and confidant of prime ministers, he was persuaded by Mr. Smallwood to forsake the corridors of power to become an outport MP. Adding the fisheries component would drive UI payments in Newfoundland and Labrador to nearly three-quarters of a billion dollars annually by the 1980s.)

In his later years, Mr. Smallwood addressed readers of *The Time Has Come to Tell* as follows:

"Do you sincerely believe that I was such a chump, such a jackass, such a traitor to Newfoundland, as to tell Newfoundland's fishermen to destroy the very means they had to make a living for themselves and their families: to burn their boats? If you are one of the diminishing band who still get orgiastic pleasure for themselves out of hating my very guts, I withdraw the question. We know your answer—You've given it many times and doubtless you'll give it many times again.

"For the record: I never said it.

"This was just one of a dozen slanders and libels put about by my enemies.

"Or perhaps you don't believe that I had enemies.

"So now that the facts are on the record, we've heard the last of that one? Are you kidding?

"The hour I entered upon my career as Premier of the new Province I inherited the 'ecstasy and the agony' of the fisheries, as most of the premiers before me had done.

"Our great, historic, famous, always troubled fisheries.

"The main reason and means of our very existence during all of the 16th, 17th, 18th, and 19th centuries, and at least the first quarter of the 20th: our fisheries.

"For over 400 years they gave us everything we had: our food, clothing, houses, furniture, schools, churches, hospitals, everything.

"They gave grudgingly to the great majority of us, so stingily that tens, scores of thousands rebelled and left the country to seek something better elsewhere, anywhere.

"Our population today would be one to two millions if our fisheries had only been something like as generous during at least the last of those centuries as they have suddenly become now that we near the 21st Century…"

Mr. Smallwood passed away on December 17, 1991, and thus was spared the unbelievable, ultimate agony of the traditional fishery—and the 250 to 300 communities that depended on it, in the main, for their economic lifeblood—namely the moratorium on Northern Cod imposed only seven months later by none other than an old political foe, John C. Crosbie, now federal Minister of Fisheries.

Fortunately a solid, new foundation had been constructed for the ancient industry in the Smallwood years, which others would build upon. The infrastructure of plants and wharves and community stages and marine haulouts had been immeasurably improved. Small boats now meant, rather than dories and trap-skiffs, multi-purpose longliners of which there was a fleet crowding 1,000 vessels, with skippers and crews indoctrinated in advanced harvesting methods, navigation, electronics and marine engineering thanks to the College of Fisheries.

Instead of a fishery tied to bays and near-shore waters, they ranged long distances to sea under the quasi-protection of the 200-mile limit, otherwise known as Canada's Economic Zone, brought in on the Premier's urging during the stewardship of Don Jamieson as Member of Parliament for Burin-St. George's and Canada's Minister of Industry. True, the "nose and tail" of the Grand Banks remain outside the limit, providing opportunity for foreign fleets to continue to operate on the continental shelf with impunity, but even the sternest critics agreed an important advance was made.

The industry now had, or was presumed to have, a more scientific base, and diversification was well underway in terms of both the species harvested, and the catching methods employed. Consequently, when the Northern Cod moratorium struck the province like a thunderclap, its force was blunted to the degree that large-scale diversion was possible and practical, mainly into high-value shellfish, so that the situation in many communities was to a significant degree saved.

That said, it is a surreal experience to revisit a decade later the "Independent Review of the State of the Northern Cod Stock," turned in to Crosbie's predecessor Tom Siddon by former Memorial University president Leslie Harris as head of the Northern Cod Review Panel in February 1990. It seems rather incredible that only twenty-nine months before the fishery was shut down—for as short a period as two years, it was stated then—the signs of imminent disaster were barely recognized.

"Early in 1989," according to Harris, "it became clear that there were serious discrepancies in the (stock) assessment figures. It now seemed that total stock size was significantly smaller than had been predicted from all previous estimates …The revised position was that while the stock had not declined relative to previous years, it had not grown at a sufficiently rapid rate to justify the TAC (total allowable catch) of a year earlier, i.e., 266,000 tonnes. In essence, the new calculations indicated that the previous estimate of fishing mortality had been too low with the consequence of offering a brighter view of stock growth than had been warranted." It was recommended that to encourage an increase in the growth rate of the spawning stock, "the TAC would have to be reduced by one-half." Ottawa's response to this alarming advice was to reduce the TAC for 1989-90 by about 15%, rather than 50%, and create an independent review.

Meantime, fears grew of a massive catch failure, requiring equally massive government intervention. Two hundred demonstrators in Clarenville demanded action to save the "failing fishery" and provide emergency help for the people. The Northwest Atlantic Fisheries Organization (NAFO) voiced concern about the "dismal" outlook, advising Canada quotas must be cut further. In St. Anthony, effects of the "fishery crisis" already were reported to leave people without means to put food on the table. In Carbonear, a veteran Labrador Coast fisherman declared the industry there was finished.

What would the Fisheries minister do? With demands for action on all sides, Crosbie told the House of Commons he was considering a broad range—from further cuts in the TAC to a complete halt of the $700 million-a-year ocean harvest. When the decision finally came it was anticlimax: a moratorium lasting from two to five years. (A decade later Northern Cod recovery still has not set in, and there are growing concerns that the last-resort shellfish sector might go the same way.)

I was at the front of the media contingent in the Delta (then Radisson) Hotel ballroom the night of July 2, 1992 when Crosbie announced the ban on fishing Northern Cod—anticipated weeks earlier by *The Evening Telegram*, of which I was then managing editor, as "the unbelievable, the unthinkable … a *fait accompli*, namely complete shutdown." Two hundred fishermen barred from the press conference beat on the locked doors, giving those inside the sense of being inside a huge bass drum: having seen the announcement on TV in the hotel lobby the demonstrators saw at once that they would bear the brunt of both a suspended fishery and inadequate compensation.

"They don't need to go berserk … trying to frighten me," Crosbie growled, his protest all but lost in the din as police and hotel security escorted him and his wife, Jane, to safety. "I don't frighten, and I'm not going to be bullied!"

Harris had emphasized the "overriding significance" of the Northern Cod to the economies of the East and Northeast Coasts of Newfoundland and the coast of Labrador, with 63 per cent of all the province's fishermen, and 69 per cent of fish plant workers, living or working contiguous to the 2J3KL fishing zone.

"In actual numbers, this means approximately 8,100 full-time fishermen, 8,200 part-time fishermen, and 18,600 plant workers for a total contribution to employment of 34,900, which does not include deep-sea fishermen and plant workers from South Coast communities that also depend, in part, upon access to Northern Cod.

"In a province in which the unemployment rate is in excess of 16 per cent, some 35,000 jobs is a matter of very great consequence and completely overshadows the fact that the fishery, as a whole, contributes only 6% to the gross provincial product."

It was suddenly clear that Crosbie had touched off the worst economic disaster in Newfoundland history.

# CHAPTER 22

## SETTING THE STAGE FOR HIBERNIA

T he stage for the Hibernia offshore oil development—as for Terra Nova and White Rose and others to follow—was set soon after Newfoundland became a province of Canada in 1949 when, spurred by gathering events in the North Sea, the Smallwood government began to entertain visions of the wealth beneath the Grand Banks.

Harvesting "black gold" from beneath the Earth's crust was still a relatively new pursuit on dry land in Canada. No one had yet attempted, and few had even thought seriously about, searching for and extracting liquid hydrocarbons from under the sea.

But in Alberta, on the impoverished, "have-not" Prairies, dust bowl of the 'Thirties, everything changed after they struck oil one February day in 1947 at Leduc, a railway whistle-stop and telegraph terminus between Edmonton and Calgary. The Leduc No.1 well opened up large deposits, followed by discovery of the Woodbend, Redwater and Pembina fields, and later development of the extensive oil sands. Thanks to an estimated 45,000 producing wells, Alberta today is arguably Canada's richest province.

Geologists have identified some 40 potential fields in Canada, with the best prospects for further discovery and development of petroleum and natural gas being in the Atlantic Ocean off Newfoundland and in the Arctic. However, the question of who owns the resources under the ocean floor, or should—whether the provinces, or the federal government in right of all Canadians—is a major source of frustration for the people of Newfoundland and Labrador. It spells the difference between a "have-not" province (or territory) and a "have" province as Alberta is today.

Joseph R. Smallwood, Newfoundland's first Premier, was well aware of what was transpiring in post-war Alberta. He also knew from his research that in this country resources constitutionally belong to the provinces. And, he was the proposer of the resolution in the National Convention that led to union with Canada, as well as the most knowledgeable member of the Newfoundland team that negotiated and signed the Terms of Union. Term 2 (out of a total of 50) was written to protect Newfoundland's territorial interest, and provides as follows:

*2. The Province of Newfoundland shall comprise the same territory as at the date of Union, that is to say, the island of Newfoundland and the islands adjacent thereto, the Coast of Labrador as delimited in the report delivered by the Judicial Council of His Majesty's Privy Council on the first day of March, 1927, and approved by His Majesty in His Privy*

---

*He proposed that Ottawa cede offshore resources to the provinces as they had northern lands to Quebec, Ontario and Manitoba ...*

PHOTOS CLOCKWISE:
■ Interest in offshore oil and gas development on the part of the Newfoundland government encouraged some 15 firms to file for exploration rights by the 1960s, leading to a busy drilling program and in time, discovery of Hibernia and other fields (GN);
■ Establishment at Marystown of a modern shipyard where a number of offshore service vessels were built was complemented by provision of the nearby Cow Head rig repair facility, making the Marystown area the focus of offshore-related activity (GN); ■ The Smallwood administration contested the federal claim to offshore oil and gas in court, and unsuccessful there, the Premier called on Ottawa to cede the resources to contiguous provinces (TA).

*Council on the twenty-second day of March, 1927, and the islands adjacent to the said Coast of Labrador.*

But there is also Term 37, vital to the question of offshore resources ownership, and natural resources in general:

*37. All lands, mines, minerals and royalties belonging to Newfoundland at the date of Union, and all sums then due or payable for such lands, mines, minerals, or royalties shall belong to the Province of Newfoundland, subject to any trusts existing in respect thereof, and to any interest other than that of the Province in the same.*

The Attorney General of Newfoundland went to court in 1982 seeking a declaration that "the lands, mines, minerals, royalties or other rights ... to the seaward limit of the continental shelf or any part thereof belong or otherwise appertain" to Newfoundland. It was pointed out that all the provinces that entered the Union after 1867 and before Newfoundland joined "did so on a basis of equality with the original provinces (Ontario, Quebec, Nova Scotia and New Brunswick) insofar as ownership of their natural resources was concerned (and) in each case, it was only those natural resources which were located within the province which belonged to them." Against this, pointed out James J. Greene, Q.C., former PC Leader of the Opposition and the government's lead lawyer, "the significance of the Newfoundland Terms of Union relating to natural resources may be clearly seen."

When Newfoundland became a province—the only province to do so with the status of a British Dominion—"the restriction of ownership of natural resources to those 'within the province' or 'situate' within the province was omitted," Greene said, a clear signal that Newfoundland's interest outside its strict land boundaries was recognized.

"Equally significant," he went on, "is the abandonment of the concept expressed so clearly in the 1930 agreements with Alberta, Saskatchewan and Manitoba that the new provinces 'were to be in the same position as the original Provinces of Confederation ... in virtue of Section 109 of the British North America Act, 1867.' If it had been intended that Newfoundland should be in the same position as the other provinces and that only those resources situated within the province should belong to it, it would have been simple to say so."

Then Greene added this: "There was moreover a sound reason for the change in wording. Newfoundland, unlike any other province, entered Confederation as an international person and with such rights in International Law attributed in respect *inter alia* of the natural resources of its internal waters, territorial sea and continental shelf."

The judges of the Newfoundland Court of Appeal were less than impressed. On February 17, 1983 Chief Justice Arthur Mifflin, Mr. Justice Herbert Morgan and Mr. Justice James Gushue handed down a unanimous finding: "The resources (of the continental shelf) do not fall within the meaning of Term 37 of the Terms of Union," they wrote, "and thus do not belong to Newfoundland." Ownership, they declared, lay with the Government of Canada, just as the Supreme Court of Canada had determined in the British Columbia reference in 1967, and would reconfirm in 1984. They ruled:

"1. Continental shelf rights are, in pith and substance, an extra-territorial manifestation of external sovereignty.

"2. Canada has the right to explore and exploit in the continental shelf off Newfoundland because:
  (a) any continental shelf rights available at international law in 1949 would have been acquired by the Crown in right of the United Kingdom, not the Crown in right of Newfoundland;
  (b) even if Newfoundland could have held continental shelf rights prior to Union, they would have passed to Canada by virtue of the Terms of Union;
  (c) in any event, international law did not recognize continental shelf rights in 1949; such rights were not indisputably recognized before the Geneva Convention of 1958;

(d) Canada has legislative jurisdiction in relation to the right to explore and exploit in the continental shelf of Newfoundland by virtue of the peace, order and good government power in its residual capacity.

"In short, in our opinion both questions [as to (a) the right to explore and exploit, and (b) the right of legislative jurisdiction] should be answered in favour of Canada."

As Publisher of *The Daily News* I had chosen to report on the case myself so as to ensure my familiarity with the critically important issues involved. It is obvious to me that had the question been framed differently—acknowledging that while "jurisdiction over the lands ... to the seaward limit of the Continental Shelf lies with Canada," in conformity with *The Constitution Act* (formerly *The British North America Act), 1867* as amended, "the mines, minerals, royalties, or other rights belong or otherwise appertain to the province"—then the answer should also have been otherwise.

One hesitates to question the findings of learned judges, but there is a substantial irony here, not to say a serious conflict: The Newfoundland Supreme Court ruled nearly a full year after patriation—the making of Canada's "supreme law" into a statute of Canada, rather than of the United Kingdom. As well, broad updating was made to this former legislation of the British Parliament that had served as Canada's Constitution for nearly 120 years, greatly strengthening the position of the provinces in respect of natural resources.

Given Royal Assent by Her Majesty, Queen Elizabeth on Parliament Hill, Ottawa on April 17, 1982, The Constitution Act, 1982 contains an expansive Section 92A dealing with "Non-Renewable Natural Resources, Forestry Resources, and Electrical Energy." It provides, pursuant to the division of powers in the federal state that is Canada, that "In each province, the Legislature may exclusively make laws in relation to (a) exploration for non-renewable natural resources in the province; (b) development, conservation and management of non-renewable natural resources and forestry resources in the province, including laws in relation to the rate of primary production therefrom; and (c) development, conservation and management of sites and facilities in the province for the generation and production of electrical energy."

The exclusive right to make laws regarding exploration, development, conservation and management comes very close, in my opinion, to actual ownership—*conferred upon the provinces, not the central government!* Our Supreme Court finding that the right to explore and exploit, and to exercise legislative jurisdiction, "should be answered in favour of Canada" directly contradicts *The Constitution Act, 1982* based on the questionable, at best technical, proposition that before 1949 Newfoundland had no rights to its offshore resources—but Canada exclusively acquired them soon after. The weight of the "supreme law" strongly in its favour, Newfoundland must revisit this whole matter—the burning question being why, in two decades, have we not done so already?

The Terms of Union did not, and in the circumstances, a decade prior to the Geneva Convention, perhaps could not determine ownership of the Grand Banks, the Strait of Belle Isle and the Labrador Sea beyond three or twelve miles, still considered international waters. However, in all logic the ocean areas south, east and north of the Island of Newfoundland and east of Labrador could not have appertained to Canada and do so today only as a consequence of Confederation. International law aside, so far as Canada's internal governance is concerned, it seems clear this province's constitutional power in the area of property and civil rights ought to be the determinant in respect of the ownership of the oil and gas resources offshore.

This was the reasoning that led to Mr. Smallwood's proposal, in response to the unfavourable 1967 Supreme Court of Canada decision in the British Columbia reference, Ottawa cede the offshore resources to contiguous provinces—in the same way federal northern lands, and resources contained therein, were ceded to Quebec, nearly doubling its size, and Ontario and Manitoba.

The Smallwood government proceeded to bring to the House of Assembly in 1965 the *Petroleum and Natural Gas Act, No. 56*, and a complete set of regulations, generally patterned after those of Canada and Alberta, was drawn up. However, promulgation was deferred pending settlement of the jurisdictional issue on which the Supreme Court of Canada had ruled in favour of Ottawa. (Tory Premier Brian Peckford would find himself in the same frustrating predicament two decades later.)

Federal assertions of jurisdiction notwithstanding, Newfoundland commenced issuing permits for offshore exploration in the 1960s and by 1966 two relatively shallow wells were drilled on the Grand Banks by

Pan American and Imperial Oil. Fifteen companies had permits or provisional agreements on the Newfoundland continental shelf, including the Gulf of St. Lawrence. Over the next three decades some 140 offshore wells were "spudded" and more than $3.5 billion spent on seismic, drilling and other activity, producing a score of significant oil and gas discoveries on the Grand Banks and the Labrador Shelf.

However, because of the unsettled jurisdiction—ministerial discussions between St. John's and Ottawa seeking, if not an offshore settlement, then an equitable working arrangement, continued up to the very day of the 1971 General Election—companies took out both federal and provincial permits in order to protect their interests no matter what the outcome.

To highlight Newfoundland's claim to the wealth under the Atlantic seabed, the Premier arranged for a diving team to install a plaque on the floor of the Grand Banks, one more attempt by Mr. Smallwood to bring to the attention of fair-minded Canadians everywhere the fact that resources that this province literally brought into Confederation—there was no way physically that they could have belonged to Canada—would not be available as they should to help the Canadians who live here to become self-supporting citizens of this great land.

The area of the Continental Shelf off Newfoundland and Labrador is estimated in excess of one and a half million square kilometres. By the 1990s, after some three decades of exploration activity, less than one per cent of this vast area was held under licence by various oil companies, but discoveries to that time of oil and gas resources were estimated at 1.6 billion barrels and 7.5 trillion cubic feet respectively.

The rather cautious judgment of Newfoundland government geologists of the 1960s, that prospects for development were "very good," is increasingly confirmed.

# CHAPTER 23

## CULTIVATING THE TOURIST PLANT

Long years before he became Premier of Newfoundland, Joseph R. Smallwood had taken to loudly singing Newfoundland's praises as a prime, albeit largely undiscovered, destination for tourists, especially from the United States.

The province, of course, is generously endowed with natural resources—lakes and rivers, spectacular coastline and mountainous terrain, extensive forest lands, abundant wildlife, and as well, historic and archeological treasures to rival other areas of the New World. These include evidences of European industrial enterprise dating back five centuries at Red Bay, the 1,000-year-old remains of Norse habitation at L'Anse aux Meadows, and the remains of 15th Century colonial settlement at Cupids and Ferryland.

They take us back in time several thousand years to the time of Maritime Archaic Indian and Dorset Eskimo people at Port au Choix and elsewhere, and to the former habitations and burial grounds of the tragically extinct Beothuk Indians.

His awareness of Newfoundland's prominence as a virtual crossroads of New World exploration and settlement, as well as her future prospects which he believed to be no less than spectacular, caused Smallwood the journalist to turn to what nature had fitted him to do, and do well—write about it.

One of his early books was *The New Newfoundland* (Macmillan, New York, 1931.) The preface states that it was written "primarily for the 150,000 Newfoundlanders and Newfoundlanders-by-descent who reside in the United States and Canada," many of whom had been away for ten or twenty years, but whose interest in Newfoundland was "practically undiminished."

Then there were "a great many businessmen in both countries who trade with Newfoundland" and would welcome a book "that tells them many of the things they will wish to know" about the country.

And finally, there were the "thousands of Americans and Canadians in the past few years (who had been) visiting Newfoundland as tourists and sportsmen. The number … is growing rapidly year after year (but) despite the many books that have been written about Newfoundland there is not in print at the present time a solitary book that a visitor can purchase." His intention, of course, was to change that, which *The New Newfoundland* set out to do, providing a description of improved roads and other means of travel, and hotel and fishing and hunting accommodations available.

"Too much cannot be said," he wrote, "in connection with the big drive for more tourists …"

*He approached the owner of Irving Oil Ltd. offering choice locations along the Trans Canada. (He) accepted, and the results are there for all to see and enjoy.*

PHOTOS CLOCKWISE:
■ Joey Smallwood the journalist wrote about the tourist potential of Newfoundland, and once in office as Premier launched programs to promote the province in a big way and became personally involved (MA); ■ The Smallwood government built over 50 provincial parks and signed agreements with Ottawa for Newfoundland's two National Parks, Gros Morne (pictured) and Terra Nova (TA); ■ The government's emphasis on highways development was a major factor in development of the tourism industry (TA); ■ When "name" hoteliers declined all efforts to entice them to Newfoundland, the Smallwood government built its own quality hotels and leased them to a Holiday Inn franchisee to operate (GN); ■ Sports fishing, and big and small game hunting, were promoted as prime tourist attractions (TA).

Formed in 1925, the Newfoundland Tourist and Publicity Commission had, he wrote, "done wonderful work for Newfoundland, and the phenomenal increase in the number of tourists visiting Newfoundland is due in very large part to their efforts."

There then followed a detailed description of the work of the Commission and the regularly increasing number of tourists—in 1927, "some 6,900, exclusive of commercial travellers, returning natives, etc." had registered, over 7,200 in 1928, and more than 8,300 in 1929. The Commission, accepting the Canadian estimate of $100 per tourist, forecast that some 9,000 visitors would spend in excess of $900,000 in 1930.

Of course, Mr. Smallwood saw a glowing future for the fledgling industry.

"It is agreed by now," he wrote, "that these figures represent no more than a mere beginning. It is quite confidently expected that within a few years the annual totals will have reached 25,000 tourists with an expenditure within Newfoundland each year of $50 million." (The latest [2001] numbers are 427,700 and the expenditures $620 million.)

The Great Depression intervened, and then the Second World War, but fifteen years later he had gotten himself into a position to develop tourism into a major economic factor for Newfoundland. As Premier and Minister of Economic Development, he turned at once to creation of the Division of Tourist Development within his own department with O.L. Vardy as the first director with Margaret "Peg" Godden as his deputy. E.P. "Ted" Henley was another notable occupant of the director's office.

In 1950 his government asked the House of Assembly to approve legislation entitled the Tourist Establishments Act, which for the first time set standards of health and safety for the industry and made it mandatory for tourist operators to be licensed. To spur construction of hotels, motels and other facilities to cater to tourists, the Tourist Development Loan Board was established in 1953 and would provide unprecedented government support for the growing industry.

The principal infrastructure required for a successful travel industry—though clearly not the only requirement—is a network of highways and secondary and trunk roads, almost nonexistent before Confederation. It was provided mainly in the construction of the Trans Canada Highway across the Island, all 565 miles of it, from St. John's to Port aux Basques, at a cost of some $120 million. Other major undertakings included the Burin Peninsula Highway, the Great Northern Peninsula Highway, and the Argentia Highway.

Completion of the Trans Canada in 1965 was celebrated with a huge three-day motorcade and the unveiling of the Pearson's Peak memorial shaft near Grand Falls by the Premier and Prime Minister L.B. Pearson. It was followed by a Come Home Year celebration in 1966 when many tens of thousands of Newfoundlanders, some of whom had been away for decades, returned to marvel at what had been wrought.

Various segments of the transportation and other systems enjoyed significant improvement beginning almost immediately following Union in 1949. Pursuant to Term 31 of the Terms of Union, Canada was obligated to take over a variety of public services, relieving the new province of the tremendous costs involved.

These included, in order, (a) the Newfoundland Railway, including steamship and other marine services; (b) the Newfoundland Hotel; (c) postal and publicly owned telecommunication services; (d) civil aviation, including Gander Airport; (e) customs and excise; (f) defense; (g) protection and encouragement of fisheries and operation of bait services; (h) geographical, topographical, geodetic and hydrographic surveys; (i) lighthouses, fog alarms, buoys, beacons, and other public works and services in aid of navigation and shipping; (j) marine hospitals, quarantine, and the care of shipwrecked crews; (k) the public radio broadcasting system; and (l) other public services similar in kind to those provided at the date of Union for the people of Canada generally.

Virtually every one of these provisions played a major, if not a critical part, in support of the tourist industry. This was even more clearly evident in Term 32 of the Confederation compact, dealing with the single most important aspect of tourist travel to the province, and transportation in general:

"Canada will maintain in accordance with the traffic offering a freight and passenger steamship service between North Sydney and Port aux Basques, which, on completion of a motor highway between Corner Brook and Port aux Basques, will include suitable provision for the carriage of motor vehicles."

The provision paved the way for radical improvements in the types and size of ships assigned to the Cabot Strait crossing, beginning with the MV *William Carson,* and creation of modern terminal facilities at Port aux Basques and later Argentia for both passengers and vehicles, including ultimately huge numbers of transport trucks.

There was also substantial development and improvement in air services, as the former wartime military facilities at Gander, Stephenville and Goose Bay, and to some extent Argentia, increasingly supported and then were turned entirely to civil aviation, and with St. John's were joined by full-service airports at Deer Lake,Wabush and St. Anthony and several lesser strips.

The Smallwood government placed extraordinary emphasis on the development of parks as a key branch of the tourist "plant." Very early on, in 1952, it brought to the House of Assembly the Provincial Parks Act, and soon opened the first of more than seventy—the Sir Richard Squires Memorial Park at Big Falls on the Humber River. As well, a network of some 120 prepared picnic grounds was developed in conjunction with the Newfoundland Forest Protection Association.

Subject of a negotiated agreement with Ottawa, the first of two National Parks, Terra Nova in Central Newfoundland, opened in 1957. A Memorandum of Agreement providing for the development of Gros Morne in Bonne Bay, at the base of the Great Northern Peninsula, was signed in October 1970, and in the meantime, National Historic Parks were designated and developed in many parts of the province, principally Signal Hill in St. John's, L'Anse aux Meadows near St. Anthony, Red Bay on the Labrador Coast, and Castle Hill at Placentia.

Information, about various attractions, about transportation schedules, about accommodation—this is the lifeblood of the tourist industry. In the 1960s, as highways were built and extended, information chalets began to sprout, the first just outside Corner Brook. But to attract the world, more was required including first-class, or better said, world-class accommodation and highway services. However, these were in woefully short supply; when Newfoundland became a province of Canada there were few hotels or motels, no camping or picnic parks, a complete absence of National and Historic parks, few historic sites marked or recognized, and no provincial museum or archives to provide visitors an insight into our long and colourful history.

On the information side, the province concentrated at first on hunting and fishing, with luminaries such as internationally known sportsman Lee Wulff involved in the production of promotional films. The Newfoundland Museum—closed by the Commission of Government to save money—was reopened and began once again to display precious artifacts of Newfoundland history not lost or destroyed.

With the Trans Canada Highway completed and paved the numbers of auto-borne travellers mounted, and the need for gasoline and automobile repair services multiplied. As well, travellers like to eat, and rest stops are a decided necessity. But little interest was displayed on the part of those who traditionally provide such conveniences.

Finally, Mr. Smallwood telephoned the owner of Irving Oil Ltd., Kenneth C. Irving. I was with him when he offered a choice of Crown land locations across the Island if the company would agree to establish a chain of first-class service station-restaurants. The New Brunswick industrialist agreed, and for more than three decades the results have been there for all to see and enjoy.

It was much the same with hotels, or lack thereof—no one was interested. This is not in any way to denigrate the efforts of local entrepreneurs, often with the help of the government's own Tourist Development Loan Board, to provide comfortable, high quality accommodation. But the absence of "name" hotels with their international promotion and reservation systems, presented an insurmountable problem when it came to encouraging international travellers to visit Newfoundland.

Having had no luck, after numerous attempts, in attracting the "majors," the Premier was finally successful in getting Jack Adams, owner of Atlific Inns of Montreal, a Holiday Inn franchisee, to come to the province. The government would finance and build proposed hotels to company design and standard at St. John's, Clarenville, Gander and Corner Brook. The company would buy them back over time. (They also acquired a privately owned hostelry in Port aux Basques.) The arrangement served the province well, and its financing obligation was discharged in accordance with the agreement made in the 1960s.

It has been estimated that only the commercial fishery and the construction industry employ more people than receive their livelihood directly and indirectly from tourism, bearing out yet another Smallwood prophecy.

As with so many things in Newfoundland and Labrador—whether industrial development, the fisheries, education, health care, transportation or municipal development—the foundations of the tourist industry were well and truly laid in the Smallwood years under the leadership of the man who led the province into the Canadian family.

They continue to sustain Newfoundlanders and Labradorians yet today.

# Chapter 24

## Are the People Better Off?

How to judge the success of Confederation? Let us count the ways:

Are the ordinary people better off than they were under the unelected Commission of Government, as Mr Smallwood put it, "voiceless in their own land"?

Or than they would have been under restoration of Responsible Government "as it existed in 1934"?

Are they better educated and trained? Are health care services incomparably better? Are job prospects much improved? Workers far better paid?

What of today's system of social services, pensions for workers and seniors, and support for the unemployed? Are they not more expansive and incredibly more generous than Newfoundlanders had experienced previously? Is not the same true of housing availability and quality? Municipal services? Streets and highways?

In the second half-century of Newfoundland's Union with Canada, the answer must be a resounding "Yes!"on all counts.

Not that, as a province, we have reached perfection, a condition unlikely ever to come to pass. But for all the decades of Confederation the services provided by the government to the people have been immeasurably improved over anything earlier available or contemplated.

In short, what has been achieved in only a generation or two in building up the province is remarkable, the progress nothing short of startling.

Newfoundland joined Canada in 1949 against the background of the Commission of Government's stringent fiscal policies and a war-generated economic boom already beginning to recede. By the winter of 1940-41, they were turning the memory of persistent budget deficits of earlier times into revenue balances—and leaving office could boast an accumulated surplus of $30 million net of an interest-free, wartime loan of $12 million to the Mother Country.

However, the human and societal consequences were not much unlike those precipitated by the Old Colony's participation in the First World War. Fish prices in the 1914-18 period reached historic levels to match exceptional catches, and a wave of optimism fuelled by high levels of employment and business activity swept the land. However—and no disrespect is intended—increasing the public debt by $10 million mainly to support a regiment in the field would, in time, prove catastrophic in the rollercoaster economy. The Great War ended in 1918, and the post-war economic slump of

*"I became a Confederate when I discovered (it) would give our people a half-decent chance in life..."*

PHOTO OPPOSITE:
■ The province's children are its future, and Premier Smallwood was committed to them with huge expenditures calculated to provide on day schools and teachers, children's health and dental programs, a degree-granting university with free tuition and allowances, and a system of district vocational schools topped by trades and fisheries colleges. To the question "Are the people better off?" the answer, so far as the future of the children was concerned, could only be answered with an unqualified "Yes!" (TA)

the 1920s soon made its effects felt. Business bankruptcies were common, fish prices in foreign markets collapsed to half their previous levels, and whole communities were forced onto inadequate public relief.

Journalist A.B. Perlin recalled in *The Story of Newfoundland, 1497-1959* that in spite of all efforts to develop the country and build a prosperous economy "unemployment remained a serious problem, and able-bodied relief had eventually to be dealt with by straight distribution of dole. In this whole post-war period revenue was unequal to the demands upon it." By 1928, the public debt had reached a pinnacle for that time of $87 million and interest costs were almost half the income of the government.

"In 1927, the Finance minister, Sir John Crosbie (Perlin's own father-in-law) predicted ultimate bankruptcy. His ominous prediction was soon to be fulfilled."

A period of significant, if slow, improvement occurred as fish prices recovered somewhat, Newfoundland's second pulp and paper mill—the so-called "hum on the Humber"—started up in Corner Brook, a base metals mine began producing in Buchans, and Wabana iron ore found new demand in Germany and Holland. But the government had been forced to take over the financially strapped Newfoundland Railway and its ancillary services, including steamships, at a capital cost of $2 million and faced operating subsidies in excess of $1 million annually.

The 1927 ruling of the Judicial Committee of the Imperial Privy Council confirming Newfoundland's ownership of Labrador may have been cause for rejoicing. However, it offered no improvement in the general condition—any more than did the 1931 Statute of Westminster conferring the opportunity of full political independence, goal of all self-respecting peoples, that Newfoundland had to decide it could not afford.

The country had now begun, as S.J.R. Noel in *Politics in Newfoundland* (University of Toronto Press, 1971) points out, to feel the effects of the world depression in international trade: "Fish prices dropped to their lowest level since 1913, thus reducing incomes in general, and as incomes fell government revenues also fell, for incomes were largely spent on imported goods, on which *ad valorem* tariffs formed the main source of revenue. At the same time, government expenditure was growing under pressure to provide 'able-bodied relief' to the unemployed and the destitute."

The government faced a deficit of $4 million, in addition to which redemption of loans coming due would cost $3 million and $1 million was required for the city of St. John's. The Squires government had no choice but to invite tenders for a loan of $8 million "but the stream of willing tenders had at last dried up. No tenders were received."

According to Noel: "For Newfoundland the blind financial course pursued by successive governments over many years ended where it almost certainly had to end: on the rocks of financial ruin … It would, of course, be wholly wrong to suggest that the government in power was responsible for this state of affairs. They were but the hapless victims of a trap constructed by preceding governments, one of which had been Squires's own, and devastatingly sprung by economic forces beyond their control."

It was, of course, inescapable that the general condition of the country—the burden of a struggling economy, of a government hard-pressed to continue public services of whatever kind—would fall hard upon the population. The truth is that Newfoundland was in no condition to withstand the Great Depression of the 1930s when exports, having peaked at $40 million, fell off by more than a third, and export prices for salt cod declined by half. Government revenues, reported at nearly $12 million two years earlier, in 1931-32 fell to $8 million. In the winter of 1932 a quarter of the people found themselves on the dole.

The public debt stood at $43 million in 1920-21. A decade later it had nearly doubled, and in 1933 reached $98.5 million. At that point interest charges amounted to a debt of some $5 million, over 60 per cent of the government's total income.

"It was strongly argued at the time," Perlin recalled, "that the government should have suspended the service of the debt until it had met some of the most pressing needs of the people. The argument was supported by the belief that default, because of the repercussions it might have throughout the Commonwealth, would have spurred Great Britain and Canada to offer substantial aid to Newfoundland."

But the government "preferred to travel as best it could the more orthodox ways of public finance" and introduced "heroic measures" to try to deal with the crisis:

"School teachers, civil servants, war and civil pensioners, suffered reductions of half their incomes. The government was more than a year behind with the payment of bills to merchants who had supplied relief, and endorsed relief accounts were the only means by which many small tradesmen could settle their debts with their wholesalers. The wonder is that the whole structure of civil administration did not collapse."

The scandal-plagued Squires Liberals were driven from office in the General Election of June 11, 1932 and the new United Newfoundland Party government of Prime Minister Frederick C. Alderdice, which won all but two of the 27 House of Assembly seats, could see only one solution, the one he proposed to pursue if elected: Government by Commission. The British agreed to appoint an inquiry to examine into Newfoundland's future, and in particular its financial prospects.

The result was the Amulree Report, a 283-page document presented in the Fall of 1933, which blamed political corruption rather than historic misfortune for Newfoundland's problems: "... (R)eckless waste and extravagance (and) the absence of constructive and efficient administration, engendered by a political system which for a generation had been abused and exploited for personal or party ends."

It called for a rest from party politics to enable "a speedy and effective recovery" from the present difficulties, a respite that would be provided by Alderdice's proposed Commission made up of three Newfoundlanders and four British members, including the Governor who would always have the final say.

Noel is unconvinced by the Amulree Commission's rationale.

"That there was, in fact, political corruption on no small scale is beyond doubt," he wrote, and "in the long run the weaknesses and abuses of the political system were in large measure responsible."

But it was equally clear that the immediate financial crisis was caused, not by corrupt politics, but by the effects of the Depression on world trade—and other countries, including Britain herself, were in similar straits.

Accordingly, Amulree "could scarcely have maintained that this alone was sufficient reason to justify indefinite suspension" of Newfoundland's elected legislature and government.

Therefore the "extreme remedy" had to be justified on the grounds the political system was corrupt "beyond all hope of redemption."

To conclude a detailed discussion of the question, Noel asks whether with "a less extreme view of the iniquities of the political system" Amulree could not have found "some means of reconciling Whitehall control with the continuation of at least one freely elected body in Newfoundland, however limited" its actual powers.

It may be said, however, that in their circumstances of grinding poverty and economic uncertainty—that is, not knowing if, or when, a man might be lucky enough to find a job and earn a decent living for himself and his family, and whether and for how long the children, in particular, could survive in the face of rampant disease and widespread malnutrition—there were few who much concerned themselves about the form of government.

## JRS: WHY I BECAME A CONFEDERATE

In perhaps his finest speech of a lifetime of speeches, a futile appeal to the delegates of the National Convention, or a majority of them, on January 23, 1948 to agree to recommend that Confederation should be on the national referendum ballot paper, Mr. Smallwood said this, in small part:

"I know our Newfoundland people. I am one of them. I am blood of their blood, bone of their bone, soul of their soul. I am descended from a family that has lived in Newfoundland for over 150 years. My ancestors were fishermen, farmers, shopkeepers, manufacturers, skilled workmen, and artisans.

"I have dug deep into my country's history, and in so doing I have paid special attention to the story of our people's labours, their battles against nature and against injustice, the story of their endless search for a square deal. I have travelled my country, North, East, South and West, into a thousand of the 1,300 settlements in it. I have been closely and intimately associated with our people. I have fished with the fishermen, logged with the loggers; I have gone down underground with the miners; held trade union meetings right inside the paper mills.

"I was never so close to our toilers as during those years of the dole, and always, so long as I live, I will remember those friends of mine, those toilers who were stricken down by beri-beri, those children who felt the pinch of hunger. I saw the heartbreak in the eyes of patient mothers who had not enough to give their little ones. I saw the baffled, sullen rage of fishermen whose greatest toil and endurance could not provide their families with enough to eat or wear.

"I attended meetings of the unemployed here in St. John's, but who was I to refuse their invitation to go and speak to them? I saw them in their despairing hundreds waiting around the street corners, waiting for the jobs that never turned up, and around the Dole Office, and helped to gather second-hand clothes to distribute to those who were half-naked, not for a day or a week or a year, but all through the Depression.

"I saw them, and I swore an oath to myself that never would I be a party to allowing such things to come back to our people again. I would never be a party to any form of government that would make us know that thing again, and that's why I became a Confederate. I became a Confederate, and discovered that Confederation would give our people a half-decent chance in life, and wipe away some of the worst obstacles in their life and remove some of the millstones that hung around their necks."

After years of organizing paper mill workers, fishermen and railway section hands, and still later, living in the booming melting-pot of Gander where thousands came for wartime work from all over Newfoundland, Mr. Smallwood knew only too well what the people thought and what they felt, as captured in *I Chose Canada*:

"The feeling was one of considerable respect for the integrity, efficiency, and goodwill of the Commission of Government. Most people thought it was the best government we had ever had. Only the most thoughtful people were very much disturbed by the non-representative nature of the Commission" or the fact it was answerable, not to Newfoundlanders, but to the British government in London.

But of course, it could not and would not last. The British had all but decided that in the throes of their own difficult recovery from the Second World War, they could not be responsible for Newfoundland's reconstruction. This would particularly be so if its people, in an anticipated public referendum, chose to go their own way, a visiting delegation from the National Convention was told in no uncertain terms.

The Commission's mandate was much earlier determined to be limited to that of caretaker and nothing more. Under it there would be little or no development of Newfoundland and its resources. Moreover, Responsible Government as it had existed prior to 1934 had been thoroughly discredited.

James K. Hiller, in *Confederation: Deciding Newfoundland's Future, 1934-1949* (Newfoundland Historical Society, 1988) says the British had decided to be financially inflexible since they "did not want to encourage a return to Responsible Government, and in this it was backed, with almost indecent enthusiasm, by the Commission."

Was there, then, a conspiracy to force Newfoundland to join Canada?

Hiller points to the "crucial, early decisions about procedure" that were made at a time when the British (and most people, for that matter) assumed that Confederation, however desirable, was unlikely to come about. As the idea only developed after "the (Commission's) reconstruction plan had collapsed, and Canadian officials had shown their interest," the conspiracy theory hardly seems credible.

Rather, the Confederation movement succeeded "because of Joseph Smallwood (who) understood that the grim days of the Depression and the prosperity of the war years had changed Newfoundland society significantly, and political attitudes as well. Many Newfoundlanders were nervous about resuming independence, nervous about economic collapse …

"Smallwood and Bradley were certainly helped in significant ways by the Canadian and British governments, but it was their achievement that by the time the (National) Convention ended early in 1948 Confederation was a live issue and a real constitutional alternative."

Mr. Smallwood found in the prospect of Union with Canada the "missing condition to successful Responsible Government in Newfoundland" of which he had earlier spoken—maximum freedom of political choice, coupled with membership in a prosperous nation—and then persuaded a majority of voters to support it.

He knew at once that the challenge of building a modern North American society in Newfoundland—of ending the impoverished, hand-to-mouth existence of the vast majority of people, of overcoming widespread ill health and disease, of giving the children the chance of an education and a real future—would have to be met otherwise than under either of the other alternatives.

"I remembered," he recalled, "the long walks and talks that Gordon Bradley and I had had, back in 1930, around Quidi Vidi Lake, and Bradley's determined voice declaiming to me, 'Joe, you mark my words! Confederation with Canada is our only hope, our only salvation!'"

◆　◆　◆

The beginning question is answered, clearly and without reservation: The people *are* better off … not, perhaps, as well off as we would like, either as a province or as individuals. Still, we receive the same Canada and Old Age and Veterans Pensions as other Canadians, the same Family Allowances and Employment Insurance, essentially the same Medicare, and benefit from a myriad of other federal programs and services ranging from assistance to highway construction and the cleanup of polluted harbours, to public services (Canada Post, the Coast Guard and the CBC) and funding for research and development. And there are imponderables—the uncounted benefits that accrue simply and automatically from belonging to a large and respected nation, with the freedom to travel and live and work anywhere in its huge expanse.

As well, there is the reality that Newfoundland and Labrador is not alone as a "have-not" province. It is one of seven whose fiscal capacity is inadequate to support levels and standards of public services that meet predetermined Canadian averages. All require and receive transfers of federal funds to offset disparities in this regard, consistent with a constitutional principle that all citizens of Canada, regardless of where they live, should be treated in a reasonably comparable way, in support of which in the mid-1990s some 44 per cent of revenues of the Government of Newfoundland and Labrador derived from federal transfers. (This compared with 43 per cent in Nova Scotia, 41 per cent in Prince Edward Island, and 39 per cent in New Brunswick.)

As this book is delivered into the hands of the printers, a Royal Commission on "Renewing and Strengthening Newfoundland and Labrador's Place in Canada" conducts what it describes as "a critical assessment" of the province's strengths and weaknesses in Confederation, 54 years after the fact. It intends to recommend "how best to achieve prosperity and self-reliance"—clear implication that we have fallen short of both—and suggests the province "still has not found its rightful place in Canada," whatever that may be. It sees "a serious gap between the hopes and expectations with which we entered Confederation and the level of prosperity we have achieved today" and wants to "envisage what a prosperous and self-reliant Newfoundland and Labrador would look like in the next decade and beyond …"

The rhetoric is interesting. The concept of "prosperity" relates to economic well-being, "self-reliance" to having confidence in and exercising the powers of judgment in order to achieve it. These are laudable in themselves, but the sentiment seems more in keeping with aspirations of the impoverished, mainly rural society that Newfoundland used to be.

Rather, the Young Commission must find answers to the essential dilemma of Newfoundland and Labrador today. The real challenge is to expose, and to suggest how best to achieve breakthrough, in the exasperating struggle against political and bureaucratic barriers to development of the abundant natural resources of Newfoundland and Labrador for the maximum benefit of those who live here. An essential element in that, of course, is an appropriate measure of political equality in Canada.

This is how to pursue prosperity in the context of the 21$^{st}$ Century. This is how to grow our province. This is how to keep our people.

# PART THREE

## A TIME FOR TRIBUTES

*Two decades ago, to honour his 80th birthday, friends and admirers of Joseph R. Smallwood gathered to pay tribute to the man considered Newfoundland's greatest son. The following pages are reproduced directly from documentation assembled on that occasion to attest to Mr. Smallwood's achievements during twenty-three years as Premier of Newfoundland and Labrador.*

# A TESTAMENT

*By Gregory Power*

Of gold I've nothing to bestow,
    and little else to give,
But Lord, I want my friends to know
    How good it was to live;
To tell how I communed with seeds
    About the styles of May,
And you arranged the Autumn beads
    To make my garden gay;
How you conspired to let me doubt
    The truth of your control,
Then brought the first white crocus out
    And touched it to my soul;
How you prescribed for every pain
    A countervailing grace—
The whispered sympathy of rain,
    The sunlight on my face.
At twilight time, to paths reserved,
    You bade me come and dine,
And learn how roses should be served,
    And harmless ways for wine.
Although you gave me little store
    To gauge by wants of men,
You sent me lilacs, and my door
    Was of a mansion then.
And there was one small taste of fame
    To set my soul alight,
And compensate for tears that come
    Unbidden in the night.
I pray that you'll communicate
    This mystic legacy
To friends who pause outside my gate
    In years I shall not see.
And so it is, O Lord, I know
    Ere my appointments cease,
You'll groom my birches for the snow
    And give me time for peace.

*—Courtesy of Dr. W.L. "Roy" Goodwin*

*Gregory Power*

# WE
# CELEBRATED

THE

80TH BIRTHDAY

OF

JOSEPH R. SMALLWOOD

MAIN DINING HALL

MEMORIAL UNIVERSITY OF NEWFOUNDLAND

THURSDAY, FEBRUARY 5, 1981

# The Celebration Committee

Dr. Roy Goodwin

Joseph D. Ashley

Verona Woodford

Steven A. Neary

Alma Babcock

William R. Callahan

Gregory J. Power

Joan Cook

Ted Garland

Dale Russell Fitzpatrick

Ray Gallagher

Eric Dawe

Who received willing assistance from
many well-wishers

# Head Table Guests
## Dr. Roy Goodwin, Chairman

Mrs. Joseph R. Smallwood
Gregory J. Power
Mrs. S.A. Neary
Senator R.W. Rowe
Mrs. Charles R. Granger
S.A. Neary, M.H.A.
Mrs. (Senator) F.W. Rowe
Pastor Graham Noble
Mrs. Patrick J. Canning
George Baker, M.P.
Ted Garland

Mrs. Gregory J. Power
Hon. Joseph R. Smallwood
Mrs. Roy Goodwin
Rev. Canon R.R. Babb
Mayor Wyatt
Hon. E.J.A. Harnum
Mrs. Graham Noble
Hon. Charles R. Granger
Mrs. (Canon) R.R. Babb
Patrick J. Canning
Harry Steele

# From Across Canada
# Came Messages of
# Congratulations and Goodwill

## The Governor General

### Right Honourable Edward Schreyer, Governor General of Canada

Tonight, your many friends are joining to help you celebrate your 80th birthday. I avail myself of this opportunity to extend congratulations and warm wishes to you on this important occasion.

You were born at the same time as a new century and you grew along with your century. You actually extended your country by ensuring the entry of your Province into the Canadian Confederation in 1949. Newfoundland and Canada are grateful for your efforts and dedication on their behalf. Tonight's banquet offers me a chance to wish you many more years of health, happiness and the peace that comes from pride in a job well done.

Long live the last surviving Father of Confederation!

## The Prime Minister

### Right Honourable Pierre Elliott Trudeau, Prime Minister of Canada

It is with the greatest of pleasure that I join my voice to all those paying tribute to The Honourable Joey Smallwood here tonight. Joey, a Politician and Provincial leader par excellence, taught many Liberals all that they know about politics. As leader of his Province's Government for twenty-three consecutive years, he had much to teach us. He is the grand old man of the Liberal Party, but far from resting on his many laurels, he is still in there fighting the good fight and giving us the benefit of his experienced views.

I understand that Joey recently threatened to retire—at some far distant time in the future. We'll believe that when we see it. With all good wishes.

## The Former Governor General

### Right Honourable Roland Mitchener, Former Governor General of Canada

My wife and I offer you felicitations as you reflect in the company of many friends on a long life of achievement for your Province and Country. Furthermore as a newly arrived octogenarian myself, I welcome you to our healthy band, still young enough in spirit to look ahead with confidence and pleasure.

# Canada's Party Leaders

### Right Honourable Joe Clarke, former Prime Minister of Canada

This event reflects the high esteem in which you are held by your associates and friends, and is a fitting tribute to your many years of dedication and service to the people of Newfoundland and of Canada. The leadership qualities and spirit of political determination which you have demonstrated throughout your career are an example to us all, regardless of political affiliation. I know I join with many in wishing you the best for your 80th year, as well as health and happiness in the years ahead.

### Mr. Ed Broadbent, Leader of the New Democratic Party of Canada

On behalf of the Federal New Democratic party and my colleagues in the House of Commons I send you heartiest congratulations on this joyous occasion. Your contributions to Newfoundland and Canada are recognized by us all and we thank you. All the best.

### Mr. Claude Ryan, Leader of the Liberal Party of Quebec

I am glad to add my personal wishes to those that you will be receiving from your countless friends upon your 80th birthday. Your historic leadership of Newfoundland into Confederation and your dynamic role in the affairs of your Province and Canada, will always be remembered with gratitude. May God give you many more years of health and happiness.

# Ministers of the Crown

### Honourable William Rompkey, Newfoundland's Minister in the Government of Canada

The birthday of one without whose efforts Canada would not be complete is a reminder to all of us of the privilege of being Canadian. I thank you for fighting for Canada in the past and at present. I hope more Newfoundlanders will fight as hard. For fight we must to keep a Country that I believe is every bit worth the effort.

### Honourable Monique Begin, Canada's Minister of Health and Welfare

You obviously have found the elixir of youth and, as Federal Minister of Health, I wish I could command you to share your secret and your real love for Canada with other Canadians. But, since, as you know, we in Ottawa never command those in the Province, I'll content myself with wishing you a very happy birthday.

### Honourable Gerald Regan, Minister of Sport and former Premier of Nova Scotia

Both Carole and I extend our very warm wishes to you, Joey, on this occasion, and may our "Living Father of Confederation" enjoy many more years of health and happines..

### Honourable Mark McGuigan, Canada's Secretary
### of State for External Affairs

35 years ago the Secretary of State for External Affairs would have had official dealings with the Government of Newfoundland. As it is, largely because of Mr. Smallwood, Canada has joined Newfoundland in Confederation, for which feat he is rightly known as a Father of Confederation. I hope that Mr. Smallwood's next eighty years are as successful as his first eighty.

### Honourable Jean Cretien, Canada's
### Attorney General and Minister of Justice

Congratulations on your birthday, sorry to miss the banquet in your honor. It is a great opportunity to remind all Canadians of your outstanding contribution to the development of our great country.

### Honourable Donald Johnston, President of
### Treasury Board of Canada

Very best wishes for the years to come.

### Honourable Eugene Whelan, Canada's Minister of Agriculture

Your achievements on behalf of your Province are recognized by all of Canada and I know that all of Canada is indeed proud of their only living Father of Confederation. To all present, my kind regards, and to Joey—may you have many more.

### Honourable R.J. Perrault, Leader of the
### Government in the Senate

I am delighted to be able to extend to you congratulations and best wishes on your eightieth birthday.

### Honourable Bob Kaplan, Canada's Solicitor General

This evening will be an enjoyable and memorable one for you and all those attending and I hope you will enjoy many more birthday celebrations. Congratulations and my very best wishes.

# From Within the Province

### The Most Reverend Alphonsus L. Penny,
### Archbishop of St. John's

I am pleased to associate myself with the assembly honouring you on your eightieth birthday. Scripture says that the span of man's life is three score and ten, and if he is strong, another decade will be added. No doubt you are aspiring, notwithstanding the Holy Writ, to create a new precedence. I wish you continuing length of years, along with good health and happines..

I take this opportunity to express my thanks for your unfailing courtesy and availability, as well as for the occasions when you went along with, or even improved on suggestions made by delegations of which I was a member.

### The Most Reverend P.J. Skinner,
### former Archbishop of St. John's

On the occasion of the celebration of your 80th birthday may I join my best wishes to so many others. At the same time I am happy to recall our cordial relations through the years. May I assure you of my constant esteem and gratitude along with kindest personal regards.

## The Most Reverend Robert L. Seaborn, former Archbishop of Newfoundland

May I extend to you my best wishes and congratulations on your 80th birthday. Yours has been and still is, a remarkable life, full of achievements and vision.

I regret my absence from this dinner being held in your honour, but my retirement duties as Bishop Ordinary to the Canadian Forces has taken me to the Mainland.

## The Right Reverend John A. Meaden, former Lord Bishop of Newfoundland

I feel that I must send you a word of congratulations on your attaining your 80th birthday and on the vision and enthusiasm with which you pursue your researches, studies and writings of our Newfoundland life and history, extending your original purpose to make "Newfoundland better known to Newfoundlanders" to include the whole of Canada and perhaps beyond.

The older Newfoundlanders will not, on this occasion, forget the part you played in bringing about our Confederation with Canada, which has brought so many benefits, both politically and socially; and perhaps the younger generation will pause to remember the contribution you have made in providing the educational opportunities they now enjoy, both in high school, University and technical Institutions.

## Dr. Moses Morgan, President and Vice-Chancellor of Memorial University of Newfoundland

It gives me great pleasure on behalf of the University community to extend to you, an Honourary Graduate and a most generous benefactor, sincere greetings and best wishes.

We will not soon forget at this University that it was your first Administration that, in 1949, shortly after Confederation, introduced into the House of Assembly the bill that was to elivate the Memorial University College to university status. Your succeeding administrations provided the new campus on Elizabeth Avenue with its 5 academic buildings, with its Paton College, and its Burton's Pond apartments. It was also your Administration that extended the campus across the Parkway and provided the Engineering building, the central heating plant, the vivarium and the Health Sciences Centre. It was your personal broad vision of the contribution the university could make to the development of the university and its people, and your enthusiastic support of that concept, that made possible the growth of the university, in the breadth of its programs and in the number of its students. It is therefore in grateful remembrance that we salute you on this happy occasion.

## Dr. C.R. Barrett, President of The College of Fisheries, Navigation, Marine Engineering and Electronics

I would like to take this opportunity on behalf of the students, staff and faculty of the College of Fisheries, Navigation, Marine Engineering and Electronics to extend to you our regards and best wishes on the anniversary of your 80th birthday.

Of your many accomplishments while you were Premier of this Province we believe one of the most important was the creation of our College which has served so well the fishing and allied marine industries of this Province, the nation and the world since its founding in 1964. For this accomplishment all of us are very grateful.

## Mr. Kenneth F. Duggan, President of the College of Technology

I was very pleased to learn that the Honourable Joseph R. Smallwood is being honoured at a birthday dinner on Thursday, February 5th. Would you please convey to him my personal congratulations and those of the members of our college fraternity.

## Mr. D.J. Kelland, Executive Director of the Janeway Health Child Centre

The Board of Directors, Administration and Staff of the Dr. Charles A. Janeway Child Health Centre extend sincere congratulations to the Hon. Joseph R. Smallwood on the occasion of his 80th birthday with the wish for continued health and happiness.

### MR. R.D. Moore, Secretary of the General Hospital Corporation

Congratulations on attainment of your 80th birthday and best wishes for many more happy and productive years.

### Mr. Harry Steele, President and Chief Executive Officer
### of Eastern Provincial Airways

I want to join with all your friends in wishing you a very happy birthday and best of luck in all your endeavours.

# Premiers and Former Premiers

### Honourable Angus MacLean, Premier of Prince Edward Island

On behalf of myself and my colleagues, I am pleased to extend our best wishes as you celebrate this milestone in a life filled with achievement. May you enjoy continued good health in the days ahead.

### Honourable Allan Blakeney, Premier of Saskatchewan

Dear Joey: Along with your many friends who are with you this evening I join in honouring your long and rich service to your Province and Country. As the only living Father of Confederation you certainly deserve an evening and more of special recognition for your contribution to National Unity. Because of your vision Canada is truly a Nation which stretches "from coast to coast to coast." The people of Saskatchewan share your belief in a strong unitied country within which our diverse regions can express their uniqueness. So on their behalf I wish you a happy evening and many more years of active public life.

### Honourable John Robarts, former Premier of Ontario

May I extend to you my best wishes and congratulations on this occasion in honour of your 80th birthday. I wish you health, happiness and all the best for '81.

### Senator G.I. Smith, former Premier of Nova Scotia

Please accept my warmest congratulations on your having reached this great milestone in your energetic, lively, productive and very distinguished career, and my best wishes for "many happy returns of the day."

### Honourable William Davis, Premier of Canada's
### most populous Province, Ontario

At a time when much attention is being focused on forging a new constitution and a new Confederation, an occasion such as this gives us the opportunity to pause and reflect on the vision and dedication of our forefathers through whose initiative the B.N.A. act came into being. We could well ponder on the solid foundation which they laid for nation-building, a foundation on which much has been accomplished in just over a century, it was with considerable pride and sense of achievement that you led Newfoundland into Confederation and thus brought into the Canadian family a land whose colourful history pre-dated that of her nine sister provinces to the west. You have been an ardent and vocal partisan politician, as were those leaders in 1867, yet you have presented to Canadians, as did they, a sense of nationhood which transcends partisan politics.

It could well be that no greater tribute could be paid to the only living Father of Confederation in Recognition of this milestone in your life, and to the memory of those other Fathers of Confederation who showed wisdom beyond their own understanding, if Canadians would put aside regional diferences and political bickering and renew their commitment to build an ever stronger and more united nation. Again, Joe, my respectful congratulations. As you begin a new decade in your rich and full life, may I extend deep appreciation for all that you have contributed to Canada and my earnest hope that you will long continue to be a positive force within the Canadian community.

### Honourable Richard Hatfield, Premier of New Brunswick

You proved that it was possible to be at the same time a Newfoundlander, a Canadian and a citizen of the world and in so doing enlarged both your Province and your Country. You have put on the mantle of the elder statesman without feeling obliged to advocate as the national gadfly. To you who has given the patriots so much light and laughter I say—Long may your big jib draw.

### Tommy Douglas, former Premier of Saskatchewan and former leader of the N.D.P.

Heartiest congratulations on reaching your 80th birthday with your zest for living still unimpaired.

I have happy memories of your first attendance at a Federal-Provincial conference where you were the latest addition to the Fathers of Confederation. Your contribution has made Canada richer in its diversity and wiser in its outlook.

It was a pleasure to have been associated with you in our mutual desire to do what was best for the people we represented.

May I extend to you an old Scottish wish,
"Land may your lum reek,
And may the mouse ne'er leave
Your meal poke wi'a tear in his 'ee."

### Senator Henry D. Hicks, former Premier of Nova Scotia

Please express my warmest greetings and congratulations to the Honourable Joseph R. Smallwood. My acquaintance with him goes back to the mid 50's when I was Premier of Nova Scotia.

He is a great Newfoundlander and has become a great Canadian.

### Honourable W.R. Bennett, Premier of British Columbia

It is impossible to adequately express the tremendous debt of gratitude that is owed by all Canadians to that handful of valiant Politicians of your generation who made—and in your case, continue to make—such an outstanding contribution to the development of this country. You have served in many fields, have pioneered in some, and have excelled in all, and I am more than delighted to join in honouring you and to express to you my warmest congratulations, and those of the people and the Government of British Columbia.

### Senator Duff Roblin, former Premier of Manitoba

When I reflect upon our productive meetings in days gone by around the first Ministers' conference tables I am prompted to send you this warm expression of congratulations on the occasion of your 80th birthday with sincere good wishes for many happy days.

Your record in Canadian public life is truly unique and must be a source of great satisfaction to you.

### Senator John J. Connolly, former Premier of Nova Scotia

I have today learned of a special event to mark the 80th birthday of the Honourable Joseph R. Smallwood. I wish I could be present.

He was always a great friend and a tower of strength. He may be 80 in the count of years, but I am sure he will always be an energetic, resilient person of great ability and with a great capacity for friendship. I wish him many more years in a fruitful and happy life.

### Honourable John Buchanan, Premier of Nova Scotia

It gives me great pleasure to be among those who are extending greetings and wishing you well this evening. May the coming years be as productive and happy as the first 80 have been. With warmest good wishes.

# Members of Canada's Parliament

### Honourable James A. McGrath, St. John's East

Please convey to Mr. Smallwood my greetings and best wishes as you meet to celebrate his birthday and to honour him for his public life and service to Newfoundland.

### Mr. Stanley Knowles, M.P.

May I join with your many friends in wishing you very hearty congratulations on your 80th birthday. I wish you many happy returns!

### Honourable Sinclair Stevens, M.P. for York Peel

Your visit to our riding is remembered fondly by many of our constituents. At this time, we would like to join with your family and friends from all across Canada in extending you best wishes for this happy and special birthday.

### Mr. Lloyd Francis, Ottawa West

Congratulations to an outstanding Canadian who has devoted his life to our Nation.

### Mr. John L. Evans, M.P., Ottawa Centre

Along with those paying tribute to you on February 5th, I am sure that I share the thoughts of all Canadians that you will continue for many more years to inspire us with your love of Canada and your dedication to a happier union of all Provinces within our Constitution. Happy Birthday.

### Mr. Raymond Savard, M.P. Verdun-St. Paul

It is a special privilege for me to pay tribute to a great Canadian, on this your 80th birthday.

All Canadians are aware of your efforts and ultimate successes, at making this country complete. Your skills as a negotiator, your influence over the destiny of Newfoundland, your charm, and your wit, have made you not only a Father of Confederation but a true part of Canadian history.

I know the citizens of Verdun-Saint-Paul, as well as all the people of Canada, join me in wishing you their very best on this great occasion, and in expressing their gratitude for your service in Canada.

### Mr. David C. Dingwall, M.P., Cape Breton

Canadians from all walks of life and in all regions of our great nation are proud of the dedication and service Mr. Smallwood continues to give to his Country.

### Mr. Tom Sidden, M.P., Richmond South Delta

I join with your many friends and colleagues in extending to you congratulations and best wishes for the occasion of your 80th birthday Anniversary.

I feel privileged to be able to acknowledge this happy event and I do hope you have a great day.

### Mr. Roland De Corneille, M.P. Eglinton-Lawrence

It is with the greatest pleasure that I take this opportunity to extend to you my congratulations on the occasion of the celebration of your 80th birthday.

This is certainly a memorable occasion and I wish you all the best in the years to come.

With warmest regards.

### Mr. George Henderson, M.P. for Egmont

I would like to take this opportunity to extend my most hearty congratulations on the occasion of your 80th birthday, and may the future years hold much health, happiness and prosperity for you.

And from many personal friends within Canada and beyond came messages of congratulations and goodwill.

# The Toast

He was born in Dunville, Placentia in 1909 and was educated at St. Bon's College, Methodist College and Memorial University College. He started in track and field at St. Bon's and was Victor Ludorum in the junior, intermediate and senior divisions. He was captain of the first Memorial College track team and he still holds the all-Newfoundland records for the high hurdles and the triple jump. He was a member of the Newfoundland team at the first British Empire Games at Hamilton, Ontario, in 1930, and he placed fifth. Through high school and at Memorial he was a top student.

He was in the forefront during the whole of the Confederation Campaign, and it is well-nigh impossible to exaggerate his contribution to the cause. Throughout the campaign he was Mr. Smallwood's right-hand man, and he was the chief editor of **The Confederate**, and agree or disagree with it, but you would be hard-pressed to find anything in political writing to equal the satire and brilliant propoganda of the "Sacred Cow".

After Confederation he was executive assistant to the Premier and the Chairman of the Board of Liquor Control. In 1951 he was elected to the House of Assembly by Placentia East and was appointed Minister of Finance and President of the Treasury Board. In 1956 he became Minister of Highways. Since his retirement from Politics he operated Newfoundland's three largest poultry farms.

Athlete, scholar, journalist, politician, businessman—all these he has been; put perhaps over-riding all this he is a poet. His poems have been included in our schools and used in English courses at Memorial University and in the University of New Brunswick. One of his poems, **A Testament**, was considered by the late Dr. A.C. Hunter of Memorial to be one of the most beautiful lyrics in the language. It was written in the early thirties when TB had cut short this most promising athletic and scholastic of careers. It gives expression to the thoughts of a young man who was face to face with death.

It is my pleasure to present Mr. Greg Power.

# Proposal

Mr. Chairman, Ladies and Gentlemen. I would like to thank Dr. Goodwin for that very kind introduction. Of course, my gratification is tempered a little by the knowledge that Dr. Goodwin is always generous in his estimate of people — that's the mark of a mature personality. I am especially grateful for his appreciation of my poem, **A Testament**, and I might add, the only reward one gets for writing poetry is the assurance that somebody likes it.

I am also delighted to have the privilege of proposing a toast to the guest of honour, not alone because he is the most distinguished Newfoundlander of our time, but because I was closely associated with him in the great battle for Confederation, and as a member of the Provincial Government for the first nine years of its existence and incidentally, we are the only two people alive today who know the inside story of how all of us became Canadians.

It's quite a story, and now that the shouting and the tumult is over, we often get together, and hit the Bristol Cream while we reminisce about the wonderful events of the past 35 years.

There are a lot of exciting things to recall — the bitter fight to get Confederation on the ballot paper; — the launching of the confederate association at a meeting in the Newfoundland hotel on almost this very night 33 years ago — the opening of our campaign headquarters at 158 Water Street — the publishing of our newspaper **The Confederate** — the campaign around the Island by plane and motorcar — our narrow escape from the mob after a meeting at the C.L.B. Armory — our elation on the night of July 22, 1948, when it became evident that we had accomplished the impossible — the thrill of taking over control of the tenth Province in 1949; and hundreds of other incidents, good and bad, that were the raw material of a social and economic revolution.

To appreciate the kind of Newfoundland that Mr. Smallwood led into Confederation, one should glance back at our beginnings, and at the kind of environment that made us what we were. It goes without saying that the bold kindred who first landed in these lonely coves, and built a nest in the rock, were self-reliant and rich in spirit. They had little else to sustain them in their battle for survival. But they did survive, in spite of all the conspiracies of wind and weather, and they did succeed in creating here a simple, frugal way of life, that for all its shortcomings is still dear to the hearts of those of us who are old enough to remember.

For generations without end, the salt cod fishery was the only means of livelihood. It was a subsistence industry, controlled by a few families in St. John's, and over the centuries it produced little beyond a condition of indentured poverty.

Time seemed to stand still here until the building of the cross-country railway. This opened up the interior, and resulted in the Grand Falls and Humber Developments, and from then on these were the two bright spots in our economy.

Then came the first world war, and an increased demand for our forest, mineral, and fishery products. This in turn brought about a short-term improvement in the quality of life, but the postwar collapse introduced the worst period of privation in living memory.

Then came the second world war, and the building of the American bases. This was a real shot in the arm, and for the first time, ever, our people had money to spend on things other than the bare necessities. We thought it was prosperity, but in retrospect it was merely the reduction of poverty to a more tolerable level.

Then in 1949, Confederation with Canada — the first real turning point in our island story, and a date that will forever mark the boundary between the squalor of the past, and the hope of the future.

Our purpose in being here tonight is to honour the man who more than anyone else was responsible for bringing this change about. It was he who spearheaded the campaign, and co-ordinated the efforts of all the rest of us, and you can take it from one who was there — Confederation would not have come without him.

In those less sophisticated days anyone who advocated social or economic reform was immediately suspected of being an agent of Moscow. So it wasn't surprising that they christened us "The Bolsheviks," and we were revolutionaries in the sense that we were under nobody's thumb. We were free spirits, and we did our own thinking instead of humbly accepting the guidelines of the establishment.

A local columnist, who was somewhat to the right of the John Birch Society in his thinking, used to refer to us as: "Joseph and his motly gang". He contended that those who had no stake in the country should have no say in the selection of its future form of government, and he continually accused the British Government of betraying Newfoundland by asking the people to decide the issue in a national Referendum. He gave one the impression that the British Government could have more honourably discharged its constitutional responsibilities by simply referring the issue to the City Club.

(Although we've come a long way in our political thinking since then. I can't help noticing that "Referendum" is still a dirty word among several of our Provincial Premiers.)

The Responsible Government leader resurrected the old bogey of property taxes — I can hear him now: "My dear friends, if you listen to the renegades who are trying to sell our dear little country, and allow them to railroad you into Confederation, everything you have will be taxed — every hen will be taxed — every pane of glass will be taxed — even your chopping-block will be taxed, and don't forget that failure to pay these taxes will result in your homes being seized and sold at public auction."

This was potent propaganda among people who had an inherent fear of direct taxation, especially among those of Irish descent, whose forefathers had experienced the horrors of mass eviction in Ireland.

Of course we Confederates denounced all this as nonsense and claptrap, but it was our no against their yes, and most people were inclined to believe the worst anyway.

We finally decided that ridicule was the best weapon against such exaggerated propaganda. So we lampooned their contentions in satirical verse; we tried their leader in what we called the People's Court; and we gave ridiculous accounts of their meetings in the stable of the Sacred Cow — the sacred cow was Responsible Government.

The feedback from all this was so encouraging that we continued this tactic throughout the whole campaign.

At that time the Responsible Government League had a radio program on which the leader of the Responsible Government side, a financial wizard in his own right, would answer questions posed by a group they called the Young Voters.

I was listening one evening, when one of the Young Voters inquired "Sir, can you tell me if we will have a surplus when we get back Responsible Government?" His leader had no trouble with that one, and predicted a surplus of $517,418.16 in the first glorious year of restoration. The young voter was reassured and said, "I understand it all very clearly now." His leader was pleased and enjoined him: "Look at Prince Edward Island!" This was the place he always held up as an example of the failure of Confederation.

In the next meeting of Responsible Government supporters in the stable of the Sacred Cow, we had the Responsible Government leader exhorting the boys to put on their thinking caps, and think up something else that he could say would be taxed after Confederation.

One of the Young Voters was the first to come up with an idea, and clapping his hands, joyfully inquired, "What about a tax on hens?" His leader informed him wearily that he had already foamed at the mouth about the tax on hens. "But," insisted the Young Voter, "if my memory serves me correctly, you neglected to include the Roosters, thereby conveying the impression that after Confederation Roosters would continue to strut around as if nothing at all had happened."

Seeing the enormity of his omission, the Responsible Government leader sprang from his stool and shouted: "Look at the Roosters in Prince Edward Island!" where, he contended, Federal Feed subsidies had reduced a once proud breed of birds to the level of Capons. He couldn't understand how the owner of any enterprising Rooster could be so false to his trust as to support Confederation, in the hope of saving a few cents on feed. Off the cuff he estimated that the Rooster tax would cost the people of Newfoundland $262,316.11 annually.

The boys gave him a standing ovation, and we hung the Rooster tax around his neck for the rest of the campaign.

One of our worst experiences was the discovery that Margarine could not be manufactured or sold in Canada.

At that time a locally manufactured product, called Green Label, sold for 33¢ a pound, but butter cost

90¢, and tens of thousands of Newfoundlanders had never even tasted it. Unless this restriction was lifted, we knew we could never win Confederation.

Our opponents were quick to capitalize on this, and the **Daily News** carried a banner headline which said: "Newfoundlanders will be denied their spread for bread."

To argue with them would have made matters worse so we decided to make a joke of it while Mr. Smallwood was negotiating to have the restriction lifted. This gave birth to the Ballad of Oleo Margarine:

I pray that I shall never know
A future without oleo,
Or live to see my little ones
Turn up their noses at my buns;
But there is one with soul so dead,
Who'd sacrifice our spread for bread,
And ban from every Newfie table
Our wholesome, rich, improved Green Label.

Besides its worth in stews and juices
It has other magic uses,
Superceding every phony
Means to forward matrimony.
Now, Myrtle, Eloise and Mabel
Don't give a damn for Betty Grable,
Since any unromantic ruffin'
Is tamed by spreading on his muffin
That fortified, improved, delicious
Blend of cottonseed and fishes.

I have heard my neighbors mutter
About a substitute called butter,
Which Mr. Wayfarer avows
Was wrung from discontented cows;
An overmilked, exploited breed,
Always lowing to secede.
He says Joe would expose the nation
To this strange, bovine creation,
And pass a law — now can you beat it —
Compelling everyone to eat it!

My late grandad, who fished for cod,
Just missed being used as cannon wad.
He rated it his closest shave,
And brought that memory to his grave.
Now in his bright, celestial hall,
I'll bet that Gramp is on the ball,
Convincing all the powers that be
That if his little progeny
Can't have some margarine on buns,
They might as well be shot from guns.

The wonder was that we **did** win considering the powerful forces that were arrayed against us — the two wealthy paper companies that had never paid any corporation tax up to that time — the majority of the business fraternity who feared that increased competition would break their snug hold on local trade, and some very powerful men of the cloth. I have never heard a logical reason for their opposition.

When Smallwood administration came to power in 1949 its first priority was the building of the Trans Canada Highway from St. John's to Port Aux Basques, and a network of feeder roads to connect up the hundreds of settlements along the way.

We build a road down the Burin Peninsula connecting all the settlements from Marystown to Terranceville in Fortune Bay.

We built a road along the North side of Bonavista Bay through Valleyfield and Wesleyville, and up along the Straight Shore through Musgrave Harbour to Gander Bay, and on to Gander.

We built a road from Bishop's Falls to St. Alban's in Bay Despair.

We built the road to the Isles connecting Twillingate, Lewisporte and dozens of other settlements in Notre Dame Bay.

We built a road from South Brook to Pilley's Island connecting up the settlements of Roberts Arm and Brighton.

We built a road to Springdale and connected up the settlements in Green Bay.

We built a road from Hampden to Sop's Arm and on to Jackson's Arm.

We built a road the length and breadth of the Bay Verte Peninsula.

We built a road from Bonne Bay up the Great Northern Peninsula to St. Anthony and across the Peninsula from Brig Bay to Roddickton.

We built a road along the South Side of Bay of Islands from Petries to Lark Harbour.

We built a bridge on the Lower Humber and connected up the settlements on the North Side of Bay of Islands.

We built a road opening up Stephenville, Lourdes and other communities on the Port au Port Peninsula.

We built a road from Port aux Basques to connect Isle au Morts, Burnt Island and Harbour LeCou, and in 1958 Mr. Smallwood and I had the thrill of being the first persons to drive across the Island from St. John's to Port aux Basques.

It was all done within the space of about 10 years. It was a labour of love, and I am sure that THE GREATEST DAY THAT EVER DAWNED IN ST. ANTHONY IN THE NORTH, IN ST. ALBAN'S IN THE SOUTH, IN MUSGRAVE HARBOUR ON THE STRAIGHT SHORE, AND IN HUNDREDS OF OTHER ISOLATED SETTLEMENTS, WAS THE WONDERFUL DAY THE BULLDOZERS BROKE THROUGH. IT CHANGED THE FACE OF NEWFOUNDLAND.

While all this was taking place, new schools were being built, new hospitals were being put into operation, water and sewer systems were being installed, new skating rinks were going up — Newfoundland was **finally** on the march, and if it had all ended there, it would have been the greatest leap forward in all our history, but more great things were to come — the building of Trade Schools — the building of Arts and Culture Centers, and above all the building of this great University, and in **tonight's** setting it isn't trite to say: — if you seek his monument, look around you.

Mr. Smallwood didn't tell the fishermen to burn their boats — that was a cheap fabrication, but he might well have told the people to throw away their kerosine lamps, because his great Hydro-electric development at Bay Despair made rural electrification possible.

I notice that those who have made a career of maligning Mr. Smallwood have one thing in common: They themselves have never done anything worth mentioning to improve the quality of life in Newfoundland; they were probably too busy criticizing what he was doing. They make great capital of Mr. Smallwood's mistakes. Of course there were mistakes during his 23 years of office, but the sum total of these mistakes is overwhelmed by the variety and magnitude of his achievements.

Let us consider just one of the great benefits that came to Newfoundland as a result of Confederation — the unemployment insurance scheme. During the past year, some 230 million dollars were paid out in Newfoundland in these insurance benefits.

This is more than was earned in either the fishing, mineral or forest industry. It was twice blest: it shielded the families of the unemployed from privation and it kept the economy moving. If it disappeared tomorrow, the collapse would be swift and devastating.

I think any fairminded person who knows the story of the past 32 years will agree with me when I say — that **MR. SMALLWOOD HAS BEEN DIRECTLY AND INDIRECTLY RESPONSIBLE FOR PUTTING MORE FOOD ON MORE TABLES, MORE CLOTHES ON MORE BACKS, AND MORE HOPE INTO MORE HEARTS THAN ANY OTHER MAN IN ALL THE HISTORY OF NEWFOUNDLAND.**

That's a tremendous thing to say about anyone, yet it's the simple truth, and long years hence, when all the political smog has drifted away, and objective historians are assessing the events of the past 35 years they will I think immortalize the man who led Newfoundland out of its age-old poverty and isolation, and made it the kind of place that our children were proud to inherit.

We have gathered here tonight to re-emphasize the truth, and to wish him well in the eightieth year of his life, so I ask you, now, to rise with me and drink a toast to the only living father of Confederation — the man who dreamed an impossible dream, and had the energy to make it come true.

To Mr. Smallwood

# Response

Mr. Chairman, my dear friends:

My first word is one of heart-felt gratitude to all of you who have so highly honoured me by your friendship: by your support through the years, and by your presence tonight. I am grateful to you beyond the power of words to tell. Your friendship is my most precious possession. Did ever public man have so many true friends in Newfoundland before or have their friendship so long? I am grateful — believe me, I am grateful.

Woodrow Wilson had his Colonel House, Franklin D. Roosevelt his Harry Hopkins, Mackenzie King his Ernest Lapoint, Winston Churchill his Lord Beaverbrook — how fortunate for them and for **their** cause that they **did** — and fortunate for me and for our cause that Greg Power threw every ounce of his talent, his wit, his humour and his unique sardonic common sense — above all, his superior intellect — into the great fight: Gregory Power, Poet, Athlete, Farmer, my friend.

We didn't have too much money, we Confederates, in that fight 32-34 years ago, but what we lacked in money we more than made up with the ardent help of dozens at first, then hundreds and finally tens of thousands of Newfoundlanders who brought the glorious ultimate triumph of 1949 — those Newfoundland men and women who not only changed the very course of Canadian history but at the same time were setting their own homeland at last on the road to prosperity and success — surely one of the most successful exercises in democracy carried out anywhere in the world in the past 100 years. We wouldn't be here tonight — not one of us — but for that remarkable accomplishment.

And I want you, and all Newfoundland, to know that in that historic battle there was no greater or more Valiant warrior than Gregory Power.

You are generously noticing my 80th birthday tonight, but really we shouldn't take the matter of age too seriously.

There's a lot of wrong thinking about age. But I have to confess to you tonight that I do get some satisfaction from the fact that of all the men elected to be Premier of Newfoundland since 1855 there have been no more than three who have lived longer than I have. I have for instance lived longer than Sir Richard Squires, 61, F.C. Alderdice, 64; Sir James Winter, 66; John Kent, 67; Sir Robert Thorburn, 70; Sir Robert Bond, 70; Philip Francis Little, our first Premier, 73; Sir Edward (later lord) Morris, 76.

The two that I'm keeping an eye on are the great Sir William Whiteway, the greatest of our Premiers, who lived to be a little over 80, and Walter Monroe who died at 81. Somehow, barring accidents, I have some confidence in my luck to exceed them. If I do I'll then be left with one great mountain to climb: 90. I'm exceedingly eager to climb that mountain and go even higher and become the longest-lived Newfoundlander ever to be elected Premier. For you see the man I have to beat is one of the greatest of all Premiers, a man who changed the very course of our history, the man who in 1869 defeated Confederation: Charles Fox Bennett. Surely fate is not going to allow an anti-Confederate to snatch that victory from me.

I am not despondent about it, for I happen to be a member of one of the longest-lived families in Newfoundland. On my father's side and on my mother's we have had them **in dozens** who lived up to their late eighties, their early and mid **nineties**, and some who reached the **century** mark and a few who went beyond. I had one great-great-great aunt who danced the Highland Fling on her 100th birthday and died one day before her 111th birthday. A great-great-great

Uncle was so old that nobody **knew** how old he was. They said that he eventually just dried up and blew away.

One of my family was a farmer in Freshwater Valley, beside St. John's, a bare few 100 yards from where we are tonight.... and when he was over **100** he actually did some ploughing of his land in the month of January that year. He was farmer Crampton, which some people shortened to Cramp. He died at 106.

On pages 550 to 557 inclusive of my book **I Chose Canada** I spell out the names, dates and some details of some of my relatives. There are **175** of them who lived to an age between 80 and 90 — 175 of them, and don't imagine that I'm not proud of **them**! But that's not all — there are 55 others who lived to an age of 90 or over —— 55 of them. And that's not all, , for 6 or the 55 went over 100.

Yet, you know, there is — there really is — a lot of superstition about this matter of age. **Verdi** was composing his masterpiece **Falstaff** at 79; Michaelangelo created his **Pieta** at 80; Robert Bridges was publishing his great **Testament of Beauty** at 85; Robert Frost was writing some of his best poetry at 89, the year he died; John Wesley was preaching at 88; Fanny Crosbie, who wrote 2000 hymns, died at 95.

Bertrand Russell, one of the greatest of this century's philosphers (and I'm so glad that I knew him personally) lived to be 96.

And don't overlook the **politicians**: the great de Gaulle was president of France up to a year before he died at 80. Mao Tsetung ruled the largest nation of the world until he died at 83. Marshall Tito lived to be 87. Conrad Adenauer ruled Western Germany until he was 87, and he lived for years after that.

And our own immortal Churchill: Churchill was Prime Minister of England until he was 87, and lived to be 91.

On Churchill's **90th** birthday a great contingent of journalists crowded into his house for an interview. The last of them to leave the house was a young fellow of 19 or 20, and as he passed out through the entrance hallway and had his hand shaken by Churchill be blurted emotionally: "It is a wonderful honour that you shake my hand, Sir. I do most fervently hope that I'll have the honour to see you a year from today!"

Churchill was all solicitude:

"Why," he asked, "Aren't you feeling well?"

• • • • • • • • •

I think that we'd all agree that this meal wouldn't be going on in this dining hall tonight if we Confederates had not won that greatest of all battles in our history.

In another 17 years we Newfoundlanders will have been here in Newfoundland a full 500 years since Cabot sailed in through the Narrows. I have looked across the world, and into a hundred years of history, but **looked in vain** to find a parallel of the veritable cloudburst of transformation that has been experienced in our homeland in these meteoric 32 years since 1949. Nothing like it — nothing resembling it — nothing the equal of it — has ever occurred anywhere else in Canada, or anywhere else in North America — this all but unbelievable **cleansweep convulsion** of change that has converged upon us almost faster than we could breathe — all of it in our own lifetime, before our very eyes, leaving not even one Newfoundlander untouched by the wonder and healing of it: and that convulsion going irresistably on to new heights and new triumphs straight ahead.

You think you get a **glimpse** of the **wonder** of our Confederation Revolution when you see that since 1949 we've built over 1200 **beautiful new schools;** that **our teachers,** now so much better trained and better paid, have increased in number from 2400 to 9000; — (there were hardly that many fishermen 10 years ago) from 169 teachers of **university grade** then to the **present** fact that **all** teachers have it now. You think you glimpse, but it's **only** a glimpse, "seen through a glass darkly."

And for a moment you think that you've sensed the **abundance** of it when you see another of Confederation's wonders — **this magnificent university** and the thousands of young Newfoundland men and women who have come here, and continue to come, from every coast and shore of Labrador and Newfoundland, from every Bay, from hundreds of our communities, to sit at the feet of Gamaliels who have themselves arrived here from all the continents of land and continents of thought to teach and inspire the students to fashion a better Newfoundland and a better Canada.

And then when you see that we Newfoundlanders now have our magnificent **College of Fisheries, Navigation, Marine Engineering and Electronics,** this great teacher that attracts students from all parts of our Province and from many parts of the world; and our **College of Technology...** and our **College of Engineering....**and our College of Nursing....and our **College of Medicine.** Tens and tens of thousands have studied in them, and tens of thousands more will do so—why, these new confederation marvels are in themselves a mightly Newfoundland revolution.

And there are all the perfectly magnificent **new hospitals** we have now... the beautiful **Janeway Health Centre,** for example, that has already treated nearly a million Newfoundland children medically and will treat a million more.... Great Hospitals all around the Province now, served by 500 Doctors, 3000 Nurses and 5000 other workers, that are helping to make us a healthier people than we ever were in the past — that, dear friends, that is **revolution**... that is Confederation.

And how could we be indifferent to the presence of vigorous, thriving **Arts and Culture Centers** at Corner Brook, Stephenville, Grand Falls, Gander, St. John's, Grand Bank... They cost millions to put there... they have already attracted and served Newfoundlanders and other Canadians numbering hundreds of thousands ...more such culture centers, population considered, than in any other Canadian Province.

We take due note and we are delighted to take note of the 75,000 fine **new dwelling houses** built at a cost of over a 1000 million dollars of federal, Provincial and personal money in hundreds of communities: dwellings of a **quality now** that only a few well-to-do families could afford to have before 1949.

And certainly not to be missed is the marvel of the 6000 miles of **absolutely new roads** built since

1949.... costing over 1000 million dollars to build, most of it from Ottawa... 3000 miles of them **paved**.... yes, those magical 6000 miles of new roads that destroyed the **ancient curse**, Newfoundland is ancient curses — **isolation** — putting an end to what too often was benumbing, lonely, certainly hindering **isolation** for the Newfoundlanders living in 900 settlements around 6000 miles of our coast.

So many of those Confederation sign-posts! **Public Libraries**: 26 in 1949, 104 now; 64,000 books then, ¾ million now... **6 Radio Stations** before, 69 now; **no T.V.** stations before, 112 now, 6 **newspapers** before, 17 now; an occasional new book on Newfoundland before, dozens of them now; about a dozen popular and "Combo" **Bands** before, over 400 of them now.

Of course, with all those roads we will not be **too** surprised to know that since 1949 the number of **automobiles** has increased from 9000 to 141,000, **trucks and busses** from 4400 to 60,000. Not counting the tens of thousands of Motor-bikes, Mini-bikes, Trailers, motor homes, snowmobiles and motor tobaggans that our people have spent scores and scores of millions to buy and use.

And the Marvellous **Trans Canada Highway!** That dream of Newfoundlanders for half a dozen generations! If nothing else whatsoever had come to us from Confederation, nothing but the Trans Canada Highway, **that one blessing**, it would have been handsomely well worth the vote that we gave for union with Canada, probably the richest bargain in our history. In no other 32 years of all our history was such a blessing of travel, of communication and of companionship witnessed. $120,000,000 it cost, most of it a gift from Ottawa — the most wondrous single miracle, perhaps of Confederation.

And **Medicare!** It's only a dozen years old, Medicare, this completely glorious Canadian blessing, but already nearly 3,000,000 Newfoundland patients have received nearly 20,000,000 treatments from 500 Doctors in Newfoundland — surely that one fact makes it unbearable to think that we Confederates might have lost in 1949! No wonder we're a **healthier** people now.

Since 1949 the money has rained: poured, showered upon us ... not hundreds, but thousands of millions: that is, billions of Canadian dollars.

Hundreds of millions for the fisheries; hundreds of millions for DREE; hundreds of millions for housing; hundreds of millions for the C.N.R.; hundreds of millions for schools, colleges, university; hundreds of millions for health; hundreds of millions for roads; hundreds of millions for business loans; hundreds of millions for welfare; hundreds of millions for the unemployed; hundreds of millions for old-age security; hundreds of millions for civil and military pensions; hundreds of millions to civil servants. So many hundreds of millions that they mount up into the billions.

The consequences have been staggering.

Here's one of the consequences: From 1949 the total amount of **Life Insurance** in force in our Province has come up from **$115** million in 1949 — 115 million — about one-tenth of a billion — to nearly 50 times that: **$5** bilion; 570 million. Yes, I said **$5** billion! The total amount of life insurance in force in this Province was **$5** billion **$570** million, and that

was 1978, and it's more now, an astonishing, almost unbelievable figure, up about 5000% above 1949 — nearly 50 time as much! 5000% increase, in the life insurance in Force in our Province. From about **one-tenth** of **one** billion up to over 5 billion.

And now I bring to your attention a sign-post of Confederation that you're not going to believe. You'll think it must be false. It has to do with the amount of **money** in **Newfoundlanders' pockets, then** and **now, the before and after: 1949** and **1978; before** confederation and **since.**

In 1949 there were 18,000, nearly 19,000 personal income tax payers in Newfoundland and Labrador — 19,000. That was 1949, as we began our history as a Province; Almost 19,000 Newfoundlanders who had enough taxable income that year to require them to pay income tax. By **1978** the number of tax-payers had risen **from** 18,000 to — hold your breath: 285,000. The number of Newfoundlanders with taxable income increased 1500% in the first 29 years of Confederation: 1500%.

In 1949 those 19,000 tax-payers had a total taxable income of **$57¾**: For the year: **$57-58** million. From $57 or $58 million income in that year the total by 1978 — 29 years later — had risen to — hold your breath — $2,355,000,000: almost **$2½ billion**, or in simpler terms $2300 million. That was an increase of 4000% in the personal income of Newfoundlanders: From 58 million a year to 2300 million a year.

In 1978 Newfoundlanders paid in personal income tax $316,000,000, or 70 times as much as in 1949 — an increase of 7000%!

The **number** of personal income tax payers in our Province increased 1500%; Their taxable **income** increased 4000%; the income tax they paid increased 7000%.

Is it any wonder that 60,000-70,000 Newfoundlanders are now able to go for **winter holidays** in Florida, Bermuda, Bahamas, Jamaica, Portugal and the Mediterranean every year, and that the number is increasing every year. Is it any wonder that as you look around, you see scores and hundreds of signs and evidences of our new prosperity.

••••••••

In the National Convention you may remember that I made the figure **21** rather famous — I referred frequently to the 21 millionaires and multi-millionairs in Newfoundland. It really did become a famous statistic: That 21.

Well, Confederation has made that 21 a pretty pathetic statistic! There are today about **300 millionaires and multi-millionaires** in our Province, and they are backed up by about 1500 ½ millionaires and about 3000 ¼ millionaires: We have about **4800** quite **wealthy** Newfoundlanders in Newfoundland and Labrador today, compared with perhaps one hundred on the day we became a Province: From 100 to 4800 wealthy Newfoundlanders in 29 years.

These are astounding figures; these are figures of growth that cannot be equalled anywhere else in North America in a similar span of time. Those are figures that represent revolution — bloodless revolution, yes, but revolution unequalled and unparalled on this continent.

And by the way, if you have any sensation of shock from these figures of considerable wealth, let me try to put your fears at rest. This is precisely how the industrial, commercial and financial success of all the free-enterprise countries of the world began; this is how the **generation of capital** began; this is always, except in Communist lands, this is how the generation and accumulation of investment capital happens..

In our own Newfoundland case let us hope that our millionaires and multi-millionaires, our half and quarter millionaires, and all Newfoundlanders who have more money than they need for their actual living expenses, will use their spare money as capital that they'll invest in productive industry here in our own Province. That might very well turn out to be the way of progress and patriotism, both, for Newfoundland.

Some of you, especially the younger of you, perhaps feel that I linger too much and too long over what I call the wonder of Confederation — its mighty accomplishments, its healing success in Newfoundland, its veritable moonsoon of blessings. If I dwell long on the Confederation miracle it's because I have reached my 80th birthday — which means you see that I lived nearly 50 of my years in **pre-Confederation** Newfoundland, when there were no **roads**, very little electricity, too few hospitals and too few good schools, **no** university, **no** medicare, **no** trade schools, **no** arts and culture centers, **no** children's hospital, practically no public libraries, **no** Veterans Charter, no **C.N.R.**, no unemployment insurance, no **Canada Pension**, no **DREE**, no Family Allowance, only a wretchedly and miserably mean Old Age Pension. The contrast is something that you just don't know and can't know, if you're under 42 or even 52. But I'm not under 42, or even 52, so I do remember; and remembering, I have no choice but to be a loyal Newfoundlander and a grateful Canadian, as every honest Newfoundlander of 40 odd years is bound to be.

So I'm sure that you'll forgive me when I praise Confederation and thank God for it.

Now, having given you this part-catalogue of the hard cash benefits of Confederation — and believe me it's only a part-catalogue — I do hope that you won't infer from my remarks that I am so stupid or so lacking in knowledge or imagination as to think that all of these Federal dollars are the total answer to Newfoundland's problems. Not so. Far from it.

········

I'm one person who never said (for I never believed) that Confederation would solve all our problems.

I knew that Confederation wouldn't give us more good soil than we had, or more forest than we had, or more minerals than we had, or more waterpower than we had, or more all-weather harbours than we had, or more fish than we had.

Confederation wouldn't give us more natural wealth than God had already given us. Confederation could, however, help us to discover, to map, to blueprint, to develop the God-given resources that we did have. It couldn't help us in the least to acquire natural wealth — nobody, nothing could do that — but it could and it did help us with cash to bring about the sequence that would lead to the development of the natural resources that we brought with us into Confederation.

The first thing that had to be done, however, was to raise our standard of living: the level of personal, family, community living. That came first. That had to be the beginning. That had to be the foundation.

Our sights had to rise. Our ambition had to rise. Our purpose had to rise.

We had to be implacably, unchangeably, stubbornly determined that we were not going to turn from being a colony of Britain to one of Canada. We had to be good Canadians but not less good Newfoundlanders.

Confederation has helped nobly in these purposes.

What real difference did Confederation make for us, anyway?

It gave us Canada's glorious social welfare system, yes: Family Allowances, Old Age assistance, Unemployment Insurance, Veterans Charter, and all the rest of the great catalogue. A great, world-famous, Heaven-blessed Canadian revelation of social justice.

This Confederation indubitably did accomplish, and hundreds of thousands of Newfoundlanders, with millions of mainland Canadians, share the benevolence of the system.

Who is going to condemn the system, imperfect as it may be, flawed by weaknesses as it undoubtedly is?

But when all due and proper praise is in fairness accorded to this side of Confederation, the question still is:

What real difference has it made for us?

It has indeed made us into Canadians, into citizens of a great country that is trusted and respected by the world.

It has truly made us co-heirs to a large-hearted heritage.

It has assuredly revived, renewed and reinforced our particular Newfoundland affiramtion.

Anything else?

It has made us healthier.

It has destroyed the ancient isolation of a thousand of our communities.

It has destroyed the inferiority complex that cursed our existence.

It has ingested us into North American life.

It has created the climate in which it became inevitable that Newfoundlanders would develop a tenacious self-confidence.

It has enabled us to have representative, responsible, democratic government which, however we abuse or misuse it, is, as Churchill said, "the worst form of government except for all the others."

Confederation has not made our Newfoundland economy sound, strong, vigorous. We never had a right to expect that it would.

It is our own job to do that.
It is our own responsibility.

Confederation helps, smoothes some of the path, removes some of the obstacles, provides some of the cash, and unless we want to become just a colony of Canada that's as much as we have a right to expect.

If, with all that Confederation does to lighten the burden, to remove obstacles, if we don't build a flourishing Newfoundland economy then the fault is with us, not with Ottawa.
      . . . . . .
Ladies and Gentlemen, those of you who shared with Greg Power and me the task of persuading the voters of Newfoundland and Labrador to vote in favour of joining Canada will agree wholeheartedly with me now when I say that we had quite a job on our hands back there 32 or 33 years ago. Believe me, quite a job!

But if **that** was a tough job, consider for a moment the monumental, the mountanious task, the **horrend ous** task there would be for any crusader in New-foundland who would today try to argue Newfound-landers into **leaving Canada!** Suppose there was a new referendum, and Newfoundlanders were asked to vote in a secret ballot for separation from Canada.

There are today some 236,000 voters in our Pro-vince, 236,000, and it would be they who would mark  he ballot papers in a new referendum.

Now to start with, 43,000 or those 236,000 voters are men and women who, it so happens, are accept-ing Old Age Security cheques from Canada every month; and there are 100,000 adult Newfoundland-ers who are now accepting free Canada Medicare treatments each year, at Ottawa's expense.

There are 60,000 adults who are accepting the benefit of Unemployment cheques every fortnight from Canada.

There are 5,000 other adults who are accepting the benefits of Veterans' cheques from Canada.

And then we have 8,000 Federal Civil servants who get their fortnightly cheques from Ottawa, and 5,000 other personnel who get their cheques every fort-night from the C.N.R., C.N.T., Marine Services, Hotels, Airports and Lighthouses.

As you know, we have about 10,000 Civil Servants and other employees of the Newfoundland Govern-ment, more than half of whose fortnightly payment comes to them from the Canadian Government, not directly but through the Provincial Government; and 10,000 Teachers, 8,000 Doctors and Nurses and so forth, and 8,000 students, staff and faculty at Memor-ial University, and The Technical College, The Fi-sheries College, and the Trade Schools, half or even more than half of whose payment originates in Ot-tawa.

Then we have another 30,000 Newfoundlanders who work in shops and offices serving those New-foundlanders who receive hundreds of millions of dollars from Ottawa every year; and another 30,000 Newfoundlanders operating taxies, trucks, busses and working the Garages, serving people many of whom get most of their salaries directly from Ottawa, or a large portion of them from Ottawa via the New-foundland Government.

On top of all that we have 35 members of the House of Assembly and 17 Ministers of the Crown who derive over half of their income from Ottawa.

If you bother to add up those figures, they come to a total of 456,000 adults altogether.

There is, of course, a lot of overlapping and dupli-cation in those figures; but when you account for the overlapping, the end result is that you have in New-foundland today about 387 independent voters 387 — who get nothing from Ottawa so far as they know, and who thus can be hailed and praised as com-pletely independent voters with no conflict of inter-est; 387 voters out of the 236,000 voters that we have in this Province today.

The anti-Confederates might perhaps be justified in counting on the votes of half, or nearly half, of those 387 voters. The remaining 236,000 voters will have no trouble whatsoever to restrain any mad desire to separate from Canada and from those fort-nightly or monthly cheques, so the only hope the Newfoundland separatists would have would be to bring a couple of hundred thousand in from Quebec.

And so I make now a bold forecast of the result of a new referendum if it is ever held:

Against separation: 200 votes.

For separation: 187 votes.

And the minute the result came out a new mental hospital would be ordered to house 187 new pa-tients—because of course you couldn't take the risk of having that many at large.
      . . . . . . . . .
In my book I **CHOSE CANADA** I wrote:

"Scores of years after Newfoundlanders first settled on the Island, other settlers from Europe made feeble clearings in the forest on the mainland of what is now Canada and cultivated half-acre by half-acre, seeding between the stumps. By 1900 they had coaxed millions of acres into smiling green meadows and prosperous fields, with their barns and stone dwellings and livestock and local roads and post offices, and a degree of material prosperity that Newfoundland had never known, had never im-agined in all its generations.

"Newfoundlanders cultivated, too; but at the end of the first 400 years of toil, they had no productive meadows, almost no local or any other roads, pre-cious few substantial houses, and no standard of material prosperity anywhere near that known in any other part of North America. For during those four centuries, their cultivation was of the unquiet, infur-iate North Atlantic Ocean. They toiled as no farmers ever toiled in North America, risking death daily, and all the toil and danger had not won an acre for them or earned them much more, for most of the time, than unending scarcity on land and on sea and in the home."

Which reminds me of the grain that they found in Tutankhamen's tomb.

The boy-king Tutankhamen of Egypt died 1332 years before Christ.

In 1922 his tomb was discovered and yielded the most marvellous collection of many of the rarest and most precious and priceless objects known to man's history.

A large earthenware vase was found in the tomb. Its mouth was sealed, and when the seal was broken the vase was seen to contain cereal grain — corn or some other. The grain seemed to be in perfect condition after all the 3311 years it had been sealed.

Scientists decided to find out whether that grain really did still have life in it.

They planted it in the earth — it took root, grew, fructified. Life was in it all those thirty centuries!

Newfoundland was something like that.

The English, Irish, Scottish, Welsh and other people who came to Newfoundland centuries ago, carried in their very genes the greatness of the peoples of whom they were a part.

The Newfoundland environment — the hard life, the hard times — was not ideal for the sprouting of the seed that was within them.

But the seed was there!

It was sealed, but it was there.

All that was needed to bring about rich germination was to break the seal by a transformation of the environment.

In short: Confederation.

Now we're enjoying the richest harvest-time that we've ever known.

The stuff was in us all the time.

CONFEDERATION MAY NOT YET HAVE BROUGHT US TO A LAND OF MILK AND HONEY, BUT IT HAS BROUGHT US OUT OF THE LAND OF PHAROAH.

I would ask no better epitaph.

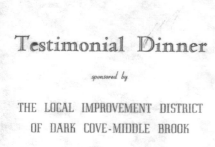

# Testimonial Dinner

*sponsored by*

## THE LOCAL IMPROVEMENT DISTRICT OF DARK COVE-MIDDLE BROOK

honouring our favourite native son

## HON. JOSEPH R. SMALLWOOD,

P.C., D.C.L., LL.D., D. Litt., M.H.A.

PREMIER OF NEWFOUNDLAND AND LABRADOR

SMALLWOOD ACADEMY, DARK COVE, B.B.

Saturday, November 7th., 1970

*"The place where first he breathed, who can forget!"*

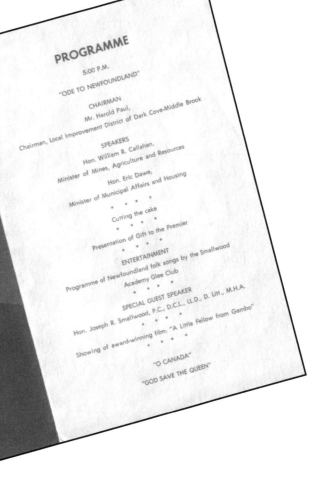

## PROGRAMME

5:00 P.M.

"ODE TO NEWFOUNDLAND"

CHAIRMAN
Mr. Harold Paul,
Chairman, Local Improvement District of Dark Cove-Middle Brook

SPEAKERS
Hon. William R. Callahan,
Minister of Mines, Agriculture and Resources

Hon. Eric Dawe,
Minister of Municipal Affairs and Housing

* * * *

Cutting the cake

* * * *

Presentation of Gift to the Premier

* * * *

ENTERTAINMENT
Programme of Newfoundland folk songs by the Smallwood
Academy Glee Club

* * * *

SPECIAL GUEST SPEAKER
Hon. Joseph R. Smallwood, P.C., D.C.L., LL.D., D. Litt., M.H.A.

* * * *

Showing of award-winning film. "A Little Fellow from Gambo"

* * * *

"O CANADA"

"GOD SAVE THE QUEEN"

Office of the
Prime Minister

CANADA

Cabinet du
Premier ministre

O T T A W A
November 15, 1974

Personal and confidential

Dear Joey:

I am writing this letter not to
congratulate you on a battle well fought, because
with millions of Canadians I simply take it for
granted that any battle you are in will be well
fought; nor do I intend to offer my sympathy at
the outcome, because I know you to be a man who
has no time to listen to sympathy when there is
a future full of further challenges to be faced.

I am writing simply as any man would
to a friend who has encountered a turning point in
his life.  I am writing to reaffirm that friendship,
to express my admiration for you as a person and as
a prodigious benefactor of Newfoundland and of
Canada as a whole, and, finally, to express once
again a deeply felt sense of personal gratitude.

.../2

The Honourable J.R. Smallwood,
    Roache's Line,
        Conception Bay,
            Newfoundland.

...2

I will never forget a major turning
point in my own life -- the national leadership
campaign in 1968 -- a time when I needed support
and you gave it to me.  You gave it strongly,
without reservation, and at a time when your support
could influence convention delegates all across
Canada.  I have no hesitation in acknowledging the
great debt I owe you.  Indeed, I willingly share
with you the credit for whatever good I and other
members of the government have been able to
accomplish for Canadians since 1968.

But you do not need the warmth of
reflected credit, when you have earned so much in
your own right as Premier of Newfoundland.  I cannot
think of a single living Canadian who has accomplished
so much for his people as you have.  Not only did you
re-shape Confederation, and the destiny of Newfoundlanders as full-fledged partners in that union, but
you were also the chief architect of a social and
economic revolution of massive proportions in the
province you have loved and served so well.

It is given to few people in this life
to make a real difference in the lives of their fellow
men.  You are a man who has made an historic difference
of unique quality -- a difference which will continue
to have a beneficial impact upon your province and
your country long after you and I have departed from
the scene.

And so I am doubly grateful: to you as
a friend who has helped me; and to you as a Canadian
who helped our country to become greater than it would
have been without you.

.../3

...3

       Long-standing tradition, rooted in the
principle of non-interference of national leaders in
the affairs of provincial political parties, persuaded
me to take no part, directly or indirectly, in the
recent Newfoundland Liberal Leadership Convention.
I want to assure you that neither I, nor anyone acting
on my behalf, exercised any concerted influence for
or against any of the leadership candidates.

       Now that the convention is over, only
those who do not know you very well will believe that
you are ready to retreat to a well-earned retirement.
I know that, despite your unique record of achievement
in public service, you still have much to contribute
to Newfoundland and to Canada.  I will watch, with
great interest and continuing fascination, the new chapters
you will write in a life story which has few equals in
our history.

*With personal good wishes and warm regards, to you and to your family.*

# PROGRAMME

Chairman: Honourable W.R. Callahan
7:00-8:00 P.M.          Cocktail Hour

———————

BANQUET

8:00 P.M.          Ode to Newfoundland
Grace:  Clyde K.Wells, M.H.A.
Fruit Cup au Bonne Bay—Curling Seafood Cocktail

Pilley's Island Duckling a l'Orange
Codroy Potatoes—Glazed Cormack Carrots
French Shore Peas *amandine*

Dessert
St. Pierre Rum-au-Smuggle

Black Bark Switchel

*Wine Served Throughout*

———————

Newfoundland Folk Songs by *The Sand Peddles*

9:00 P.M.

Tribute to the Honourable J.R. Smallwood
*The Chairman*

Special Address
*Honourable T. Alex Hickman*

THE QUEEN

Television sets will be placed throughout the Hall for
viewing of Confederation Banquet at St. John's from
the gathering will be addressed by the Honourable the
Premier and the Right Honourable and Prime Minister
of Canada.

O CANADA

## TRIBUTE TO THE PREMIER
## OF NEWFOUNDLAND AND LABRADOR
## BY
## THE MINISTER OF MINES, AGRICULTURE
## AND RESOURCES
## CONFEDERATION ANNIVERSARY DINNER
## CORNER BROOK, 31 MARCH 1969

I am pleased and honoured beyond words to have been invited to chair this banquet tonight.

But my principal duty is to propose a tribute to the Premier of Newfoundland and Labrador - the only one we've ever had. I consider that an even greater privilege.

Ladies and Gentlemen, it used to be said in Newfoundland that the cornerstone of our civilization and its stability were the "holy trinity" - the merchant, the clergyman and the doctor. Certainly, they played and still play their part.

Indeed, it was a physician - Dr. William Carson - who despite his necessary preoccupation of fighting epidemics of disease, and patching up the victims of duels and brawls in boisterous 19th Century St. John's, found time to lead the fight for Responsible Government.

Who will gainsay the part the Church played in our essential development - in the "civilization," if you like (principally through involvement in education) - of what started out as a rough-and-ready rumpot of a fishing station in the Western Atlantic?

And down through the years - in fact, since the beginning - the stability of Newfoundland, such as it was or could be, and her continuing existence as a community, and as an identifiable political and social entity, depended in the main upon the continuation of trade and commerce ... which is another way of saying that whatever the faults of the merchants, and the merchant system, it and they comprised for most of our history the lifeblood of our existence.

The mercantile system was, in fact, the government of Newfoundland until Responsible Government came along in the 1850s, and even today it has not displaced the natural "establishment" completely. The so-called "holy trinity" continue to exert a strong influence on what we Newfoundlanders think and what we do, and that is not necessarily good - but certainly not of necessity bad.

That said, it was neither doctor nor clergyman nor merchant who finally cut the bonds of our ancient isolation, and dragged Newfoundland kicking and screaming into her own particular "alliance for progress." The man who won the 80-year argument as to whether Newfoundland should throw in her lot with the rest of British North America was born in Gambo, Bonavista Bay, on Christmas Eve 1900. A couple of decades later, it is said, he was introduced to his future mother-in-law by a friend who declared, "Mrs. Oates, this is Clara's beau; he's not very big, but he's sure to grow!"

He is a newspaperman by trade.

He is a "bayman" and proud of it.

And while looking forward to his 70th birthday, he continues to confound his critics, and ofttimes to scare the daylights out of his friends, by his willingness to plunge into situations that cause men of average courage to blanch.

It is trite to say that an active man of many years is "years young" rather than "years old." I think the late Robert F. Kennedy's description of "youth" fits Mr. Smallwood to a "T":

Youth, he declared, is "not a time of life, but a state of mind, a temper of the will, a quality of the imagination, a predominance of courage over timidity, of the appetite for adventure over the love of ease." In those terms, we all know people who, being young in years, are in fact ancient spirits!

To continue the late United States Senator's analogy, there is a state of mind and spirit which abhors futility - the belief that there is nothing one man or one woman can do against the enormous array of the world's ills. That certainly is NOT the story of the past twenty years ...

There is, however, a state of mind and spirit that recognizes no basic inconsistency between ideals and realistic possibilities. In Senator Kennedy's words, "Only those who dare to fail greatly can ever achieve greatly." The Premier of this Province falls precisely into this category. His is a state of mind and spirit that abhors timidity, and resists firmly the temptation to follow easy and familiar paths of personal ambition and financial success - the temptation simply to be comfortable. I think no one can accuse Joseph Roberts Smallwood of yielding to that.

Few men are willing to brave the disapproval of their fellows, the censure of colleagues, the wrath of society; he is one of that small number. It has been written there is nothing more difficult to take in hand, more perilous to conduct, or more uncertain in its success, than to take the lead in introducing a new order of things. Uncommon courage is required, and it inspires the man we honour tonight and his achievements!

Senator Kennedy outlined these precepts not long before he was overtaken by tragedy at the instant he reached the highest plateau of success in the drive to lead his nation to seek and find a newer world. They are precepts that form, perhaps, a classic mold - one in which the Premier of our province could familiarly fit. They might have been written for him. He is a man devoid of any sense of futility; burned up with the ideal of building a new province; lacking absolutely in timidity; and clearly not given to the pursuit of the easy and the comfortable.

I believe all Newfoundlanders, partisan politics aside, recognize in him the incarnation of the spirit of the land we love, as we wish it to be. And so, it is right that we have paid him tribute.

Ladies and Gentlemen, I give you the health of the Premier of Newfoundland and Labrador.

# PART FOUR

## A CONFEDERATION CHRONOLOGY

National Convention delegate Joseph R. Smallwood (Bonavista Centre) addresses session.

# NATIONAL CONVENTION TERMS OF REFERENCE

The 45 members of the National Convention were elected in June 1946 to assist Newfoundlanders in arriving at "a free and informed decision as to their future form of government."

The terms of Reference by which the Convention would do this were as follows:

To consider and discuss amongst themselves as elected representatives of the Newfoundland people, the changes that have taken place in the financial and economic situation of the Island since 1934 and, bearing in mind the extent to which high revenues of recent years have been due to wartime conditions, to examine the position of the country and to make recommendations to His Majesty's Government as to possible forms of future government to be put before the people at a national referendum.

In February 1947 the National Convention passed a resolution to send a delegation to Ottawa to determine "what fair and equitable basis may exist for federal union of Newfoundland and Canada." A similar delegation was sent to England with clearly unsatisfactory results; a resolution to send a delegation to the United States was roundly defeated.

From June to September a Newfoundland delegation of seven members held discussions with a committee of the Canadian Cabinet. Then, on October 27, a statement of terms that the government would be prepared to recommend to Parliament as a basis for union was sent by the Canadian prime minister to the governor of Newfoundland for the Convention.

After protracted debate the Convention, on January 29, 1948, recommended to the United Kingdom government that two choices only be placed on a referendum ballot restoration of Responsible Government and continuation of the Commission of Government. A motion to include confederation with Canada was rejected by a vote of 29-16.

The British government, however, decided to add the Canadian option to the ballot on the grounds "it would not be right that the people … should be deprived of an opportunity" of considering this alternative.

A two-stage referendum completed, and union with Canada approved by a majority of approximately 7,000 votes—18 electoral districts showing a preference for Confederation to seven for Responsible Government—attention turned to final negotiation of the Terms of Union. This took place between Oct. 5 and Dec. 11, 1948 when the terms were signed.

A Bill to approve the Terms was passed by the Canadian Parliament on February 16 and 17, 1949 and signed into law a few days before the official date of Newfoundland's entry on March 31, 1949.

# A CONFEDERATION CHRONOLOGY

**DECEMBER 11, 1945**

In Montreal, en route back to Gander from a visit to hog operations in Ontario, pig farmer Joseph R. Smallwood learns from a report in *The Gazette* that the British Government is ready to permit Newfoundlanders to decide their political future

**MARCH 1, 1946**

With the cooperation of Publisher John S. Currie, Smallwood launches in *The Daily News* a series of eleven Confederation Letters extolling union with Canada

**JUNE 21, 1946**

Newfoundlanders go to the polls for the first time since 1932 electing 45 delegates, including Smallwood (Bonavista Centre), to the National Convention

**SEPTEMBER 11, 1946**

Convention called to order by its Chairman, Mr. Justice Cyril J. Fox, former Member and Speaker of the House of Assembly; he would die suddenly two months later

**NOVEMBER 5, 1946**

By a vote of 25-18, the Convention rejects Smallwood's resolution to ascertain the Canadian attitude to union and the terms and conditions that might apply

**NOVEMBER 23, 1946**

In private session, the Convention elects one of its members, F. Gordon Bradley, as Chairman, succeeding Fox who died suddenly November 16

**FEBRUARY 4, 1947**

Hon. R.B. Job's resolution to request permission to investigate all options passes 38-8, but Commission of Government forbids approach to U.S.

**FEBRUARY 28, 1947**

The Convention accepts resolutions to send delegations to London (Malcolm Hollett) and Ottawa (Smallwood), each to be led by Bradley

**APRIL 11, 1947**

Delegation leaves for London to determine, opting for either Responsible or Commission of Government, what help to expect; short answer: little or none

**JUNE 19,1947**

Delegation leaves for Ottawa to determine benefits to be expected from union with Canada, anticipating one month's absence; returns in early October

**OCTOBER 10, 1947**

The Convention resumes Oct. 10; facing censure due to lengthy absence of the Ottawa delegation, Bradley resigns to be replaced by lawyer John B. McEvoy

**NOVEMBER 6, 1947**

The Convention receives the Canadian Terms of Union; the issue of joining Canada dominates a raucous Third Session (Fall 1947)

**DECEMBER 4, 1947**

The third session of the Convention ends abruptly during a Smallwood speech when many delegates walk out, depriving the proceedings of a quorum

**JANUARY 23, 1948**

Smallwood moves that confederation with Canada based on the Terms of Union tabled Nov. 6, 1947 be placed on the ballot for the forthcoming referendum

**JANUARY 27, 1948**

By a vote of 29-16, the Convention rejects Smallwood's resolution to place Confederation with Canada on the referendum ballot

**JANUARY 28, 1948**

The Convention votes 45-0 to place on the referendum ballot (a) Responsible Government as it existed prior to 1934 and (b) Commission of Government

**JANUARY 30, 1948**

The National Convention meets for the last time; delegates return to their respective districts to prepare for the referendum on Newfoundland's future

**FEBRUARY 2, 1948**

Rejecting decision of "twenty-nine dictators" keeping Confederation off the ballot, Smallwood launches petition to have decision reversed

**FEBRUARY 7, 1948**

National Convention delegate C.A. Crosbie (St. John's) moves for U.S. economic union earlier advocated by D.I. Jackman (Bell Island)

**FEBRUARY 9, 1948**

In response to Bradley radio speech prepared by Smallwood, over 50,000 telegraph support petition which is presented to Governor MacDonald

**FEBRUARY 26, 1948**

Newfoundland Confederate Association forms with Bradley as President and Smallwood as General Secretary and Campaign Manager

**MARCH 2, 1948**

Broadcasting Corp. of Newfoundland announces from Government House the British decision on the petition: Confederation will be on the ballot

**APRIL 5, 1948**

The Confederation battle is joined as *The Confederate* newspaper comes out against *The Independent* of the Responsible Government League

**JUNE 3, 1948**

Results of the first leg of a two-stage referendum: Responsible Government 69,400, Confederation 64,066, Commission of Government 22,311

**JULY 2, 1948**

Results of the second leg of the referendum: Confederation 78,323, Responsible Government 71,334

**OCTOBER 6, 1948**

Seven-man delegation led by Commissioner for Justice Albert J. Walsh negotiating with Canadian Cabinet committee the final Terms of Union

**DECEMBER 11, 1948**

The Terms of Union are signed during a formal ceremony in the Senate chamber on Parliament Hill in Ottawa

**FEBRUARY 16, 1949**

Canada's House of Commons approves the negotiated Agreement and a petition to King George VI for confirmatory U.K. legislation

**FEBRUARY 17, 1949**

Approved by the Senate, Royal Assent given by Chief Justice Thebadeau Rinfret, the package "is sent on its way with 'God Save the King'"

**FEBRUARY 21 - MARCH 9, 1949**

The Commission of Government and the British House of Commons and House of Lords approve legislation for Newfoundland-Canada union

**MARCH 28, 1949**

Former Speaker of the House of Assembly and Commissioner for Justice, Albert J. Walsh, is Knighted and appointed Lieutenant-Governor

**MARCH 31, 1949**

Newfoundland becomes the tenth province of Canada a few minutes before midnight

**APRIL 1, 1949**

Joseph R. Smallwood sworn in as Premier and head of an interim government pending a General Election scheduled for May 27

**MAY 27, 1949**

Newfoundland's first House of Assembly election in 15 years. Results: 22 Liberals, 5 PCs and 1 Independent

**JULY 11, 1949**

The House of Assembly opens for business for the first time since 1933

# CONVENTION AFTERMATH
# LEADS TO VICTORY

*UNWILLING TO ACCEPT THE DECISION OF "TWENTY-NINE DICTATORS" WHO REFUSED TO ALLOW CONFEDERATION ON THE BALLOT, SMALLWOOD PREPARED A RADIO SPEECH FOR BRADLEY CALLING UPON NEWFOUNDLANDERS TO EXPRESS SHOCK AND ANGER THAT THEY WERE BEING CHEATED OUT OF THE OPPORTUNITY "TO EXERCISE THEIR OWN JUDGMENT ABOUT (THE FUTURE OF) THEIR OWN COUNTRY." IT URGED:*

*"IF YOU THINK THAT CONFEDERATION SHOULD BE PLACED ON THE BALLOT PAPER, SO THAT PEOPLE CAN VOTE FOR OR AGAINST IT ACCORDING TO THEIR OWN FREE AND INDEPENDENT WILL, SEND INSTANTLY YOUR TELEGRAMS DEMANDING THAT CONFEDERATION BE PUT ON THE BALLOT PAPER, AND YOUR DEMANDS WILL BE DELIVERED TO THE BRITISH GOVERNMENT."*

Mr. Smallwood displays telegraphed petitions—estimated at nearly 60,000—asking that confederation be a choice on the Referendum ballot. The British government agreed.

*IN ABOUT A WEEK, BETWEEN 50,000 AND 60,000 PEOPLE HAD RESPONDED AND SMALLWOOD CALLED UPON THE GOVERNOR, GORDON MACDONALD, "TO INFORM HIM THAT I WISHED TO PRESENT THE TELEGRAMS AND PETITIONS TO HIM AT HIS EARLIEST CONVENIENCE" FOR TRANSMISSION TO LONDON.*

*THE "INTERMINABLE, INTOLERABLE, MADDENING WAIT" FOR THE BRITISH REPLY ENDED EARLY ON MARCH 2, 1948 WHEN THE BROADCASTING CORPORATION OF NEWFOUNDLAND WAS INVITED TO GO TO GOVERNMENT HOUSE TO RECEIVE AND BROADCAST IT" HIS MAJESTY'S GOVERNMENT DID NOT THINK IT RIGHT TO DENY NEWFOUNDLANDERS THE OPPORTUNITY TO PRONOUNCE ON THE QUESTION OF CONFEDERATION WITH CANADA.*

*SMALLWOOD WAS ECSTATIC:*

*"WE HAD WON! GLORY HALLELUJAH!"*

# THE STATUTE OF WESTMINISTER

## PREAMBLE

During the reign of King Edward I (1239-1307) two statutes were passed bearing the title "Statute of Westminster."
The Statute of Westminster, 1275 contained 51 clauses covering a wide swath of legislation including common rights, free elections, etc. The Statute of Westminster, 1285 set out the principles of fundamental land law.

The Statute of Westminster, 1931 established the foundations for the modern-day British Commonwealth. Its principal provision reads as follows:

"Dominions are autonomous communities within the British Empire, equal in stature, in no way subordinate to one another in their domestic or external affairs though united by a common allegiance to the Crown, and freely associated as members of the British Commonwealth of Nations."

## DOMINION STATUS

"Dominion status" was an expression often used before 1939 to describe the position of British countries then known as the Dominions, namely Canada, the Commonwealth of Australia, New Zealand, the Union of South Africa, Eire and Newfoundland. Though there was no formal definition of dominion status, a pronouncement of the Imperial Conference of 1926 described Great Britain and the Dominions as "autonomous communities within the British Empire, equal in status ... as members of the British Commonwealth of Nations." (Full text following)

The main characteristics of dominion status were considered to be complete legislative authority as provided in the Statute of Westminster (1931) and, in the executive sphere, the right of dominions ministers to direct access to the sovereign, in contrast to the previous position whereby advice on dominion matters could be tendered only by United Kingdom ministers.

Internationally, it connoted recognition of the dominions as separate and distinct states, entitled to have separate representation in the League of Nations and other international bodies, to appoint their own ambassadors, and to conclude their own treaties. (Newfoundland, near bankruptcy, declined to exercise the new mantle of autonomy and instead, the Alderdice government agreed to suspension of the legislature in favour of a British-appointed Commission of Government.) At the same time, the dominions were not considered to stand in the same relationship to the United Kingdom, or among themselves, as foreign countries.

## MEMBERS OF THE COMMONWEALTH

After 1947 use of the expression "dominion status" was abandoned as it was thought in some quarters to imply some form of subordination, and the phrase "members of the Commonwealth" came into use to describe the United Kingdom and the dominions enumerated above except the Republic of Ireland, which left the Commonwealth in 1949 (and Newfoundland which became a province of Canada the same year), as well as India, Pakistan, Ceylon, Ghana and the Federation of Malaya, all of which later attained the same status.

The declaration of 1926 was modified by another arising from the Commonwealth Prime Ministers' meeting of 1949. According to this, India, which intended to adopt a republican form of constitution, but desired to retain membership in the Commonwealth, accepting the British sovereign as the symbol of the free association of independent member nations, continued its membership on those terms. A similar declaration relating to Pakistan was issued by the Commonwealth Prime Ministers' meeting of 1955.

By the year 2000 more than 50 former colonies, having become independent states, maintained membership in the free association of the Commonwealth, the declared aim being to promote democracy and encourage economic cooperation among former members of the Empire.

Designed to function without formal constitution or specific treaty, its members being bound together by common historical, economic or cultural interests with the British Crown as their common symbol.

Sources: *Encyclopedia Britannica*, Vs. 7 & 23, 1961
*Concord Desk Encyclopedia*, 1982
*Canadian Global Almanac*, 1999

# THE STATUTE OF WESTMINISTER

## THE TEXT

STATUTE OF WESTMINSTER, 1931
22 GEORGE V, CHAPTER 4

An Act to give effect to certain resolutions passed by Imperial Conferences held in the years 1926 and 1930.

[*11th December, 1931.*]

Whereas the delegates of His Majesty's Governments in the United Kingdom, the Dominion of Canada, the Commonwealth of Australia, the Dominion of New Zealand, the Union of South Africa, the Irish Free State and Newfoundland, at Imperial Conferences holden at Westminster in the years of our Lord nineteen hundred and twenty-six and nineteen hundred and thirty did concur in making the declarations and resolutions set forth in the Reports of the said Conferences:

And whereas it is meet and proper to set out by way of preamble to this Act that, inasmuch as the Crown is the symbol of the free association of the members of the British Commonwealth of Nations, and as they are united by a common allegiance to the Crown, it would be in accord with the established constitutional position of all the members of the Commonwealth in relation to one another that any alteration in the law touching the Succession to the Throne or the Royal Style and Titles shall hereafter require the assent as well of the Parliaments of all the Dominions as of the Parliament of the United Kingdom:

And whereas it is in accord with the established constitutional position that no law hereafter made by the Parliament of the United Kingdom shall extend to any of the said Dominions as part of the law of that Dominion otherwise than at the request and with the consent of that Dominion:

And whereas it is necessary for the ratifying, confirming and establishing of certain of the said declarations and resolutions of the said Conferences that a law be made and enacted in due form by authority of the Parliament of the United Kingdom:

And whereas the Dominion of Canada, the Commonwealth of Australia, the Dominion of New Zealand, the Union of South Africa, the Irish Free State and Newfoundland have severally requested and consented to the submission of a measure to the Parliament of the United Kingdom for making such provision with regard to the matters aforesaid as is hereafter in this Act contained:

Now, therefore, be it enacted by the King's most Excellent Majesty by and with the advice and consent of the Lords Spiritual and Temporal, and Commons, in this present Parliament assembled, and by the authority of the same, as follows:—

1. In this Act the expression "Dominion" means any of the following Dominions, that is to say, the Dominion of Canada, the Commonwealth of Australia, the Dominion of New Zealand, the Union of South Africa, the Irish Free State and Newfoundland.

2. (1) The Colonial Laws Validity Act, 1865, shall not apply to any law made after the commencement of this Act by the Parliament of a Dominion.

(2) No law and no provision of any law made after the commencement of this Act by the Parliament of a Dominion shall be void or inoperative on the ground that it is repugnant to the law of England, or to the provisions of any existing or future Act of Parliament of the United Kingdom, or to any order, rule or regulation made under any such Act, and the Powers of the Parliament of a Dominion shall include the power to repeal or amend any such Act, order, rule or regulation in so far as the same is part of the law of the Dominion.

3. It is hereby declared and enacted that the Parliament of a Dominion has full power to make laws having extra-territorial operation.

4. No Act of Parliament of the United Kingdom passed after the commencement of this Act shall extend or be deemed to extend, to a Dominion as part of the law of that Dominion, unless it is expressly declared in that Act that that Dominion has requested, and consented to, the enactment thereof.

5. Without prejudice to the generality of the foregoing provisions of this Act, sections seven hundred and thirty-five and seven hundred and thirty-six of the Merchant Shipping Act, 1894, shall be construed as though reference therein to the Legislature of a British possession did not include reference to the Parliament of a Dominion.

6. Without prejudice to the generality of the foregoing provisions of this Act, section four of the Colonial Courts of Admiralty Act, 1890 (which requires certain laws to be reserved for the significa-tion of His Majesty's pleasure or to contain a suspending clause), and so much of section seven of that Act as requires the approval of His Majesty in Council to any rules of Court for regulating the practice and procedure of a Colonial Court of Admir-alty, shall cease to have effect in any Dominion as from the commencement of this Act.

7. (1) Nothing in this Act shall be deemed to apply to the repeal, amendment or alteration of the British North America Acts, 1867 to 1930, or any order, rule or regulation made thereunder.

(2) The provisions of section two of this Act shall extend to laws made by any of the Provinces of Canada and to the powers of the legislatures of such Provinces.

(3) The powers conferred by this Act upon the Parliament of Canada or upon the legislatures of the Provinces shall be restricted to the enactment of laws in relation to matters within the competence of the Parliament of Canada or of any of the legis-latures of the Provinces respectively.

8. Nothing in this Act shall be deemed to confer any power to repeal or alter the Constitution or the Constitution Act of the Commonwealth of Australia or the Constitution Act of the Dominion of New Zealand otherwise than in accordance with the law existing before the commencement of this Act.

9. (1) Nothing in this Act shall be deemed to authorize the Parliament of the Commonwealth of Australia to make laws on any matter within the authority of the States of Australia, not being a matter within the authority of the Parliament or Government of the Commonwealth of Australia.

(2) Nothing in this Act shall be deemed to require the concurrence of the Parliament or Gov-ernment of the Commonwealth of Australia, in any case where it would have been in United Kingdom with respect to any matter within the authority of the States of Australia, not being a matter within the authority of the Parliament or Government of the Commonwealth of Australia, in any case where it would have been in accordance with the constitu-tional practice existing before the commencement of this Act that the Parliament of the United King-dom should make that law without such con-currence.

(3) In the application of this Act to the Com-monwealth of Australia the request and consent referred to in section four shall mean the request and consent of the Parliament and Government of the Commonwealth.

10. (1) None of the following sections of this Act, that is to say, sections two, three, four, five and six, shall extend to a Dominion to which this section applies as part of the law of that Dominion unless that section is adopted by the Parliament of the Dominion, and any Act of that Parliament adopt-ing any section of this Act may provide that the adoption shall have effect either from the com-mencement of this Act or from such later date as is specified in the adopting Act.

(2) The Parliament of any such Dominion as aforesaid may at any time revoke the adoption of any section referred to in subsection (1) of this section.

(3) The Dominions to which this section applies are the Commonwealth of Australia, the Dominion of New Zealand and Newfoundland.

11. Notwithstanding anything in the Interpreta-tion Act, 1889, the expression " Colony " shall not, in any Act of the Parliament of the United King-dom passed after the commencement of this Act, include a Dominion or any Province or State form-ing part of a Dominion.

12. This Act may be cited as the Statute of Westminster, 1931.

# Part Five

## The Terms of Union
### of
### Newfoundland and Canada

## Signatories to the Terms

*On behalf of Canada:*

*[signature: Louis S. St. Laurent]*

*[signature: Brooke Claxton]*

*On behalf of Newfoundland:*

*[signature: Albert J. Walsh]*

*[signature: F.G. Bradley]*

*[signature: Philip Gruchy]*

*[signature: John B. McEvoy]*

*[signature: Joseph R. Smallwood]*

*[signature: G.A. Winter]*

Signatories to the Terms of Union were: For Canada, Prime Minister Louis S. St. Laurent and Acting External Affairs Minister Brooke Claxton; for Newfoundland, Albert J. Walsh, F.G. Bradley, Philip Gruchy, J.B. McEvoy, J.R. Smallwood, and G.A. Winter. The seventh Newfoundland delegate, Chesley A. Crosbie, refused to sign on the grounds the Terms were fiscally inadequate.

SIGNED IN THE SENATE

Canad's Senate chamber (top photo) was the setting for the signing of the Terms of Union of Newfoundland with Canada. In the below photo, Prime Minister Louis S. St. Laurent and Newfoundland delegation chairman Albert J. Walsh are surrounded by members of the respective negotiating teams. In the bottom photo Mr. St. Laurent and Mr. Smallwood shake hands (MA).

Memorandum of Agreement entered into on the Eleventh Day of December, 1948, between Canada and Newfoundland.

Whereas a delegation appointed from its members by the National Convention of Newfoundland, a body elected by the people of Newfoundland, consulted in 1947 with the Government of Canada to ascertain what fair and equitable basis might exist for the union of Newfoundland with Canada;

Whereas, following discussions with the delegation, the Government of Canada sent to His Excellency the Governor of Newfoundland for submission to the National Convention a statement of terms which the Government of Canada would be prepared to recommend to the Parliament of Canada as a fair and equitable basis for union, should the people of Newfoundland desire to enter into confederation;

Whereas the proposed terms were debated in the National Convention in Newfoundland and were before the people of Newfoundland when, by a majority at a referendum held on the twenty-second day of July, 1948, they expressed their desire to enter into confederation with Canada;

Whereas the Governments of the United Kingdom, Canada and Newfoundland agreed after the referendum that representatives of Canada and Newfoundland should meet and settle the final terms and arrangements for the union of Newfoundland with Canada;

And whereas authorized representatives of Canada and authorized representatives of Newfoundland have settled the terms hereinafter set forth as the Terms of Union of Newfoundland with Canada;

It is therefore agreed as follows:

# TERMS·OF UNION

## UNION

1. On, from, and after the coming into force of these Terms (hereinafter referred to as the date of Union), Newfoundland shall form part of Canada and shall be a province thereof to be called and known as the Province of Newfoundland.

2. The Province of Newfoundland shall comprise the same territory as at the date of Union, that is to say, the island of Newfoundland and the islands adjacent thereto, the Coast of Labrador as delimited in the report delivered by the Judicial Committee of His Majesty's Privy Council on the first day of March, 1927, and approved by His Majesty in His Privy Council on the twenty-second day of March, 1927, and the islands adjacent to the said Coast of Labrador.

## APPLICATION OF THE BRITISH NORTH AMERICA ACTS

3. The British North America Acts, 1867 to 1946, shall apply to the Province of Newfoundland in the same way and to the like extent as they apply to the provinces heretofore comprised in Canada, as if the Province of Newfoundland had been one of the provinces originally united, except insofar as varied by these Terms and except such provisions as are in terms made or by reasonable intendment may be held to be specially applicable to or only to affect one or more and not all of the provinces originally united.

## REPRESENTATION IN PARLIAMENT

4. The Province of Newfoundland shall be entitled to be represented in the Senate by six members, and in the House of Commons by seven members out of a total membership of two hundred and sixty-two.

5. Representation in the Senate and in the House of Commons shall from time to time be altered or readjusted in accordance with the British North America Acts, 1867 to 1946.

6. (1) Until the Parliament of Canada otherwise provides, the Province of Newfoundland shall for the purposes of the election of members to serve in the House of Commons, be divided into the electoral divisions named and delimited in the Schedule to these Terms, and each such division shall be entitled to return one member.

(2) For the first election of members to serve in the House of Commons, if held otherwise than as part of a general election, the Governor General in Council may cause writs to be issued and may fix the day upon which the polls shall be held, and, subject to the foregoing, the laws of Canada relating to by-elections shall apply to an election held pursuant to any writ issued under this Term.

(3) The Chief Electoral Officer shall have authority to adapt the provisions of The Dominion Elections Act, 1938, to conditions existing in the Province of Newfoundland so as to conduct effectually the first election of members to serve in the House of Commons.

## PROVINCIAL CONSTITUTION

7. The Constitution of Newfoundland as it existed immediately prior to the sixteenth day of February, 1934, is revived at the date of Union and shall, subject to these Terms and the British North America Acts, 1867 to 1946, continue as the Constitution of the Province of Newfoundland from and after the date of Union, until altered under the authority of the said Acts.

### Executive

8. (1) For the Province of Newfoundland there shall be an officer styled the Lieutenant-Governor, appointed by the Governor General in Council by instrument under the Great Seal of Canada.

(2) Pending the first appointment of a Lieutenant-Governor for the Province of Newfoundland and the assumption of his duties as such, the Chief Justice, or if the office of Chief Justice is vacant, the senior judge, of the Supreme Court of Newfoundland, shall execute the office and functions of Lieutenant-Governor under his oath of office as such Chief Justice or senior judge.

9. The Constitution of the Executive Authority of Newfoundland as it existed immediately prior to the sixteenth day of February, 1934, shall, subject to these Terms and the British North America Acts, 1867 to 1946, continue as the Constitution of the Executive Authority of the Province of Newfoundland from and after the date of Union, until altered under the authority of the said Acts.

10. The Lieutenant-Governor in Council shall as soon as may be after the date of Union adopt and provide a Great Seal of the Province of Newfoundland and may from time to time change such seal.

11. All powers, authorities, and functions that under any statute were at or immediately prior to the date of Union vested in or exercisable by the Governor of Newfoundland, individually, or in Council, or in Commission,

(a) as far as they are capable of being exercised after the date of Union in relation to the Government of Canada, shall be vested in and shall or may be exercised by the Governor General, with the advice, or with the advice and consent, or in conjunction with, the King's Privy Council for Canada or any member or members thereof, or by the Governor General individually, as the case requires, subject nevertheless to be abolished or altered by the Parliament of Canada under the authority of the British North America Acts, 1867 to 1946; and

(b) as far as they are capable of being exercised after the date of Union in relation to the Government of the Province of Newfoundland, shall be vested in and shall or may be exercised by the Lieutenant-Governor of the Province of Newfoundland, with the advice, or with the advice and consent, or in conjunction with, the Executive Council of the Province of Newfoundland or any member or members thereof, or by the Lieutenant-Governor individually, as the case requires, subject nevertheless to be abolished or altered by the Legislature of the Province of Newfoundland under the authority of the British North America Acts, 1867 to 1946.

12. Until the Parliament of Canada otherwise provides, the powers, authorities, and functions vested in or imposed on any member of the Commission of Government of Newfoundland, as such member or as a Commissioner charged with the administration of a Department of the Government of Newfoundland, at or immediately prior to the date of Union in relation to matters other than those coming within the classes of subjects by the British North America Acts, 1867 to 1946, assigned exclusively to the Legislature of a province, shall in the Province of Newfoundland be vested in or imposed on such person or persons as the Governor General in Council may appoint or designate.

13. Until the Legislature of the Province of Newfoundland otherwise provides, the powers, authorities, and functions vested in or imposed on any member of the Commission of Government of Newfoundland, as such member or as a Commissioner charged with the administration of a Department of the Government of Newfoundland, at or immediately prior to the date of Union in relation to matters coming within the classes of subjects by the British North America Acts, 1867 to 1946, assigned exclusively to the Legislature of a province, shall in the Province of Newfoundland be vested in or imposed on such person or persons as the Lieutenant-Governor in Council may appoint or designate.

*Legislature*

14. (1) Subject to paragraph two of this Term, the Constitution of the Legislature of Newfoundland as it existed immediately prior to the sixteenth day of February, 1934, shall, subject to these Terms and the British North America Acts, 1867 to 1946, continue as the Constitution of the Legislature of the Province of Newfoundland from and after the date of Union, until altered under the authority of the said Acts.

(2) The Constitution of the Legislature of Newfoundland insofar as it relates to the Legislative Council shall not continue, but the Legislature of the Province of Newfoundland may at any time re-establish the Legislative Council or establish a new Legislative Council.

15. (1) Until the Legislature of the Province of Newfoundland otherwise provides, the powers, authorities, and functions vested in or imposed on a Minister or other public officer or functionary under any statute of Newfoundland relating to the Constitution of the Legislature of Newfoundland as it existed immediately prior to the sixteenth day of February, 1934, shall, subject to these Terms and the British North America Acts, 1867 to 1946, be vested in or imposed on such person or persons as the Lieutenant-Governor in Council may appoint or designate.

(2) Until the Legislature of the Province of Newfoundland otherwise provides,

(a) the list of electors prepared pursuant to The List of Electors Act, 1947, shall be deemed to be the list of electors for the purposes of The Election Act, 1913, subject to the provisions of The Election Act, 1913, respecting supplementary lists of electors;

(b) the franchise shall be extended to female British subjects who have attained the full age of twenty-one years and are otherwise qualified as electors;

(c) the Coast of Labrador together with the islands adjacent thereto shall constitute an additional electoral district to be known as Labrador and to be represented by one member, and residents of the said district who are otherwise qualified as electors shall be entitled to vote; and

(d) the Lieutenant-Governor in Council may by proclamation defer any election in the electoral district of Labrador for such period as may be specified in the proclamation.

16. The Legislature of the Province of Newfoundland shall be called together not later than four months after the date of Union.

## EDUCATION

17. In lieu of section ninety-three of the British North America Act, 1867, the following Term shall apply in respect of the Province of Newfoundland:

In and for the Province of Newfoundland the Legislature shall have exclusive authority to make laws in relation to education, but the Legislature will not have authority to make laws prejudicially affecting any right or privilege with respect to denominational schools, common (amalgamated) schools, or denominational colleges, that any class or classes of persons have by law in Newfoundland at the date of Union, and out of public funds of the Province of Newfoundland provided for education,

(a) all such schools shall receive their share of such funds in accordance with scales determined on a non-discriminatory basis from time to time by the Legislature for all schools then being conducted under authority of the Legislature; and

(b) all such colleges shall receive their share of any grant from time to time voted for all colleges then being conducted under authority of the Legislature, such grant being distributed on a non-discriminatory basis.

## CONTINUATION OF LAWS

### General

18. (1) Subject to these Terms, all laws in force in Newfoundland at or immediately prior to the date of Union shall continue therein as if the Union had not been made, subject nevertheless to be repealed, abolished, or altered by the Parliament of Canada or by the Legislature of the Province of Newfoundland according to the authority of the Parliament or of the Legislature under the British North America Acts, 1867 to 1946, and all orders, rules, and regulations made under any such laws shall likewise continue, subject to be revoked or amended by the body or person that made such orders, rules, or regulations or the body or person that has power to make such orders, rules, or regulations after the date of Union, according to

26110—2

their respective authority under the British North America Acts, 1867 to 1946.

(2) Statutes of the Parliament of Canada in force at the date of Union, or any part thereof, shall come into force in the Province of Newfoundland on a day or days to be fixed by Act of the Parliament of Canada or by proclamation of the Governor General in Council issued from time to time, and any such proclamation may provide for the repeal of any of the laws of Newfoundland that

(a) are of general application;

(b) relate to the same subject matter as the statute or part thereof so proclaimed; and

(c) could be repealed by the Parliament of Canada under paragraph one of this Term.

(3) Notwithstanding anything in these Terms, the Parliament of Canada may with the consent of the Legislature of the Province of Newfoundland repeal any law in force in Newfoundland at the date of Union.

(4) Except as otherwise provided by these Terms, all courts of civil and criminal jurisdiction and all legal commissions, powers, authorities, and functions, and all officers and functionaries, judicial, administrative, and ministerial, existing in Newfoundland at or immediately prior to the date of Union, shall continue in the Province of Newfoundland as if the Union had not been made, until altered, abolished, revoked, terminated, or dismissed by the appropriate authority under the British North America Acts, 1867 to 1946.

### Supply

19. Any statute of Newfoundland enacted prior to the date of Union for granting to His Majesty sums of money for defraying expenses of, and for other purposes relating to, the public service of Newfoundland, for the financial year ending the thirty-first day of March, one thousand nine hundred and fifty, shall have effect after the date of Union according to its terms, until otherwise provided by the Legislature of the Province of Newfoundland.

## Patents

20. (1) Subject to this Term, Canada will provide that letters patent for inventions issued under the laws of Newfoundland prior to the date of Union shall be deemed to have been issued under the laws of Canada, as of the date and for the term thereof.

(2) Canada will provide further that in the event of conflict between letters patent for an invention issued under the laws of Newfoundland prior to the date of Union and letters patent for an invention issued under the laws of Canada prior to the date of Union

(a) the letters patent issued under the laws of Newfoundland shall have the same force and effect in the Province of Newfoundland as if the Union had not been made, and all rights and privileges acquired under or by virtue thereof may continue to be exercised or enjoyed in the Province of Newfoundland as if the Union had not been made; and

(b) the letters patent issued under the laws of Canada shall have the same force and effect in any part of Canada other than the Province of Newfoundland as if the Union had not been made, and all rights and privileges acquired under or by virtue thereof may continue to be exercised or enjoyed in any part of Canada other than the Province of Newfoundland as if the Union had not been made.

(3) The laws of Newfoundland existing at the date of Union shall continue to apply in respect of applications for the grant of letters patent for inventions under the laws of Newfoundland pending at the date of Union, and any letters patent for inventions issued upon such applications shall, for the purposes of this Term, be deemed to have been issued under the laws of Newfoundland prior to the date of Union; and letters patent for inventions issued under the laws of Canada upon applications pending at the date of Union shall, for the purposes of this Term, be deemed to have been issued under the laws of Canada prior to the date of Union.

(4) Nothing in this Term shall be construed to prevent the Parliament of Canada from providing that

26110—2½

no claims for infringement of a patent issued in Canada prior to the date of Union shall be entertained by any court against any person for anything done in Newfoundland prior to the date of Union in respect of the invention protected by such patent, and that no claims for infringement of a patent issued in Newfoundland prior to the date of Union shall be entertained by any court against any person for anything done in Canada prior to the date of Union in respect of the invention protected by such patent.

## Trade Marks

21. (1) Canada will provide that the registration of a trade mark under the laws of Newfoundland prior to the date of Union shall have the same force and effect in the Province of Newfoundland as if the Union had not been made, and all rights and privileges acquired under or by virtue thereof may continue to be exercised or enjoyed in the Province of Newfoundland as if the Union had not been made.

(2) The laws of Newfoundland existing at the date of Union shall continue to apply in respect of applications for the registration of trade marks under the laws of Newfoundland pending at the date of Union and any trade marks registered upon such applications shall, for the purposes of this Term, be deemed to have been registered under the laws of Newfoundland prior to the date of Union.

## Fisheries

22. (1) In this Term, the expression "Fisheries Laws" means the Act No. 11 of 1936, entitled "An Act for the creation of the Newfoundland Fisheries Board", the Act No. 14 of 1936, entitled "An Act to Prevent the Export of Fish Without Licence", the Act No. 32 of 1936, entitled "An Act to Amend the Newfoundland Fisheries Board Act (No. 11 of 1936)", the Act No. 37 of 1938, entitled "An Act further to Amend the Newfoundland Fisheries Board Act, 1936", the Act No. 10 of 1942, entitled "An Act Respecting Permits for the Exportation of Salt Fish", the Act No. 39 of 1943, entitled "An Act Further to Amend the Newfoundland Fisheries Board Act, 1936", the Act No. 16 of 1944,

entitled "An Act Further to Amend the Newfoundland Fisheries Board Acts, 1936-38", and the Act No. 42 of 1944, entitled "An Act Further to Amend the Newfoundland Fisheries Board Act, 1936", insofar as they relate to the export marketing of salted fish from Newfoundland to other countries or to any provinces of Canada.

(2) Subject to this Term, all Fisheries Laws and all orders, rules, and regulations made thereunder shall continue in force in the Province of Newfoundland as if the Union had not been made, for a period of five years from the date of Union and thereafter until the Parliament of Canada otherwise provides, and shall continue to be administered by the Newfoundland Fisheries Board; and the costs involved in the maintenance of the Board and the administration of the Fisheries Laws shall be borne by the Government of Canada.

(3) The powers, authorities, and functions vested in or imposed on the Governor in Commission or the Commissioner for Natural Resources under any of the Fisheries Laws shall after the date of Union respectively be vested in or imposed on the Governor General in Council and the Minister of Fisheries of Canada or such other Minister as the Governor General in Council may designate.

(4) Any of the Fisheries Laws may be repealed or altered at any time within the period of five years from the date of Union by the Parliament of Canada with the consent of the Lieutenant-Governor in Council of the Province of Newfoundland and all orders, rules, and regulations made under the authority of any Fisheries Laws may be revoked or altered by the body or person that made them or, in relation to matters to which paragraph three of this Term applies, by the body or person that under the said paragraph three has power to make such orders, rules, or regulations under the Fisheries Laws after the date of Union.

(5) The Chairman of the Newfoundland Fisheries Board or such other member of the Newfoundland Fisheries Board as the Governor General in Council may designate shall perform in the Province of Newfoundland the duties of Chief Supervisor and Chief Inspector of the Department of Fisheries of the Government of Canada, and employees of the Newfoundland Fisheries Board shall become employees in that Department in positions comparable to those of the employees in that Department in other parts of Canada.

(6) Terms eleven, twelve, thirteen and eighteen are subject to this Term.

## FINANCIAL TERMS
### Debt

23. Canada will assume and provide for the servicing and retirement of the stock issued or to be issued on the security of Newfoundland pursuant to The Loan Act, 1933, of Newfoundland and will take over the Sinking Fund established under that Act.

### Financial Surplus

24. (1) In this Term the expression "financial surplus" means the balances standing to the credit of the Newfoundland Exchequer at the date of Union (less such sums as may be required to discharge accounts payable at the date of Union in respect of appropriations for the public services) and any public moneys or public revenue (including loans and advances referred to in Term twenty-five) in respect of any matter, thing, or period prior to the date of Union recovered by the Government of the Province of Newfoundland subsequent to the date of Union.

(2) Newfoundland will retain its financial surplus subject to the following conditions:

(a) one-third of the surplus shall be set aside during the first eight years from the date of Union, on deposit with the Government of Canada, to be withdrawn by the Government of the Province of Newfoundland only for expenditures on current account to facilitate the maintenance and improvement of Newfoundland public services, and any portion of this one-third of the surplus remaining unspent at the end of the eight-year period shall become available to the Province of Newfoundland without the foregoing restriction;

(b) the remaining two-thirds of the surplus shall be available to the Government of the Province of Newfoundland for the development of resources and for the establishment or extension of public services within the Province of Newfoundland; and

(c) no part of the surplus shall be used to subsidize the production or sale of products of the Province of Newfoundland in unfair competition with similar products of other provinces of Canada, but nothing in this paragraph shall preclude the Province of Newfoundland from assisting industry by developmental loans on reasonable conditions or by ordinary provincial administrative services.

(3) The Government of the Province of Newfoundland will have the right within one year from the date of Union to deposit with the Government of Canada all or any part of its financial surplus held in dollars and on the thirty-first day of March and the thirtieth day of September in each year to receive with respect thereto interest at the rate of two and five-eighths per centum per annum during a maximum period of ten years from the date of Union on the minimum balance outstanding at any time during the six-month period preceding payment of interest.

### Loans

25. (1) The Province of Newfoundland will retain its interest in, and any securities arising from or attaching to, any loans or advances of public funds made by the Government of Newfoundland prior to the date of Union.

(2) Unless otherwise agreed by the Government of Canada, paragraph one of this Term shall not apply to any loans or advances relating to any works, property, or services taken over by Canada pursuant to Term thirty-one or Term thirty-three.

### Subsidies

26. Canada will pay to the Province of Newfoundland the following subsidies:

(a) an annual subsidy of $180,000 and an annual subsidy equal to 80 cents per head of the population of the Province of Newfoundland (being taken at 325,000 until the first decennial census after the date of Union), subject to be increased to conform to the scale of grants authorized by the British North America Act, 1907, for the local purposes of the Province and the support of its Government and Legislature, but in no year shall sums payable under this paragraph be less than those payable in the first year after the date of Union; and

(b) an additional annual subsidy of $1,100,000 payable for the like purposes as the various fixed annual allowances and subsidies provided by statutes of the Parliament of Canada from time to time for the Provinces of Nova Scotia, New Brunswick, and Prince Edward Island or any of them and in recognition of the special problems of the Province of Newfoundland by reason of geography and its sparse and scattered population.

### Tax Agreement

27. (1) The Government of Canada will forthwith after the date of Union make an offer to the Government of the Province of Newfoundland to enter into a tax agreement for the rental to the Government of Canada of the income, corporation income, and corporation tax fields, and the succession duties tax field.

(2) The offer to be made under this Term will be similar to the offers to enter into tax agreements made to other provinces, necessary changes being made to adapt the offer to circumstances arising out of the Union, except that the offer will provide that the agreement may be entered into either for a number of fiscal years expiring at the end of the fiscal year in 1952, as in the case of other provinces, or for a number of fiscal years expiring at the end of the fiscal year in 1957, at the option of the Government of the Province of Newfoundland, but if the Government of the Province of Newfoundland accepts the latter option the agreement will provide that the subsequent entry into a tax agreement by the Government of Canada with

any other province will not entitle the Government of the Province of Newfoundland to any alteration in the terms of its agreement.

(3) The offer of the Government of Canada to be made under this Term may be accepted by the Government of the Province of Newfoundland within nine months after the date of the offer but if it is not so accepted will thereupon expire.

(4) The Government of the Province of Newfoundland shall not by any agreement entered into pursuant to this Term be required to impose on any person or corporation taxation repugnant to the provisions of any contract entered into with such person or corporation before the date of the agreement and subsisting at the date of the agreement.

(5) If the Province of Newfoundland enters into a tax agreement pursuant to this Term the subsidies payable under Term twenty-six will, as in the case of similar subsidies to other provinces, be included in the computation of tax agreement payments.

### Transitional Grants

28. (1) In order to facilitate the adjustment of Newfoundland to the status of a province of Canada and the development by the Province of Newfoundland of revenue-producing services, Canada will pay to the Province of Newfoundland each year during the first twelve years after the date of Union a transitional grant as follows, payment in each year to be made in equal quarterly instalments commencing on the first day of April, namely,

| | |
|---|---|
| First year | $6,500,000 |
| Second year | 6,500,000 |
| Third year | 6,500,000 |
| Fourth year | 5,650,000 |
| Fifth year | 4,800,000 |
| Sixth year | 3,950,000 |
| Seventh year | 3,100,000 |
| Eighth year | 2,250,000 |
| Ninth year | 1,400,000 |
| Tenth year | 1,050,000 |
| Eleventh year | 700,000 |
| Twelfth year | 350,000 |

(2) The Government of the Province of Newfoundland will have the right to leave on deposit with the Government of Canada any portion of the transitional grant for the first eight years with the right to withdraw all or any portion thereof in any subsequent year and on the thirty-first day of March and the thirtieth day of September in each year to receive in respect of any amounts so left on deposit interest at the rate of two and five-eighths per centum per annum up to a maximum period of ten years from the date of Union on the minimum balance outstanding at any time during the six-month period preceding payment of interest.

### Review of Financial Position

29. In view of the difficulty of predicting with sufficient accuracy the financial consequences to Newfoundland of becoming a province of Canada, the Government of Canada will appoint a Royal Commission within eight years from the date of Union to review the financial position of the Province of Newfoundland and to recommend the form and scale of additional financial assistance, if any, that may be required by the Government of the Province of Newfoundland to enable it to continue public services at the levels and standards reached subsequent to the date of Union, without resorting to taxation more burdensome, having regard to capacity to pay, than that obtaining generally in the region comprising the Maritime Provinces of Nova Scotia, New Brunswick, and Prince Edward Island.

## MISCELLANEOUS PROVISIONS

### Salaries of Lieutenant-Governor and Judges

30. The salary of the Lieutenant-Governor and the salaries, allowances, and pensions of the judges of such superior, district, and county courts as are now or may hereafter be constituted in the Province of Newfoundland shall be fixed and provided by the Parliament of Canada.

### Public Services, Works and Property

31. At the date of Union, or as soon thereafter as practicable, Canada will take over the following services

and will as from the date of Union relieve the Province of Newfoundland of the public costs incurred in respect of each service taken over, namely,

    (a) the Newfoundland Railway, including steamship and other marine services;

    (b) the Newfoundland Hotel, if requested by the Government of the Province of Newfoundland within six months from the date of Union;

    (c) postal and publicly-owned telecommunication services;

    (d) civil aviation, including Gander Airport;

    (e) customs and excise;

    (f) defence;

    (g) protection and encouragement of fisheries and operation of bait services;

    (h) geographical, topographical, geodetic, and hydrographic surveys;

    (i) lighthouses, fog alarms, buoys, beacons, and other public works and services in aid of navigation and shipping;

    (j) marine hospitals, quarantine, and the care of ship-wrecked crews;

    (k) the public radio broadcasting system; and

    (l) other public services similar in kind to those provided at the date of Union for the people of Canada generally.

32. (1) Canada will maintain in accordance with the traffic offering a freight and passenger steamship service between North Sydney and Port aux Basques, which, on completion of a motor highway between Corner Brook and Port aux Basques, will include suitable provision for the carriage of motor vehicles.

(2) For the purpose of railway rate regulation the Island of Newfoundland will be included in the Maritime region of Canada, and through-traffic moving between North Sydney and Port aux Basques will be treated as all-rail traffic.

(3) All legislation of the Parliament of Canada providing for special rates on traffic moving within, into, or out of, the Maritime region will, as far as appropriate, be made applicable to the Island of Newfoundland.

33. The following public works and property of Newfoundland shall become the property of Canada when the service concerned is taken over by Canada, subject to any trusts existing in respect thereof, and to any interest other than that of Newfoundland in the same, namely,

    (a) the Newfoundland Railway, including rights of way, wharves, drydocks, and other real property, rolling stock, equipment, ships, and other personal property;

    (b) the Newfoundland Airport at Gander, including buildings and equipment, together with any other property used for the operation of the Airport;

    (c) the Newfoundland Hotel and equipment;

    (d) public harbours, wharves, break-waters, and aids to navigation;

    (e) bait depots and the motor vessel Malakoff;

    (f) military and naval property, stores, and equipment;

    (g) public dredges and vessels except those used for services that remain the responsibility of Newfoundland and except the nine motor vessels known as the Clarenville boats;

    (h) the public telecommunication system, including rights of way, land lines, cables, telephones, radio stations, and other real and personal property;

    (i) real and personal property of the Broadcasting Corporation of Newfoundland; and

    (j) subject to the provisions of Term thirty-four, customs houses, and post-offices and generally all public works and property, real and personal, used primarily for services taken over by Canada.

34. Where at the date of Union any public buildings of Newfoundland included in paragraph (j) of Term thirty-three are used partly for services taken over by Canada and partly for services of the Province of Newfoundland the following provisions shall apply:

    (a) where more than half the floor space of a building is used for services taken over by Canada the building shall become the property of Canada and where more than half the floor space of a building is used for services of the Province of Newfoundland the building shall remain the property of the Province of Newfoundland; ·

(b) Canada shall be entitled to rent from the Province of Newfoundland on terms to be mutually agreed such space in the buildings owned by the Province of Newfoundland as is used for the services taken over by Canada and the Province of Newfoundland shall be entitled to rent from Canada on terms to be mutually agreed such space in the buildings owned by Canada as is used for the services of the Province of Newfoundland;

(c) the division of buildings for the purposes of this Term shall be made by agreement between the Government of Canada and the Government of the Province of Newfoundland as soon as practicable after the date of Union: and

(d) if the division in accordance with the foregoing provisions results in either Canada or the Province of Newfoundland having a total ownership that is substantially out of proportion to the total floor space used for its services an adjustment of the division will be made by mutual agreement between the two Governments.

35. Newfoundland public works and property not transferred to Canada by or under these Terms will remain the property of the Province of Newfoundland.

36. Without prejudice to the legislative authority of the Parliament of Canada under the British North America Acts, 1867 to 1946, any works, property, or services taken over by Canada pursuant to these Terms shall thereupon be subject to the legislative authority of the Parliament of Canada.

### Natural Resources

37. All lands, mines, minerals, and royalties belonging to Newfoundland at the date of Union, and all sums then due or payable for such lands, mines, minerals, or royalties, shall belong to the Province of Newfoundland, subject to any trusts existing in respect thereof, and to any interest other than that of the Province in the same.

### Veterans

38. Canada will make available to Newfoundland veterans the following benefits, on the same basis as they are from time to time available to Canadian veterans, as if the Newfoundland veterans had served in His Majesty's Canadian forces, namely,

(a) The War Veterans' Allowance Act, 1946, free hospitalization and treatment, and civil service preference will be extended to Newfoundland veterans who served in the First World War or the Second World War or both;

(b) Canada will assume as from the date of Union the Newfoundland pension liability in respect of the First World War, and in respect of the Second World War Canada will assume as from the date of Union the cost of supplementing disability and dependants' pensions paid by the Government of the United Kingdom or an Allied country to Newfoundland veterans up to the level of the Canadian rates of pensions, and, in addition, Canada will pay pensions arising from disabilities that are pensionable under Canadian law but not pensionable either under the laws of the United Kingdom or under the laws of an Allied country;

(c) The Veterans' Land Act, 1942, Part IV of the Unemployment Insurance Act, 1940, The Veterans' Business and Professional Loans Act, and The Veterans Insurance Act will be extended to Newfoundland veterans who served in the Second World War;

(d) a re-establishment credit will be made available to Newfoundland veterans who served in the Second World War equal to the re-establishment credit that might have been made available to them under The War Service Grants Act, 1944, if their service in the Second World War had been service in the Canadian forces, less the amount of any pecuniary benefits of the same nature granted or paid by the Government of any country other than Canada;

(e) Canada will assume, as from the date of Union, the cost of vocational and educational training of Newfoundland veterans of the Second World War on the same basis as if they had served in His Majesty's Canadian forces; and

(f) sections six, seven, and eight of The Veterans Rehabilitation Act will be extended to Newfoundland veterans of the Second World War who have not received similar benefits from the Government of any country other than Canada.

## Public Servants

39. (1) Employees of the Government of Newfoundland in the services taken over by Canada pursuant to these Terms will be offered employment in these services or in similar Canadian services under the terms and conditions from time to time governing employment in those services, but without reduction in salary or loss of pension rights acquired by reason of service in Newfoundland.

(2) Canada will provide the pensions for such employees so that the employees will not be prejudiced, and the Government of the Province of Newfoundland will reimburse Canada for the pensions for, or at its option make to Canada contributions in respect of, the service of these employees with the Government of Newfoundland prior to the date of Union, but these payments or contributions will be such that the burden on the Government of the Province of Newfoundland in respect of pension rights acquired by reason of service in Newfoundland will not be increased by reason of the transfer.

(3) Pensions of employees of the Government of Newfoundland who were retired on pension before the service concerned is taken over by Canada will remain the responsibility of the Province of Newfoundland.

## Welfare and Other Public Services

40. Subject to these Terms, Canada will extend to the Province of Newfoundland, on the same basis and subject to the same terms and conditions as in the case of other provinces of Canada, the welfare and other public services provided from time to time by Canada for the people of Canada generally, which, in addition to the veterans' benefits, unemployment insurance benefits, and merchant seamen benefits set out in Terms thirty-eight, forty-one, and forty-two respectively, include family allowances under The Family Allowances Act, 1944, unemployment insurance under The Unemployment Insurance Act, 1940, sick mariners' benefits for merchant seamen and fishermen under the Canada Shipping Act, 1934, assistance for housing under The National Housing Act, 1944, and, subject to the Province of Newfoundland entering into the necessary agreements or making the necessary contributions, financial assistance under The National Physical Fitness Act for carrying out plans of physical fitness, health grants, and contributions under the Old Age Pensions Act for old age pensions and pensions for the blind.

## Unemployment Insurance

41. (1) Subject to this Term, Canada will provide that residents of the Province of Newfoundland in insurable employment who lose their employment within six months prior to the date of Union and are still unemployed at that date, or who lose their employment within a two-year period after that date, will be entitled for a period of six months from the date of Union or six months from the date of unemployment, whichever is the later, to assistance on the same scale and under the same conditions as unemployment insurance benefits.

(2) The rates of payment will be based on the individual's wage record for the three months preceding his loss of employment, and to qualify for assistance a person must have been employed in insurable employment for at least thirty per centum of the working days within the period of three months preceding his loss of employment or thirty per centum of the working days within the period since the date of Union, whichever period is the longer.

### Merchant Seamen

42. (1) Canada will make available to Newfoundland merchant seamen who served in the Second World War on British ships or on ships of Allied countries employed in service essential to the prosecution of the war, the following benefits, on the same basis as they are from time to time available to Canadian merchant seamen, as if they had served on Canadian ships, namely,

(a) disability and dependants' pensions will be paid, if disability occurred as a result of enemy action or counter-action, including extraordinary marine hazards occasioned by the war, and a Newfoundland merchant seaman in receipt of a pension from the Government of the United Kingdom or an Allied country will be entitled, during residence in Canada, to have his pension raised to the Canadian level; and

(b) free hospitalization and treatment, vocational training, The Veterans' Land Act, 1942, and The Veterans Insurance Act will be extended to disability pensioners.

(2) Vocational training, Part IV of The Unemployment Insurance Act, 1940, and The Veterans Insurance Act will be extended to Newfoundland merchant seamen who were eligible for a Special Bonus or a War Service Bonus, on the same basis as if they were Canadian merchant seamen.

(3) The Unemployment Insurance Act, 1940, and The Merchant Seamen Compensation Act will be applied to Newfoundland merchant seamen as they are applied to other Canadian merchant seamen.

### Citizenship

43. Suitable provision will be made for the extension of the Canadian citizenship laws to the Province of Newfoundland.

### Defence Establishments

44. Canada will provide for the maintenance in the Province of Newfoundland of appropriate reserve units of the Canadian defence forces, which will include the Newfoundland Regiment.

### Economic Survey

45. (1) Should the Government of the Province of Newfoundland institute an economic survey of the Province of Newfoundland with a view to determining what resources may profitably be developed and what new industries may be established or existing industries expanded, the Government of Canada will make available the services of its technical employees and agencies to assist in the work.

(2) As soon as may be practicable after the date of Union, the Government of Canada will make a special effort to collect and make available statistical and scientific data about the natural resources and economy of the Province of Newfoundland, in order to bring such information up to the standard attained for the other provinces of Canada.

### Oleomargarine

46. (1) Oleomargarine or margarine may be manufactured or sold in the Province of Newfoundland after the date of the Union and the Parliament of Canada shall not prohibit or restrict such manufacture or sale except at the request of the Legislature of the Province of Newfoundland, but nothing in this Term shall affect the power of the Parliament of Canada to require compliance with standards of quality applicable throughout Canada.

(2) Unless the Parliament of Canada otherwise provides or unless the sale and manufacture in, and the interprovincial movement between, all provinces of Canada other than Newfoundland, of oleomargarine and margarine, is lawful under the laws of Canada, oleomargarine or margarine shall not be sent, shipped, brought, or carried from the Province of Newfoundland into any other province of Canada.

### Income Taxes

47. In order to assist in the transition to payment of income tax on a current basis Canada will provide in respect of persons (including corporations) resident in Newfoundland at the date of Union, who were not resident in Canada in 1949 prior to the date of Union, and in respect of income that under the laws of Canada

in force immediately prior to the date of Union was not liable to taxation, as follows:

(a) that prior to the first day of July, 1949, no payment will be required or deduction made from such income on account of income tax;

(b) that for income tax purposes no person shall be required to report such income for any period prior to the date of Union;

(c) that no person shall be liable to Canada for income tax in respect of such income for any period prior to the date of Union; and

(d) that for individuals an amount of income tax for the 1949 taxation year on income for the period after the date of Union shall be forgiven so that the tax on all earned income and on investment income of not more than $2,250 will be reduced to one-half the tax that would have been payable for the whole year if the income for the period prior to the date of Union were at the same rate as that subsequent to such date.

### Statute of Westminster

48. From and after the date of Union the Statute of Westminster, 1931, shall apply to the Province of Newfoundland as it applies to the other Provinces of Canada.

### Saving

49. Nothing in these Terms shall be construed as relieving any person from any obligation with respect to the employment of Newfoundland labour incurred or assumed in return for any concession or privilege granted or conferred by the Government of Newfoundland prior to the date of Union.

### Coming into Force

50. These Terms are agreed to subject to their being approved by the Parliament of Canada and the Government of Newfoundland; shall take effect notwithstanding the Newfoundland Act, 1933, or any instrument issued pursuant thereto; and shall come into force immediately before the expiration of the thirty-

first day of March, 1949, if His Majesty has theretofore given His Assent to an Act of the Parliament of the United Kingdom of Great Britain and Northern Ireland confirming the same.

Signed in duplicate at Ottawa this eleventh day of December, 1948.

*On behalf of Canada:*

LOUIS S. ST. LAURENT

BROOKE CLAXTON

*On behalf of Newfoundland:*

ALBERT J. WALSH

F. GORDON BRADLEY

PHILIP GRUCHY

JOHN B. McEVOY

JOSEPH R. SMALLWOOD

G. A. WINTER

# SCHEDULE

In this Schedule the expression "District" means District as named and delimited in the Act 22 George V Chapter 7 entitled "An Act to amend Chapter 2 of the Consolidated Statutes of Newfoundland (Third Series) entitled 'Of the House of Assembly' ".

*Grand Falls-White Bay* shall consist of the Districts of White Bay, Green Bay, and Grand Falls, and all the territory within a radius of five miles of the Railway Station at Gander, together with the Coast of Labrador and the Islands adjacent thereto.

*Bonavista-Twillingate* shall consist of the Districts of Twillingate, Fogo, Bonavista North, and Bonavista South, but shall not include any part of the territory within a radius of five miles from the Railway Station at Gander.

*Trinity-Conception* shall consist of the Districts of Trinity North, Trinity South, Carbonear-Bay de Verde, Harbour Grace, and Port de Grave.

*St. John's East* shall consist of the District of Harbour Main-Bell Island and that part of the Province bounded as follows, that is to say: By a line commencing at a point where the centre line of Beck's Cove Hill intersects the North shore of the Harbour of St. John's, thence following the centre line of Beck's Cove Hill to the centre of Duckworth Street, thence westerly along the centre line of Duckworth Street to the centre of Theatre Hill, thence following the centre line of Theatre Hill to the centre of Carter's Hill, thence following the centre line of Carter's Hill and Carter's Street to the centre of Freshwater Road, thence following the centre line of Freshwater Road to its intersection with the centre of Kenmount Road, and thence along the centre line of Kenmount Road to its intersection with the North Eastern boundary of the District of Harbour Main-Bell Island, thence along the said North Eastern boundary of the District of Harbour Main-Bell Island to the shore of Conception Bay and thence following the coastline around Cape St. Francis and on to the Narrows of St. John's Harbour and continuing along by the North Shore of St. John's Harbour to a point on the North shore of the said Harbour intersected by the centre line of Beck's Cove Hill, the point of commencement.

*St. John's West* shall consist of the Districts of Placentia-St. Mary's and Ferryland, and that part of the Province bounded as follows, that is to say: By a line commencing at the Motion Head of Petty Harbour and running in a straight line to the Northern Goulds Bridge (locally known as Doyle's Bridge) thence following the centre line of Doyle's Road to Short's Road, thence in a straight line to a point one mile west of Quigley's, thence in a straight line to the point where the North Eastern boundary of the District of Harbour Main-Bell Island intersects Kenmount Road, thence along the centre line of Kenmount Road and Freshwater Road to Carter's Street, thence down the centre line of Carter's Street and Carter's Hill to Theatre Hill and thence along the centre line of said Theatre Hill to the centre line of Duckworth Street and thence easterly along the centre line of Duckworth Street to the top of Beck's Cove Hill, thence from the centre line of said Beck's Cove Hill to the shore of St. John's Harbour and thence following the shore of St. John's Harbour and, passing through the Narrows by the North of Fort Amherst and thence following the coastline Southerly to the Motion Head of Petty Harbour, the point of commencement.

*Burin-Burgeo* shall consist of the Districts of Placentia West, Burin, Fortune Bay-Hermitage, and Burgeo and LaPoile and all the unorganized territory bounded on the North and West by the District of Grand Falls, on the South by the Districts of Burgeo and LaPoile and Fortune Bay-Hermitage, on the East by the Districts of Trinity North, Bonavista South and Bonavista North.

*Humber-St. George's* shall consist of the Districts of St. George's-Port au Port, Humber, and St. Barbe, and all the unorganized territory bounded on the North by the District of Humber, on the East by the District of Grand Falls, on the South by the District of Burgeo and LaPoile, and on the West by the District of St. George's-Port au Port.

# Part Six

## The Smallwood Electoral Record

I respectfully request your support and vote in this election

Sincerely yours,

*Joseph R. Smallwood*

Liberal candidate for
HUMBER WEST

The name of Joseph R. Smallwood appeared on an election ballot paper for the first time in 1932 when he stood for the Liberals in Bonavista South, only to be swamped 3,528 votes to 812 by Conservative Herman W. Quinton.

It would be his only personal defeat in four decades in elective politics. (Interestingly, he appointed Quinton to his original elected Cabinet as Finance minister in 1949. The First World War veteran, school teacher, future member of the Commission of Government and eventual Senator ran successfully as a Liberal in Burgeo and Lapoile in the first General Election following Confederation.)

Meanwhile, Mr. Smallwood's mentor, Liberal Prime Minister Sir Richard Squires, who in 1928 had received in Humber the largest ever percentage of the popular vote, 82.7%—no doubt in reward for establishment of the Corner Brook paper mill, the so-called "hum on the Humber"—switched to Trinity South in 1932. There he lost badly to incumbent Tory Harold Mitchell 2,366 to 1,686.

At the same time Squires's wife, Helena Strong Squires, the first woman ever returned to the House of Assembly with 81% of the vote in a 1930 by-election, went down to defeat defending her seat in Twillingate.

Squires's third administration took office following its ouster of the Monroe Conservatives on October 29, 1928. Its first year was full of hope based on an improved climate of industrialization, but by 1930 the Great Depression had devastated fish markets resulting in unemployment in the thousands. In 1931 Newfoundland's deficit reached $4 million. Conventional borrowing was impossible, and only Canadian intervention by way of bank loans and help to meet loan payments staved off bankruptcy.

Three days before the legislature was to open, on February 1, 1932, with the long-suffering public looking to the government for relief, its Minister of Finance and Customs dropped a bombshell. Major Peter Cashin suddenly resigned, and from the Opposition benches charged Squires with falsifying Cabinet minutes and with the misappropriation of War Reparations funds. Other members of the government were accused of corrupt practices.

The House adjourned while Governor Sir John Middleton investigated the allegations, which he declared baseless, but when it reconvened on March 22, the government announced increases in tariffs on imported goods and cuts in war veterans' pensions. More government resignations ensued—Minister without Portfolio H.M. Mosdell, and MHAs Philip Fudge and John Parsons.

The night of April 4, a huge public protest meeting was staged by the Opposition—a meeting from which Mr. Smallwood, attempting to

*PHOTOS CLOCKWISE:*
■ Premier Smallwood campaigning in Humber West (MA); ■ The Liberal condidate is surrounded by supporters, including many prominent citizens, on the steps of the Corner Brook City Hall (TA); ■ Simple, low-key request for support was part of the successful 1966 Smallwood campaign in Humber West (TA).

defend his mentor Squires, was summarily ejected. The following day a protesting crowd gathered in the grounds of the Colonial Building spawned a destructive mob that vandalized building and contents. Trapped inside for a time, Squires and his wife were lucky to escape unharmed. Few were surprised when the House was dissolved for a General Election on June 11.

Squires's re-election platform offered stimulation of fisheries and agriculture, further industrialization, and a balanced Budget. But it was much too little, too late.

The Conservatives under Opposition Leader Frederick Alderdice, nephew of former Prime Minister Walter S. Monroe, changed their name to the United Newfoundland Party. The only promise was to investigate the feasibility of establishing a commission of government whose first duty would be to tackle the economy—but only if the people agreed to the proposal by way of a referendum. This proved highly popular, and the Liberals were stripped of all but two seats while 24 UNP members and one Independent were elected in a legislature now reduced from 40 members to save money.

The government lost little time agreeing to the British proposal of an inquiry (the Amulree Royal Commission, which was appointed February 17, 1933) to look into Newfoundland's future. Its recommendations came down eight months later, calling principally for the Commission of Government the prime minister earlier proposed, and were quickly accepted. The legislative majority agreed to formally request that London suspend the country's constitution to make way for the new regime. Thus on February 16, 1934 Newfoundland voted itself out of existence as an independent country, the only member state of the British Empire ever to do so—but without benefit of the public referendum Alderdice had promised.

A decade later, on December 12, 1945, in Montreal, Mr. Smallwood picked up a newspaper and was startled to read the headline: "SELF-RULE IS PLAN FOR NEWFOUNDLAND: Colony Soon to Have Own Government, After 12 Years of Commission." For the former journalist and broadcaster-turned-pig-farmer, it opened the next, and by far the most important phase of his life, a career in politics.

In fact, what the Labour government of Prime Minister Clement Atlee announced was a process by which Newfoundlanders would decide the form of their future governance. London had determined the nature of that process: it would be, in effect, a constitutional convention with members elected from all over the country.

Their "duty and functions" would be, after due deliberation, to recommend to their fellow citizens and to the British government "possible forms of future government to be put before the people at a national referendum."

The National Convention Act, passed by the Commission of Government on May 21, 1946, provided for the election one month later of 45 members in 38 districts, with residents of Labrador enabled to vote in their own constituency for the first time.

All were designated as single-member districts with the exception of the most populous—St. John's City East (3) and West (3); the principal industrial centres of Grand Falls (2) and Humber (2); and the rural area of Harbour Main (2). The district of Bonavista Centre nominated two out of the total of 123 candidates who put their names forward for Newfoundland's first General Election in nearly two decades. They were Kitchener Pritchett, who came away with 277 votes, and Joseph R. Smallwood, who campaigned vigorously on a confederation platform and received 2,129 or 88.4% of the popular vote. He thus surpassed Squires's record nearly two decades earlier.

The Convention was called to order by its first Chairman, Mr. Justice Cyril J. Fox, on September 11. Mr. Smallwood promptly established himself as informal leader of the pro-confederation forces which, according to historian James K. Hiller in *CONFEDERATION, Deciding Newfoundland's Future, 1934-49* (Newfoundland Historical Society, 1998), were believed to number about a quarter of the members.

This was borne out after he submitted, on October 25, a resolution to send a delegation to Ottawa to ascertain Canada's attitude to possible union and the terms and conditions that might apply. The resolution, and the speech that accompanied it, set forth the issues and concerns better and more succinctly than others would do, addressing alternatives for the future and sparking the first major debate of the Convention. The speech was enhanced by the fact microphones had just been installed in the chamber; the broadcasting veteran (the "Barrelman") knew his words would be carried far and wide:

"Our people never enjoyed a good standard of living, and never were able to yield enough taxes to maintain the government. The difference was made up by borrowing or grants-in-aid.

"We can indeed reduce our people's standard of living: we can force them to eat and use and have much less than they have; and we can deliberately lower the level of governmental services. Thus we might manage precariously to maintain independent national status. We can resolutely decide to be poor but proud. But if such a decision is made it must be made by the 60,000 families who would have to do the sacrificing, not the 5,000 families who are confident of getting along pretty well in any case.

"We have … a perfect right to decide that we will turn away from North American standards of public services, and condemn ourselves as a people and government deliberately to long years of struggle to maintain even the little that we have. We may, if we wish, turn our backs upon the North American continent beside which God placed us, and resign ourselves to the meaner outlook and shabbier standards of Europe, 2,000 miles across the ocean. We can do this, or we can face the fact that the very logic of our situation on the surface of the globe impels us to draw close to the progressive outlook and dynamic living standards of this continent …

"We can, of course, persist in isolation, a dot on the shore of North America, the Funks of the North American continent, struggling vainly to support ourselves and our greatly expanded public services. Reminded continually by radio, movies and visitors of greatly higher standards of living across the Gulf, we can shrug incredulously or dope ourselves into the hopeless belief that such things are not for us. By our isolation from the throbbing vitality and expansion of the continent we have been left far behind in the march of time, the 'sport of historic misfortune,' the 'Cinderella of the Empire.' Our choice now is to continue in blighting isolation or seize the opportunity that may beckon us to the wider horizons and higher standards of unity with the progressive mainland of America."

Anticipating charges that he was ready to betray and sell out Newfoundland—Cashin thundered that Judas Iscariot "at least had the decency to hang himself"—Mr. Smallwood went on:

"I am not one of those, if such there be, who would welcome federal union with Canada at any price … I insist that as a constituent part of the federation we should continue to be quite free to hold to our love of our own dear land (and) pledge myself to this House and to this country that I will base my ultimate stand in this whole question of Confederation upon the nature of the terms that are laid before the Convention and the country. If the terms are such as clearly to suggest a better Newfoundland for our people I shall support and maintain them. If they are not of such a nature I shall oppose them with all the means I can command."

On November 5, by a vote of 25-18, the Convention rejected the Smallwood resolution. However, he was successful on the second try on February 28 the following year when it was decided to send delegations to Ottawa and London (the Commission of Government ruled against a similar approach to the U.S.) for the same purpose. The London visit had a clearly disappointing result, but the discussions in Ottawa produced later in the year preliminary Terms of Union (the "Black Books") that were introduced November 20 and became the subject of heated debate until the session adjourned in disorder for the Christmas recess on December 12.

Debate resumed on January 5, 1948 and with the Convention winding down, on January 19 St. John's East delegate John G. Higgins moved that Responsible Government as it existed in 1934, and Commission of Government, be recommended to the United Kingdom for inclusion on the ballot for the National Referendum. On January 22 it carried unanimously.

The next day Mr. Smallwood moved, seconded by W.J. Banfield, "That the National Convention desires to recommend … that the following form of Government be placed before the people of Newfoundland in the forthcoming Referendum, namely, Confederation with Canada upon the basis submitted to the National Convention on November 6 by the Prime Minister of Canada." On January 27 the resolution was voted down 29-16. Mr. Smallwood promptly labelled the majority as "29 dictators … (cheating Newfoundlanders out of the opportunity) to exercise their own judgment" about the future of their country.

On January 30 the Administrator, Chief Justice L.E. Emerson, presided as the Convention met for the last time, its work complete.

But for Mr. Smallwood the matter was far from finished. He was especially mindful of the cold logic of the position given the delegation to London the previous year: Simply, if Newfoundland was ready to return to independent nationhood, she should not require continuing financial support. If, however, support would be needed, then she not only was not ready for self-government, but Britain, struggling to recover from the war, would be hard-pressed to provide it. He knew that only union with Canada offered Newfoundland the opportunity of "Responsible Government under conditions that will give Responsible Government a real chance to succeed."

He knew, as well, that much earlier—in 1942 during a Newfoundland visit—Attlee, as deputy prime minister in Sir Winston Churchill's wartime coalition and Dominions Secretary, had privately expressed similar concerns. However, in a radio address from Government House, a press conference for the St. John's media, and remarks to a blue-chip dinner audience he glossed over the issue. Instead, the people of Newfoundland were praised for their war effort and merely reminded that important decisions would need to be made once the conflict was over.

Against this background the pro-confederates set in motion a petition requesting the British government to place Confederation with Canada on the ballot. It began with a broadcast appeal by F. Gordon Bradley, second chairman of the Convention following the death of Fox, and who would become president of the Newfoundland Confederate Association. As well, Mr. Smallwood took to the airwaves with a series of broadcasts urging signatures to the petition. Meanwhile, Cashin went on the air to defend the Convention's decision, a movement for Economic Union with the United States was launched, and more than 30 prominent St. John's lawyers cabled London calling for the recommendation of the Convention to be upheld.

However, by early February Mr. Smallwood reported a huge response to the appeal, and at mid-month announced that 49,769 signatures had been received, more than 2,000 in excess of the number that voted to elect members to the Convention. Finally, on March 2, the British government forwarded to Governor Gordon MacDonald their decision that Confederation with Canada would be on the ballot for the National Referendum.

On June 3, 155,777 Newfoundlanders went to the polls—more than 88 per cent of those eligible—but the result was inconclusive, no alternative receiving a clear majority. Responsible Government received 69,400 (44.55%), Confederation 64,066 (41.13%) and Commission of Government 23,311 (14.32%). In a runoff second stage of the Referendum on July 22, with Commission of Government dropped from the ballot, just under 85 per cent of those eligible voted with the result that Confederation received 78,323 (52.34%) and Responsible Government 71,334 (47.66%).

In conventional political terms, Confederation had won 18 of the 25 referendum districts and Responsible Government 7, as follows:

Confederation—Burgeo and Lapoile, Burin, Fortune Bay and Hermitage, St. Barbe, Labrador, White Bay, Twillingate, Bonavista North, Green Bay, Humber, Trinity North, Fogo, Trinity South, St. George's-Port au Port, Grand Falls, Placentia West, Carbonear-Bay de Verde, and Bonavista South;

Responsible Government—Port de Grave, Harbour Grace, St. John's West, St. John's East, Placentia-St. Mary's, Harbour Main-Bell Island, and Ferryland.

The first General Election to return members to the restored House of Assembly took place on May 27, 1949 with the results amazingly similar: 22-5.

The Smallwood electoral record over more than two decades follows:

| DATE | PREMIER | LIB | % | PC | % | NDP | % | OTH | % | VOTING |
|------|---------|-----|------|----|------|-----|------|-----|-----|--------|
| 27/05/49 | SMALLWOOD | 22 | 65.2 | 5 | 32.7 | – | – | 1 | 1.6 | 95.6% |
| 26/11/51 | SMALLWOOD | 24 | 63.2 | 4 | 35.3 | – | – | 0 | 0.9 | 75.1% |
| 02/10/56 | SMALLWOOD | 32 | 65.7 | 4 | 31.7 | – | – | 0 | 1.7 | 61.0% |
| 20/08/51 | SMALLWOOD | 31 | 57.6 | 3 | 25.2 | 0 | 7.1 | 2 | 9.5 | 94.4 % |
| 19/11/62 | SMALLWOOD | 34 | 58.3 | 7 | 36.3 | 0 | 3.6 | 1 | 1.1 | 58.5% |
| 08/09/66 | SMALLWOOD | 39 | 61.3 | 3 | 33.7 | 0 | 1.8 | 0 | 2.4 | 62.3% |
| 28/10/71 | SMALLWOOD | 20 | 44.0 | 2 | 50.9 | 0 | 1.7 | 1 | 2.5 | 87.9% |

DATE: 16/09/75          DISTRICT: TWILLINGATE

| | |
|---|---|
| Joseph R. Smallwood (Lib. Ref.) | 1,467 |
| Woodrow Philpott (Lib.) | 1,200 |
| Thomas Doyle (PC) | 877 |
| Roderick Woolridge (NDP) | 85 |

# EPILOGUE

Hon. Joseph R. Smallwood, PC, OC
Farewell Speech to the
House of Assembly

Hon. Joseph R. Smallwood in the House of Assembly. His farewell speech took place on June 8, 1977, when the then former Premier was the Liberal Reform MHA for Twillingate (TA).

# Farewell to the House of Assembly

Excerpt from HANSARD,
Newfoundland House of Assembly,
June 8, 1977, 3:18:13-3:33:00 P.M.

The House met at 3:00 P.M.

Mr. Speaker in the Chair.

| | |
|---|---|
| **MR. SPEAKER:** | Order Please! |
| | I recognize the Hon. Minister of Justice. |
| **MR. HICKMAN:** | Mr. Speaker, before we move to statements by Ministers, I move that the rules of this House be suspended for today to permit the coverage by radio and television of the proceedings of this House whilst the Hon. Member for Twillingate (Mr. Smallwood), the Hon. Premier and the Hon. Leader of the Opposition are speaking in relation to a statement that it has been indicated to me that the Hon. Member for Twillingate will make. |
| **MR. SPEAKER:** | The Hon. Leader of the Opposition. |
| **MR. ROBERTS:** | I wish to second the motion, Sir. My understanding is that it is in respect only of the opening procedures and that following the statements of the gentleman from Twillingate and the Premier and myself, and any other Hon. Member who wishes to speak, in respect of that matter, we will then revert to the regular procedure. Sir, we gladly consent. Sir, I think it would be wrong in every of us not to consent. We gladly do consent. |
| **MR. SPEAKER:** | Order, please! |
| | I must ask whether the Hon. Minister of Justice has leave to move this motion? |
| **MR. NEARY:** | The Hon. Minister of Justice has my approval, Sir, to move the motion. I think this milestone in our history should be recorded, Sir. |
| **MR. SPEAKER:** | The Hon. Member for St. John's North. |
| **MR. J. CARTER:** | No, Mr. Speaker. |
| **SOME HON. MEMBERS:** | Boo! Boo! Boo! |
| **MR. SPEAKER:** | Order, please! |
| **MR. NEARY:** | Shame! Shame! Shame! |
| **MR. SMALLWOOD:** | Mr. Speaker— |

**SOME HON. MEMBERS:**    Hear, hear!

**MR. SPEAKER:**    The Hon. Member for Twillingate.

**MR. SMALLWOOD:**    On a point of personal privilege.

Mr. Speaker, I am now in my twenty-fifth year as an elected member of this House, but long before I was elected I had had a lot of experience of this House, for it is now sixty years, over sixty years, since as a schoolboy at Bishop Feild College and later as a working newspaperman, I began to sit in the gallery to listen to such parliamentary giants as Sir Robert Bond, Sir Edward Morris, W.F. Coaker, A.B. Morine, Michael P. Cashin, W.J. Higgins, John R. Bennett, Cyril J. Fox, James Mary Kent, W.J. Walsh, Sir Richard Squires, Doctor Arthur Barnes, L.E. Emerson, and others whose names used to be household words in Newfoundland and in some cases still are. When I first began to haunt the House of Assembly as a visitor there were still hundreds of people living in Newfoundland who remembered the coming of Representative Government in 1832. There were thousands still living who took part, who had taken part in the election of the first House of Assembly under Responsible Government in 1855. There were still living many of those who had campaigned in the 1869 general election that was fought primarily on the question of Confederation with Canada. My own grandfather, David Smallwood, was one of them.

I had had the honour to know personally every Premier of Newfoundland in the present century, the Right Honourable Sir Robert Bond, the Right Honourable Sir Edward Morris, the Right Honourable Sir William Lloyd, Sir Michael Cashin, the Right Honourable Sir Richard Squires, W.R. Warren, Albert E. Hickman, W.S. Monroe, F.C. Alderdice and the Premier of the present time, five of them elected by the people, five of them who held office for short periods only. Now whether or not the general public pay anything more than passing interest, the irrefragable fact is that this is Newfoundland's supreme and sovereign lawmaking body, the body to which the government are always responsible, the high court of parliament, the only elected representative of all the people. Membership here is a high honour for any man or women, for this House, more than any other body in the Province, has the power to make or break Newfoundland.

As I have said, I am now in my twenty-fifth year as a member of this House and for months past I have been wondering why I am here. It is not as though I get much pleasure from being here. I was too long at the helm not to know the nature of the work, the ceaseless cares, the ceaseless crises and the ceaseless complexities of the Premiership. I was at the helm too long to be happy or efficient now in the daily round of criticism. I am not good at it, Mr. Speaker, I have not taste for it, and while I sit here as an Opposition backbencher I feel that I am but occupying the seat of someone who would be more useful to my colleagues, to my district, to the House and to the Province. Of course, if the Premier cared to exchange seats with me I might reconsider the matter. I am not sure, however, that my colleagues here would welcome the Premier to their caucus, or that the members across would exult to have me in theirs.

**MR. LUNDRIGAN:**    Go on over, "Frank."

**MR. SMALLWOOD:**    Now in that matter, Mr. Speaker, allow me to give the House fair warning that it had better not jump to the conclusion that when I leave here today it will have seen the last of the Smallwoods. For in the gallery at this very moment there are two other Smallwoods, another Joey Smallwood, my grandson, and his infant son, Joey Smallwood III, my great-grandson.

**SOME HON. MEMBERS:**    Hear, hear!

**MR. SMALLWOOD:**    I have reminded the House already that my own life overlapped the lives of some Newfoundlanders who were alive in 1932. If my great-grandson Joey lives to be as old as I am now he will then represent nearly two and a quarter centuries of Newfoundland political history, and I wish no worse luck on Ray Guy and Wickford Collins than that they should have the ineffable pleasure, unendurable prolonged, to imagine Newfoundland in the year 2052 as the locale of a joyous political contest between my great-grandson, Joey, and the present Premier's grandson, Frankie, perhaps with Ed's grandson, Eddie, leading the NDP, that is unless Steve's grandson succeeds in capturing that leadership, always bearing in mind however the possibility of John Crosbie's grandson, Johnnie, leading the seventh or eighth political party graced by the well-known, lovable Crosbie charisma.

**SOME HON. MEMBERS:** Hear, hear!

**MR. SMALLWOOD:** Mr. Speaker, this will be my last day here as a member of the House, and in case there should be any curiosity as to how I intend to occupy my mind and my time my answer is that I will write and edit books and publish them, one book a year, and that they will all be about our Province and our people and our Province's history and they will try to portray the strength and greatness, the romance and poetry, the beauty and courage of Newfoundland and Labrador both. And I will endeavour thereby to inform and stimulate the pride and confidence of Newfoundlanders and their Province and in themselves, and at the same time to strive to help our fellow Canadians to better understand Newfoundland and Newfoundlanders and to understand what Canada gained as well as what she gave when we became part of her.

In 1937 I published Volumes I and II of the *Book of Newfoundland*, thirty years later, in 1967, Volumes III and IV, in 1975 Volumes V and VI. My ambition is to publish Volumes VII and VIII in 1982, and Volumes IX and X in 1986. All of this, of course, *Deo Volonte* which means God Willing. I feel sincerely that I can perhaps serve Newfoundland better with books than I can do with speeches to be made from this desk. For many parts of Canada I continue in increasing numbers to receive invitations to address schools and colleges, Rotary Clubs and Canadian Clubs, churches and Chambers of Commerce, learned societies and a variety of other bodies. I have in the past accepted only a very small number of these invitations, but in the present state of national affairs in Canada, especially the danger of Quebec separatism, I wonder whether it might be useful to the country of my choice, Canada, if I participate more often in the public discussion across our nation. But this would conflict severely with my duty to this House and to the district that I represent here. So I had to make a choice. Of all the provinces of Canada, Newfoundland would suffer more grievously from the breakup of Canada and I incline to the view that I can perhaps serve Newfoundland better by joining actively in the effort to preserve the unity of Canada than I can do by continuing to sit here as a backbench member of the Opposition.

I go from this House today with gratitude in my heart for the kindness shown me here, for the graciousness of the people of Twillingate district, and for the long and patient generosity of the people of Newfoundland and Labrador, given almost undeviatingly to me down through the years. In my twenty-fifth year as one of its members I leave this House of Assembly as I entered it, a life-long believer in the principles of Liberalism, and enthusiastic Confederate and Canadian, and with unchanging faith in the destiny of this Province.

**SOME HON. MEMBERS:** Hear Hear!

# Photo Legend

LEGEND: BN (Book of Newfoundland), CP (Crocker Photography), GN (Government of Newfoundland and Labrador), HC (Harry Cuff Publications), JN (John A. Nolan), MA (Memorial University CNS Archives), NH (Newfoundland Herald, RL (A.C. Hunter Research Library), RN (Royal Newfoundland Constabulary Archives), SH (Smallwood Heritage Foundation); TA (Tower Consultants Archives)

---

# Selected Bibliography

*A World Unto Itself, the Political Memoirs of Don Jamieson*, Volume 2, Breakwater Books, 1991

Building New Highroads to a Better Life, The Liberal Blueprint for Newfoundland's Biggest Years, 1966

*Call Me Joey*, James R. Thoms, Harry Cuff Publications, 1990

*Canada and the Constitution, 1979-1982*, Edward McWhinney, University of Toronto Press, 1982

Chartbook of Selected Statistics for Newfoundland and Labrador, Government of Newfoundland and Labrador, 1987

*Confederation: Deciding Newfoundland's Future, 1934-1949*, James K. Hiller, Newfoundland Historical Society, 1998

*Education and Culture in Newfoundland*, Frederick W. Rowe, McGraw-Hill Ryerson, 1976

*Encyclopedia of Newfoundland and Labrador*, J.R. Smallwood /Cyril F. Poole Editor-in-Chief, Newfoundland Book Publishers (1967) Ltd./Harry Cuff Publications Ltd., Vols. 1-5

*Grits*, Christina McCall-Newman, Mcmillan of Canada, 1982

*Hansard*, Official Record of Debates (House of Assembly Proceedings), 1964, 1977, 1979, 1996

Historical Statistics of Newfoundland and Labrador, Government of Newfoundland and Labrador, 1970

*I Chose Canada*, J.R. Smallwood, Macmillan, Toronto, 1973

*Just Call Me Joey*, James R. Thoms, Creative Printers & Publishers

*Life at the Crossroads of the World*, Gander Seniors' Club, 1988

*Newfoundland: Canada's Happy Province*, Government of Newfoundland and Labrador, 1966

*Newfoundland: Canada's New Province*, Government of Canada, King's Printer, Ottawa, 1950

Newfoundland and Labrador: Budget, 1999, Government of Newfoundland and Labrador

*Newfoundland in the North Atlantic World, 1929-1949*, Peter Neary, McGill-Queens Press, 1998

*No Apology from Me*, J.R. Smallwood, Newfoundland Book Publishers (1967) Ltd.

*No Holds Barred*, John C. Crosbie, McClelland & Stewart, 1997

*No Place for Fools, the Political Memoirs of Don Jamieson*, Volume 1, Breakwater Books, 1989

Our Choices, Our Future, Our Time: Platform of the Liberal Party of Newfoundland and Labrador, 1999

*Politics in Newfoundland*, S.J.R. Noel, University of Toronto Press, 1971

Proceedings, Federal-Provincial Conference 1955, Queen's Printer, Ottawa, 1955

Ready for a Better Tomorrow: Platform of the Liberal Party of Newfoundland and Labrador, 1996

*Rene, A Canadian in Search of a Country*, Peter Desbarats, McClelland and Stewart, 1976

Report, Newfoundland Royal Commission, 1933 (The Amulree Report), His Majesty's Stationery Office, London, 1933

Report, Royal Commission on Dominion-Provincial Relations, Queen's Printer, Ottawa, 1954

*Smallwood, the Unlikely Revolutionary*, Richard Gwyn, McLelland and Stewart, 1968, 1999

*The Book of Newfoundland*, J.R. Smallwood, Editor-in-Chief, Newfoundland Book Publishers (1967) Ltd., Vols 1-6

*The Time Has Come to Tell*, J.R.Smallwood, Newfoundland Book Publishers Ltd., 1979

Various reports and documents of the Government of Canada and the Newfoundland and Labrador

Various files of: *The Daily News*, *The (Evening) Telegram*, *The Western Star*, *The Newfoundland (Sunday) Herald*, *Barrons Weekly*, *The Halifax Chronicle-Herald* in the Centre for Newfoundland Studies Archives, Memorial University of Newfoundland

Viewbook, College of the North Atlantic, Second Edition (undated)

# Index

Deutsch, John, 23
Development Conference, 63, 74
Dicks, Paul, 95
Diefenbaker, John G., 14, 16, 21, 23-26
diphtheria, 116, 155
District Vocational Schools, 116, 171, 173, 203
Division of Tourist Development, 198
Dominion Drama Festival, 15
Dominion Steel and Coal Company (DOSCO), 90
Donald D. Dick Limited, 111
Doody, C. William, 97, 110
Dorset Eskimo, 197
Downey, Michael J., 117
Doyle, Gerald S., 23
Doyle, John Christopher, 32, 76, 99, 105, 106, 109-112, 119
Doyle, Thomas, 266
Drew, George, 138
Drover, Sam, 52
Duffy, A.M., 25
Duffett, Harold, 5
Duggan, Alphonsus, 156
Duley, Margaret, 178
Dunfield, Brian, 147
Dustan, Harry G., 186
E. & B. Cowan, 110
Earle, H.R.V., 29, 33, 40, 42, 43
Eastern Provincial Airways, 83, 89, 107
Eaton, Campbell, 78
Edema, Gerard, 178
Efford, John, 78
Electric Reduction Company (ERCO), 89
El Panama Hotel, 112
Emerson, L.E., 265, 270
*Encyclopedia of Newfoundland and Labrador*, 6, 48, 78, 159, 161, 172, 179
Engineering Services Limited, 112
Ennis Sisters, 177
Ernest Harmon Air Force Base, 29, 89, 106
*Evening Telegram*, 4, 8, 16, 18, 25, 26, 39, 43, 47, 56, 63, 65, 79, 96, 99, 106, 112, 138, 139, 187
Ewing, J.R., 179
expenditures, 39, 41, 67, 84, 95, 100, 101, 155, 198, 203
Exploits River, 89, 160
Farm Products Corporation, 72, 91
Ferryland, 139, 197, 266
Figgy Duff, 177
Finn, Ed, 25
First World War, 75, 107, 131, 139, 171, 203, 263
Fisher, John, 15, 16
Fisheries College, 86, 87, 92
Fisheries Development Authority, 92, 119, 186
Fisheries Loan Board, 92, 119, 183, 185, 186
Fishermen's Protective Union, 30, 92, 140, 165, 184
fishermen's unemployment insurance, 186
Forsey, Philip S., 71, 122, 138, 139
Fox, Cyril J., 25, 128, 133, 134, 239, 264, 266, 270
Fraser, Alister, 84
Frecker, George Alain, 29, 33, 38, 71, 89, 172

Front de Liberation du Quebec (FLQ), 31, 59
Fudge, Philip, 263
Fudge, Pierce, 75, 128
Fulton, Davie, 14
Fund, 59
Fund for Rural Economic Development (FRED), 31, 59
Furey, Albert E., 25
Furlong, Robert Stafford, 26, 51, 52
Gambo, 3, 75, 79, 133, 160, 233
Gander Airport, 198
Garland, Charles, 139, 141
Gauthier, Georges-Etienne, 16
Geneva Convention, 192, 193
Geoffrion, Henri, 110
Gill, F. Burnham "Burn", 5, 14, 120-122, 177, 180
Gimby, Bobby, 13, 17
*Globe and Mail*, 168
Glynmill Inn, 5, 14
Godden, Margaret "Peg", 198
Golden Eagle oil refinery, 106
Golden Eagle Refining Co. of Canada, 108
Goldfarb, Martin, 74
Golding, Jack, 16
Goodridge, Harold B., 14, 179
Goose Bay U.S. Air Force Base, 68, 89, 199
Goose Hilton, 68
Gordon, Donald, 67
Gover, Frederick, 83
Government by Commission, 205
Government House, 3, 26, 52, 78, 240, 241, 266
Government of Canada, 22, 23, 108, 119, 161, 167, 184, 192
Grand Bank, 42, 147
Grand Banks, 83, 85-87, 148, 187, 191, 193, 194
Grand Falls, 7, 17, 18, 37, 41, 79, 89, 91, 117, 141, 147, 156, 160, 161, 165, 166, 174, 179, 198, 264, 266
Granger, Charles R., 29, 33, 43
Great Big Sea, 177
Great Depression, 4, 153, 154, 198, 204, 263
Great Fire, 107
Great War, 203
Greene, James J., 25, 51, 65, 86, 192
Greene, Richard J., 25
Grenfell, Wilfred, 172
Griffin, Frederick, 7
Griffin, Patrick, 91
Grimes, Roger, 99
Gros Morne National Park, 47, 71-73, 83, 88, 162, 197, 199
Gruchy, Philip S., 23
Guinchard, Rufus, 177
Gulf of St. Lawrence, 31, 72, 194
Gunn, Gertrude E., 4
Gushue, James, 192
Guy, John, 159
Gwyn, Richard, 6, 8, 23, 75
Hale, Arthur D., 77
Hall's Bay Line, 160
Hamilton River, 63, 67, 167
*Hansard*, 84, 111, 269-271

Land Rover safari, 15, 159, 161
Lane, C. Max, 29, 33, 40, 90, 184
Lang, Charlie, 5
L'Anse aux Meadows, 47, 73, 88, 197, 199
LaPorte, Pierre, 64
Lawrence, Ross, 17
Leadership Convention, 37, 38, 41, 42, 56, 57, 99
Leduc, 86, 191
Legge, Roy C., 33
Lesage, Jean, 8, 165, 167
Lessard, Jean-Claude, 66, 168
Lévesque, René, 64, 167
Lewington, James, 89
Lewis, Bob, 5
Lewis, Philip J., 23, 25, 29, 33, 42, 71, 171
Liberalism, 140, 141, 271
Liberal Party, 29, 30, 32-34, 37, 38, 41-44, 48, 51, 52, 55-57, 74, 78, 98, 108, 138-142
Liberal Reform Party, 48, 75, 141
Lieutenant-Governor, 3, 5, 52, 74, 75, 78, 122, 137, 138, 171, 173, 240
Lilly, Hugh, 86
Lions Club, 42, 109
Local Government Act, 147
Lockhart, Bob, 5
Long Harbour, 84, 89
Lower Churchill, 66-68, 99, 131, 162
Lukins, Fred, 92
Lundrigan, Arthur, 105, 106, 108
Lundrigan, William James, 106
MacDonald, Gordon, 133, 240, 241, 266
MacKay, Alexander M., 165, 166
Mademoiselle Toulinguet, 177
Mahoney, John A., 29, 33, 41, 42
Majestic Theatre, 76
Major, Ed, 47
Major, Kevin, 178
Majumdar, Shawn, 178
make-work projects, 159
Malone, Gerald, 83, 87
Maloney, Aiden J., 29, 33, 38, 40, 71, 131, 185
maternal mortality, 154
Maynard, Ed, 48, 51, 52, 110
Maple Leaf, 15, 161
Marchand, Jean, 59, 63
*Margaret P.*, 76
Marine Institute, 172
Maritime Archaic Indian, 197
Maritime Fruit Carriers, 87
Maritime History Archive, 172
Marshall, William, 43
Martin, Cabot, 168
Marystown Shipyard, 87, 92, 119, 183
Maynard, Arthur, 18
McCann, Phil, 47
McCormack, George, 47
McEvoy, John B., 25, 239
McGrath, Desmond, 91

McGrath, James A., 5, 24, 78
McGrath, James M., 29, 33, 38-40, 153
McIsaac, Hazel, 13
McIsaac, Martin, 47
McKay, Muriel, 5
McKillop, John, 90
McLean, John, 63
McNair, John B., 23-26
McParland, Donald J., 66-68, 162, 167, 168
McSween, Joe, 13
Meaney, John T., 141
Medical Care Commission, 154
Medical Care Program (MCP), 116
Medicare, 16, 116, 153, 154, 207
Meeker, Howie, 5
Melville Pulp and Paper Company, 76
Memorandum of Agreement, 21, 47, 73, 199
Memorial University College, 116, 171, 172
Memorial University Extension Choir, 180
Memorial University of Newfoundland, 171, 173
Memorial University School of Engineering, 116, 172
Memorial University School of Fine Arts, 116, 172
Memorial University School of Medicine, 116, 153, 172
Memorial University School of Music, 116, 172, 178
Memorial University School of Nursing, 116, 153, 172
Memorial University School of Pharmacy, 116, 153, 172
Mercer, Rick, 178
Mercy Congregation, 178
Methodist College Literary Institute, 120
Mews, Henry G.R., 139
Middleton, John, 263
Mifflin, Arthur, 59, 192
Miller, Leonard A., 128, 154
Millman, Wally, 5
Mitchell, Harold, 263
Monroe, Walter S., 141, 263, 264, 270
Montgomerie, Andrew, 29
Montreal Engineering Company, 165
*Montreal Gazette*, 132
Moon, Robert, 6
Moores, Frank Duff, 51, 52, 59, 66, 67, 74, 75, 87, 88, 90, 96, 97, 99-102, 109-111
moratorium on Northern Cod, 147, 148, 183, 186, 187
Morgan, Bernice, 178
Morgan, Herbert, 192
Morgan, Moses, 78
Morine, Alfred, 183, 270
Morris, Edward, 107, 183, 270
Morrissey, Donna, 178
Mosdell, H.M., 263
Moss, William J., 13, 14, 18
Mount Pleasant Cemetery, 8
Mulroney, Brian, 86, 148, 149
Municipalities Act, 148
Munro, John, 88
Murphy, Anthony J. "Ank", 29, 43
Murphy, Dennis "Dee", 17
Murphy, Noel F., 29, 30, 33

Pratt, Christopher, 179
Pratt, Mary, 177
Presentation Congregation, 178
Prince, Rupert, 184
Pritchett, Kitchener, 133, 264
Procon Limited, 109
Progressive Conservative Association, 139
Progressive Conservative Party, 18, 23, 24-26, 31, 43, 48,
    51, 52, 74-77, 92, 95, 96, 98, 99, 109, 138, 139, 141,
    148, 192, 240, 263, 264, 266
prospectus, 97, 99, 101
Provincial Debt Position, 97
Provincial Flag Society, 6
Provincial Park, 73, 84, 97, 115, 197, 199
Provincial Parks Act, 199
Prowse, D.W., 178
Public Service Electric Company, 165
Puddester, H.G., 51
Pulp, Sulphite mill union, 79, 156
Pumphrey, Ron, 6
Quebec City, 15
RMS *Queen Elizabeth 2*, 109
Quigley, Jim, 5, 13
Quinton, Herman W., 71, 138, 139, 263
Ralph, Ed, 87, 88
Ratcliffe, Edward, 120
Ratcliffe, Elinor, 120
Red Bay, 197, 199
referendum, 8, 15, 75, 80, 120, 131-134, 137, 138, 141,
    173, 177, 205, 206, 236-241, 264-266
Reform Liberals, 40
Regan, Jim, 5
Regional Development Incentives Act (RDIA), 59
Registry of Deeds and Companies, 110
Reid, Robert Gillespie, 160
Renouf, G. Rex, 24, 25
Representative Government, 140, 160, 270
Resettlement Program, 117
Responsible Government, 4, 7, 133, 134, 137, 160, 203,
    206, 207, 233, 236-240, 265, 266, 270
Responsible Government League, 139, 240
Reuters, 132, 138
Richards, John Thomas, 74
Richards, Morley, 7
Riche, Ed, 178
Rideout, Tom, 99
Rinfret, Thebaudeau, 138, 240
Roaches Line, 29, 48-50, 79
Roads to Resources Agreement, 162
Roberts, Edward M., 5, 29, 33, 38, 40, 48, 52, 59, 63, 71,
    75, 269
Roberts, Russ, 5, 13
Robinson, John Alexander, 48
Roche's Farm, 29
Rodgers, Gordon, 178
Rogers, Edward John, 4
Rogers, James P., 38
Rogers, Loretta, 38

Roosevelt, Eleanor, 21, 26
Roosevelt, Franklin D. Jr., 66
Rose, Howard, 74
Rousseau, L.Z., 83
Rousseau Royal Commission, 88
Rowe, Frederick William, 29, 33, 38, 40, 42, 58, 63, 71,
    171, 173, 179, 180
Rowe, William N., 29, 33, 40, 63, 71
Royal Canadian Mounted Police (RCMP), 14, 17, 24, 26,
    49, 77, 112, 119
Royal Commission, 21-23, 25, 83, 92, 148, 153, 155, 184, 207
Royal Commission for the National Development
    of the Arts, 179
Royal Commission on Economic Prospects, 40
Rural Electrification Program, 166
Russell, Clara Smallwood, 79
Russell, Edward "Ted", 71, 139
Russell, Merv, 5
Russwood Poultry, 50
Ryan, Albert, 5
Ryan, Amy Bailey, 6
Ryan, John J., 6
Ryan, Theresa, 32
St. Barbe South, 40, 47, 48, 51, 75
St. John's, 3, 5, 8, 13-17, 24-26, 29, 43, 52, 55-57, 59, 67,
    68, 71, 73, 76, 78, 79, 89, 91, 95, 96, 99, 100, 102,
    107, 111, 112, 115, 117, 121, 122, 132, 133, 138-141,
    147, 148, 153, 155, 159-162, 165, 168, 171, 174, 178,
    179, 185, 194, 198, 199, 204, 206, 232, 233, 240, 264-
    266, 269
St. John's Art Club, 179
St. John's Arts and Culture Centre, 13, 15, 63, 179, 177
St. John's Electric Light Company, 165, 166
St. John's General Hospital, 153, 155
St. John's Harbour, 76, 162
St. John's Housing Area, 117, 147, 148
St. John's Housing Corporation, 26
St. John's Light and Power Company, 165
St. John's Lions Club, 109
St. John's Memorial Stadium, 17, 37, 42, 43
St. John's Metropolitan Area Board, 117, 148
St. John's Rotary Club, 58
St. John's Street Railway Company, 165
St. John's Symphony Orchestra, 179
St. Laurent, Louis S., 13, 23, 138, 246
St. Lawrence, 72, 90, 101
St. Lawrence fluorspar mines, 71, 84, 89, 90
Sally's Cove, 48
Salmonier Nature Park, 87
Sametz, Zenon W., 31
Saunders, Gary, 179
Saunders, William P., 29, 52
Schumph, Stan, 47
Second World War, 4, 67, 88, 106, 111, 115-117, 121, 131,
    146, 147, 160, 166, 198, 206
*SEDCO 706*, 87
Senate, 137, 138, 141, 171, 240, 246
Senior, Aubrey, 74